Jolly Grammar Handbook

Written by

Sara Wernham and Sue Lloyd

Edited by Angela Hockley

Illustrated by Lib Stephen and Yoana Gurriz Muñoz

First Edition

Published August 2016
Reprinted December 2022

Jolly Learning Ltd
77 Hornbeam Road
Buckhurst Hill
Essex
IG9 6JX
United Kingdom

Tel: (+44 or 0) 20 8501 0405
Fax: (+44 or 0) 20 8500 1696

www.jollylearning.co.uk
info@jollylearning.co.uk

The Photocopy Sections in this book use Sassoon Infant, a typeface designed for children learning to read and write. Sassoon is a registered trademark of Sassoon and Williams. For more information, visit www.clubtype.co.uk.

The page numbers are printed within the binding at the bottom of each page so that they do not appear on copies of the photocopiable sheets.

ISBN 978-1-84414-472-3 (JL720)

Acknowledgements

Our sincere thanks go first to Professor Alice Coleman, whose work has been an inspiration to us and a profound influence on this project.

We are grateful also to Susan Sindall, Susan Hartley and the children of The Old School Henstead, Suffolk. Their hard work and support in testing our material has greatly benefited this book.

Finally, we are indebted to Mr David K. Thompson for his work on box analysis, which has inspired our sentence walls.

Contents

PART 1

Introduction   1
Teaching Ideas for Grammar   3
Teaching Ideas for Spelling   31

PART 2   Photocopiable Material

Photocopy Section 1   –   Grammar and Spelling Lesson Sheets   41

Week	Spelling	Grammar	
1	Numerical Prefixes for 1	Homophone Mix-Ups	44
2	Numerical Prefixes for 2	Simple, Continuous and Perfect Tenses	49
3	Numerical Prefixes for 3	Definite and Indefinite Articles	54
4	Numerical Prefixes for 4, 5, 6	Countable and Uncountable Nouns	59
5	Numerical Prefixes for 7, 8, 9	Parts of Speech	64
6	Numerical Prefix for 10: ‹dec-›	Direct and Indirect Objects	69
7	‹ei› and ‹eigh› for /ai/	Indirect Objects and Sentence Walls	74
8	‹ei› and ‹ie› for /ee/	Linking Verbs: 'To Be'	79
9	‹ei›, ‹eigh› and ‹eir›	Prepositional Phrases as Adverbs	84
10	‹ci› for /sh/	Prepositional Phrases as Adjectives	89
11	‹cious›	Relative Clauses	94
12	‹-eous›	Relative Clauses in Sentences	99
13	Double Letters	Coordinating Conjunctions	104
14	‹cc› for /k/	Semicolons and Compound Sentences	109
15	Doubling Rule for ‹fer›	Colons in Sentences	114
16	Spellings for Long /oo/	Subordinating Conjunctions	119
17	Spellings for /ai/	Complex Sentences	124
18	Silent ‹h› Digraphs	Simple, Compound and Complex Sentences	129
19	‹bt›, ‹te›, ‹tte›, ‹th›, ‹cht› for /t/	Adverbials	134
20	‹mb›, ‹mn›, ‹me› for /m/	Past Participles as Adjectives	139
21	Silent ‹p› Digraphs	The Active and Passive Voice	144
22	‹ui› and ‹u› for /i/	The Passive Voice	149
23	‹gh› and ‹gue›	Gerunds	154
24	‹gu›	Idioms	159

Week	Spelling	Grammar	
25	‹ough›	Verb 'To Do': Past, Present, Future	164
26	Schwa: ‹ure›	Statements and the Verb 'To Do'	169
27	Schwa: ‹our›	Questions and the Verb 'To Do'	174
28	Suffixes: ‹-ity›, ‹-ety›	Modal Verbs	179
29	Suffix: ‹-ial›	Modal Adverbs	184
30	Suffix: ‹-able›	Imperatives	189
31	‹que› for /k/	Using Paragraphs and Cohesion	194
32	‹ne› for /n/	Formal and Informal Writing	199
33	Word Mix-Ups	Alliteration	204
34	Suffix: ‹-ly›	Homophone Mix-Ups	209
35	‹ere› and /oa/	Antonyms and Synonyms	214
36	Schwas	'Grammar Consequences' Game	219

Photocopy Section 2 – Spelling List Sheets		224
Photocopy Section 3 – Extension Activity Sheets		232

Introduction

The Jolly Grammar 6 Handbook is designed to follow the Jolly Phonics Handbook and the Handbooks for Jolly Grammar 1, 2, 3, 4 and 5. It is intended to:

• extend and refine the children's understanding of the grammar already taught,
• introduce new elements of grammar,
• teach new spelling patterns systematically,
• develop a greater understanding of sentence structure,
• improve vocabulary and comprehension,
• develop dictionary and thesaurus skills, and
• reinforce the teaching in the Handbooks for Jolly Grammar 1 to 5.

The teaching is multisensory, active and progresses at a challenging pace. It places emphasis on consolidating the children's learning and helping them to apply their skills. Each part of speech is taught with its own action and colour. The actions enliven the teaching and make the learning easier. The colours, which are useful for identifying parts of speech in sentences, match those used by Montessori Schools. Like the Jolly Phonics Handbook, the Handbooks for Jolly Grammar provide all the essential teaching ideas.

Children's Achievement

The most dramatic improvements to result from using the Jolly Grammar Handbooks will be found in the children's writing. The children will spell and punctuate more accurately, use a wider vocabulary, and have a clearer understanding of how language works.

In their first year at school, the Jolly Phonics Handbook teaches children to write independently by listening for the sounds in words and choosing letters to represent the sounds. This enables the children to write pages of news and stories. It is a joy to read their work and to see the great pride and confidence they derive from their newly acquired skill. However, it is important to build on this foundation in the following years. The Jolly Grammar Handbooks provide teaching ideas for developing writing skills. The children become more aware that they are writing for a purpose: that their words are intended to be read and understood. They learn that writing is easier to understand if it is grammatically correct, accurately spelt, well punctuated and neatly written – and that if the words used are interesting too, their writing can give real pleasure. Even in the early stages, it is valuable for children to have a simple understanding of this long-term goal.

The Format of the Jolly Grammar 6 Handbook

The programme consists primarily of photocopiable activity sheets for two lessons a week. Each lesson is designed to be about one hour in duration, and material is provided for 36 weeks. Teaching ideas are offered alongside each activity sheet.

There are two elements to the programme, namely spelling and grammar. Each week the first lesson is devoted to spelling and the second to grammar. These terms are used loosely and there is some overlap: parts of speech, punctuation and vocabulary development are among the areas covered in both spelling and grammar lessons. This is a deliberate feature of the programme, as the two elements complement each other when blended together. It is very noticeable in the Handbooks for Jolly Grammar 5 and 6, where there are two Spelling Sheets per lesson; the second of these usually features one activity based on a related, or recently introduced, grammar point and another that looks at sentence structure within a grammar context.

The teaching is intended to be envisaged as part of a broader literacy programme. If two days' literacy sessions are devoted to grammar and spelling each week, this leaves three for other areas, such as comprehension, group and individual reading, formal and creative writing, and handwriting practice. The children should be shown how spelling and grammar relate to their other literacy work. For instance, if the children are studying a text that has an example of something they have recently learnt (such as a colon or semicolon, or the use of the passive voice), this should be pointed out. The children can then be encouraged to look, for example, at what goes before and after the punctuation, or identify the part of 'to be' and the past participle used to form the passive verb.

The teaching ideas alongside each activity sheet give useful suggestions and reminders. More detailed explanations and advice are provided in the following two chapters: 'Teaching Ideas for Grammar' and 'Teaching Ideas for Spelling'.

To avoid confusion, the Jolly Grammar Handbooks follow the convention of using different symbols to distinguish between letter names and letter sounds. Letter names are indicated by the symbols ‹ ›, whereas letter sounds are indicated by the symbols / /: for example, the word 'ship' begins with the letter ‹s› and starts with the /sh/ sound.

Teaching Ideas for Grammar

The benefits of learning grammar are cumulative. In the first instance, a knowledge of grammar will give the children more conscious control over the clarity and quality of their writing. Later it will also help them to understand more complicated texts, learn foreign languages with greater ease, and use Standard English in their speech.

Spoken language is living and varies from region to region. The grammar we first learn, through our speech, varies accordingly. However, sometimes there is a need for uniformity. This uniformity improves communications and is one of the main ways of uniting people in the English-speaking world. An awareness of this helps children who do not speak Standard English to understand that the way they speak is not wrong, but that it has not been chosen as the standard for the whole country. The children need to learn the standard form of English, as well as appreciating their own dialect.

In their first year of learning grammar, the Jolly Grammar 1 Handbook introduces the children to the concepts of sentences, punctuation and parts of speech. They learn about proper and common nouns, pronouns, verbs, adjectives and adverbs. They also learn to use verbs to indicate whether something happens in the past, present or future.

In Jolly Grammar 2, the children's knowledge is extended and their understanding is deepened: their knowledge of sentences is refined; they learn to punctuate with greater variety and precision; they are introduced to irregular verbs; and they also learn new parts of speech, namely possessive adjectives, conjunctions, prepositions, and comparatives and superlatives.

In Jolly Grammar 3, the children's understanding is further refined: they learn the difference between a phrase and a sentence, how to identify the subject and object of a sentence, and about organising sentences into paragraphs; in dictation, they receive regular practice in writing direct speech with the proper punctuation; they learn how to form the continuous tenses and are introduced to new parts of speech, namely collective nouns, irregular plurals, possessive pronouns and object pronouns; they also have regular dictionary and parsing practice with the aim of building their dictionary skills, improving their vocabulary and reinforcing their grammar knowledge.

Jolly Grammar 4 continues to build on the previous years' teaching: the children learn the difference between simple and compound sentences, about how statements can be turned into questions and how to distinguish between a phrase, a clause and an independent clause; they have regular parsing practice, both at sentence and verb level, to secure their understanding of parts of speech and of grammatical person and tense; they are introduced to the idea of simple subject-verb agreement, seeing what happens to the words in a sentence when a singular subject is made plural or, for example, when a sentence in the first person singular is rewritten in the third person; and they are taught new parts of speech, namely infinitives, noun phrases and concrete, abstract and possessive nouns.

Jolly Grammar 5 extends the children's understanding and reinforces their grammar knowledge: their understanding of verbs is deepened as they learn about transitive and intransitive verbs, phrasal verbs, past participles and how to form the perfect tenses; they learn that verbs can be modified by prepositional phrases as well as adverbs, and that adverbs can modify other adverbs and adjectives; they look in depth at how adverbs fall into different categories of manner, degree, place, time and frequency and how adjectives tend to be written in a certain order; they are shown how to use parentheses correctly in their writing and how to punctuate vertical lists using colons and bullet points; and they also have regular practice working with sentence walls, a simplified form of sentence diagramming, with the aim of refining their knowledge of sentence structure and deepening their understanding of how different parts of a sentence relate to one another.

Jolly Grammar 4, 5 and 6 continue to work on improving the children's vocabulary and writing, with a particular focus on developing their knowledge of antonyms and synonyms, prefixes and suffixes, and commonly confused homophones. The children are also encouraged to use onomatopoeia and different forms of comparatives and superlatives in Jolly Grammar 4, and they are introduced to homographs, homonyms and heteronyms in Jolly Grammar 5. In Jolly Grammar 6, they learn about near homophones, alliteration, idioms, paragraph structure and cohesion. They also learn to recognise the different literary styles and vocabulary used in formal and informal writing.

Jolly Grammar 6 extends, consolidates and refines the teaching of previous years. The children are introduced to many new parts of speech, namely countable and uncountable nouns; gerunds; relative pronouns; relative and modal adverbs; modal and linking verbs; coordinating and subordinating conjunctions; adverbials; and prepositional phrases, past participles and relative clauses that act as adjectives.

The children's knowledge of sentences and sentence structure is also refined: they learn the difference between the active voice (when the subject does the verb action) and the passive voice (when the subject receives the verb action), and are shown how a sentence with a direct object sometimes has an indirect object; they are taught that a complex sentence has a subordinate clause which gives us more information about the main clause, and learn how to use the verb 'to do' as an auxiliary to add emphasis or to form a question or negative statement; they are taught how to form imperatives, which usually end in a full stop but can be punctuated by an exclamation mark, and are introduced to semicolons, which can be used in compound sentences or as listing commas in complicated lists; they learn how colons can be used in sentences to introduce a list of examples, a single idea or an explanation, and they continue to parse sentences and put them into sentence walls on a regular basis.

Because the Jolly Grammar 6 Handbook builds on the teaching of the previous levels, the children's understanding of that teaching must be secure; it is important to go over anything the children are unsure of before introducing anything new.

As a result, the Jolly Grammar Handbooks provide a systematic approach to revision. This enables even the slowest learners to keep up, while ensuring that more able ones master their skills thoroughly and develop good grammatical habits. Every lesson should include some revision and there are suggestions for this in the teacher's notes alongside the activity sheets. However, every class is different, and teachers should feel free to adapt the revision, focusing on areas that need the most attention.

The term 'grammar' is used broadly. Definitions of the parts of speech, and of what constitutes a sentence, phrase and clause have necessarily been simplified to age-appropriate working definitions. As the children grow older, the definitions can be expanded and refined.

Nouns

A noun denotes a person, place or thing. On the most basic level, nouns can be divided into proper nouns and common nouns.

Proper Nouns

Proper nouns are introduced in the Jolly Grammar 1 Handbook and are revised in the subsequent levels. A proper noun starts with a capital letter and is the particular name given to:

- a person (including that person's surname and title),
- a place (such as a river, mountain, park, street, town, country, continent or planet),
- a building (such as a school, house, library, swimming pool or cinema), and
- a date (such as the days of the week, months of the year and religious holidays).

In the early Jolly Grammar Handbooks, the main focus is initially on people's names, and then on the names of the months, including their correct spelling and sequence. In Jolly Grammar 3, the focus moves to place names. The children learn that in longer place names, such as 'the Tower of London', only the important words need a capital letter, and not the short joining words.

Action: The action for proper nouns is to touch your forehead with the index and middle fingers. This is the same action as that used for 'name' in British Sign Language.

Colour: The colour for nouns is black.

Common Nouns

All nouns that are not specific names or titles are called common nouns; they can be divided into concrete nouns (such as 'table'), abstract nouns (such as 'warmth') and collective nouns (such as 'group').

As abstract nouns and collective nouns are more difficult for young children to grasp, only concrete nouns are taught in the early years, although the term itself is not introduced to the children until Jolly Grammar 4.

Everything we can see has a common name by which we can refer to it, such as 'table', 'chair' and 'pencil'. In the early years, the children are encouraged to think of nouns as the names for things they can see, touch or photograph. To help the children decide if a word is a noun, they can see whether it makes sense to say the word 'a', 'an' or 'the' before it. ('A', 'an' and 'the' are the three articles, which are explained later.)

In general, children are able to understand the concept of nouns quite easily from the beginning and have no trouble when asked to think of examples. Identifying nouns in sentences is more difficult, but comes with regular parsing practice, which is provided in the Handbooks for Jolly Grammar 3 onwards.

Action: The action for common nouns is to touch your forehead with all the fingers of one hand.

Colour: The colour for nouns is black.

Collective Nouns

Collective nouns, which are introduced in Jolly Grammar 3, are words that describe a group of people, animals or things: for example, a **crowd** of people, a **herd** of cows or a **fleet** of ships. They also describe ideas and emotions (as in 'a **host** of ideas'), but these are abstract nouns, which are introduced in the following year.

Collective nouns are usually used in the singular (as in 'a bunch', 'a band', 'a flock') because they are describing the group as a whole; whereas the nouns that make up the group are plural because there are many of them (as in 'a bunch of **flowers**', 'a band of robbers', 'a flock of **birds**'). Collective nouns are a form of common noun so they do not need a capital letter.

The same collective noun can often be used to describe different things: for example, 'bunch' can be used to describe flowers, keys and bananas, amongst other things. Sometimes more than one collective noun can be used to describe the same item: for example, a group of whales can be described as both a 'pod' and a 'school'.

There are many collective nouns to describe animals and birds. Some are very common, such as 'herd', 'flock' and 'pride', while others, particularly the ones for birds, are rather obscure, such as 'a murder of crows'. However, there are many new ones that are not officially recognised which the children may also find entertaining, like 'a bounce of kangaroos'.

It is important not to confuse collective nouns with uncountable nouns. Nouns like 'water' and 'meat' are rarely used in the plural, while 'furniture' and 'traffic' never are; such nouns are considered uncountable and cannot be divided into smaller groups of one particular item. Collective nouns, on the other hand, can be plural and describe a group of one particular type of object (as in 'a colony of ants', 'two colonies of ants'). The children are introduced to the idea of countable and uncountable nouns in Jolly Grammar 6 (as discussed on the opposite page).

Concrete Nouns

In Jolly Grammar 4, the children learn that the things they can see, hear, smell, taste or touch – that is, things that exist in a physical form – are called concrete nouns. The children are encouraged to think about different types of concrete noun and to categorise them according to the five senses.

Action: The action for concrete nouns is to gently tap your forehead twice with your hand.

Colour: The colour for nouns is black.

Abstract Nouns

Once the children learn what is meant by concrete nouns, they can be introduced to the concept of abstract nouns. In Jolly Grammar 4, they learn that abstract nouns are things that cannot be experienced through the five senses; they are typically the names for things like ideas (as in 'justice' and 'freedom'), feelings (as in 'anger' and 'happiness'), qualities (as in 'bravery' and 'wisdom'), and actions and events (as in a 'walk' or a 'meeting').

Children should be at the stage now where they are able to understand the idea of abstract nouns, at least in principle, and with regular parsing practice they will find it easier to identify abstract nouns in their reading and writing.

Action: The action for abstract nouns is to move your hand away from your forehead in a spiral action.

Colour: The colour for nouns is black.

Possessive Nouns

In Jolly Grammar 2, the children are taught that adding ‹'s› to a person's name shows possession, so that 'Tiffany's bike' means 'the bike belonging to Tiffany'. The apostrophe is there to show that the ‹s› is not being used to make the proper noun plural. In Jolly Grammar 4, the children go on to learn that this form of the noun is called a possessive noun and is not just restricted to proper nouns but to common nouns as well, as in 'the **girl's** coat' and 'the **kangaroo's** pouch'. They are also taught that possessive nouns can be plural. Most plurals will already end in ‹s›, in which case only the apostrophe is required, as in 'the **girls'** coats' and 'the **kangaroos'** pouches'; however, if the plural is irregular and does not end in ‹s›, both the apostrophe and the ‹s› are added, as in 'the **men's** watches' or 'some **mice's** tails'.

It is important the children do not confuse 'it's', which is a contraction of 'it is' or 'it has', with the possessive adjective 'its'. Possessive adjectives (covered in more detail on pages 15 and 16) are used in place of possessive nouns, so that 'the girl's coat' becomes '**her** coat' and 'the kangaroo's pouch' becomes '**its** pouch'. Possessive adjectives already indicate possession so they do not need ‹'s›. With regular practice, the children will learn to distinguish between the two homophones and use them correctly in their writing.

Despite its name, a possessive noun acts as an adjective in a sentence because it describes another noun. The children are already familiar with this idea, knowing that nouns can act as adjectives in compound words such as '**apple** pie' and '**rabbit** hutch'.

Countable and Uncountable Nouns

In Jolly Grammar 6, the children learn that while most common nouns can be counted – and therefore take a plural – some nouns in English very rarely take a plural and are usually considered uncountable; this is usually because they are substances (such as 'dust', 'food', 'metal', 'mud', 'salt' and 'water') or abstract concepts (such as 'intelligence', 'kindness', 'music', 'news' and 'peace'), neither of which can be divided into discrete countable units. However, a small number of uncountable nouns, such as 'rice' and 'sand', for example, can be divided into discrete units (in this case, individual grains), but they are considered uncountable because it is not possible or practical to count such a great quantity.

Unlike countable nouns, uncountable nouns cannot follow an indefinite article ('a' or 'an'): we do not ask for 'an' advice or do 'a' homework, for example. Neither can they be modified directly by a number: we do not buy, for instance, three 'butters' or two 'milks'. Instead, to indicate quantity we use general descriptions like 'some', 'a lot of' or 'more', and if we want to express a specific quantity, we use noun phrases like 'one slice of cheese', 'two teaspoons of sugar' or 'a thick layer of dust'. Also, if we wish to know the quantity of an uncountable noun, we do not ask 'how many?' as we would with a countable noun, but say 'how much?' instead.

Uncountable nouns are singular and so they are always used with a singular verb, as in 'The news **is** bad' and 'Their luggage **was** in the car'. However, there are a few occasions when nouns that are normally considered uncountable become countable. This usually happens when we are referring to their different types, as in 'a selection of soft cheeses' or 'a plate of cold meats', for example. Similarly, some nouns can be countable or uncountable depending on the context. For example, if we buy a couple of chocolate **cakes** now, we can eat some **cake** later, or we can have some **chicken** for lunch before feeding the **chickens**.

Other examples of uncountable nouns include the following: art, accommodation, blood, bread, education, equipment, flour, furniture, gas, gold, honey, information, jam, juice, lightning, liquid, money, pasta, rain, silver, snow, soil, thunder, traffic, transport, weather, wood.

Uncountable nouns are also known as non-count or mass nouns.

Gerunds

The gerund, which is a verb form that functions as a noun, is introduced in Jolly Grammar 6. Rather than people or objects, gerunds name activities and they can do anything a noun can do: for example, they can function as the subject or object of a sentence (as in '**Cycling** keeps me fit' and 'I love **reading**'); they can be the head of a noun phrase (as in 'the **ticking** of the clock'); and they can function as the object of a preposition (as in 'Before **jogging**, I always do some stretches'). Gerunds are not taught earlier because they are easily confused with the present participle; this is because gerunds and present participles are both formed by adding ‹-ing› to the root verb.

Gerunds can also be used in gerund phrases, where the whole phrase acts as a noun, as in '**Learning to cook** is great fun' and 'Dad likes **ironing his shirts**', but the children can learn more about this when they are older.

Plurals

Most nouns change in the plural: that is, when they are describing more than one of something. In the early Jolly Grammar Handbooks, the two main ways of forming the plural are introduced and revised: firstly, by adding ‹-s› to a noun (as in 'dogs', 'cats', 'girls' and 'boys') and secondly, by adding ‹-es› to those nouns which end in ‹sh›, ‹ch›, ‹s›, ‹z› or ‹x› (as in 'brushes', 'dresses' and 'foxes'). These endings often sound like /z/ and /iz/, respectively, as in 'dogs' and 'foxes', so knowing that these words are plurals will help the children remember to spell the /z/ sound correctly.

In Jolly Grammar 2, the children also learn to form the plural of nouns ending in ‹y›: if the letter immediately before the ‹y› is a vowel, the plural is simply made in the usual way by adding ‹-s› (as in 'days', 'boys' and 'monkeys') but, if the letter immediately before the ‹y› is a consonant, ‹y› is replaced by ‹i› before adding ‹-es› (as in 'flies', 'babies' and 'puppies'). The children should already know that 'shy ‹i›' does not like to be alone at the end of a word and is often replaced by 'toughy ‹y›'. This helps them understand that while we would be unlikely to find 'shy ‹i›' at the end of a word like 'puppy', we will find it in the plural 'puppies', when 'shy ‹i›' is no longer at the end of the word.

The weekly spelling lists also introduce some common plurals that are irregular, or 'tricky': for example, 'children', 'women' and 'mice' (for 'child', 'woman' and 'mouse', respectively). Tricky plurals can be formed by modifying the root word, altering its pronunciation, adding an unusual ending, or a combination of the three; sometimes the pronunciation of the root word alters even when the spelling does not: for example, the letter ‹i› makes a long /ie/ sound in 'child', whereas it makes a short /i/ sound in 'children'.

Some plurals, such as 'sheep', 'fish' and 'deer', are tricky because they have the same form for both singular and plural, and these are introduced in Jolly Grammar 3. In this level, the children also learn that nouns ending in ‹o› usually take the ‹-es› suffix, except when the word is foreign, abbreviated, or has a vowel before the ‹o›, as in 'pianos', ' kilos' and 'studios'.

In Jolly Grammar 4, the children learn that other plurals are tricky because their singular forms end in ‹f› or ‹fe›, whereas their plurals are made by removing the ending and adding ‹-ves›, as in 'shelves' and 'knives'. Not all singular nouns ending in ‹f› or ‹fe› make their plurals in this way, so the spellings have to be learnt.

The children are also taught that not only do they have to think about the spelling of a plural in a sentence, but they also have to make sure that the other words connected to it agree (as discussed in Grammatical Agreement on page 27). While most children will be making these adjustments automatically in their language, the teaching is made more explicit in Jolly Grammar 4.

Jolly Grammar 5 introduces the irregular plural ‹-i›, which is added to some words that have a Latin origin. It is irregular because not all words that derive from Latin and which end in ‹us› take this plural; in fact most are formed in the regular way by adding ‹-es›, as in 'viruses' and 'choruses'.

However, a small number of scientific or academic words like 'nuclei' and 'alumni' do use this plural and even more can take either plural, such as 'hippopotamus', 'cactus', 'crocus' and 'fungus'. In order to be sure, the children should look up words that end in ‹us› in the dictionary.

Pronouns

Pronouns are the little words used to replace nouns; without them, language would become boring and repetitive. They can be divided into personal pronouns (such as 'I' and 'me'), possessive pronouns (such as 'mine'), relative pronouns (such as 'who') and reflexive pronouns (such as 'myself').

Only personal pronouns are taught in the early Handbooks, and possessive pronouns are introduced in Jolly Grammar 3. The children learn about relative pronouns in Jolly Grammar 6, but reflexive pronouns can be taught when the children are older.

Personal Pronouns

The early Handbooks introduce and revise the eight personal pronouns: 'I', 'you', 'he', 'she', 'it', 'we', 'you' and 'they'. In modern English, we use the same word, 'you', for both the singular and plural second person pronoun, but this is not the case in many foreign languages. In order to make learning such languages easier later on, the children learn the distinction between 'you' used in the singular and 'you' used in the plural.

In Jolly Grammar 3, the children learn how to identify the subject and object of a sentence and are taught that the personal pronouns can change, depending on whether they are the subject or the object. The personal pronouns that the children know already are subject pronouns; the corresponding object pronouns are 'me', 'you', 'him', 'her', 'it', 'us', 'you' and 'them'.

In Jolly Grammar 4, the children are taught that personal pronouns are called 'personal' because they mostly relate to people: when talking about ourselves, we use 'I' and 'we'; when talking directly to one or more people, we say 'you'; and when talking about someone or something else, we use 'he', 'she' and 'it' for the singular and 'they' for the plural. The children learn that these three groups are known as first, second and third person and they can be singular or plural.

Once the children are introduced to grammatical person, they are given regular practice parsing the verb in the spelling lessons. They also learn that when the person in a sentence is changed, the verb and the rest of the sentence must agree.

The children practise using the subject pronouns whenever they conjugate verbs; they do the actions and say, for example, 'I smile, you smile, he smiles, she smiles, it smiles, we smile, you smile, they smile'. The same actions can also be used to revise the object pronouns:

		Subject		Action	Object
1st person singular:		I	–	point to yourself	– me
2nd person singular:		you	–	point to someone else	– you
3rd person singular:		he	–	point to a boy	– him
3rd person singular:		she	–	point to a girl	– her
3rd person singular:		it	–	point to the floor	– it
1st person plural:		we	–	point in a circle to yourself & others	– us
2nd person plural:		you	–	point to two other people	– you
3rd person plural:		they	–	point to the class next door	– them

Colour: The colour for pronouns is pink.

Possessive Pronouns

In Jolly Grammar 3, the eight possessive pronouns are introduced: 'mine', 'yours', 'his', 'hers', 'its', 'ours', 'yours' and 'theirs'. These pronouns correspond to the personal pronouns ('I/me', 'you/you', 'he/him', 'she/her', 'it/it', 'we/us', 'you/you' and 'they/them') and the possessive adjectives ('my', 'your', 'his', 'her', 'its', 'our', 'your' and 'their'). Possessive pronouns replace a noun and its possessive adjective, so that 'my hat' becomes 'mine' and 'their house' becomes 'theirs'. These pronouns are possessive because they indicate who the noun that they are replacing belongs to. Possessive pronouns can be practised using the same colour (pink) and actions as for the personal pronouns.

Relative Pronouns

Relative pronouns are introduced in Jolly Grammar 6, alongside relative adverbs and relative clauses (see pages 17 and 22). The most common relative pronouns are 'who', 'which', 'that', 'whom' and 'whose'. They are often used at the beginning of a relative clause – which is a special kind of dependent clause that acts as an adjective – to relate the clause to the person or thing that it is describing.

   The relative pronouns 'who' and 'whom' are used for people: 'who' is used for the subject of the clause and 'whom' for the object, as in 'the girl **who** won the race' and 'the boys **whom** we met yesterday'. We use 'which' to refer to things, as in 'the book **which** you lent me', while 'that' can be used for both people and things, as in 'the scarf **that** I bought' or 'the nurse **that** bandaged my knee'. The relative pronoun 'whose' is used to indicate possession, as in 'the chef **whose** recipes we like'.

Verbs

A verb denotes what a person or thing does or is. It can describe an action, an event, a state or a change. From the beginning, the children are encouraged to talk about verbs in the infinitive form ('to run', 'to hop', 'to sing', 'to play') rather than as gerunds. (Gerunds, such as 'running', 'hopping', 'singing' and 'playing', are the noun form of a verb.) Early on, the children think of this as the 'name' of the verb, but gradually the term 'infinitive' can be introduced. In Jolly Grammar 4, the children learn that the infinitive can be used in a sentence (as in 'I want **to stay**'), although it is never the main verb and does not have a subject. Jolly Grammar 6 also introduces the bare infinitive, which is the infinitive form of the verb without 'to'. The children learn to use it with either modal verbs (as in 'You **must**

go home') or the auxiliary 'to do' (as in 'I **do like** ice cream'), or when forming imperative sentences, like '**Sit** down over there'.

When the children are young, they find it easiest to think of verbs as 'doing' words. This is the working definition used throughout the Handbooks for Jolly Grammar 1 to 5. However, during this time the children's understanding is gradually refined. For example, from Jolly Grammar 3 onwards, they learn about auxiliary verbs, which do not stand alone but are found 'helping' another verb in the sentence (such as the auxiliaries 'will' and 'shall', which indicate the future). In Jolly Grammar 6, they also learn that some verbs are more accurately described as 'being' words, because they describe a state of being or change. Rather than taking a direct object, these verbs link the subject of the sentence to its complement. A complement is so called because it completes our understanding of the subject. It does this either by identifying the subject as a noun, noun phrase or pronoun (as in 'Kate is an **engineer**') or by describing it using an adjective, or adjective phrase (as in 'Kate is very **clever**'). The children learn that 'doing' words are more commonly called action verbs and that 'being' words are known as linking (or copular) verbs. The most common linking verb is 'to be', but other common examples include 'to seem', 'to appear', 'to become', 'to remain', 'to look', 'to sound', 'to smell', 'to taste' and 'to feel'. Most linking verbs can also act as action verbs, so the children need to think about what the verb is doing in the sentence before they decide what type it is.

Verb Tenses and Conjugation

The children are introduced to verbs in Jolly Grammar 1, where they learn to conjugate regular verbs in the present, past and future. (Since verbs in English are very complicated, only the simple tenses are introduced initially.) Conjugating means choosing a particular verb and saying the pronouns in order with the correct form of the verb after each one. Conjugating verbs aloud with the pronoun actions is very good for children. It promotes a strong understanding of how verbs work, which helps them make sense of their own language, and it is invaluable when they come to learn foreign languages later on. Revise the conjugations regularly, using the pronoun actions:

Simple past	Simple present	Simple future
I talked	I talk	I shall/will talk
you talked	you talk	you will talk
he talked	he talks	he will talk
she talked	she talks	she will talk
it talked	it talks	it will talk
we talked	we talk	we shall/will talk
you talked	you talk	you will talk
they talked	they talk	they will talk

The children need to remember the following points:

- In the simple present tense, the verb changes after the singular pronouns 'he', 'she' and 'it': For regular verbs, ‹-s› is added to the root, unless the word ends in ‹sh›, ‹ch›, ‹s›, ‹z› or ‹x›, when ‹-es› is added. This is called the third person singular marker.
- The simple past tense of regular verbs is formed by adding the suffix ‹-ed› to the root. If the root ends in ‹e› (as in 'bake'), the final ‹e› must be removed before ‹-ed› is added. The suffix ‹-ed› can be pronounced in one of three ways: /t/ (as in

'slipped'), /d/ (as in 'smiled') or /id/ (as in 'waited').

- In the simple tense, we add the auxiliary verbs 'shall' or 'will' to the root verb to denote the future. The auxiliary 'will' can be used with all the pronouns, but 'shall' should only be used with 'I' or 'we'.

In Jolly Grammar 2, the children learn that every sentence must contain a verb, and so time is spent helping them to identify verbs with confidence. They revise regular conjugations and are introduced to some of the most common irregular verbs and their 'tricky' past forms: for example, the verbs 'to sit' and 'to run', which have the tricky pasts 'sat' and 'ran'. In addition, they learn to conjugate and identify the irregular verb 'to be' in both the present and past tenses. This is especially useful for those children who are not in the habit of using standard forms in their speech: children who say, for example, 'we was' instead of 'we were'. Chanting the conjugations regularly will help these children avoid making mistakes in their written work. In truth, this is good practice for all children, as most of them will find it difficult to identify 'to be' in a sentence until they become familiar with its irregularities.

The verb 'to be' is used frequently in English, both as a main verb and as an auxiliary. In Jolly Grammar 3, the children learn how to conjugate 'to be' in the simple future and are introduced to the continuous tenses. The continuous tenses use 'to be' as an auxiliary, followed by the present participle, as in 'I am walking', 'I was walking', 'I shall be walking'. Later, in Jolly Grammar 5, the children learn the perfect tenses, which use 'to have' as an auxiliary, followed by the past participle, as in 'I had walked', 'I have walked', 'I shall have walked'. Participles are discussed in more detail on the opposite page.

Once the children have learnt a new tense, it is important that they practise identifying all the verb tenses taught so far. It is also important that they develop their ability to write sentences in those tenses. The Handbooks for Jolly Grammar 4 and 5 provide lots of practice in both these skills. As a result, the children should be able to distinguish between the simple, continuous and perfect forms more easily, and this in turn will help them understand how the different tenses are used. For now it is enough that the children understand that the simple past and future describe actions that start and finish within a specific time, while the simple present describes repeated or usual actions (as in 'I swim in the pool every day'); the continuous tenses describe actions that have started and are still happening, either at that very moment or as a longer action in progress (as in 'I am learning to swim'); and the perfect tenses are used to describe actions that have already been completed, especially general experiences, events that happen at unspecified times (as in 'I have swum in that pool several times), or actions that – although complete – still have some connection to the present (as in 'I had just finished swimming in the pool'). For reference, the table below shows all three forms in past, present and future:

	Past	Present	Future
Simple	sailed	sail	will sail
Continuous	was sailing	is sailing	will be sailing
Perfect	had sailed	have sailed	will have sailed

Technically there is no future tense in English, since, unlike the past tense, the future is not formed by modifying the root verb itself. However, at this stage it is helpful for the children to think of verbs as taking place in the past, present or future. The complexities can be taught when the children are older.

Participles

The ‹-ing› suffix, which is added to root verbs, is introduced in Jolly Grammar 2. In Jolly Grammar 3, the children learn that this form of the verb is called the present participle, and it is used with the verb 'to be' to form the continuous tenses. In Jolly Grammar 4, they learn that present participles can be used as adjectives, as in 'There is no running water'. Present participles should not be confused with gerunds, the noun form of a verb, which are introduced in Jolly Grammar 6 (see page 8).

Past participles are introduced in Jolly Grammar 5, in preparation for the perfect tenses. Past participles of regular verbs have the same form as the simple past tense. However, past participles of irregular verbs are 'tricky' and they have to be learnt. Jolly Grammar 5 introduces two of the more common forms. Verbs like 'to swim' change their vowel sound to indicate tense: 'swim' is used in the simple present, 'swam' in the simple past and the past participle 'swum' in the perfect tenses. Verbs like 'to write' and 'to fall' change their vowel sound in the simple past, but keep the original vowel letter and add either ‹-n› or ‹-en› to form the past participle, as in 'write, wrote, written' and 'fall, fell, fallen'. A good dictionary will always list the irregular parts of a verb, so if the children are not sure which form to use in their writing, encourage them to look it up.

In Jolly Grammar 6, the children learn that past participles – like present participles – can be used as adjectives. Present participles that are used in this way usually indicate an action carried out by the noun it is describing; this action is either still happening or happens regularly, as in a 'galloping horse' or a 'talking parrot'. Past participles, on the other hand, usually indicate an action that has already happened and that is done to the thing it is describing, as in 'buried treasure' or a 'mixed salad'. Past and present participles also differ when they concern feelings: for example, an activity might be 'interesting', 'frightening' or 'boring', and we, in turn, may be 'interested', 'frightened' or 'bored' by the activity. Present participles describe the thing that makes us feel a certain way and past participles describe the way it makes us feel.

Phrasal Verbs

Phrasal verbs are introduced in Jolly Grammar 5. They consist of a verb plus one or more other words, which are usually prepositions or adverbs. Put together, these words make a new verb with a new meaning, such as 'to break down' (meaning 'to stop working') or 'to break out' (meaning 'to escape'). Like other verbs, phrasal verbs often have more than one meaning, so 'to break down' can also mean 'to collapse' and 'to break out' can mean 'to flare up'.

The words in a phrasal verb are sometimes separated by the object (including any modifiers), so we can say either 'I **brought back** your book' or 'I **brought** your book **back**'. However, other phrasal verbs, such as 'to look for' cannot be separated in this way, so we would never say, for example, 'I looked him for'. Nevertheless, If a phrasal verb can be separated, an object pronoun will always do so, as in 'I brought it back' (and not 'I brought back it').

Modal Verbs

Jolly Grammar 6 introduces the children to modal verbs, which are a special kind of auxiliary. Modal auxiliaries are used with the 'bare' infinitive of the main verb (the infinitive form without 'to') to help express things like certainty ('You **will** see me tomorrow'), obligation ('You **must** see me tomorrow'), permission ('You **may** see me tomorrow') or ability

('You **can** see me tomorrow'). They are also used to give advice ('You **should** see me tomorrow') or make suggestions ('You **could** see me tomorrow'). The most common modal verbs are 'will', 'shall', 'can', 'could', 'may', 'might', 'should', 'would' and 'must'. Unlike other auxiliaries, they do not change depending on the grammatical person (so the verb stays the same whichever pronoun is used).

Imperatives

The children also learn about imperatives in Jolly Grammar 6, which get their name from the Latin verb 'imperare', meaning 'to command'. The imperative is a special form of the verb that is used not only to give commands ('Sit down!'), but also to give warnings ('Beware of the bull!'), instructions ('Add a pinch of salt') and advice ('Read the instructions first'); they can also be used to make suggestions ('Taste this ice cream'), invitations ('Come back anytime') and requests ('Please close the door'). When we talk directly to someone we usually use the second person, 'you', but this is not the case in imperative sentences; instead we use the bare infinitive and leave the subject unstated (although it can be used to add emphasis, as in 'You be quiet'). Negative imperatives are formed by using 'to do' as an auxiliary, as in 'Do not disturb', although 'do not' is often contracted to 'don't' in speech.

The Active and Passive Voice

Sentences can be written in either the active voice or the passive voice. The children have been learning how to write in the active voice since Jolly Grammar 1, although the term itself is not used until Jolly Grammar 6. It is at this point that the children learn how to write in the passive voice, which uses 'to be' as an auxiliary, together with the past participle of the main verb (as in 'The painting **was stolen** in the night'). There is more information on both the active and passive voice at the bottom of page 20.

Actions: The action for **verbs** is to clench both fists and move your arms backwards and forwards at your sides, as if running.

The action for the **present tense** is pointing towards the floor with the palm of the hand.

The action for the **past tense** is pointing backwards over the shoulder with a thumb.

The action for verbs which describe the **future** is pointing to the front.

Colour: The colour for verbs is red.

Adjectives

An adjective is a word that describes a noun or pronoun. It can be used either directly before the noun or pronoun, as in 'the big dog', or elsewhere in the sentence, as in 'The dog was big'. Throughout the Jolly Grammar Handbooks, the children are encouraged to use adjectives imaginatively in their writing. They learn how to use them before a noun in Jolly Grammar 1, but in Jolly Grammar 2 they start to recognise adjectives wherever they are in the sentence.

In the Handbooks for Jolly Grammar 3 and 4, the children learn that some adjectives are formed by adding a suffix to a noun or verb: for example, ‹-y› and ‹-al› can be added to a noun, as in 'windy' and 'salty', 'accidental' and 'logical'; and ‹-less›, ‹-ful› and ‹-able› can be added to nouns and verbs to make adjectives like 'worthless', 'helpful' and 'enjoyable'. The children also learn that other parts of speech can sometimes act as adjectives: for example, in the compound word '**apple** pie', the first noun 'apple' is describing the main noun 'pie'; in the phrase 'the **running** water', the present participle 'running', which is a verb form, is describing the water; and possessive nouns always act as adjectives to describe another noun, as in the '**peacock's** tail'.

Similarly, in Jolly Grammar 6, the children learn that past participles (as in 'the **lost** boy') and prepositional phrases (as in 'the flowers **in the vase**') can also act as adjectives, while relative clauses (as in 'the letter **that I wrote**') always act as an adjective in a sentence (see pages 13, 18 and 22).

Before this, however, the Jolly Grammar 5 Handbook refines the children's understanding of adjectives by introducing them to adjective order. In English, we tend to write adjectives in a certain order, depending on which category they belong to. The children learn that there are seven general categories, which are often written in the following sequence:

1. Determiners (such as 'a', 'an', 'one', 'two', 'some', 'many', 'any', 'this', 'that')
2. Opinion (such as 'lazy', 'good', 'nasty', 'expensive', 'bad')
3. Size and shape (such as 'fat', 'thin', 'small', 'broad', 'rectangular', 'oval')
4. Condition and age (such as 'broken', 'battered', 'hungry', 'full', 'ancient', 'recent')
5. Colour and pattern (such as 'black', 'brown', 'white', 'tartan', 'zigzag')
6. Origin (such as 'Welsh', 'Polish', 'African', 'Japanese', 'Australian')
7. Material, including nouns acting as adjectives (such as 'leather', 'iron', 'diamond')

This is only a general rule and sometimes the order changes; for example, when shape and age are both included in a description, age tends to come before shape, as in 'the old square box'. However, as a general guide it can be useful, especially for non-native English speakers.

Action: The action for adjectives is to touch the side of your temple with your fist.

Colour: The colour for adjectives is blue.

Possessive Adjectives

The children's understanding of adjectives is extended in Jolly Grammar 2 to include the eight possessive adjectives: 'my', 'your', 'his', 'her', 'its', 'our', 'your' and 'their'. These correspond to the personal pronouns ('I/me', 'you/you', 'he/him', 'she/her', 'it/it', 'we/us', 'you/you' and 'they/them') and possessive pronouns ('mine', 'yours', 'his', 'hers', 'its', 'ours', 'yours' and 'theirs').

A possessive adjective replaces one noun and describes another by saying whose it is. For example, in the sentence 'Lucy fed her cat', the possessive adjective 'her' is used in place of 'Lucy's', and it also describes 'cat' by saying whose cat it is.

As possessive adjectives also function as pronouns, they are sometimes referred to as the weak set of possessive pronouns, but to avoid confusion with the strong set (which include 'mine' and 'yours') the Jolly Grammar Handbooks do not use this terminology.

Comparatives and Superlatives

In Jolly Grammar 1, the children are introduced to adjectives that describe a noun or pronoun without comparing it to anything else, as in 'The young girl' or 'The girl is young'. These are known as 'positive' adjectives, although this term is not used with the children.

In the Handbooks for Jolly Grammar 2 and 3, comparatives and superlatives are introduced and revised. These adjectives describe a noun or pronoun by comparing it to other items: a comparative is used when comparing a noun to one or more other items, as in 'Sam is **younger** than Jim and Ted'; and a superlative is used when comparing a noun to all the other items in its group, as in 'Sam is the **youngest** boy in the team'. Short adjectives usually form their comparatives and superlatives with the suffixes ‹-er› and ‹-est›, respectively, and applying these correctly is the main focus in Jolly Grammar 2 and 3 (see the rules for adding suffixes on pages 39 and 40).

In Jolly Grammar 4, the children learn that longer adjectives often use the words 'more' and 'most', so we say 'harder' and 'hardest', but 'more difficult' and 'most difficult'. Some two-syllable adjectives also make their comparative and superlative by adding 'more' and 'most', especially ones which have a suffix, as in 'most careful', 'more helpless', 'most daring', 'more shaded' and 'most famous'. The children need to listen and decide which sounds right in the sentence. As well as learning about 'more' and 'most', the children also learn about other comparative and superlative forms, such as 'less' and 'least', 'better' and 'best', 'worse' and 'worst'.

Adverbs

In the first four years of learning grammar, the children are taught that adverbs are similar to adjectives but describe verbs rather than nouns. Adverbs often describe how, where, when, how much or how often something happens and, in Jolly Grammar 5, the children learn that these types of adverb are called adverbs of manner, place, time, degree and frequency.

Adverbs are first introduced in Jolly Grammar 1, and at the beginning it helps the children to think of them as words that usually end in ‹-ly›. In Jolly Grammar 2, the children are encouraged to identify less obvious adverbs by looking for the verb and deciding which word describes it: for example, in the sentence 'They arrived late last night', the adverb 'late' tells us something more about when they arrived. Identifying adverbs like this is quite difficult for young children, so it is important to point out examples in texts whenever possible to help them develop their understanding.

In subsequent years they learn that adjectives can sometimes be turned into adverbs by adding the suffix ‹-ly›, as in 'quickly', 'slowly' and 'softly' (Jolly Grammar 3), or by adding ‹-ly› or ‹-ally› when the adjective ends in ‹-ical› or ‹-ic›, as in 'musica**lly**' and 'basic**ally**' (Jolly Grammar 4).

In Jolly Grammar 5, the children look at how adverbs do not always go next to the verb; they also learn that adverbs do not always describe verbs: they can modify other adverbs (as in '**really** quickly'), as well as adjectives (as in '**quite** surprising').

In Jolly Grammar 6, the children learn about modal adverbs and relative adverbs. Modal adverbs, like modal verbs, can be used to express degrees of certainty, as in 'Ann will **certainly** go to town', 'Ann will **probably** go to town' and '**Perhaps** Ann will go to town'. They can be used with modal verbs like 'will', as in the previous examples, or with main verbs, as in 'He **clearly** loves music'. Because modal verbs and adverbs express varying degrees of certainty, some do not work well together: for example, 'perhaps', which expresses a low level of certainty, is not usually used with 'must', which expresses a high degree of certainty.

Relative adverbs are adverbs that are commonly used to replace the more formal phrases 'in which', 'on which', 'at which' and 'for which' that are sometimes used in relative clauses. For example, we are more likely to use the adverb 'when' than say 'the day <u>on which</u> I was born' or the adverb 'where' in 'the house <u>in which</u> I was born'. Similarly, it is more common to use 'why' to replace 'for which' in a noun phrase like 'the reason **why** he was late'. There is more information about relative clauses on page 22.

Action: The action for adverbs is to bang one fist on top of the other.

Colour: The colour for adverbs is orange.

Adverbials

In Jolly Grammar 6, the children are introduced to the term 'adverbial', which is used to describe any word, phrase or clause that acts as an adverb in a sentence. The most common adverbials are adverbs themselves, along with noun phrases, prepositional phrases and subordinate clauses. Adverbial noun phrases express time, telling us when something happens ('this Wednesday', 'next year', 'yesterday morning'), how often it happens ('every time', 'each winter'), or how long it takes ('all afternoon', 'the whole day'). Other adverbials can modify the verb in a range of ways, most commonly telling us more about how ('loudly', 'without complaint'), where ('in the house', 'wherever I go'), when ('during the week', 'after we had eaten') or why ('for their wedding anniversary', 'because it was raining').

Like adverbs, adverbials do not always appear next to the verb: when one is placed at the beginning of a sentence it is called a fronted adverbial, and it is usually separated from the rest of the sentence by a comma. In parsing, the children should be encouraged to identify adverbials by putting orange brackets around all the words in the phrase or clause (adverbs can be underlined in orange, as usual).

Prepositions

A preposition is a word that relates one noun or pronoun to another: for example, in the sentence 'He climbed over the gate', the preposition 'over' relates the pronoun 'he' to the noun 'gate'. If the latter noun is part of a noun phrase, the preposition is always placed before all the words in it, as in '**under** the bridge', '**in** my purse', '**after** a long pause', '**on** Sally's bicycle' and '**from** her dearest friend'.

Prepositions, as introduced in Jolly Grammar 2, often describe where something is or the direction it is moving in. They can be practised by calling out examples and asking the children to suggest nouns to go with them: for example, the children might suggest 'a box' or 'the classroom' to follow 'in', and 'the mat' or 'the table' to follow 'under'. Many prepositions are short words like 'at', 'by', 'for', 'of', 'in', 'on', 'to' and 'up'. Other common examples include 'above', 'after', 'around', 'behind', 'beside', 'between', 'down', 'from', 'into', 'past', 'through', 'towards', 'under' and 'with'. Care must be taken, however, as many of these words function as adverbs if they do not come before a noun or pronoun: in the sentence 'I fell down', for example, 'down' is an adverb describing 'fell', whereas in 'I fell down the stairs', it is a preposition relating 'I' to 'stairs'. It helps to remember that 'preposition' has the prefix ‹pre-›, meaning 'before', and the root word 'position', meaning 'to place', so a preposition is always <u>placed before</u> a noun or pronoun.

In Jolly Grammar 5, the children learn that not all prepositions are prepositions of place. Sometimes, a preposition relates something to a time or event, as in 'Owls sleep **during the day**' or 'The seasons change **throughout** the year'. They also look at phrases which start with a preposition, followed by a simple noun phrase or pronoun, and learn that these are called prepositional phrases. They are taught that such phrases often act as adverbs in a sentence, describing how, where or when something happens, as in 'I played **with my friends**', 'They ran **down the street**', or 'They arrived **in the afternoon**'.

In Jolly Grammar 6, the children learn that prepositional phrases acting as adverbs are also known as adverbials, as is any word, phrase or clause that fulfils this function. (It is best to avoid the term 'adverbial phrase' until the children are older, as it is so close to 'prepositional phrase' that it can be confusing.) The children also learn that some prepositional phrases act as adjectives rather than adverbs, answering the question 'which one?' or 'what kind?' as in 'the girl **with red hair**' or 'a bar **of milk chocolate**'. They also look at longer prepositional phrases, which usually consist of two shorter phrases put together, as in '<u>at</u> the front <u>of</u> the stage)', '<u>in</u> the heat <u>of</u> the moment' and '<u>by</u> the house <u>on</u> the corner'.

Action: The action for prepositions is to point from one noun to another.

Colour: The colour for prepositions is green.

Conjunctions

A conjunction is a word used to join parts of a sentence which usually, but not always, contain their own verbs. Conjunctions allow the children to write longer, less repetitive sentences: for example, instead of writing 'I eat fish. I eat chips. I like the taste', the children can use the conjunctions 'and' and 'because' to write 'I eat fish and chips because I like the taste'. Whereas the shorter sentences are stilted and repetitive, the longer one flows because it joins together ideas that are closely related.

The ability to vary the length of their sentences will greatly improve the quality of the children's writing. Young children often string sentences together using 'and', so it is a good idea to display a list of common conjunctions in the classroom to encourage them to use other words instead: examples include 'although', 'if', 'now', 'once', 'since', 'unless', 'until', 'when' and 'whether'.

Conjunctions can often be categorised by meaning: for example, 'and' adds extra information, whereas 'nor' excludes it; 'or' provides an alternative and 'so' reveals the consequences; 'though', 'while', 'although', 'but' and 'yet' provide a contrast; 'for', 'because', 'since' and 'as' provide an explanation; and 'if' and 'unless' imply a condition. Many indicate time, including 'as', 'while', 'when', 'after', 'before', 'until', 'since' and 'whenever', and a few, such as 'where', 'wherever' and 'everywhere', indicate place.

Conjunctions are introduced in Jolly Grammar 2, where the focus is on six of the most useful ones: 'and', 'but', 'because', 'or', 'so' and 'while'. Later, the children learn that certain conjunctions can be used to join two simple sentences together in a compound sentence (Jolly Grammar 4) and later still (Jolly Grammar 6) they learn that there are two types of conjunction: those that coordinate parts of a sentence and those that subordinate one part to another.

Coordinating Conjunctions

The coordinating conjunctions are so called because they join together words, phrases or clauses of equal importance. There are only seven coordinating conjunctions: 'for', 'and', 'nor', 'but', 'or', 'yet' and 'so', which can be remembered by the acronym FANBOYS. Some are used more often than others: 'and', 'or', 'so', 'but' and 'yet' are used quite widely; 'nor' is used to join a negative clause to one in which the subject and verb are inverted (as in 'She was <u>not</u> at home, nor <u>was she</u> at work'); and 'for' – which introduces an explanation – is very formal and is rarely used in everyday speech.

The coordinating conjunctions are most notably used to join two simple sentences together in a compound sentence, which the children learn in Jolly Grammar 4. 'And', 'nor', 'but' and 'or' are also used in pairs of correlative conjunctions, as in 'He is <u>neither</u> tall <u>nor</u> handsome', but the children can learn about this when they are older.

Subordinating Conjunctions

A subordinating conjunction joins the main clause in a sentence to a subordinate one. 'Subordinate' means 'ranked below', so a subordinating conjunction indicates that the clause it belongs to is less important than the other. For example, in the sentence 'They went home once it got dark', the conjunction 'once' tells us that the clause 'once it got dark' is subordinate to (or dependent on) the main clause, 'They went home'. A clause with a subordinating conjunction is an adverbial (see page 17), so it can be placed at the beginning of a sentence, as in 'Once it got dark, they went home'.

Action: The action for conjunctions is to hold your hands apart with the palms facing up. Move both hands so one is on top of the other.

Colour: The colour for conjunctions is purple.

A / An / The

The words 'a', 'an' and 'the' are known as articles: 'the' (the definite article) can be used before both singular and plural nouns, whereas 'a' and 'an' (the indefinite articles) are only used before singular nouns. Articles, which belong to a group of words called determiners, are a special type of adjective because they always modify a noun. Determiners appear at the start of a noun phrase to show (or determine) the following: how known it is (articles); how many there are (quantifiers like 'some', 'few', 'more' and 'any'); who it belongs to (possessive adjectives like 'my' and 'ours'); and which particular one is referred to (the demonstratives 'this', 'that', 'these' and 'those').

In Jolly Grammar 1, the children learn when to use 'an' instead of 'a'. They are taught to look at the word that follows the article: if it starts with a vowel sound, the correct article is 'an' (as in 'an ant', 'an egg', 'an itch', 'an octopus' and 'an umbrella'); otherwise, the article is 'a'. This makes it easier to say the two words together fluently. Note that it is the first sound that is important, not the first letter; if a word starts with a silent consonant and the first sound is actually a vowel, it takes 'an', as in 'an hour', whereas one beginning with the long vowel /ue/, pronounced /y-oo/, takes 'a', as in 'a unicorn'.

In Jolly Grammar 6, the children look more closely at when we use the different articles. They learn that 'definite' means 'clearly known', so 'the' indicates that the noun it refers to is one we are likely to know already because, for example, it has been mentioned or is what we are expecting; it is also used before a superlative, because there can only be one thing or one group that is, for example, the tallest or the strongest. 'Indefinite' has the prefix ‹in-›, meaning 'not', and so 'a' and 'an' are used to indicate that the nouns they refer to are unknown and are being introduced for the first time. The children are also introduced to the actions for the articles: they make a capital T with their hands for 'the' and hold up their left hand, palm out, and point to their thumb for 'a' and 'an'. These actions, along with those for the other parts of speech, are used in the Grammar Action Sentences (Grammar Lesson 5) and the Grammar Consequences game (Grammar Lesson 36).

Simple, Compound and Complex Sentences

The full definition of a sentence is complicated and so, in the Jolly Grammar Handbooks, a simple working definition is gradually expanded and refined.

In Jolly Grammar 1, the children learn that a sentence must start with a capital letter, end with a full stop and make sense, and in Jolly Grammar 2, the children learn that a sentence must always have a verb and end with a full stop, question mark or exclamation mark. This definition is further refined in Jolly Grammar 3, when the children learn that a sentence always has a subject and may have an object; the subject is the noun or pronoun that **does** the verb action, as in '**Sam** hit the ball', and the object is the noun or pronoun that **receives** the verb action, as in 'The ball hit **Sam**'. The children then learn in Jolly Grammar 4 that when two or more sentences are joined together with one of the coordinating conjunctions (see page 19), it is called a **compound** sentence, and the two original sentences are called **simple** sentences.

Later, in Jolly Grammar 5, the children are introduced to the idea that subjects and objects can also have simple and compound forms: the simple subject or object is what the children are encouraged to identify when parsing or writing on the sentence walls (see pages 28 and 29) and consists of the head noun only, rather than the whole noun phrase; a compound subject or object consists of two or more subjects or objects in one simple sentence, as in '**Jack** and **Jill** went up the hill', or 'He bought two **shirts** and a **tie**'. The children are also introduced to the idea that at its most basic level, a sentence has two parts: the **subject**, including any words that modify it, and then everything else, including the verb, which is known as the **predicate**. They are also taught that verbs which have an object are called **transitive** and those that do not are called **intransitive**.

In Jolly Grammar 6, the children are taught that a compound sentence may be joined by a **semicolon** – rather than by a coordinating conjunction – as long as the two independent clauses are closely related. They learn that a sentence with a main (or independent) clause and a subordinate (or dependent) clause is called a **complex** sentence. They are also introduced to the idea that a sentence with a **direct object** may also have an **indirect object** for whom or to whom the verb action is done, as in 'The twins made <u>Dad</u> a birthday card'.

The children also learn that a sentence can be written in either the **active voice** or the **passive voice**. In the active voice, the subject and object function in the usual way, but in the passive voice the subject of the sentence is the **receiver** of the verb action and the **agent,** who does the verb action, may not be mentioned at all: if it is, it is introduced in a prepositional phrase, as in 'The ball was hit **by Sam**'. The passive voice is used when the agent of the verb is not known or is considered unimportant and the verb is formed by using the auxiliary 'to be' with the past participle.

Statements, Questions and Exclamations

In Jolly Grammar 1 and 2, the children learn to recognise a question as a sentence that asks for further information and ends in a question mark. They are also taught the ‹wh› question words ('what', 'why', 'when', 'where', 'who', 'which' and 'whose') and how to use them to make questions. Subsequently, the children's knowledge is extended as they are introduced to exclamation marks, which are used at the end of exclamations to show that the writer or speaker feels strongly about something (Jolly Grammar 2); they also learn how to write questions and exclamations in direct speech (Jolly Grammar 3).

In Jolly Grammar 4, the children learn that sentences ending in a full stop are called statements, and they look at some simple ways to turn statements into questions. For example, if a statement's main verb is 'to be', it can be made into a question by putting the verb at the beginning and replacing the full stop with a question mark; as a result, 'This **is** the way to the park' becomes '**Is** this the way to the park?' Similarly, if there is a main verb and an auxiliary, it is the auxiliary verb that is moved to the front; in this way, 'I **can** go to the park' becomes '**Can** I go to the park?'

Later, in Jolly Grammar 6, the children learn that statements written in the simple past and simple present cannot be turned into questions in the usual way, because they have no auxiliary verb. Instead, the verb 'to do' is used as an auxiliary, together with the bare infinitive of the main verb. This means that a sentence like 'You **went** to the park' can be turned into the question '**Did** you **go** to the park?' The children also learn that 'to do' can be used in a similar way to add emphasis to a positive statement ('I **do like** ice cream') or to make a statement negative ('She **does** not **like** ice cream').

Phrases

Jolly Grammar uses a simple working definition to identify a phrase as a group of words that makes sense but has no verb or subject. This helps the children to distinguish between a sentence and a phrase in Jolly Grammar 3. Then, in Jolly Grammar 4, the children learn that a noun, together with the words that describe (or modify) it, is called a noun phrase. There can be more than one noun phrase in a sentence and each noun phrase can be replaced with a pronoun. For example, in the sentence 'I took <u>three juicy apples</u> from <u>the big wooden bowl</u>' there are two noun phrases, which can be replaced by the pronouns 'them' and 'it' and still make sense: 'I took them from it'. The children also learn that not all words in a noun phrase come before the noun, as can be seen in 'a girl with blonde hair'. This kind of noun phrase generally has a main noun (in this example it is 'girl') and another noun helping to describe it ('hair').

In Jolly Grammar 5, the children are introduced to prepositional phrases. These are phrases that start with a preposition followed by a simple noun phrase or pronoun, as in 'down the steep hill', or 'between them'. They learn that prepositional phrases often act as adverbs of manner ('He sat **in silence**'), place ('She walked **to the door**') or time ('They jog **in the morning**'); then, in Jolly Grammar 6, the children are taught that they can also act as adjectives, as in 'the room **at the top**' or 'a tube **of toothpaste**'.

Clauses

Clauses are introduced in Jolly Grammar 4. A clause is a group of words that contains a verb and subject and makes sense. This is much like the working definition of a sentence; indeed, some clauses can stand alone as sentences, such as those in the compound sentence 'Gran baked a cake and the children decorated it'. Such clauses are known as independent clauses. However, not all clauses are independent. In the sentence 'While he waited, he read his book', the clause 'he read his book' could stand alone as a simple sentence, but 'While he waited' could not. This is because – despite having a verb and subject – the clause does not represent a complete thought: it leaves us to ask what else the subject did during that time. This type of clause is called a dependent or subordinate clause. It is dependent because it relies on further information to express its full meaning, and it is subordinate (meaning 'ranked below') because its function is to give us extra information about the main (or independent) clause.

In Jolly Grammar 6, the children learn that a sentence with a main clause and a subordinate one is called a complex sentence. They also learn more about the type of information that a subordinate clause provides. Clauses starting with a subordinating conjunction act as adverbs by telling us more about when, where or why something happens, as in 'We went inside before it started to rain'; 'It rained wherever we went'; and 'We went inside because it was raining'.

However, clauses that start with a relative pronoun or relative adverb, as in 'the key that I found' or 'the street where you live', always act as adjectives. Sometimes the information in the relative clause is interesting, but it could easily be left out. The children learn to punctuate this type of relative clause with bracketing commas. However, some information is essential because it tells us what we need to know in order to identify which person or thing is meant. Relative clauses are therefore described as either **defining** or **non-defining** clauses (or sometimes as restrictive and non-restrictive clauses). As they fulfil the adjective function, relative clauses are also known as adjectival clauses; however, this is not a term that is used with the children at this stage.

Paragraphs and Cohesion

Paragraphs are used to organise information in a piece of writing so that it is easy to read and understand. Instead of one large block of text, the writing is broken down into smaller groups of sentences called paragraphs. Each paragraph starts on a new line (which is usually indented) and is made up of sentences that describe one idea or topic. By putting paragraphs in a particular order, a piece of writing can move from one idea to another in a way that makes sense.

In Jolly Grammar 3, the children learn how to plan their work and write in paragraphs. They think about what they want to say and note down their ideas, arranging them under topic headings. The children are then able to expand their thoughts into proper sentences and put their paragraphs in a logical order. Once they can do this, the children should be encouraged to use paragraphs in their writing, organising their ideas before they write anything down. It is also a good idea to point out paragraphs in the texts the children are studying. This will help them appreciate how a well-structured piece of writing flows and keeps the reader interested.

In Jolly Grammar 6, the children look more closely at the structure of a paragraph. They learn that it needs a beginning, a middle and an end: the first sentence, called the topic sentence, usually explains what the whole paragraph is about; the sentences that follow provide the evidence to support the main idea; and the final sentence usually acts as a conclusion, summing up what the paragraph is about (although not all paragraphs do this). This pattern echoes the structure of a longer piece of writing, which would normally have an introductory and closing paragraph. Writing in this way helps the children to avoid repeating or contradicting themselves.

The children also learn about cohesion, which is the use of words and phrases to link ideas or paragraphs in a fluid way. Many adverbs and conjunctions provide cohesion, as do phrases that act as these parts of speech. They are often referred to as 'connectives' and can be categorised by function. They include, for example, words that indicate time or sequence ('meanwhile', 'next', 'then', 'firstly', 'secondly', 'thirdly'); an opening ('at first', 'to begin with', 'initially'); a summing-up ('finally', 'after all', 'in conclusion'); place ('nearby', 'around the corner', 'down the road'); cause and effect ('because', 'since', 'therefore', 'as a result'); additional information ('also', 'as well as', 'moreover'); and contrast ('instead', 'although', 'however', 'unless').

Punctuation

Jolly Grammar 2 places particular emphasis on the importance of punctuation: the children revise what they learnt in Jolly Grammar 1 (full stops, question marks and speech marks) and are introduced to exclamation marks, commas and apostrophes. The teaching aims to help the children understand that their writing will be easier to read if it is accurately punctuated.

In Jolly Grammar 3 and 4, the focus is on using the correct punctuation when writing direct speech, as in '"I'm tired," said Tim', where the words are written exactly as they are said; this should not be confused with reported speech, such as 'Tim said he was tired'. The children revise how to use speech marks, full stops, commas and contractions, and they learn how to use question marks and exclamation marks in direct speech; they are also introduced to some of the more straightforward uses of hyphens (Jolly Grammar 4).

In Jolly Grammar 5, the children are shown how to use parentheses correctly in their writing and learn how to punctuate vertical lists using a colon and bullet points. Their knowledge is further extended in Jolly Grammar 6, when they learn that colons can be used in a sentence to introduce things like an idea, a list of examples, or an explanation. They are introduced to semicolons, which can be used to replace commas in a complicated list or to join closely related clauses in a compound sentence. They also learn how to punctuate imperative sentences, non-defining relative clauses and fronted adverbials.

Question Marks

The children need to understand what a question is and how to form a question mark correctly. If a sentence is worded in such a way that it expects an answer, then it is a question and needs a question mark ‹?› instead of a full stop. If a question is written as direct speech, the question mark is kept at the end and is not replaced with a comma.

Exclamation Marks

When someone cries out suddenly, especially in anger, surprise or pain, they are said to exclaim or to make an exclamation. An exclamation mark ‹!› is used at the end of a sentence, instead of a full stop, to show that the speaker or writer feels strongly about something. It is also used after interjections (such as 'Hi!' 'Well!' and 'Sorry!') and in some imperative sentences, if these express a forceful order, command or warning. If an exclamation is written as direct speech, the exclamation mark is kept at the end and is not replaced with a comma.

Commas

Sometimes it is necessary to indicate a short pause within a sentence to help the reader separate one idea from another. For this sort of pause we use a comma ‹,› rather than a full stop. The children are probably used to being told to pause when they see a comma in their reading, but learning when to use commas in their writing is more difficult. Jolly Grammar 2 introduces two of the most straightforward ways commas are used:

- We use commas to separate items in a list of more than two items, as in 'red, white and blue', or 'Grandma, Grandpa, Aunt or Uncle'. (In Jolly Grammar 6, the children learn that if an item already has a comma, they can punctuate the list using semicolons instead.) A comma is not used before the last item in a list: instead, it is replaced by the word 'and' or 'or'.

- We also use commas in sentences with direct speech to indicate a pause between the words spoken and the rest of the sentence. If the speech comes before the rest of the sentence, the comma belongs inside the speech marks, after the last word spoken, as in ' "I am hungry," complained Matt.' (If the words spoken form a question or exclamation, a question mark or exclamation mark is used instead of a comma in the same position.) If the speech comes after the rest of the sentence, the comma goes at the end of the word that comes before the speech marks, as in 'Matt complained, "I am hungry." '

Later, in Jolly Grammar 6, the children learn that a fronted adverbial is usually separated from the rest of the sentence by a comma, as in 'When I got home, I went to bed'. They are also taught that a non-defining relative clause should be bracketed with commas, unless the clause appears at the end of the sentence, when the second comma is unnecessary. The commas show that the information, while interesting, is not essential, as in 'The house, which has four bedrooms, is currently for sale'.

Apostrophes

Apostrophes are very often incorrectly used, although the rules on how and when to use them are pretty straightforward. It is therefore important to teach the rules early on, before any children develop bad habits in their writing. Jolly Grammar 2 introduces both of the main ways that an apostrophe ‹'› can be used:

- An apostrophe with the letter ‹s› is used after a noun to indicate possession, as in 'Ben's new toy' or 'the girl's father'. The apostrophe is needed to show that the ‹s› is not being used to make a plural. Understanding this will help the children use apostrophe ‹s› correctly. Encourage them to think about the meaning of what they write and whether each ‹s› is being used to make a plural or the possessive case.
  In Jolly Grammar 4, the children learn that this type of noun is called a possessive noun. They also learn how to make possessive nouns plural (as in 'the boys' room' or 'the women's hats'), as described on page 7. Later, the children can learn how to use apostrophe ‹s› with names that end in ‹es› (as in 'James' cat').
  Although the possessive adjectives (such as 'my', 'your', 'his', 'her' and 'its' indicate possession, there is no risk of confusion with the plural, so they do not need an apostrophe. Knowing this will help the children avoid the common

mistake of writing the possessive adjective 'its' as 'it's'.

- An apostrophe is also used to show that one or more letters is missing in a contraction. Sometimes we contract words by joining them together and leaving out some of their letters, as in 'I'm' for 'I am', 'didn't' for 'did not' and 'you'll' for 'you will'. The apostrophe indicates where the missing letter(s) used to be.

  There are many common contractions and when the children come across them, they should be encouraged to listen to the word and identify which sound(s) are missing. This will help them leave out the appropriate letter(s) and put the apostrophe in the right place, thereby avoiding some common mistakes. In 'haven't', for example, the /o/ of 'not' is missing, so the apostrophe goes between ‹n› and ‹t› to show where ‹o› used to be; it does not go between ‹e› and ‹n› to make 'have'nt'.

  Knowing that 'it is' and 'it has' can be contracted in this way will also help the children not to confuse 'it's' and 'its'. For example, if the word to be written is short for either 'it is' or 'it has', as in 'It's late' or 'It's fallen in the water', the children should remember to use an apostrophe.

  It is important that the children learn how to spell and punctuate contractions correctly. However, contractions should only be used in direct speech or in informal notes; they are not traditionally used in formal writing.

Hyphens

Sometimes it is necessary to show that two or more words (or parts of words) are linked closely together, either in use or meaning. This helps the reader understand the text properly and avoids any ambiguity. To do this we use a hyphen ‹-›, and it is found mostly in compound words and in some words with a prefix. Using hyphens makes a word like 'brother-in-law' easier to read and allows us to distinguish, for example, between 're-cover' and 'recover'.

However, not all compound words or words with a prefix need a hyphen, and hyphens are not used so commonly now as they once were; whether or not a hyphen is used often changes over time, and varies between dictionaries. Also, the rules for when to use hyphens are quite complex for children of this age, and so they should be encouraged to use a dictionary and make sure that their spelling is consistent.

Nevertheless, there are some instances in which a hyphen is nearly always used and these, along with the term 'hyphen', are introduced in Jolly Grammar 4. The children learn to use a hyphen when the numbers between 21 and 99 are written as words, as in 'twenty-one' or 'thirty-three', and when the first part of a compound word is a capital letter, as in 'X-ray' and 'T-shirt'. Later, children can learn about other common uses of the hyphen. These include joining fractions (as in 'three-quarters' and 'two-thirds') and compound adjectives (but only when the adjective comes before the noun it is describing, as in 'the well-known phrase'). For now it is enough that the children understand what a hyphen is and how it can be used to make meaning clearer.

Colons and Bullet Points

In Jolly Grammar 5, the children learn how to write lists vertically down a page. Vertical lists are often used in presentations and reports or for practical reasons, like making a shopping list, as the layout makes the list easier to read at a glance. However it is written, a list always needs an introduction. The children learn that a vertical list's introduction has a colon at the end, which is a punctuation mark written as two small dots, one above the other ‹:›. Like full stops and commas, a colon marks the place where we should pause in speaking: it is a longer pause than a comma, but not as long as a full stop. In normal writing, an introduction that ends in a colon should be able to stand alone as a simple sentence, but in vertical lists this is not so important.

The items in a vertical list are not separated by commas. Instead, each item starts on a new, slightly indented, line with a special symbol at the front. This symbol, known as a bullet, can vary in design, but most commonly appears as a large dot or circle. Both the symbol itself and the items in the list are called bullet points, although not all vertical lists use them; instead, the items could be numbered 1, 2, 3, or A, B, C, for example. Unlike a traditional list, the 'and' or 'or' before the final item does not usually appear.

A vertical list item can be a word, phrase or clause and it can either have an open punctuation style (no full stop at the end and a lower-case letter at the start, except when writing proper nouns) or be more formally punctuated; either way is acceptable as long as the style is consistent, although it is more common for clauses to be punctuated as sentences. The wording itself also has to be consistent, so that the list makes sense. For example, if a vertical list begins 'At school I:' and the first two bullet points are 'study hard' and 'play sports', the other items should follow the same format, starting with a verb in the simple present tense; it would not make sense to change style by changing the tense, using a participle, or writing a whole sentence, for example.

In Jolly Grammar 6, the children look at how a colon can be used in a sentence and learn that when we see one, we know that some important information will follow, such as a list of examples, an idea or an explanation. As in a vertical list, the colon is used as part of the introduction, but unlike a vertical list, the words in front of the colon must always form an independent clause. This means that we should never use a colon to separate a verb from its object or complement: instead of using an unnecessary colon in 'My sister has: two dogs, three cats and a hamster', for example, we could say, 'My sister has six pets: two dogs, three cats and a hamster'.

Semicolons

Like the colon, a semicolon marks a longer pause than a comma, but a shorter one than a full stop. Both punctuation marks look quite similar, except the semicolon has a comma-like mark rather than a bottom dot ‹;›. The children are introduced to the semicolon in Jolly Grammar 6, and learn the two main ways that it can be used in writing.

Firstly, semicolons can be used to join independent clauses in a compound sentence. Normally, this is done by using one of the coordinating conjunctions to create a flow in our writing (as explained on page 19). However, when the relationship between the two clauses is obvious, the conjunction can be replaced with a semicolon, as in 'Take your umbrella; it is going to rain'. The semicolon implies there is a connection between the two clauses without interrupting the flow.

Semicolons can also be used instead of commas to separate items in a complicated list. For example, the children learn that if any of the items already has a comma, it is better to separate them with a semicolon, as in 'In the box there was an old, chipped cup; some old Roman coins; and some torn, faded postcards'.

Parentheses

In a piece of writing, we sometimes choose to provide further information which is interesting, but not essential. In Jolly Grammar 5, the children learn that the main way to do this is to put the information in parentheses. Parentheses are round brackets that come in pairs, rather like speech marks do; an opening bracket is placed at the beginning and a closing bracket is put at the end. When something is written in parentheses, the reader knows that the sentence would still be complete even if the extra information were removed. The extra information provided can be varied, but often includes such things as dates, prices, page numbers, explanations and alternative names. It can even be a sentence, and if it is written as such, with a capital letter at the beginning and a full stop at the end, the full stop should go inside the parentheses. Parentheses can also be used in a list of options: for example, 'These shirts are available in (a) small, (b) medium or (c) large.' The children should be encouraged to read their writing through and check that it would still make sense if the words in parentheses were removed.

Grammatical Agreement

From the beginning, the children are encouraged to think about the relationship between words in a sentence and to use their grammar knowledge to make their writing as clear and as accurate as possible. They learn that the indefinite articles 'a' and 'an' are only used with a singular noun, whereas the definite article 'the' can be used for both singular and plural. They learn how to form a plural correctly and how to conjugate a verb. They also learn the possessive adjectives and possessive pronouns and are shown, for example, how 'It is my book' can be written as 'It is mine'.

This knowledge will help the children to understand grammatical agreement. In most languages, certain word relationships have to match or 'agree'; in English this agreement centres on person, number and sometimes gender. The form of a verb can change, for example, depending on which person is used for the subject: we say 'I am' for the verb 'to be' in the **first** person singular but 'he is' for the **third** person singular. Whether the subject is singular or plural (grammatical number) can also affect the verb: we say 'The rabbit **eats**' in the singular, but 'The rabbits **eat**' in the plural. When it comes to pronouns and possessive adjectives, gender can affect which word is used: in the singular, we say 'he', 'him' or 'his' for the masculine, 'she', 'her' or 'hers' for the feminine and 'it' and 'its' for the neuter.

While most children use simple grammatical agreement quite naturally in their spoken and written language, it is important that they understand the principles. This will help them as they start to produce longer, more complicated writing. The idea is introduced gradually in Jolly Grammar 4. First, the children look at what happens when certain words in a sentence are changed, starting first with object nouns and the words that describe them and then with subjects and their verbs. Then, when the children have learnt about grammatical person, they look at how changing this can affect the verb and the rest of the sentence. Encourage the children to proofread their work and to make sure that all the relevant words in the sentence agree.

Parsing: Identifying Parts of Speech in Sentences

Parsing means identifying the function, or part of speech, of each word in a sentence. The children must look at each word in context to decide what part of speech it is. This skill is worth promoting, as it reinforces the grammar teaching and helps the children to develop an analytical understanding of how our language works. Many words can function as more than one part of speech. For example, the word 'light' can be a noun ('the light'), a verb ('to light') or an adjective ('a light colour'). It is only by analysing a word's use within a sentence that its function can be identified.

The best way to introduce parsing is by writing extremely simple sentences on the board. A good example is 'I pat the dog', which is parsed like this: pronoun, verb, (article), noun.

The children can be encouraged to identify the parts of speech they know and then take turns to underline them in the appropriate colours. Gradually, when most of the children have mastered this, move on to more complicated sentences that use more parts of speech: for example, 'She cheerfully wrote a long letter to her friend'. This can be parsed as pronoun, adverb, verb (the infinitive of which is 'to write'), (article), adjective, noun, preposition, possessive adjective, noun. Ask the children to identify the nouns and verbs first, reminding them that every sentence must contain at least one verb. Also encourage them to say the verb in its infinitive form. If there is time, the children should identify as many of the other parts of speech as possible, underlining them in the appropriate colours: nouns (black), verbs (red), pronouns (pink), adjectives (blue), adverbs (orange), prepositions (green), conjunctions (purple).

From Jolly Grammar 3 onwards, there is regular parsing practice in the spelling lessons to help the children become quick and competent at this task. If any children are unfamiliar with parsing, or find it difficult, they need to work on simpler sentences and build up their confidence.

Sentence Walls

Parsing a sentence can reveal a lot about the role of the individual words. It can also help the children identify its subject and object. This in turn allows them to decide whether a verb is transitive or intransitive. However, it does not always reveal the relationship between certain words or phrases; nor does it tell us much about the structure of the sentence. Jolly Grammar 5 introduces the idea of sentence walls: a form of sentence diagramming* that has been simplified for younger children. Sentence walls represent the building blocks of a sentence in an accessible and visual way. They allow the children to see at a glance different parts of a sentence: the subject and predicate; the verb and direct object; an indirect object or subject complement; prepositional phrases acting as adverbs or adjectives; and the words that are essential to the meaning of the sentence and those that provide extra information. To give some visual interest, the sentence walls on the worksheets are portrayed as old stone walls, but they basically consist of six boxes that can be drawn on the board and discussed with the children.

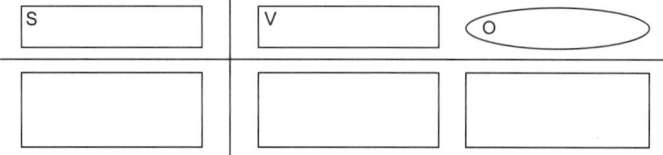

A short vertical line separates the two basic parts of a sentence: the subject and predicate. A long horizontal line separates the essential information from the extra information. Everything above the line – the simple subject, verb and simple object (if there is one) is necessary to the sentence and reads rather like a short newspaper headline. Everything below the line (such as articles, determiners, adjectives, adverbs and prepositional phrases) is additional information that modifies the words above. A simple sentence like 'The young girl has decorated her picture beautifully' can be parsed as normal, and then it can be transferred to the boxes, as shown at the top of the opposite page.

* Modern diagramming is based on Alonzo Reed and Brainerd Kellogg's work in *Higher Lessons in English: A Work on English Grammar and Composition*, first published in 1877. However, sentence walls were inspired by D. K. Thompson's work on box analysis, which is closer in format to Francis A. March's diagrams in *A Parser and Analyzer for Beginners* (1869), which were influenced by W. S. Clark and his 'balloon' system (*A Practical Grammar*, 1847).

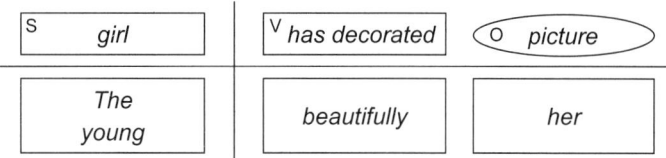

If the sentence contains a compound subject and object it will look like this:

Similarly, if the main adverb is modified by another adverb or there is a prepositional phrase acting as an adverb, the boxes are completed like this:

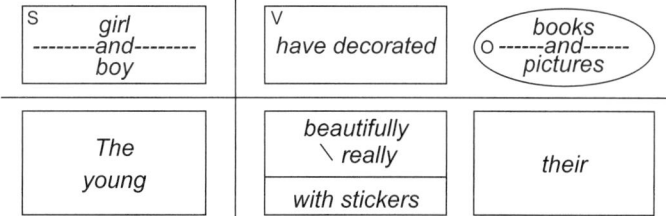

If an adverb modifies an adjective (as in '**really** beautiful'), or a prepositional phrase acts as an adjective rather than an adverb (as in 'the book <u>with stickers</u>'), they are written as above, but go in either the left- or right-hand bottom box, depending on whether they are describing the subject or object (see Grammar Lesson 10).

Similarly, if 'really beautiful' is a subject complement used with a linking verb like 'to be' (as in 'The stickers are really beautiful'), the top row is filled in like this:

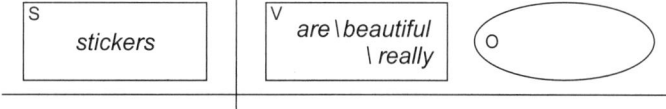

Finally, if a sentence has an indirect object, it is written like this:

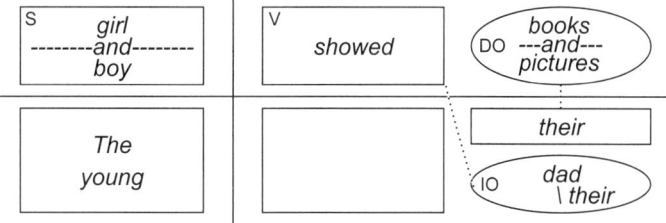

Alphabetical Order, Dictionary and Thesaurus Work

The more familiar children are with the order of the alphabet, the better they will be at using essential classroom resources like dictionaries, thesauruses and encyclopedias. In Jolly Grammar 1, the children learn the alphabet thoroughly and are taught how to navigate a dictionary. They learn to think of the dictionary as comprising four approximately equal parts, containing the following groups: 1. Aa–Ee (red), 2. Ff–Mm (yellow), 3. Nn–Ss (green), 4. Tt–Zz (blue). It is a good idea to have a copy of the alphabet, divided into the four groups, available for the children to see. The groups and colour-coding are incorporated into the Jolly Phonics Alphabet Poster and the Jolly Dictionary.

Knowing the alphabet groups saves the children time when using a dictionary. Before looking up a word, they decide which group its initial letter falls into and then narrow their search to that section of the dictionary. When looking up the word 'pony', for example, the children can turn directly to the third quarter of the dictionary because they know that the letter ‹p› is in the green group. Jolly Grammar 2 improves the children's dictionary skills by teaching them to look beyond the initial letter of each word. They practise putting into alphabetical order words that share the first two letters (such as 'sheep' and 'shoe') and then words that share the first three letters (for example, 'penny', 'pencil' and 'penguin'). This skill is reinforced in Jolly Grammar 3, 4 and 6, where a common activity involves putting words from the weekly spelling list into alphabetical order.

In Jolly Grammar 3 and 4, looking up words in the dictionary for spelling and meaning is a regular activity in the spelling lessons. It helps the children understand how useful dictionaries are and aims to develop the skills they need to become regular and proficient dictionary users. Most children can become quite proficient at using a dictionary designed for schools. When they finish a piece of writing, the children should proofread their work, identify any words that look incorrectly spelt and look them up in the dictionary. The children should also be encouraged to use a dictionary to make sure they are using the right word, especially one that is a homophone, near homophone or homograph. Homophones are words that sound similar to one another but have different spellings and meanings (as in 'hear' and 'here'). Homographs are words that share the same spelling but have different meanings. There are two types of homograph: Those that look and sound the same are called homonyms (as in 'There was a **fly** on my sandwich' and 'I will **fly** to Australia'); those that look the same but sound different are called heteronyms (as in 'The two rocky paths **wind** among the trees' and 'The **wind** blew the leaves off the tree'). There is a strong focus on homophones throughout the Jolly Grammar Handbooks, particularly in Jolly Grammar 4, while homographs are introduced in Jolly Grammar 5.

In Jolly Grammar 2, the children are introduced to thesauruses. Instead of giving a definition for a word, a thesaurus provides a group of words with a similar meaning and often suggests words with the opposite meaning. The children can make their work more interesting by using a thesaurus to find alternatives to words that are commonly overused, like 'nice' or 'said'. In Jolly Grammar 4, the children learn the technical names for the two types of word found in a thesaurus: words with similar meanings are called synonyms and their opposites are known as antonyms. The children also develop their knowledge of antonyms, learning that many prefixes and some suffixes can be used to create them: for example, ‹un-›, ‹im-› and ‹non-› mean 'not'; ‹de-› and ‹dis-› mean 'undo' or 'remove'; ‹mis-› means 'wrongly' or 'not'; and ‹ex› means 'out' or 'away from'. The suffixes ‹-less› and ‹-ful›, which mean 'without' something or 'full' of it, can be added to the same root word to make a pair of adjectives with the opposite meaning, as in 'thoughtful' and 'thoughtless'.

Having their own Spelling Word Book can help the children improve their independent writing. In it they can record the weekly spellings, as well as other useful vocabulary and examples of literacy devices (such as homophones, antonyms, synonyms, idioms and alliterative phrases). The following extension activities can be used to improve alphabet and dictionary skills, or with those children who finish their work ahead of time:

- The children take the words from a page in their Spelling Word Book and rewrite them in alphabetical order.
- Choose a word with a sound or spelling pattern that has alternative spellings. Use these spellings to write out several versions of the word on the board: for example, 'delicious', 'delitious', 'delixious' and 'deliscious'. The children use a dictionary to check which spelling of the word is correct.
- In pairs, the children race one another to find a given word in the dictionary.

Teaching Ideas for Spelling

Most children need to be taught to spell correctly. In the Jolly Grammar Handbooks, spelling is the main focus for one lesson each week. The spelling activities in Jolly Grammar 6 are designed to consolidate the children's existing knowledge and introduce new spelling patterns. Its main focus is on the more unusual spellings of the vowel sounds, less common 'silent letter' digraphs, number prefixes, and closely related suffixes like ‹-ity› and ‹-ety›, ‹-ious› and ‹-eous›, and ‹-ure› and ‹-our›.

In Jolly Phonics, the children first learn to spell by listening for the sounds in a word and writing the letters that represent those sounds. They also systematically learn the tricky words, which are frequently used words that either have an irregular spelling or use phonic knowledge that the children do not know yet. By the time they are ready to start Jolly Grammar 2, most children have a reading age of at least seven years, and they are starting to spell with far greater accuracy. As research has shown, children with a reading age of seven years or more are able to use analogy in their reasoning. This is a useful strategy for spelling. For example, children who know the word 'would' and who want to write 'should', might notice that the end of both words sound the same. They can then use this knowledge to write 'should', replacing the ‹w› with ‹sh›. If the children are unsure of a spelling, they may be able to find it by writing the word in several ways (such as 'should', 'shood' and 'shud') and choosing the version that looks correct. If they have already encountered the word several times in their reading, they will probably be able to choose the right one. By introducing groups of spelling words that each feature a particular spelling pattern, the Jolly Grammar Handbooks encourage the children to think analogically.

A focus on revising the alternative spellings of vowel sounds and learning new ones helps the children consolidate and extend their learning. The alternative vowel spellings are what make English spelling difficult and, by this stage, the children need to be not only revising the main ways of spelling the vowel sounds, but also improving their ability to remember which words take which spelling.

The Jolly Grammar 6 Handbook builds on the teaching of the previous Handbooks and assumes that the children have some knowledge of the following spelling features, which are outlined in greater detail below:

- vowel digraphs,
- alternative spellings of the vowel sounds,
- new spelling patterns,
- syllables,
- the schwa,
- silent letters,
- identifying the short vowels, and
- spelling rules.

Vowel Digraphs

The vowel digraphs are first introduced as a focus for spelling in Jolly Grammar 1, and the focus in Jolly Grammar 2 and 3 is on consolidating this learning. 'Vowel digraph' is the term for two letters that make a single vowel sound. Often, the two letters are placed next to each other in a word, as in 'h**ay**', 's**ea**', '**out**', '**oil**' and 'f**ew**'. At least one of these letters is always a vowel, and two vowel letters are usually needed to make one of the long vowel sounds: /ai, ee, ie, oa, ue/. (The long vowel sounds are the same as the names of the vowel letters: ‹a, e, i, o, u›.) Generally, the sound made by a digraph is that of the first vowel's name, hence the well-known rule of thumb: 'When two vowels go walking, the first does the talking.'

Sometimes, the long vowel sound is made by two vowels separated by one or more consonants. In monosyllabic words, the second vowel is usually an ‹e›, known as a 'magic ‹e›' because it modifies the sound of the first vowel letter. Digraphs with a magic ‹e› can be thought of as 'hop-over ‹e›' digraphs: ‹a_e›, ‹e_e›, ‹i_e›, ‹o_e› and ‹u_e›. Once again, the sound they make is that

of the first vowel's name; the magic ‹e› is silent. Children like to show with their hand how the 'magic' from the ‹e› hops over the preceding consonant and changes the short vowel sound to a long one.

The hop-over ‹e› digraphs are an alternative way of writing the long vowel sounds, and are found in words such as 'bake', 'these', 'fine', 'hope' and 'cube'. The children need to be shown many examples of such words, which are available in the Jolly Phonics Word Book. To help the children understand how magic ‹e› works, ask them to read a word twice: first with the magic ‹e› showing and then with it hidden by a piece of paper. In this way 'pipe' becomes 'pip', 'hate' becomes 'hat', 'hope' becomes 'hop' and 'late' becomes 'lat'. It does not matter if, as in the last example, the children find themselves producing nonsense words; the exercise will still help them to understand the spelling rule. When looking at words on the board or in other texts, the children can be encouraged to look for and identify words with a magic ‹e›.

Although hop-over ‹e› words are quite common, there are relatively few with the ‹e_e› spelling and they are often quite advanced: 'these', 'scheme' and 'complete' are some of the simpler examples. For this reason, ‹e_e› is not given quite as much emphasis as the other long vowel spellings, and it is not made the focus of a whole lesson until Jolly Grammar 3.

Alternative Spellings of the Vowel Sounds

Children who have learnt to read with Jolly Phonics are used to spelling new words by listening for the sounds and writing the letters that represent those sounds. This skill enables them to spell accurately the many regular words that do not use vowel sounds with more than one spelling: words like 'hot', 'plan', 'brush', 'drench' and 'sting'. However, trying to spell words like 'train', 'play' and 'make' presents a problem. All three words feature the same vowel sound, /ai/, but in each case it is spelt differently. The list below shows the first spelling taught for each sound and the main alternatives introduced:

First spelling taught for sound	Alternative spellings for sound	Examples of all spellings in words
ai	ay, a_e	rain, day, came
ee	ea	street, dream
ie	igh, y, i_e	pie, light, by, time
oa	ow, o_e	boat, snow, home
ue	ew, u_e	cue, few, cube
er	ir, ur	her, first, turn
oi	oy	boil, toy
ou	ow	out, cow
or	aw, au, al	corn, saw, haunt, talk

These vowel sounds and their alternative spellings are the main focus for spelling in Jolly Grammar 1. They are then revised in Jolly Grammar 2 and 3 and should be familiar to the children. However, it is very important to keep consolidating the teaching. This can be achieved by revising the spelling patterns regularly with flashcards, and by asking the children to list the alternative spellings for a particular sound. The children should be able to do this automatically and apply their knowledge when writing unfamiliar words. For example, with a word like 'frame', they should be able to write 'fraim, fraym, frame' on a scrap of paper, before deciding which version looks correct.

New Spelling Patterns

The Handbooks for Jolly Grammar 2 onwards introduce many of the less common spellings for familiar sounds. A few are also taught in Jolly Grammar 1. The list below shows the spelling first taught and the new spelling patterns introduced:

First spelling taught for sound(s)	New spelling for sound(s)	Examples of new spellings in words
The Jolly Grammar 1/2 Handbooks		
ai	ei, eigh	veil, eight, sleigh
cher*	ture	capture, nature, picture
e	ea	breakfast, deaf, ready
ee	ey, ie, y**	key, field, fairy**
f	ph	graph, orphan, photo
j	soft g	gem, giant, gymnast
k	ch, ck	chord, cricket
ngk	nk**	ink, bank, trunk
ool*	le	handle, little, nibble
or	ore	more, snore, wore
s	soft c	cell, city, cycle
sh	si, ti	tension, station
u	o, ou	month, touch
w	wh**	whale, whistle, why
(w)o	(w)a	swan, wasp, watch
The Jolly Grammar 3 Handbook		
ai	a	able, taste, haste
air, are, ear*	ere	ere, where, there
ar	a	koala, vase, lava
ch	tch	match, fetch, itch
ear*	eer, ere	cheer, deer, here, mere
ee	e_e, e	these, athlete, secret, reflex
f	gh	enough, cough, laugh
i	y	myth, pyramid, system
ie	i	child, wild, microwave
j	dge	edge, bridge, judge
n	gn	gnaw, resign, gnome
ng	n	trunk, finger, anchor
oa	o	only, ogre, ago
(qu)o	(qu)a	squad, squabble, quantity
ue	u	menu, emu
z	s, se, ze	easy, pause, bronze

The Jolly Grammar 4 Handbook

er	ear	earth, pearl, search
g	gh	ghost, dinghy, aghast
oo	u	truth, flu, cruel
or	ough, augh	ought, thought, caught
s	se, st	goose, false, castle, listen
v	ve	solve, curve, groove
(w)er	(w)or	worm, worst, worker

The Jolly Grammar 5 Handbook

iez	ize, ise	capsize, surprise
ij	age, ege	advantage, privilege
sh	ch, che, sch	chef, moustache, schwa
shor*	sure	sure, unsure, assure
shul*	cial, sial, tial	special, controversial, initial
shun*	ssion, cian	mission, musician
shus*	cious, xious, tious	delicious, anxious, cautious
sk	sch	school, scheme
us*	ous	famous, nervous, dangerous

The Jolly Grammar 6 Handbook

ai	ea, ey, et, e_e, aigh	great, they, ballet, fete, straight
air*	eir	their, heirloom
e	ei	heifer, leisure
ear*	eir	weir, weird
ee	ei	ceiling, receive, deceit, deceive
g	gu, gue	guess, guitar, league, dialogue
gw	gu	penguin, language, iguana
i	ei, ui, u	counterfeit, building, busy
ie	ei, eigh	feisty, eiderdown, height
ius*/us*	eous	hideous, erroneous, gorgeous, outrageous
k	cc, que	hiccup, occupy, queue, masquerade
m	mb, mn, me	numb, column, welcome
ne	n	examine, migraine, bygone
ng	gue	tongue, harangue, meringue
oa	oe, oo, ew, ou, au, ough	toe, brooch, sewn, shoulder, mauve, dough
off	ough	cough
oo	ui, ou, o, oe, ough	fruit, soup, movie, shoe, through
or	ough	bought, sought, thought
ou	ough	bough, drought
sh	ci	ancient, social, species
t	bt, te, tte, th, cht	doubt, paste, palette, thyme, yacht
uff	ough	rough, tough, enough

* This is only an approximation of the sound made by the new spelling.
** ‹y› as /ee/, ‹wh› and ‹nk› are introduced in the Jolly Grammar 1 Handbook.

The children need to memorise which words use each of the new spelling patterns. It is helpful to make up silly sentences for each spelling, using as many of the words as possible. For the ‹ie› spelling of the /ee/ sound, for example, the children could chant the following: 'I bel**ie**ve my n**ie**ce was the ch**ie**f th**ie**f who came to gr**ie**f over the p**ie**ce of sh**ie**ld she hid in the f**ie**ld'.

Jolly Grammar 2 and 3 also feature a few letter sounds that have not been a focus for spelling before. Jolly Grammar 2 introduces the new sounds /zh/ (written as ‹si›, as in 'vision') and /ear/ (written as ‹ear›, as in 'hear' and 'earring') and teaches the ‹air›, ‹are› and ‹ear› spellings of /air/ (as in 'hair', 'care' and 'bear'). In Jolly Grammar 3, the children learn that /ear/ can also be written as ‹eer› and ‹ere› (as in 'deer' and 'here'); that ‹ere› also makes the /air/ sound (as in 'there' and 'where'); and that ‹s› makes a /zh/ sound in words like 'pleasure' and 'treasure'. Later, in Jolly Grammar 6, ‹ere› is revised as an alternative spelling of both /air/ and /ear/, and the spelling pattern ‹eir› is introduced as another alternative for both sounds (as in 'their' and 'weird').

Throughout the Jolly Grammar Handbooks, the children's knowledge of the spelling pattern ‹ure› is revised and extended: In Jolly Grammar 2, the children learn that ‹ture› says /cher/ in words like 'picture' and 'future'; in Jolly Grammar 3, they look at how ‹ure› can follow other letters to make words like 'leisure', 'pressure', 'figure', 'failure' and 'conjure'; in Jolly Grammar 5, the children learn that in short words, ‹ure› usually keeps its pure sound, /ue-r/ (as in 'pure' and 'cure'), but that in words like 'sure', 'unsure' and 'ensure', ‹sure› says /shor/; and finally, in Jolly Grammar 6, the children look at how the ‹ure› in longer, multisyllabic words is often swallowed in an unstressed syllable, becoming a schwa, or neutral vowel.

In Jolly Grammar 6, the children are also introduced to ‹ough›, which is one of the trickiest spellings in English because it can say a number of different sounds: /ou/ (as in 'drought'), /uff/ (as in 'enough'), /or/ (as in 'bought'), a schwa (as in 'thorough'), /oa/ (as in 'doughnut'), /off/ (as in 'cough') and /oo/ (as in 'breakthrough'). It even says /up/ in 'hiccough', which is an alternative spelling of 'hiccup'. There are no rules to help the children work out when to use these spellings, so the words must be learnt; however, there are only a small number of common words that use ‹ough› for each of these sounds and this is why, when mastered, they can be remembered as '**oh** yo**u** g**e**t **h**appy' words!

Syllables

An understanding of syllables will help to improve the children's spelling. A number of spelling rules depend on the children's ability to identify the number of syllables in a given word and to hear where the stress is placed. Although the rules of English sometimes let us down, they are worth acquiring. The more the children know, the more skilful they become and the better equipped they are to deal with any irregularities.

In Jolly Grammar 2, the children are encouraged to count the syllables in a word by doing 'chin bumps'. This is a fun, multisensory way of teaching syllables. The children place one hand under their chin (with the hand flattened as though they are about to pat something). Then they slowly say a word and count the number of times they feel their chin go down and bump their hand. When saying 'cat', for example, the children feel one bump, which means the word has one syllable; they will feel two bumps for 'table', which has two syllables; 'any' also has two bumps and two syllables; 'screeched' has one bump and one syllable; and 'idea' has three bumps and three syllables.

In Jolly Grammar 3 and 4, the teaching of syllables is extended and refined. In Jolly

Grammar 3, the children learn that a syllable is a unit of sound which is organised around a vowel sound: If a word has three vowel sounds, for example, it will have three syllables. Words with two or more syllables are referred to as multisyllabic or polysyllabic. If a word only has one vowel sound, and therefore one syllable, it is referred to as monosyllabic. Jolly Grammar 4 introduces the idea that, in English, stress is placed on at least one of the syllables in a multisyllabic word. This is achieved by saying the syllable a little louder and lengthening the vowel slightly, which keeps the vowel sound pure. However, the vowel in an unstressed syllable is often swallowed and becomes – most commonly – a neutral schwa, sounding something like /uh/.

From Jolly Grammar 3 onwards, the children are given regular practice identifying the syllables in words. They find doing this aurally (with chin bumps or by clapping the syllables) quite easy with practice, but the children are also required to identify the syllables on paper. In Jolly Grammar 3 and 4, they do this by underlining the letters that make the vowel sounds and drawing a vertical line between the syllables. In Jolly Grammar 5 and 6, the children go through the spelling list and write each word again, with a space between the syllables. There are some simple rules that the children can learn which will help them split words with double consonants, or with ‹ck› and ‹le› spellings:

- *Double consonants:* when a consonant is doubled, the line goes between the two letters, as in 'kit/ten'. However, the children should take care with words like 'hopped', 'stopped' and 'nipped', where the ‹e› in ‹-ed› is silent. These may look like two-syllable words but they are, in fact, monosyllabic.
- *‹ck› words:* although ‹c› and ‹k› make the same sound and so act like double consonants, the line goes after the ‹k›, as in 'pock/et'.
- *‹le› words:* the sounds represented by the ‹le› spelling are the same as those for ‹el› and ‹il› and consist of a small schwa before the /l/. This swallowed vowel sound can clearly be seen in 'lab**e**l' and 'penc**i**l' but not in 'candle'. In ‹le› words, there is no written vowel to underline in the last syllable. Instead, when the children see a word like this, they must listen for the schwa and draw a line before the consonant preceding it, as in 'can/dle' and 'sad/dle'. Again, ‹ck› words are an exception; the line goes after the ‹k›, as in 'pick/le', 'cack/le' and 'buck/le'.

Exactly how a word is split into syllables often depends on stress (as in the noun '**pres**/ent' and the verb 'pre/**sent**') or whether the syllable is open or closed. Open syllables are syllables ending in a long vowel sound, and closed syllables are syllables with a short vowel that end in a consonant. A word like 'paper', for example, tends to be split into 'pa/per' rather than 'pap/er'. The type of syllable is not always easy to determine, as many long vowels become swallowed and are pronounced as schwas in English.

The guidance given in the lesson notes aims to follow these rules, but in practice there is no definitive way to split the syllables and different dictionaries will often do it in different ways. For now, the focus should be on improving the children's ability to identify the vowel sounds in a word and hear how many syllables there are.

The Schwa

In Jolly Grammar 4, the children are introduced to the schwa, which is the most common vowel sound in English. It is used when the vowel in an unstressed syllable is swallowed and loses its purity, becoming more like an /uh/ sound. Although it is the most common vowel sound, the schwa is not taught earlier because it can be made by any unstressed vowel. This means that there is no helpful spelling rule for the children to use and so the spellings have to be learnt. To help them remember the spelling, encourage the children to 'say it as it sounds', stressing the pure form of the vowel sound and saying, for example, 'doct-**or**' rather than 'doct-**uh**'. This is a useful strategy for any word that is difficult to spell. The schwa often appears in suffixes that have similar spellings, making it difficult for children to choose the correct one simply by listening for the sounds. The later Jolly Grammar Handbooks focus on this type of suffix and include the following:

- ‹-ant›, ‹-ent›
- ‹-ance›, ‹-ence›
- ‹-ancy›, ‹-ency›
- ‹-ary›, ‹-ery›, ‹-ory›
- ‹-tion›, ‹-sion›, ‹ssion›, ‹cian›, ‹-ation›
- ‹-able›, ‹-ible›
- ‹cial›, ‹tial›, ‹sial›
- ‹-ious›, ‹-eous›
- ‹tious›, ‹cious›, ‹xious›

A swallowed vowel in an unstressed syllable does not always become neutral, but sometimes changes to an /i/ sound, as can be seen in words like 'vill**a**ge', 'coll**e**ge' and 'soci**e**ty'. It happens to ‹e› in particular, especially when it appears at the beginning of a word (as in 'exam', 'enjoy', 'enough', 'extend', 'expand', 'efficient', 'enormous', 'emergency', 'encourage', 'equipment', 'embarrass' and 'essential') or is part of a prefix like ‹re-› (as in 'rely', 'remove', 'refer', 'recruit', 'revise', 'receive', 'receipt', 'relation', 'retrieve', 'revere' and 'reprieve'), ‹pre-› (as in 'prefer', 'prepare', 'pretend', 'prevent', 'predict', 'precise', 'presume', 'precede', 'presenter', 'precaution', 'precarious' and 'preliminary') or ‹de-› (as in 'deny', 'delay', 'decide', 'deliver', 'defeat', 'debate', 'deduct', 'deprive', 'despise', 'devise', 'deceive' and 'determine'). In Jolly Grammar 5 and 6, the lesson notes point out when an unstressed vowel in a spelling word changes to /i/ in this way.

Silent Letters

A number of English words contain letters that are not pronounced at all. These are known as silent letters. Some silent letters, such as the ‹k› in 'knee', show us how the word was pronounced in the past. Other silent letters, like the ‹h› in 'rhyme', indicate the word's foreign origins. Encouraging the children to 'say it as it sounds' will help them to remember these spellings. If the word 'lamb' is called out, for example, the children should respond with /lam**b**/, emphasising the /b/, which would normally be silent. The Jolly Grammar Handbooks introduce the following silent letters:

- silent ‹b›, as in 'lamb'
- silent ‹c›, as in 'scissors'
- silent ‹h›, as in 'rhubarb'
- silent ‹k›, as in 'knife'
- silent ‹w›, as in 'wrong'
- silent ‹g›, as in 'gnome'
- silent ‹t›, as in 'castle'
- silent ‹p› as in 'attempt'
- silent ‹n› as in 'hymn'
- silent ‹e› as in 'active'

The first five silent letters (shown in the left-hand column) are introduced in Jolly Grammar 2. Later, the children learn that silent letters often go with a particular letter to form a common spelling pattern. For example, in Jolly Grammar 3, the children look at how silent ‹g› comes before ‹n› in words like 'gnome', 'gnat' and 'sign'. Similarly, in Jolly Grammar 4, they learn that silent ‹t› follows ‹s› in words such as 'castle', 'listen' and 'nestle'. From Jolly Grammar 4 onwards, the children are encouraged to think of these and other examples (including ‹mb›, ‹wr›, ‹kn›, ‹wh›, ‹rh›, ‹wh›, ‹sc› and ‹gh›) as 'silent letter' digraphs. Further examples, introduced in Jolly Grammar 6, appear in more advanced words. Some of them, like the silent ‹p› digraphs in 'attempt', 'psalm' and 'pneumonia', share a common silent letter. Others use different silent letters, but make the same sound, such as the digraphs in 'numb', 'hymn' and 'some', which make the /m/ sound.

Several spelling patterns, introduced over the course of the Jolly Grammar Handbooks, include a silent ‹e› at the end, making words like 'more', 'bronze', 'geese', 'twelve' and 'examine'. A silent ‹e› should not be confused with magic ‹e›, which is explained on page 32.

Identifying the Short Vowels

One of the most reliable spelling rules in English is the consonant doubling rule. Consonant doubling is governed by the short vowels, so the children need to be able to identify short vowel sounds confidently. In the early Jolly Grammar levels, a puppet (such as the Inky Mouse puppet) and a box can be used to encourage the children to listen for the short vowels:

- For /a/, put the puppet **a**t the side of the box.
- For /e/, make the puppet wobble on the **e**dge of the box.
- For /i/, put the puppet **i**n the box.
- For /o/, put the puppet **o**n the box.
- For /u/, put the puppet **u**nder the box.

The children can then pretend that their fist is the box and their open hand is the puppet. Each time a short vowel is called out, the children listen carefully and do the appropriate action with their hands. Similarly, they can do the actions when short words with a short vowel are called out, such as 'pot', 'hat', 'bun', 'dig' and 'red'. When most of the children have mastered the short vowels, short words with a variety of vowel sounds can be used. If the children hear a word without a short vowel sound, they keep their hands still.

Once the children know the short vowel sounds, it is important that they revise them regularly. A simple way to do this is by using the vowel hand. The children hold up one hand so that their palm is facing them; then, using the index finger of their other hand, they point to the tip of each finger, saying the vowel sounds in turn. First they point to the tip of their thumb for /a/, then to their first finger for /e/, and so on. The vowel hand can also be used to revise the long vowel sounds: the children point to the base of each finger as they say /ai/, /ee/, /ie/, /oa/ and /ue/. Activities like these help to keep the children tuned in to identifying the sounds in words and, in turn, help to prepare them for the consonant doubling rules.

Spelling Rules

The ability to identify the syllables and short vowels in words will help the children apply the following rules for consonant doubling and adding suffixes.

The rules for consonant doubling are as follows:

a. When a monosyllabic word has a short vowel sound and the final consonant is ‹f›, ‹l›, ‹s› or ‹z›, that consonant is doubled, as in 'cliff', 'bell', 'miss' and 'buzz'. (Some common exceptions to this rule are the two-letter words 'as', 'if', 'is', 'of' and 'us'.)

b. When a monosyllabic word has a short vowel sound and the final consonant sound is /k/, this is spelt ‹ck›, as in 'back', 'neck', 'lick', 'clock' and 'duck'.

c. If there is only one consonant after a short, stressed vowel sound, this consonant is doubled before any suffix starting with a vowel is added, as in 'hop**ped**', 'wet**ter**', 'big**gest**', 'clap**ping**', 'fu**nny**' and 'hug**gable**'. Note that when ‹y› is a suffix, it counts as a vowel because it has a vowel sound.

   This rule does not apply to words that end in ‹x›, because /x/ is really two consonant sounds – /k/ and /s/ – blended together as /ks/. This means that consonant doubling is unnecessary in words like 'faxed', 'boxing' and 'mixer'.

   The rule can be understood more easily if the children think of the consonant(s) as a wall between two vowels. With only one consonant, the wall is not thick enough to prevent the 'magic' hopping over from the vowel in the suffix and changing the short vowel sound to a long one. With two consonants, the wall becomes so thick that the 'magic' cannot get over.

d. When a word ends in the letters ‹le› and the preceding syllable contains a short, stressed vowel sound, there must be two consonants between the short vowel and the ‹le›. This means that the consonant before the ‹le› is doubled in words like 'paddle', 'kettle', 'nibble', 'topple' and 'snuggle'. No doubling is necessary in words like 'handle', 'twinkle' and 'jungle' because they already have two consonants between the short vowel and the ‹le›.

e. The doubling rule also applies to words ending in ‹fer›, but only if the syllable containing ‹fer› is stressed once the suffix is added. This is why the ‹r› is doubled in 'preferred', 'referral' and 'conferring', but remains single in 'offered' and 'conference'. The main exception to this rule is the word 'transferable', in which ‹fer› is stressed but there is only one ‹r›.

The rules for adding suffixes are as follows:

a. If the root word ends in a consonant that does not immediately follow a short vowel sound, simply add the suffix. (So 'walk' + ‹-ed› = 'walked'; 'quick' + ‹-est› = 'quickest'; 'look' + ‹-ing› = 'looking'; and 'avoid' + ‹-able› = 'avoidable'.)

b. If the root word ends in the letter ‹e› and the suffix starts with a consonant, simply add the suffix (so 'care' + ‹-less› = 'careless'). If the suffix starts with a vowel, remove the ‹e› before adding the suffix. (So 'love' + ‹-ed› = 'loved'; 'brave' + ‹-er› = 'braver'; 'like' + ‹-ing› = 'liking'; and 'value' + ‹-able› = 'valuable'.)

   When the suffix ‹-ing› is added to a root word ending in ‹ie›, not only is the ‹e› removed, but 'shy ‹i›' is replaced by 'toughy ‹y›'. This avoids the problem of having two ‹i›s next to each other and makes the word easier to read. (So 'tie', 'die' and 'lie' + ‹-ing› = 'tying', 'dying' and 'lying', but 'tie', 'die' and 'lie' + ‹-ed› = 'tied', 'died' and 'lied'.)

One exception to this rule is when the suffix ‹-able› is added to words ending in ‹e›. Many of these words can be spelt either with or without the ‹e›: both 'lovable' and 'loveable' are correct, for example. In these cases, it is better for the children to be consistent and drop the ‹e› in their writing.

c. If the root word ends in ‹ce› or ‹ge› and the suffix is ‹-able›, do not remove the ‹e›. This is because the ‹e› is part of the 'soft' ‹c› and ‹g› spellings, making the ‹c› say /s/ and the ‹g› say /j/, as in 'noticeable' and 'changeable'.

d. If the root word ends in ‹ce› and the suffix is ‹-al›, replace ‹e› with ‹i› before adding the suffix. (So 'commerce' + ‹-al› = 'commercial', for example.)

e. If the root word ends in a consonant that immediately follows a short, stressed vowel sound and the suffix starts with a consonant, simply add the suffix (so 'sad' + ‹-ness› = 'sadness'). If the suffix starts with a vowel, however, double the final consonant before adding the suffix. (So 'stop' + ‹-ed› = 'stopped'; 'sad' + ‹-er› = 'sadder'; 'run' + ‹-ing› = 'running'; and 'control' + ‹-able› = 'controllable'.)

Remind the children that two consonants are needed to make a thicker 'wall' between the two vowels. This prevents 'magic' from the vowel in the suffix from jumping over to change the short vowel sound. (See rule 'c' for consonant doubling on page 39.)

f. If the root word ends in a letter ‹y› that immediately follows a consonant, replace 'toughy ‹y›' with 'shy ‹i›' before adding the suffix. (So 'hurry' + ‹-ed› = 'hurried'; 'dirty' + ‹-est› = 'dirtiest'; 'beauty' + ‹-ful› = 'beautiful'; 'vary' + ‹-able› = 'variable'; and 'pity' + ‹-ful› = 'pitiful'.) If the suffix starts with the letter ‹i›, however, the rule does not apply (so 'worry' + ‹-ing› = 'worrying').

The letter ‹y› is unique in being able to function as either a vowel or a consonant. As a vowel, ‹y› replaces ‹i› and, in Jolly Phonics, the children learn that 'shy ‹i›' does not like to go at the end of a word, so 'toughy ‹y›' takes its place. It is interesting to note that when ‹y› is the last syllable of a multisyllabic word, the sound it makes is somewhere between the short /i/ in 'tin' and the long /ee/ in 'bee'. (The same sound is made in the rare instances when the letter ‹i› is the final syllable in a multisyllabic word, as in 'taxi' and 'spaghetti'.) Despite this confusing pronunciation, it is important for the children to think of ‹y› as replacing 'shy ‹i›'. This will help them to remember that the ‹i› returns when such words are extended (except in words like 'worrying', where it would look odd to have two ‹i›s next to each other).

In Jolly Grammar 6, the children are introduced to the well-known spelling rule that governs whether ‹i› goes before ‹e› in our writing. This rule is usually misunderstood and often rejected because it seems to have too many exceptions: for example, the words 'weird', 'their', 'height', 'vein' and 'weight' are all spelt ‹ei› even though the preceding letter is not ‹c›. This misunderstanding occurs when an important part of the rule is omitted: as long as the children are taught that 'It's ‹i› before ‹e›, except after ‹c›, **if you want to say /ee/,**' it is a very reliable rule and will help the children with their spelling of words like 'niece', 'shriek', 'achieve', 'receive', 'deceive' and 'ceiling'. There are a few exceptions, however, and these can be remembered as '**Se**ize n**ei**ther prot**ei**n nor caff**ei**ne'.

Grammar and Spelling Lesson Sheets

For each lesson there is at least one photocopiable activity sheet for the children to complete, accompanied by a page of teacher's lesson notes. The recommendations in the notes are intended to be followed systematically. However, if a suggestion seems inappropriate for a particular class situation, it can of course be adapted to suit.

All the lesson notes feature a notepad in the top right-hand corner. This has a brief checklist of what to prepare (items which are useful, but not essential, are shown in brackets) as well as a guide to previous lessons that the teaching builds on.

The **grammar notes** all follow the same format:

a. Aim
b. Introduction
c. Main point
d. Grammar sheet
e. Extension activity
f. Rounding off

Each grammar lesson has its own particular focus, and the teacher's notes vary accordingly. However, the standard format helps to give the lessons a recognisable shape.

The **spelling notes** also follow a standard format:

a. Revision
b. Main point
c. Spelling list
d. Spelling sheets A & B
e. Dictation

Many of the teaching points are common to all the spelling lessons, so these are explained in further detail below.

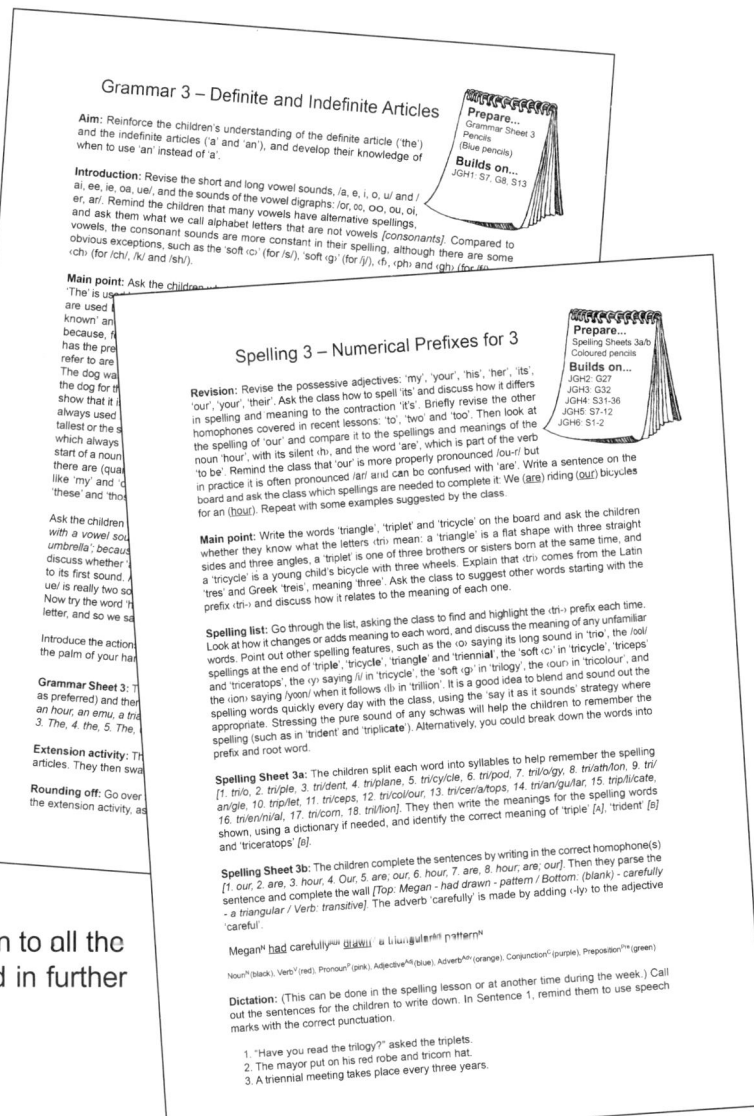

a. Revision

Each lesson should start with a short burst of revision. Early lessons concentrate on commonly confused homophones, such as 'its' and 'it's'; 'to', 'two' and 'too'; 'our', 'hour' and 'are'; 'your' and 'you're'; 'there', 'their' and 'they're'; and 'where', 'wear' and 'were'. After that, they focus on the prefixes, suffixes, spelling rules and spelling patterns introduced in recent lessons. The teacher's notes provide suitable words to write on the board and discuss with the class.

b. Main Point

In the Jolly Grammar 6 Handbook, the focus of many spelling lessons is on the more unusual vowel spellings and 'silent letter' digraphs, and on commonly used prefixes and suffixes. Analysing different parts of a word and understanding how they convey meaning, or recognising when they form a certain part of speech, can help the children enormously with their comprehension, particularly when reading unfamiliar words for the first time.

c. Spelling List

Each week the children are given some words with a particular spelling pattern to learn for a test. It is a good idea to give the spelling homework at the beginning of the week and to test at the end of the week, or on the following Monday.

The spelling words have been carefully selected to enable every child to have some success. There are eighteen words in total, arranged in three groups of six. The words in the first group are usually short, regular and fairly common; those in the second group are a bit longer and may have more alternative spellings in them; and the third group has longer, often less common words, with more varied spellings.

For those children who find spelling difficult, it may be appropriate to give them only the first six spelling words; the number can be increased when the children are ready. The number of spelling words given to the children is at the teacher's discretion, based on his or her knowledge of the children in the class.

It is not enough simply to send home a list of words for the children to learn; it is important to go over the words during the spelling lesson, discussing their meanings, and looking carefully to see which parts of a word are regular and identifying the parts that are not. The teacher's notes point out the words that need particular attention and suggest suitable learning strategies. The spelling sheet activities will also help the children become more familiar with the words and how they are spelt. Go over the spelling words as often as possible during the week; ideally, blend and sound out the words with the children every day. The class can also work in pairs, using their spelling books to test each other on their spellings in spare moments.

Each child takes the list of spellings home in a small vocabulary-size exercise book. In Photocopy Section 2 the spelling words are set out in their groups, ready for photocopying. At the beginning of the week, stick the appropriate list into each child's Spelling Homework Book or, if preferred, ask the children to write out the words themselves. If the children do the writing, check that they have copied the words clearly and accurately before the books go home.

Test and mark the spellings each week. The results should be written in for the parents to see. Write in the mark or use a coded system, if preferred, such as different coloured stars: a gold star for 18/18, a silver star for 17/18 and a coloured star for 16/18, for example. A letter of encouragement to parents is provided on page 225. Most parents like to be involved in their children's homework and are interested to see how many words were spelt correctly and which words were misspelt.

Children need to be aware that accurate spelling is important for their future. Unfortunately, there is no magic wand that can be waved to make them good at spelling. In addition to knowing the letter sounds and alternative spellings thoroughly, a certain amount of dedication and practice is needed.

d. Spelling Sheets A and B

Now that the children are older, there are two spelling sheets per lesson. As before, the focus of each spelling sheet reflects the main teaching point. Every week there are two activities on Sheet A that use the words from the spelling list. In the first activity, the children have to write out the spelling words, splitting them into syllables: the children should be familiar with doing this now, so they are given no clues and have to work out the number of syllables for themselves. (The teacher's notes show how the words should be split, but as long as the children are able to hear the syllables, which are organised around the vowel sounds, and can indicate them approximately, their work should be marked as correct. For more information on syllables, see pages 35 and 36.)

The second activity is more varied: it could be writing in the missing letters; putting words in alphabetical order; using them to solve crossword clues; finding them in word searches; identifying their meanings in quizzes and multiple-choice questions; solving anagrams; drawing pictures; making word families; adding prefixes and suffixes; matching words to their root words; writing the meanings of words; or using them in a noun phrase or sentence. These activities allows the children to actively engage with the spelling words and makes learning them more meaningful.

Sheet B has three activities: the top and bottom ones are the same every week. At the top of the sheet, lines are provided for the weekly dictation. At the bottom of the sheet, there is a parsing activity. Parsing involves identifying the part of speech for each word in a sentence and underlining it in the appropriate colour. The children then identify the subject and (if there is one) the object of the sentence, before transferring the words to the sentence wall. (Sentence walls are explained in more detail on pages 28 and 29.) The middle activity sometimes focuses on the main spelling point but, more often than not, it provides some crossover with recent grammar lessons. This consolidates the grammar the children are learning and puts it into a spelling context.

e. Dictation

As a weekly exercise, dictation is useful in a number of ways. It gives the children regular practice listening for the sounds in the words they write, and it is a good way of monitoring their progress. Dictation helps the children to develop their independent writing and encourages the slower writers to increase their speed. It also provides a good opportunity for the children to practise their punctuation, using question and exclamation marks, commas and speech marks. The lesson notes suggest what is important to point out to the children.

There are three sentences each week for dictation. All the sentences revise the spelling focus for that week and may also feature spelling patterns and grammar points from previous lessons. For example, when the spelling focus is ‹que›, the dictation sentences feature words like 'antique', 'technique', 'unique' and 'boutique', but they also use previous spelling words like 'sculpture', 'valuable', 'bought' and 'fashionable'. Furthermore, grammar points like the passive voice, questions formed by using the verb 'to do', and positive and negative imperatives all appear in the dictation sentences once they have been taught. The children can write the dictation sentences on the lines provided at the top of Spelling Sheet A. Begin by calling out the first sentence for the children to write down. Give the children a reasonable amount of time to finish writing, but not too long, and then move on to the next sentence. The few children who have not finished should leave the sentence incomplete and move on. This encourages them to get up to speed. Afterwards, it is important to go over the sentences with the children and discuss the spellings, grammar and punctuation points.

Spelling 1 – Numerical Prefixes for 1

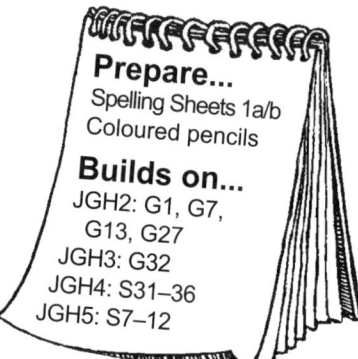

Prepare...
Spelling Sheets 1a/b
Coloured pencils

Builds on...
JGH2: G1, G7, G13, G27
JGH3: G32
JGH4: S31–36
JGH5: S7–12

Revision: Revise homophones, which are words that sound the same but have different spellings and meanings. Write 'its' and 'it's' on the board and ask the children to identify the different meanings: 'its' is a possessive adjective that describes a noun by saying who it belongs to and 'it's' is a contraction of either 'it is' or 'it has'. Write a sentence on the board and ask the class which spellings are needed to complete it: (<u>It's</u>) cold so the dog will need (<u>its</u>) coat. Ask the class to suggest other sentences using either 'its' or 'it's' and to say which spelling is needed each time.

Main point: Write the words 'unicycle' and 'monocle' on the board and ask the children whether they know what ‹uni› and ‹mono› mean: the word 'unicycle' describes a type of bicycle that only has one wheel and a 'monocle' is like a pair of spectacles (glasses) with just one lens. Explain that both prefixes mean 'one': ‹uni-› is from the Latin 'unus', meaning 'one' and ‹mono-› comes from the Greek 'monos', meaning 'alone'. Ask the class to suggest other words starting with ‹uni› and ‹mono› and discuss how each prefix relates to the meaning. Write the words on the board and put them in alphabetical order with the class. Remind them to look at the letters after each prefix to help determine the correct order.

Spelling list: Go through the list, asking the class to find and highlight the ‹uni-› or ‹mono-› prefix each time. Look at how it changes or adds meaning to each word, and discuss the meaning of any unfamiliar words. Point out other spelling features, such as the ‹y› saying /ie/ in 'unify' and 'unicycle', the 'soft ‹c›' in 'uni**c**ycle', the /ool/ spellings at the end of 'unicy**cle**', 'mono**cle**', 'monosyllab**le**' and 'univers**al**', the ‹ion› saying /yoon/ when it follows ‹n› in 'union', the ‹se› saying /s/ in 'universe', the ‹gue› saying /g/ in 'monologue', the ‹y› saying /i/ in 'monosyllable', the ‹ch› saying /k/ in 'monochrome' and the ‹tion› saying /shun/ in 'unification'. It is a good idea to blend and sound out the spelling words quickly every day with the class, using the 'say it as it sounds' strategy where appropriate (stressing the pure sound of any schwas, for example), or you could break down the words into prefix and root word.

Spelling Sheet 1a: The children split each word into syllables to help remember the spelling *[1. u/nit, 2. u/ni/corn, 3. u/ni/form, 4. mon/o/gram, 5. mon/o/rail, 6. mon/o/tone, 7. u/ni/fy, 8. u/ni/cy/cle, 9. u/nion, 10. u/ni/verse, 11. mon/o/cle, 12. mon/o/logue, 13. mon/o/syl/la/ble, 14. u/ni/ver/sal, 15. mon/o/chrome, 16. mon/o/lith, 17. u/ni/fi/ca/tion, 18. mo/nop/o/ly]*. They then put the spelling words into alphabetical order *[**mono** 1. -chrome, 2. -cle, 3. -gram, 4. -lith, 5. -logue, 6. -poly, 7. -rail, 8. -syllable, 9. -tone; **uni** 10. -corn, 11. -cycle, 12. -fication, 13. -form, 14. -fy, 15. -on, 16. -t, 17. -versal, 18. -verse]*.

Spelling Sheet 1b: The children complete the sentences by writing in the correct homophone(s) *[1. its, 2. its, 3. It's, 4. its, 5. It's; its, 6. it's, 7. It's, 8. It's]*. Then they parse the sentence and complete the wall *[Top: actor - performed - monologue / Bottom: The - perfectly - the / Verb: transitive (see page 20)]*. The adverb 'perfectly' is made by adding ‹-ly› to the adjective 'perfect'.

The actor[N] performed[V] the monologue[N] perfectly[Adv].

Noun[N] (black), Verb[V] (red), Pronoun[P] (pink), Adjective[Adj] (blue), Adverb[Adv] (orange), Conjunction[C] (purple), Preposition[Pre] (green)

Dictation: (This can be done in the spelling lesson or at another time during the week.) Call out the sentences for the children to write down. Remind them to use speech marks with the correct punctuation in Sentence 3. Sentence 2 needs a question mark.

1. The man in the painting was wearing a monocle.
2. How many stars are in the universe?
3. "Turn to the first unit in your textbook," said the teacher.

Spelling List 1

 ‹uni-› ‹mono-›

Put the words in the Spelling List into alphabetical order.

1. unit
2. unicorn
3. uniform
4. monogram
5. monorail
6. monotone
7. unify
8. unicycle
9. union
10. universe
11. monocle
12. monologue
13. monosyllable
14. universal
15. monochrome
16. monolith
17. unification
18. monopoly

1. _____
2. _____
3. _____
4. _____
5. _____
6. _____
7. _____
8. _____
9. _____
10. _____
11. _____
12. _____
13. _____
14. _____
15. _____
16. _____
17. _____
18. _____

a b c d e f g h i j k l m n o p q r s t u v w x y z

Dictation: ‹uni-› ‹mono-›

1. _____

_____

2. _____

_____

3. _____

_____

'Its' and 'it's' are homophones. They are words that sound the same but have different spellings and meanings. Which one should be used to complete each sentence correctly?

1. The museum is proud of _____ collection of unicycles.

2. The school has changed _____ uniform from blue to green.

3. You should go by monorail. _____ the quickest way to the airport.

4. The union has asked _____ members to go on strike next week.

5. _____ a gloomy picture because of _____ monochrome design.

6. "Yes, _____ a huge monolith," the teacher told the class.

7. This is Dad's handkerchief. _____ got his monogram in the corner.

8. "_____ a story about a dragon and a unicorn," said the boy.

Parse the sentence and then write it on the wall.

The actor performed the monologue perfectly.

subject	verb	object
	transitive / intransitive	

Grammar 1 – Homophone Mix-Ups

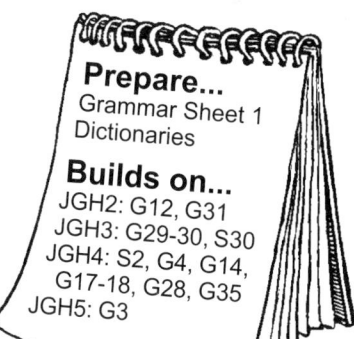

Prepare...
Grammar Sheet 1
Dictionaries

Builds on...
JGH2: G12, G31
JGH3: G29-30, S30
JGH4: S2, G4, G14,
G17-18, G28, G35
JGH5: G3

Aim: Reinforce the children's understanding of homophones and develop their ability to choose between similar-sounding words in their writing.

Introduction: Ask the children what we call words like 'its' and 'it's', which sound the same but have different spellings and meanings *[homophones]*. Remind them that some of the most commonly used homophones are possessive adjectives and contractions, such as 'your' and 'you're', 'its' and 'it's', and 'their' and 'they're', while others are parts of the verb 'to be' ('are' is often confused with 'our' and 'were' with 'where'). These are revised in Spelling Lessons 3 to 6 so now is a good time to quickly remind the class about possessive adjectives ('my', 'your', 'his', 'her', 'its', 'our', 'your', 'their'), about how an apostrophe replaces the missing letters in a contraction, and about the irregular parts of the verb 'to be'. For more information, see pages 15 and 25 in the Introduction. As well as using homophones correctly, the children also need to take care using different types of homograph: homonyms (words that look and sound the same but have different meanings, as in 'the **second** time' and 'in a **second**') and heteronyms (words that look the same but sound different and have different meanings, as in 'to **lead** the way' and 'a **lead** pencil'). Ask the children if they can think of any other examples of homophones and homographs.

Main point: Remind the children that it is important to use the correct spelling when writing homophones, otherwise their writing will not make sense. Write the homophones from Grammar Sheet 1 on the board, look at the spellings and check that the class know what they mean: led/lead, aloud/allowed, aisle/isle, precede/proceed, steal/steel, mourning/morning, bridal/bridle, compliment/complement. If the children are unsure of any meanings, ask them to look up the words in the dictionary and see who can find them first. Remind the children that they need to stop and think before writing a homophone, decide which meaning is needed, and think how the word with that meaning is spelt. Using the information they already know can sometimes help them remember the different spellings and meanings. For example, 'allowed' is the simple past tense of the verb 'allow', made by adding the suffix ‹-ed›, whereas 'aloud' is an adverb meaning 'out loud'. To 'complement' something means to create a good combination (and comes from the verb 'to complete', which explains the ‹e› spelling); so, for example, a scarf complements a dress and makes the outfit more complete. Ask the children to think of sentences for some of the homophones and discuss which spelling they would use.

Grammar Sheet 1: The children write the meaning for each homophone. Encourage them to use a dictionary, if needed, to remind them of the meaning or to check the spelling. They then use each homophone in a sentence, writing them on the back of their worksheet (or this could be done as part of the extension activity instead).

Extension activity: Write some more homophones on the board and ask the children to write meanings or sentences for them. These could be words that the children have particular problems with or other common homophones, such as one/won, be/bee, son/sun, knot/not, main/mane, fair/fare, plain/plane, ball/bawl, grate/great, heal/heel/he'll, missed/mist, scene/seen, berry/bury, accept/except, affect/effect.

Rounding off: Go over the sheet with the children, discussing their answers. If they have done the extension activity, ask some of the children to read out their sentences and meanings before checking which spelling they have used.

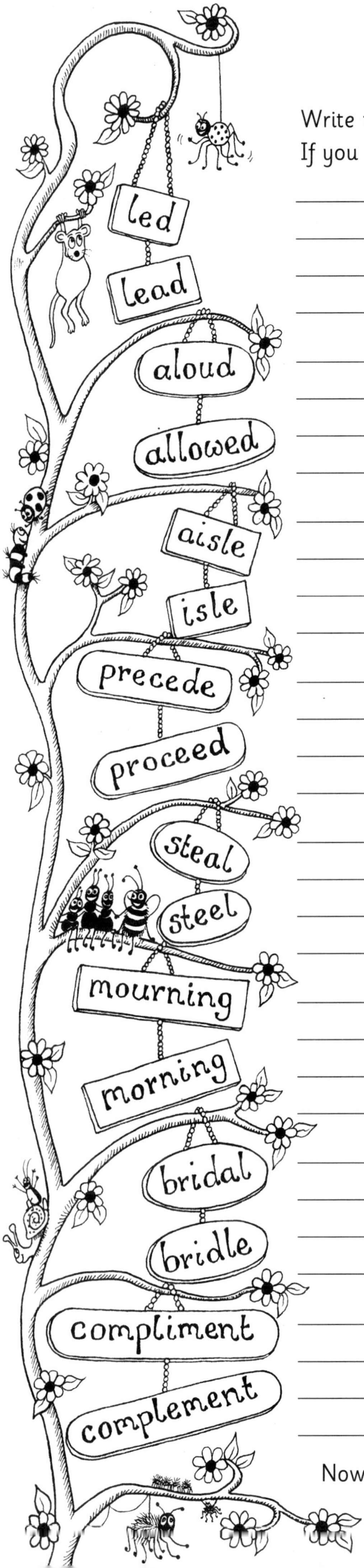

Homophone Mix-Ups

Write the meanings for these pairs of homophones.
If you are unsure, look them up in the dictionary.

led

lead

aloud

allowed

aisle

isle

precede

proceed

steal

steel

mourning

morning

bridal

bridle

compliment

complement

Now write a sentence for each word on the back of the sheet.

Spelling 2 – Numerical Prefixes for 2

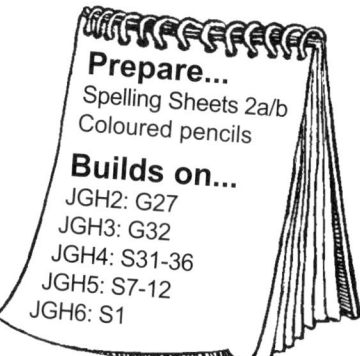

Prepare...
Spelling Sheets 2a/b
Coloured pencils

Builds on...
JGH2: G27
JGH3: G32
JGH4: S31-36
JGH5: S7-12
JGH6: S1

Revision: Revise the homophones, 'to', 'two' and 'too', discussing their spellings and meanings: 'to' is used with a verb to make the infinitive or is a preposition relating two objects, 'two' is a number, and the adverb 'too' means 'also' or 'excessively'. Write a sentence on the board and ask the class which spellings are needed to complete it: It was (<u>too</u>) late for the (<u>two</u>) girls (<u>to</u>) go out. Repeat with examples suggested by the class.

Main point: Write the words 'bicycle', 'digraph' and 'duet' on the board and ask the children whether they know what ‹bi-›, ‹di-› and ‹du-› mean: a 'bicycle' is a vehicle with two wheels, a 'digraph' is a pair of letters that make one sound and a 'duet' is a piece of music for two performers. Explain that these prefixes mean 'two', 'twice' or 'double' and come from the Latin 'duos', meaning 'two', and the Greek 'dis', meaning 'twice'. Ask the class to suggest other words starting with each prefix and discuss how it relates to the meaning.

Spelling list: Go through the list, asking the class to find and highlight the ‹bi-›, ‹di-› or ‹du-› prefix each time. Look at how it changes or adds meaning to each word, and discuss the meaning of any unfamiliar words. Point out other spelling features, such as the vowel saying its long sound in 'du**o**' and 'bicentenary', the 'soft ‹c›' in 'biceps', 'bi**c**ycle', 'bicentenary' and 'bicentennial', the ‹y› saying /i/ in 'bicycle', the /ool/ spellings at the end of 'bicy**cle**', 'du**el**', 'bienni**al**', 'bilingu**al**' and 'bicentenni**al**', the 'soft ‹g›' in 'diverge', the ‹ph› saying /f/ in 'digraph', the ‹ion› saying /yoon/ when it follows ‹ll› in 'billion' and the ‹gu› saying /gw/ in 'bilingual'. Also explain that 'bicentennial' is another word for 'bicentenary'. It is a good idea to blend and sound out the spelling words quickly every day with the class, using the 'say it as it sounds' strategy where appropriate (stressing the pure sound of any schwas, for example), or you could break down the words into prefix and root word.

Spelling Sheet 2a: The children split each word into syllables to help remember the spelling *[1. du/o, 2. du/et, 3. bi/ceps, 4. bi/plane, 5. bi/cy/cle, 6. du/el, 7. di/lem/ma, 8. bi/ath/lon, 9. bi/na/ry, 10. di/verge, 11. du/pli/cate, 12. di/graph, 13. bil/lion, 14. bi/en/ni/al, 15. bi/noc/u/lars, 16. bi/cen/te/na/ry, 17. bi/lin/gual, 18. bi/cen/ten/ni/al].* They then work out the answers to the crossword clues and write them in *[1. biceps, 2. biennial, 3. bicycle, 4. digraph (across) duet (down), 5. bicentennial, 6. duplicate, 7. dilemma, 8. diverge, 9. binoculars, 10. billion (across) biathlon (down), 11. bicentenary, 12. binary, 13. duel, 14. duo, 15. bilingual, 16. biplane].*

Spelling Sheet 2b: The children complete the sentences by writing in the correct homophone(s) *[1. too, 2. to, 3. two, 4. too, 5. two; to; to, 6. too, 7. two, 8. two; to].* Then they parse the sentence and complete the wall *[Top: Sam–and–Seth - will be competing - (blank) / Bottom: (blank) - in the biathlon - (blank) / Verb: intransitive].* The 'and' can be bracketed with dotted lines to show it is not one of the subjects (see page 29). 'In the biathlon' is a prepositional phrase acting as an adverb, so orange brackets can be put around it.

Sam[N] and[C] Seth[N] (will be competing)[V] (in[Pre] the biathlon[N])[Adv].

Noun[N] (black), Verb[V] (red), Pronoun[P] (pink), Adjective[Adj] (blue), Adverb[Adv] (orange), Conjunction[C] (purple), Preposition[Pre] (green)

Dictation: (This can be done in the spelling lesson or at another time during the week.) Call out the sentences for the children to write down. In Sentence 2, remind them to use speech marks with the correct punctuation.

1. There are over seven billion people on the planet.
2. "Can you make me a duplicate set of keys?" he asked.
3. My parents gave me a new bilingual dictionary.

Spelling List 2

1. duo
2. duet
3. biceps
4. biplane
5. bicycle
6. duel
7. dilemma
8. biathlon
9. binary
10. diverge
11. duplicate
12. digraph
13. billion
14. biennial
15. binoculars
16. bicentenary
17. bilingual
18. bicentennial

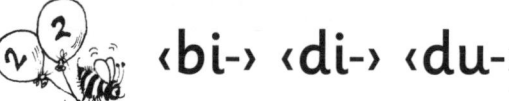

‹bi-› ‹di-› ‹du-›

Work out the answers to the clues and complete the crossword. All of the answers are words in the Spelling List.

1. large muscles, one at the front of each upper arm
2. happening once every two years
3. a two-wheeled vehicle with a saddle and pedals
4. (across) 2 letters making one sound, like ‹ch› and ‹ai›
4. (down) a piece of music for two singers or players
5. another word for 'bicentenary'
6. to make an exact copy of something
7. a problem forcing you to decide between two things
8. to branch off in different directions
9. special glasses that help you see things far away
10. (across) the number 1,000,000,000 or 1,000,000,000,000
10. (down) a two-sport event (skiing and rifle-shooting)
11. the 200th anniversary of an important event
12. having two parts or involving two things
13. a fight between two people with pistols or swords
14. two people who sing, play or perform together
15. able to speak two languages well
16. an early type of aircraft with two pairs of wings

Dictation: ‹bi-› ‹di-› ‹du-›

1. _____

_____

2. _____

_____

3. _____

_____

'To', 'two' and 'too' are homophones. They are words that sound the same but have different spellings and meanings. Which one should be used to complete each sentence correctly?

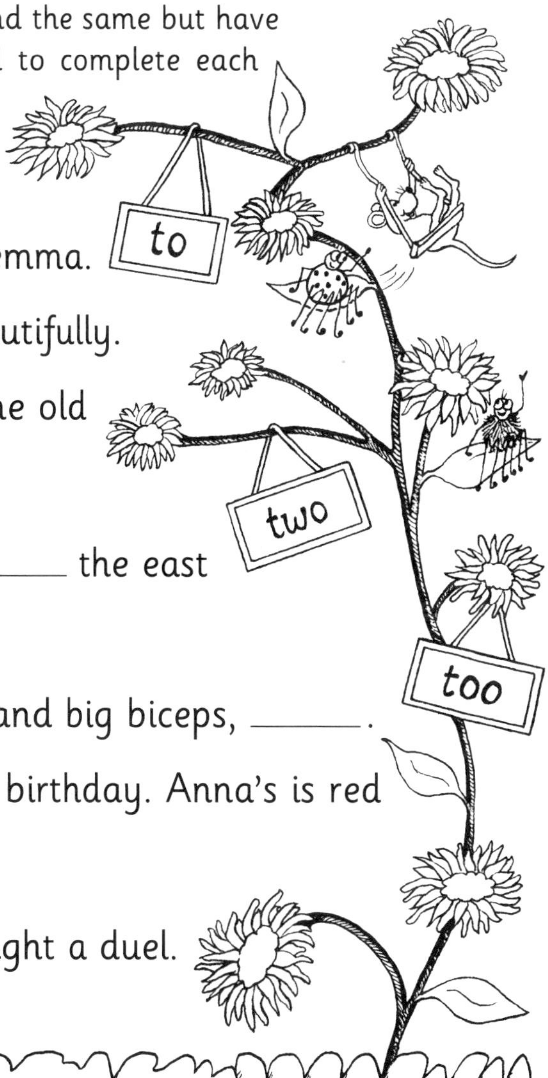

1. Was the pair of binoculars _____ expensive?

2. A good friend helped me _____ solve my dilemma.

3. The _____ young singers sang their duet beautifully.

4. The air museum has jets, helicopters, and some old biplanes, _____ .

5. The _____ roads diverged, with one going _____ the east and the other _____ the west.

6. A weightlifter has a strong back, sturdy legs and big biceps, _____ .

7. We bought the twins _____ bicycles for their birthday. Anna's is red and Kay's is green.

8. The _____ great swordsmen agreed _____ fight a duel.

Parse the sentence and then write it on the wall.

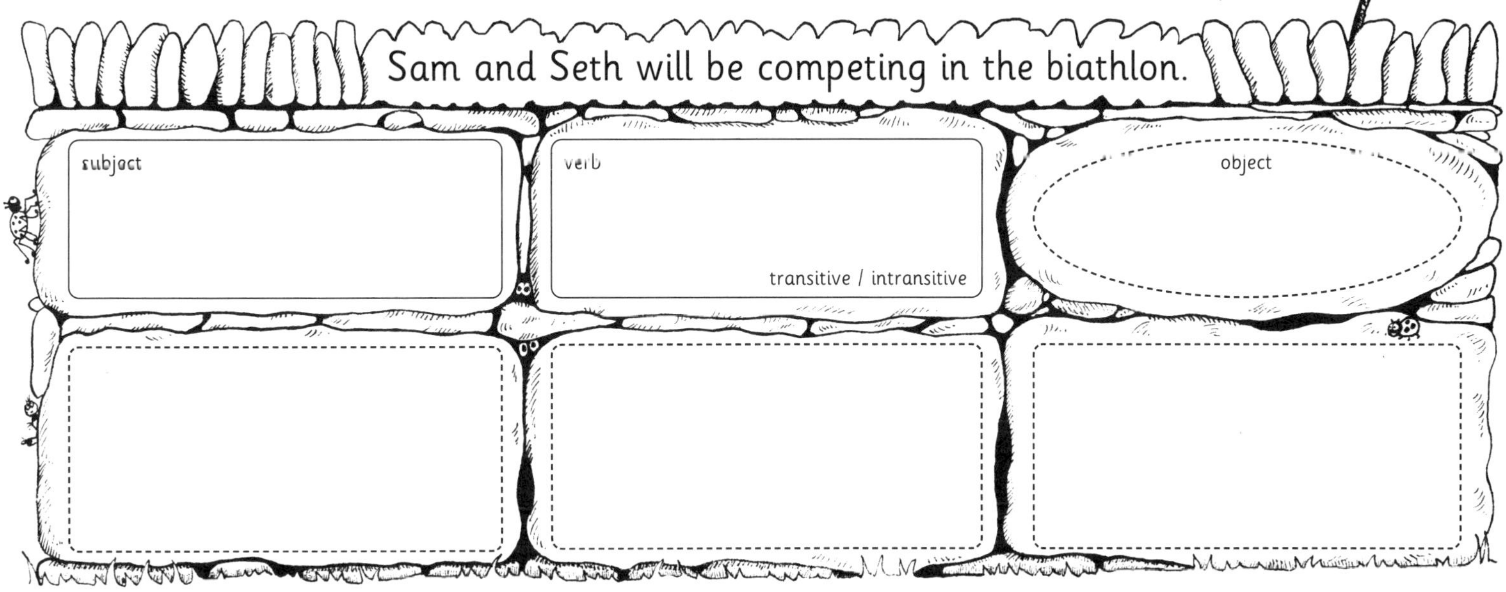

Sam and Seth will be competing in the biathlon.

subject	verb	object
	transitive / intransitive	

Grammar 2 – Simple, Continuous and Perfect Tenses

Prepare...
Grammar Sheet 2
Red pencils
Dictionaries

Builds on...
JGH1: G15-18
JGH2: G16-18,G21
JGH3: G8-9,G17,G36
JGH4: G1-2,G13,G36
JGH5: G4-7,G9-10,G17

Aim: Reinforce the children's understanding of the simple, continuous and perfect tenses, and develop their ability to identify tenses in sentences.

Introduction: Write 'to push' on the board and ask what form of the verb this is [*the infinitive*]. Discuss with the class how the infinitive is the name of the verb and without more information we cannot say who did the pushing or when it was done. Draw a simple grid of nine boxes on the board (or make it look like the Tense Tent on Grammar Sheet 2), reminding the children that verbs describe what is happening in the past, present or future. Then ask the children what tenses they know [*simple, continuous and perfect*] and label the grid as shown below. Fill in the grid with the class, discussing how each tense is formed (see Verbs: pages 11 and 12), and remind the children that the third person singular in the present tense takes the suffix ‹-s›, unless the verb ends in ‹sh›, ‹ch›, ‹s›, ‹z› or ‹x›, when ‹-es› is added. The verbs 'to be' and 'to have', which act as auxiliary verbs in the continuous and perfect tenses respectively, are irregular, so now is a good time for the class to conjugate them in the simple past and present tense, using the pronoun actions.

	Past	Present	Future
Simple	*pushed*	*push/pushes*	*shall/will push*
Continuous	*was/were pushing*	*am/are/is pushing*	*shall/will be pushing*
Perfect	*had pushed*	*have/has pushed*	*shall/will have pushed*

Main point: Write the sentences 'We rode our bicycles yesterday', 'We were riding our bicycles to school' and 'We have ridden our bicycles recently' on the board. Discuss these sentences and remind the class that the simple tenses describe actions that start and finish within a specific time, the continuous tenses describe actions that have started and are still happening, and the perfect tenses describe general experiences that have already been completed, usually at an unspecified point in the past. Also remind the class that while present participles (used in the continuous tenses) are completely regular, past participles (used in the perfect tenses) are often irregular and can be formed in a variety of ways, with no clear rules for which verbs take which spellings. Revise the two most common patterns: 'swim, swam, swum', where a change in vowel letter indicates a change in tense, and 'ride, rode, ridden', where ‹-n› or ‹-en› is added to the root verb to form the past participle. Point out that the ‹d› is doubled in 'ridden' to keep the short vowel sound /i/, and remind the children of the spelling rules for adding a suffix that starts with a vowel (see pages 39 and 40).

Grammar Sheet 2: Write the following verbs on the board: to play, to carry, to wear, to sing, to drink, to eat, to read, to run away (a phrasal verb). The children write inside the outlined word Verbs, using a red pencil, and then choose a verb, writing it in each tense to complete the Tense Tent. A good dictionary will always list the verb name and irregular past tense and past participle of a verb, so encourage the children to look these up where necessary. [*Six of the verbs are irregular: wear/wore/worn; sing/sang/sung; drink/drank/drunk; eat/ate/eaten; read/read/read (pronounced /reed, red, red/); run/ran/run*].

Extension activity: The children think of a sentence, using a verb from the board, and write it out nine times on the back of their grammar sheet, changing the tense each time.

Rounding off: Go over the sheet with the children, discussing their answers. If they have done the extension activity, ask some of them to read out a sentence and say which tense is being used.

Verb Tenses

Verbs — Red

Past

Present

Future

Simple

Continuous

Perfect

Spelling 3 – Numerical Prefixes for 3

Prepare...
Spelling Sheets 3a/b
Coloured pencils

Builds on...
JGH2: G27
JGH3: G32
JGH4: S31-36
JGH5: S7-12
JGH6: S1-2

Revision: Revise the possessive adjectives: 'my', 'your', 'his', 'her', 'its', 'our', 'your', 'their'. Ask the class how to spell 'its' and discuss how it differs in spelling and meaning to the contraction 'it's'. Briefly revise the other homophones covered in recent lessons: 'to', 'two' and 'too'. Then look at the spelling of 'our' and compare it to the spellings and meanings of the noun 'hour', with its silent ‹h›, and the word 'are', which is part of the verb 'to be'. Remind the class that 'our' is more properly pronounced /ou-r/ but in practice it is often pronounced /ar/ and can be confused with 'are'. Write a sentence on the board and ask the class which spellings are needed to complete it: We (are) riding (our) bicycles for an (hour). Repeat with some examples suggested by the class.

Main point: Write the words 'triangle', 'triplet' and 'tricycle' on the board and ask the children whether they know what the letters ‹tri› mean: a 'triangle' is a flat shape with three straight sides and three angles, a 'triplet' is one of three brothers or sisters born at the same time, and a 'tricycle' is a young child's bicycle with three wheels. Explain that ‹tri› comes from the Latin 'tres' and Greek 'treis', meaning 'three'. Ask the class to suggest other words starting with the prefix ‹tri-› and discuss how it relates to the meaning of each one.

Spelling list: Go through the list, asking the class to find and highlight the ‹tri-› prefix each time. Look at how it changes or adds meaning to each word, and discuss the meaning of any unfamiliar words. Point out other spelling features, such as the ‹o› saying its long sound in 'tri**o**', the /ool/ spellings at the end of 'trip**le**', 'tricy**cle**', 'trian**gle**' and 'trienni**al**', the 'soft ‹c›' in 'tri**c**ycle', 'tri**c**eps' and 'tri**c**eratops', the ‹y› saying /i/ in 'tric**y**cle', the 'soft ‹g›' in 'trilo**g**y', the ‹our› in 'tricol**our**', and the ‹ion› saying /yoon/ when it follows ‹ll› in 'trillion'. It is a good idea to blend and sound out the spelling words quickly every day with the class, using the 'say it as it sounds' strategy where appropriate. Stressing the pure sound of any schwas will help the children to remember the spelling (such as in 'trid**e**nt' and 'triplic**ate**'). Alternatively, you could break down the words into prefix and root word.

Spelling Sheet 3a: The children split each word into syllables to help remember the spelling [1. tri/o, 2. tri/ple, 3. tri/dent, 4. tri/plane, 5. tri/cy/cle, 6. tri/pod, 7. tril/o/gy, 8. tri/ath/lon, 9. tri/an/gle, 10. trip/let, 11. tri/ceps, 12. tri/col/our, 13. tri/cer/a/tops, 14. tri/an/gu/lar, 15. trip/li/cate, 16. tri/en/ni/al, 17. tri/corn, 18. tril/lion]. They then write the meanings for the spelling words shown, using a dictionary if needed, and identify the correct meaning of 'triple' [A], 'trident' [B] and 'triceratops' [B].

Spelling Sheet 3b: The children complete the sentences by writing in the correct homophone(s) [1. our, 2. are, 3. hour, 4. Our, 5. are; our, 6. hour, 7. are, 8. hour; are; our]. Then they parse the sentence and complete the wall [Top: Megan - had drawn - pattern / Bottom: (blank) - carefully - a triangular / Verb: transitive]. The adverb 'carefully' is made by adding ‹-ly› to the adjective 'careful'.

Megan[N] had carefully[Adv] drawn[V] a triangular[Adj] pattern[N].

Noun[N] (black), Verb[V] (red), Pronoun[P] (pink), Adjective[Adj] (blue), Adverb[Adv] (orange), Conjunction[C] (purple), Preposition[Pre] (green)

Dictation: (This can be done in the spelling lesson or at another time during the week.) Call out the sentences for the children to write down. In Sentence 1, remind them to use speech marks with the correct punctuation.

1. "Have you read the trilogy?" asked the triplets.
2. The mayor put on his red robe and tricorn hat.
3. A triennial meeting takes place every three years.

Spelling List 3

1. trio
2. triple
3. trident
4. triplane
5. tricycle
6. tripod
7. trilogy
8. triathlon
9. triangle
10. triplet
11. triceps
12. tricolour
13. triceratops
14. triangular
15. triplicate
16. triennial
17. tricorn
18. trillion

‹tri-›

Write the meaning for each of these spelling words.

1. trio _____
   _____
2. triplane _____
3. tricycle _____
4. trilogy _____
5. triangle _____
6. triplet _____
7. triceps _____

Which of these meanings correctly describes the spelling word?

8. **triple**
   A. being three times as large as something
   B. existing as three identical copies
   C. happening every three years

9. **trident**
   A. a three-legged stand that supports a camera
   B. a long-handled weapon with three sharp points
   C. a hat with its brim turned up on three sides

10. **triceratops**
    A. a three-sport event (running, swimming, cycling)
    B. a type of dinosaur with three horns on its head
    C. a flag divided equally into three different colours

Join the dots to reveal one of the spelling words.

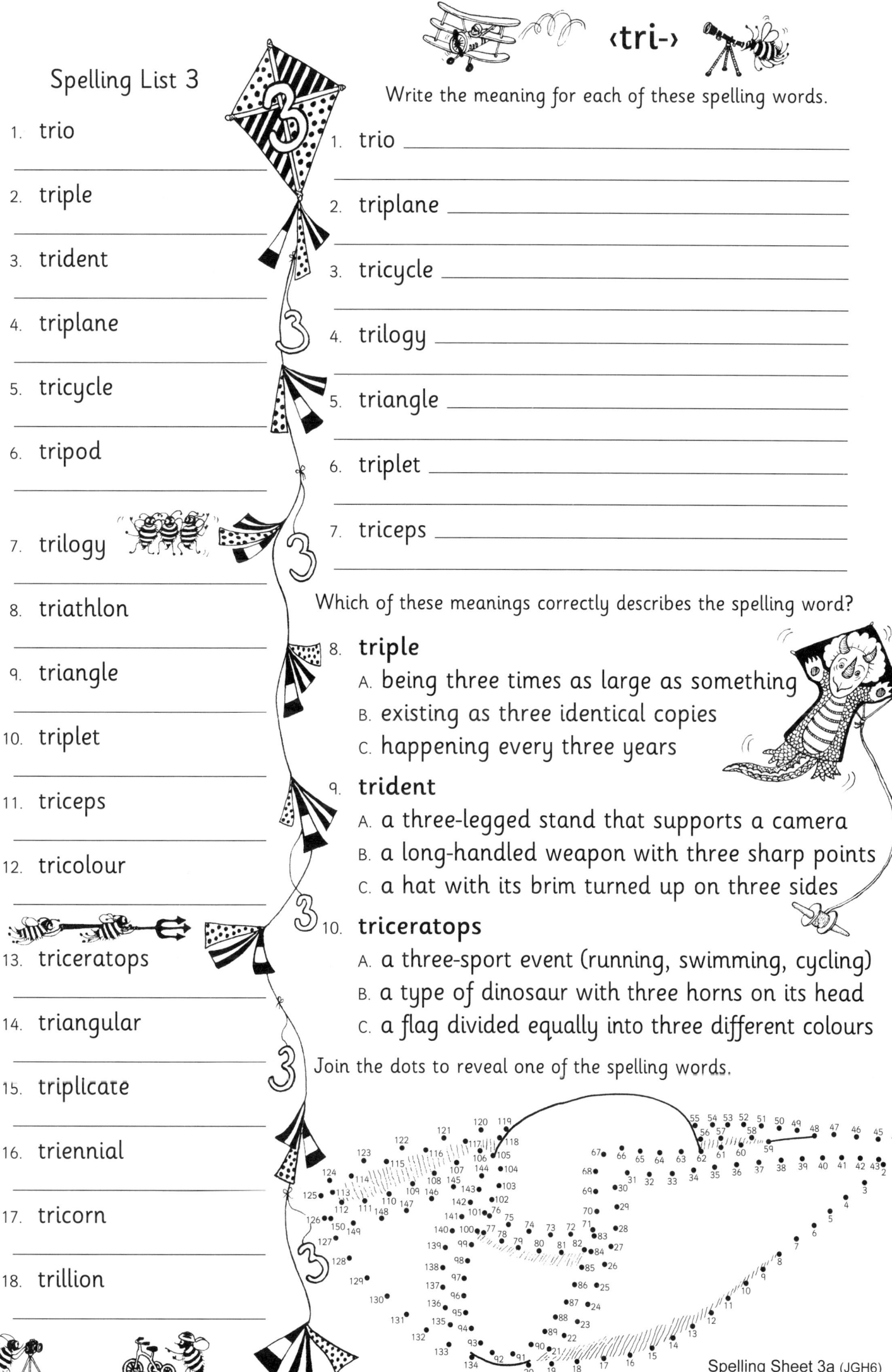

Spelling Sheet 3a (JGH6)

Dictation: ‹tri-›

1. _____
_____

2. _____
_____

3. _____
_____

'Hour', 'our' and 'are' are homophones. They are words that can sound the same but have different spellings and meanings. Which one should be used to complete each sentence correctly?

1. I am wearing a tricorn hat in _____ school play.

2. The lives of three families _____ told in the trilogy.

3. It took less than an _____ to complete the forms and print them in triplicate.

4. "_____ acrobats do six triple somersaults in a row," said the ringmaster, proudly.

5. We _____ taking two cameras, three lenses and a tripod on _____ next trip.

6. The trio of musicians will be performing for two _____s.

7. There _____ three equal sides and three equal angles in an equilateral triangle.

8. In an _____ we _____ going to see _____ friend in the triathlon.

hour

our

are

Parse the sentence and then write it on the wall.

Megan had carefully drawn a triangular pattern.

subject	verb	object
	transitive / intransitive	

Grammar 3 – Definite and Indefinite Articles

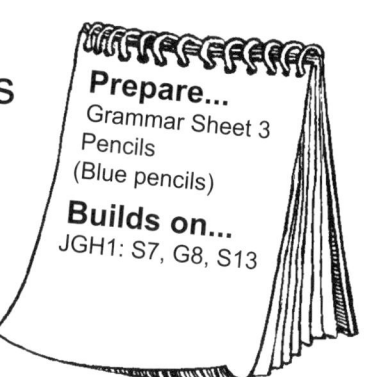

Prepare...
Grammar Sheet 3
Pencils
(Blue pencils)

Builds on...
JGH1: S7, G8, S13

Aim: Reinforce the children's understanding of the definite article ('the') and the indefinite articles ('a' and 'an'), and develop their knowledge of when to use 'an' instead of 'a'.

Introduction: Revise the short and long vowel sounds, /a, e, i, o, u/ and /ai, ee, ie, oa, ue/, and the sounds of the vowel digraphs: /or, oo, oo, ou, oi, er, ar/. Remind the children that many vowels have alternative spellings, and ask them what we call alphabet letters that are not vowels [consonants]. Compared to vowels, the consonant sounds are more constant in their spelling, although there are some obvious exceptions, such as the 'soft ‹c›' (for /s/), 'soft ‹g›' (for /j/), ‹f›, ‹ph› and ‹gh› (for /f/), and ‹ch› (for /ch/, /k/ and /sh/).

Main point: Ask the children what they think is the most frequently used word in English [the]. 'The' is used before singular and plural nouns and is called the 'definite article', while 'a' and 'an' are used before singular nouns and are called the 'indefinite articles'. 'Definite' means 'clearly known' and 'the' is used to determine that the noun it refers to is one we are likely to know because, for example, it has already been mentioned or is what we are expecting. 'Indefinite' has the prefix ‹in-›, meaning 'not', and so 'a' and 'an' are used to determine that the nouns they refer to are unknown and are being introduced for the first time. Write 'I saw a dog in the park. The dog was barking' on the board and discuss the use of 'a' and 'the': 'a' is used to introduce the dog for the first time and after that it can be referred to as 'the dog'; 'the' is used with 'park' to show that it is the familiar, local park, rather than an unspecified one. Also point out that 'the' is always used before a superlative, because there can only be one thing or one group that is the tallest or the strongest, for instance. The articles belong to a group of words called 'determiners', which always modify a noun and so are a special type of adjective. Determiners appear at the start of a noun phrase to show (or determine) the following: how known it is (articles); how many there are (quantifiers like 'some', 'few', 'more', 'any'); who it belongs to (possessive adjectives like 'my' and 'ours'); and which particular one is referred to (the demonstratives 'this', 'that', 'these' and 'those').

Ask the children when and why they would use 'an' instead of 'a' [when the word following it starts with a vowel sound, as in 'an ant', 'an arm', 'an empty nest', 'an eel', 'an inch', 'an order', 'an umbrella'; because it makes it easier to say the words together fluently]. Call out some words and discuss whether 'a' or 'an' should be used. End with 'unicorn' and ask the class to listen carefully to its first sound. As it starts with a long vowel, /ue/, we would expect to say 'an unicorn', but /ue/ is really two sounds – /y-oo/ – and so we say 'a unicorn', because /y/ is a consonant sound. Now try the word 'hour' and remind the class that it is the first sound that is important, not the first letter, and so we say 'an hour' because the ‹h› in 'hour' is silent.

Introduce the actions for 'the' (making a capital 'T' with your hands) and for 'a' and 'an' (showing the palm of your hand and pointing to your thumb).

Grammar Sheet 3: The children write inside the outlined words the, a and an (in pencil or blue, as preferred) and then fill in the correct article to complete the noun phrases [an ostrich, a horse, an hour, an emu, a triangle, a shell, a bicycle, a unicorn, an umbrella] and sentences [1. a, 2. an, 3. The, 4. the, 5. The, 6. the, 7. an, 8. a, 9. a, 10. the, 11. The, 12. The; a].

Extension activity: The children write down their own sentences, leaving blank spaces for the articles. They then swap them with a partner and fill in the missing words.

Rounding off: Go over the sheet with the children, discussing their answers. If they have done the extension activity, ask some of them to read out a few sentences.

Definite and Indefinite Articles

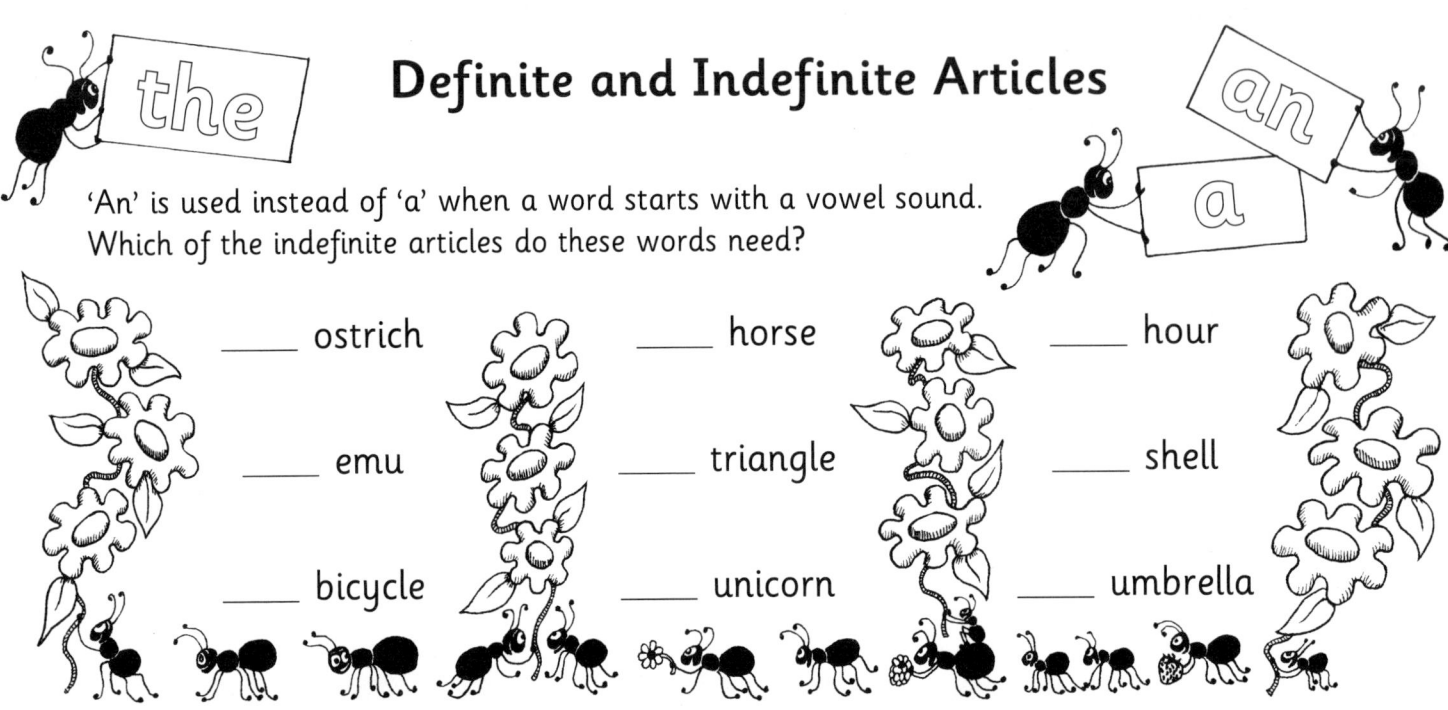

'An' is used instead of 'a' when a word starts with a vowel sound.
Which of the indefinite articles do these words need?

____ ostrich   ____ horse   ____ hour

____ emu   ____ triangle   ____ shell

____ bicycle   ____ unicorn   ____ umbrella

Which article should it be? Write in 'a', 'an' or 'the' to complete each sentence correctly.

1. I have lost _____ shoe.

2. It was _____ honest mistake.

3. _____ triplets are three years old.

4. Ravi and his friends are in _____ kitchen.

5. _____ hotel we are staying in is fabulous.

6. Anna is _____ best swimmer in her class.

7. They have _____ interesting dilemma.

8. We are staying in _____ fabulous hotel.

9. He bought _____ new pair of binoculars.

10. She really liked _____ kangaroos at the zoo.

11. Did you walk to school? _____ school is nearby.

12. _____ funniest clown was riding _____ unicycle.

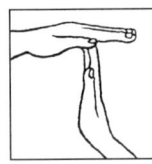

Definite Article: 'The'
Action: Make a capital 'T' with your hands, with one hand facing palm down and the other pointing up towards it.

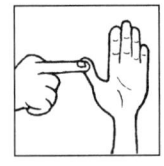

Indefinite Articles: 'A', 'An'
Action: Hold up your hand, palm facing forward, and point to your thumb.

Spelling 4 – Numerical Prefixes for 4, 5 and 6

Prepare...
Spelling Sheets 4a/b
Coloured pencils

Builds on...
JGH2: G27
JGH3: G32
JGH4: S31-36
JGH5: S7-12
JGH6: S1-3

Revision: Revise the possessive adjectives: 'my', 'your', 'his', 'her', 'its', 'our', 'your', 'their'. Ask the class how to spell 'its' and 'our' and compare them to 'it's', 'hour' and 'are'. Also revise 'to', 'two' and 'too'. Now look at the spelling of 'your' and compare it to 'you're', which is a contraction of 'you are'. Write a sentence on the board and ask the class which spellings are needed to complete it: '(You're) visiting (your) granny today. Repeat with some examples suggested by the class. Ask the children if they can remember any of the prefixes for words relating to the numbers one, two and three.

Main point: English words relating to the numbers four, five and six also have prefixes influenced by Latin and Greek. Words beginning with ‹quad(r)-› or ‹quar-› come from the Latin words 'quattuor' and 'quartus', meaning 'four' and 'fourth'. ‹Quin-› comes from the Latin word 'quinque' and ‹penta› from the Greek word 'pente', both meaning 'five'. ‹Sex-› and ‹hexa-› come from the Latin and Greek words for 'six' ('sex' and 'hex'). Ask the children if they can think of any words beginning with these prefixes.

Spelling list: Go through the list, asking the class to find and highlight the prefix each time. Look at how it changes or adds meaning to each word, and discuss the meaning of any unfamiliar words. Point out other spelling features, such as the ‹a› saying /o/ and ‹ar› saying /or/ after ‹qu› in words starting with ‹quad› and ‹quar›, and the /ool/ spellings at the end of 'quadru**le**', 'hexagon**al**', 'quadrang**le**' and 'quadrilater**al**'. It is a good idea to blend and sound out the spelling words quickly every day with the class, using the 'say it as it sounds' strategy where appropriate (stressing the pure sound of any schwas, for example, as in 'hex**ago**n'), or you could break down the words into prefix and root word.

Spelling Sheet 4a: The children split each word into syllables to help remember the spelling *[1. quad, 2. quin/tet, 3. quad/rant, 4. quar/tet, 5. sex/tet, 6. hex/a/gon, 7. pen/ta/gon, 8. quar/ter, 9. quad/ru/ple, 10. hex/ag/o/nal, 11. pen/tath/lon, 12. sex/tant, 13. quad/ran/gle, 14. pen/ta/gram, 15. quad/ru/ped, 16. pen/tam/e/ter, 17. sex/tu/plet, 18. quad/ri/lat/er/al].* They then answer each question in the quiz *[1. quartet, 2. quintet, 3. sextet, 4. four, 5. running; swimming; horse riding; fencing; shooting, 6. the pizza should be divided into four equal parts, 7. six (hexagon); four (quadrilateral); five (pentagon), 8. a picture of an animal with four legs, such as a sheep, cow, horse, etc].*

Spelling Sheet 4b: The children complete each sentence by crossing out the wrong homophone. *[The correct spellings are: 1. You're, 2. You're, 3. your, 4. you're, 5. Your, 6. your, 7. your, 8. you're].* Then they parse the sentence and complete the wall *[Top: I - divided - pizza / Bottom: (blank) - neatly/into quarters - the cheese and tomato / Verb: transitive].* 'Cheese' and 'tomato' are nouns acting as adjectives and should be underlined in blue. 'Into quarters' is a prepositional phrase acting as an adverb, so orange brackets can be put around it.

IP neatlyAdv dividedV the cheeseAdj andC tomatoAdj pizzaN (intoPre quartersN)Adv.

NounN (black), VerbV (red), PronounP (pink), AdjectiveAdj (blue), AdverbAdv (orange), ConjunctionC (purple), PrepositionPre (green)

Dictation: (This can be done in the spelling lesson or at another time during the week.) Call out the sentences for the children to write down. In Sentence 1, remind them to use speech marks with the correct punctuation. 'Miss Beech' is a proper noun with initial capital letters. Sentence 3 needs a question mark.

1. "Please draw a quadrilateral," said Miss Beech.
2. The quintet will be singing in the concert.
3. Does a pentagon have more sides than a square?

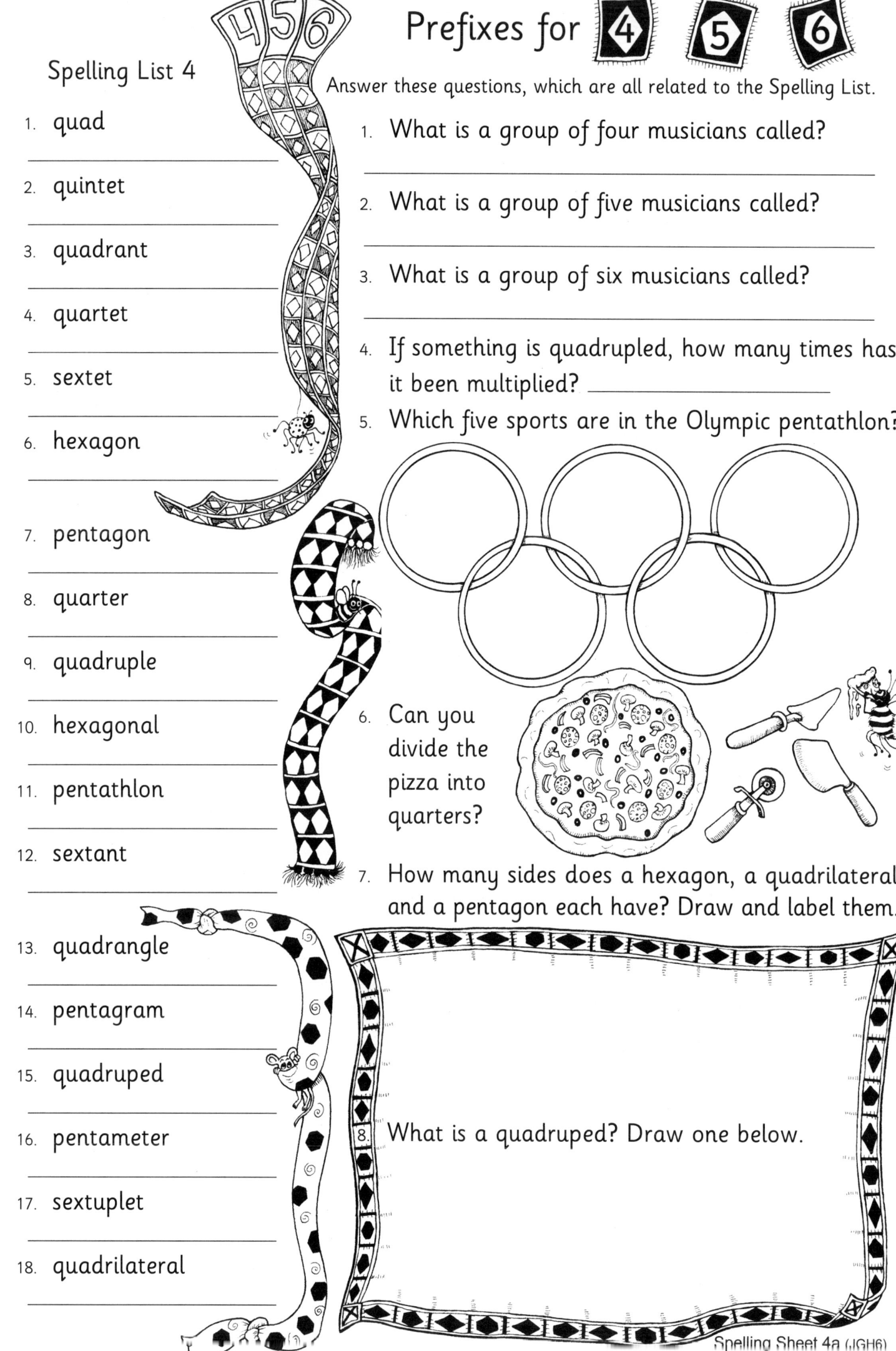

Prefixes for 4 5 6

Spelling List 4

1. quad
   _____
2. quintet
   _____
3. quadrant
   _____
4. quartet
   _____
5. sextet
   _____
6. hexagon
   _____
7. pentagon
   _____
8. quarter
   _____
9. quadruple
   _____
10. hexagonal
   _____
11. pentathlon
   _____
12. sextant
   _____
13. quadrangle
   _____
14. pentagram
   _____
15. quadruped
   _____
16. pentameter
   _____
17. sextuplet
   _____
18. quadrilateral
   _____

Answer these questions, which are all related to the Spelling List.

1. What is a group of four musicians called?
   _____

2. What is a group of five musicians called?
   _____

3. What is a group of six musicians called?
   _____

4. If something is quadrupled, how many times has it been multiplied? _____

5. Which five sports are in the Olympic pentathlon?

6. Can you divide the pizza into quarters?

7. How many sides does a hexagon, a quadrilateral, and a pentagon each have? Draw and label them.

8. What is a quadruped? Draw one below.

Dictation: Prefixes - **4, 5, 6**

1. _____
   _____
   _____

2. _____
   _____
   _____

3. _____
   _____

'Your' and 'you're' are homophones. They are words that sound the same but have different spellings and meanings. Which one should be used to complete each sentence correctly?

1. Your / You're playing the violin in the quartet next week.

2. " Your / You're going to study quadrants this week," my teacher said.

3. Have you done your / you're homework on hexagons, yet?

4. Is the book your / you're reading all about quadrupeds?

5. " Your / You're prices have quadrupled this year!" the angry customer complained.

6. Didn't your / you're cousin do well in the pentathlon?

7. Is your / you're room in the building across the quadrangle?

8. I'll peel and quarter the potatoes while your / you're chopping the carrots.

you're

you're

your

your

Parse the sentence and then write it on the wall.

I neatly divided the cheese and tomato pizza into quarters.

subject	verb	object
	transitive / intransitive	

Grammar 4 – Countable and Uncountable Nouns

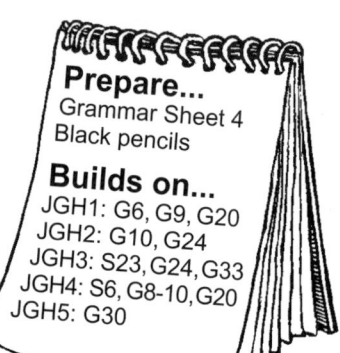

Prepare...
Grammar Sheet 4
Black pencils

Builds on...
JGH1: G6, G9, G20
JGH2: G10, G24
JGH3: S23, G24, G33
JGH4: S6, G8-10, G20
JGH5: G30

Aim: Refine the children's knowledge of nouns, and introduce the concept of countable and uncountable nouns. These are also known as 'count' nouns and 'non-count' (or 'mass') nouns.

Introduction: Revise proper nouns and common nouns. Proper nouns start with a capital letter and are the names given to particular people, places and dates. Common nouns are the names of everyday things and often have the articles 'a', 'an' or 'the' in front of them. Ask the children what kinds of common nouns they know. They should be familiar with **collective** nouns (the names for groups of people, animals or things), **concrete** nouns (things we can see, hear, smell, taste or touch) and **abstract** nouns (the names for things like ideas, feelings, actions, qualities and events); see pages 4 to 7 for more information. The class should also know about **possessive** nouns (proper and common nouns ending in ‹'s›, which show possession and act as adjectives). Revise the actions for proper, common, concrete and abstract nouns and remind the class that the colour for nouns is black. Ask the children to call out different nouns and say what type they are.

Main point: Most nouns have a singular and plural form. Call out some regular plurals and ask the children how they would spell them: 'girls', 'dogs', 'foxes', 'dishes', 'potatoes', 'pianos', 'boys', 'berries'. (See page 8 for when and how to add the suffixes ‹-s›, ‹-es› and ‹-ies›.) Now call out some irregular plurals ('men', 'women', 'children', 'mice', 'sheep', 'wolves', 'wives', 'cacti') and compare them to their singular forms ('man', 'woman', 'child', 'mouse', 'sheep', 'wolf', 'wife', 'cactus'). Explain that nouns like these, which can be counted, that can have 'a' or 'an' in front of them and have a plural form, are called 'countable' nouns. Now ask the children to imagine they are going on a picnic: what would they take? They might like some bread and butter, some honey and jam, or some cheese. Ask the children what is different about these nouns and explain that we do not usually count them or talk about them in the plural; we do not ask someone if they would like 'a bread' or buy 'two jams' at the supermarket. Instead, we use general descriptions like 'some', 'a lot of' or 'more', and if we want to express a specific quantity, we use noun phrases like 'a loaf of bread' or 'a jar of jam'. We do not ask 'how many?' as we would with countable nouns, but 'how much?' instead. This is because, in English, these things are thought of as a single idea or as something that is too hard to divide. Point out that some words can be countable or uncountable: for example, you might bring two <u>cakes</u> and a big roast chicken to the picnic (countable), then sit down and eat some <u>chicken</u> and <u>cake</u> (uncountable). Ask for suggestions of uncountable nouns and discuss them with the class. Possible words include rice, sugar, pasta, flour, milk, food, rain, snow, thunder, lightning, weather, gold, silver, money, luggage, traffic, furniture, music.

Grammar Sheet 4: The children write inside the outlined words Countable and Uncountable Nouns, using a black pencil. They then choose suitable nouns from the picture to write on the lines or in the jug and notepad *[Countable: ant, apple, banana, basket, blanket, bottle, cake, chicken, cup, dish, egg, flask, fork, grape, jar, knife, napkin, orange, plate, spoon, sandwich; Uncountable: bread, butter, cake, cheese, chicken, coffee/soup/tea, fruit, grass, honey, jam, lemonade, mustard, pepper, salt, water. Quantities: a jug of lemonade/water; two slices of bread/cake/cheese/chicken; a loaf of bread; a spoonful of honey/jam/mustard/ pepper/salt; five bottles of lemonade/mustard/water; a cup of coffee/soup/tea/lemonade/ water; three pieces of bread/cake/cheese/chicken/fruit; a jar of coffee/honey/jam/mustard].*

Extension activity: The children write some sentences, using 'much' with some suitable uncountable nouns and 'many' with some countable nouns.

Rounding off: Go over the sheet/extension activity with the children, checking their answers.

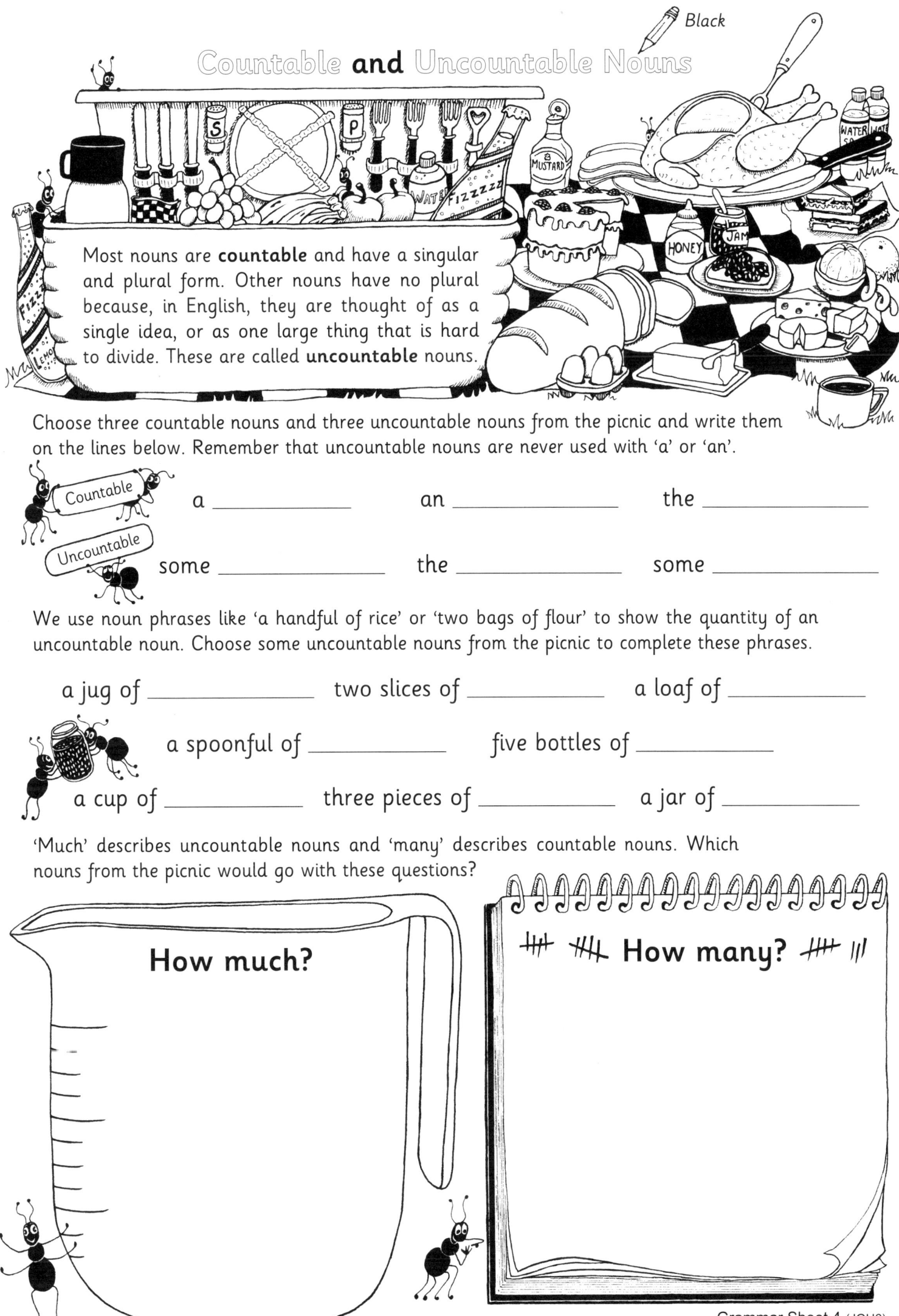

Countable **and** Uncountable Nouns

Most nouns are **countable** and have a singular and plural form. Other nouns have no plural because, in English, they are thought of as a single idea, or as one large thing that is hard to divide. These are called **uncountable** nouns.

Choose three countable nouns and three uncountable nouns from the picnic and write them on the lines below. Remember that uncountable nouns are never used with 'a' or 'an'.

Countable

a _____   an _____   the _____

Uncountable

some _____   the _____   some _____

We use noun phrases like 'a handful of rice' or 'two bags of flour' to show the quantity of an uncountable noun. Choose some uncountable nouns from the picnic to complete these phrases.

a jug of _____   two slices of _____   a loaf of _____

a spoonful of _____   five bottles of _____

a cup of _____   three pieces of _____   a jar of _____

'Much' describes uncountable nouns and 'many' describes countable nouns. Which nouns from the picnic would go with these questions?

How much?

How many?

Spelling 5 – Numerical Prefixes for 7, 8 and 9

Prepare...
Spelling Sheets 5a/b
Coloured pencils

Builds on...
JGH2: G27
JGH3: G32
JGH4: S31-36
JGH5: S7-12
JGH6: S1-4

Revision: Revise the possessive adjectives: 'my', 'your', 'his', 'her', 'its', 'our', 'your', 'their'. Ask the class how to spell 'its', 'our' and 'your' and compare them to the homophones 'it's', 'hour', 'are' and 'you're'. Also revise 'to', 'two' and 'too'. Now look at the spelling of 'their' and compare it to 'they're' (a contraction of 'they are') and 'there', which is often used as an adverb to show position or as a pronoun to introduce the subject of a sentence (There is... / There are...). Write a sentence on the board and ask the class which spellings are needed to complete it: (They're) buying (their) school uniforms (there). Repeat with some examples suggested by the class. Ask the children if they can remember any of the prefixes for words relating to the numbers one to six.

Main point: Like the numbers one to six, words relating to seven, eight and nine have prefixes influenced by Latin and Greek. ‹Sept-› comes from the Latin 'septem' and ‹hepta-› from the Greek 'hepta', both meaning 'seven'. ‹Oct-› comes from 'octo' in Latin and 'okto' in Greek, which both mean 'eight'. ‹Novem-› and ‹nona-› come from 'novem' and 'nonus', Latin words for 'nine' and 'ninth'. Ask the children if they can think of any words beginning with these prefixes.

Spelling list: Go through the list, ask the class to find and highlight the prefix each time, look at how it changes or adds meaning to each word, and discuss the meaning of any unfamiliar words. Point out other spelling features, such as the suffix ‹-al› saying /ool/ in 'octagonal', the vowel saying its long sound in 'October', 'November' and 'octahedron', and the 'soft ‹g›' and ‹a› saying /air/ in 'septuagenarian', 'octogenarian' and 'nonagenarian'. It is a good idea to blend and sound out the spelling words quickly every day with the class, using the 'say it as it sounds' strategy where appropriate (stressing the pure sound of any schwas, for example, as in 'octagon' and 'octave'), or you could break down the words into prefix and root word.

Spelling Sheet 5a: The children split each word into syllables to help remember the spelling [1. sep/tet, 2. oc/tet, 3. hep/ta/gon, 4. oc/ta/gon, 5. non/a/gon, 6. oc/to/pus, 7. oc/tave, 8. oc/tag/o/nal, 9. Sep/tem/ber, 10. Oc/to/ber, 11. No/vem/ber, 12. hep/tath/lon, 13. sep/tu/plet, 14. oc/tu/plet, 15. oc/ta/he/dron, 16. sep/tu/a/ge/nar/i/an, 17. oc/to/ge/nar/i/an, 18. non/a/ge/nar/i/an]. They then answer each question in the quiz [1. sept-/hepta- (7); oct- (8); novem-/nona- (9), 2. September/October/November, 3. seven, 4. septuagenarian/octogenarian/nonagenarian, 5. septet, 6. octet, 7. eight] and draw an octopus.

Spelling Sheet 5b: The children complete each sentence by crossing out the wrong homophone. [The correct spellings are: 1. there, 2. their; They're, 3. their, 4. There; They're, 5. there, 6. They're, 7. There, 8. Their]. Then they parse the sentence and complete the wall [Top: octopuses - slept - (blank) / Bottom: The two small - peacefully/in their aquarium - (blank) / Verb: intransitive]. The prepositional phrase 'in their aquarium' acts as an adverb, so orange brackets can be put around it. The adverb 'peacefully' is made by adding ‹-ly› to the adjective 'peaceful'.

The two^{Adj} small^{Adj} octopuses^{N} slept^{V} peacefully^{Adv} (in^{Pre} their^{Adj} aquarium^{N})^{Adv}.

Noun^{N}(black), Verb^{V}(red), Pronoun^{P}(pink), Adjective^{Adj}(blue), Adverb^{Adv}(orange), Conjunction^{C}(purple), Preposition^{Pre}(green)

Dictation: (This can be done in the spelling lesson or at another time during the week.) Call out the sentences for the children to write down. Sentence 1 needs a question mark. In Sentence 3, remind them to use speech marks with the correct punctuation. 'October' and 'Dad' are proper nouns and need a capital letter.

1. How many people sing in a septet?
2. The triplets became octogenarians last month.
3. "We will see your cousins in October," said Dad.

Spelling List 5

1. septet

_____

2. octet

_____

3. heptagon

_____

4. octagon

_____

5. nonagon

_____

6. octopus

_____

7. octave

_____

8. octagonal

_____

9. September

_____

10. October

_____

11. November

_____

12. heptathlon

_____

13. septuplet

_____

14. octuplet

_____

15. octahedron

_____

16. septuagenarian

_____

17. octogenarian

_____

18. nonagenarian

_____

Prefixes for 7 8 9

Answer these questions, which are all related to the Spelling List.

1. What are the prefix(es) for these numbers?

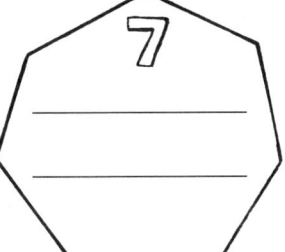 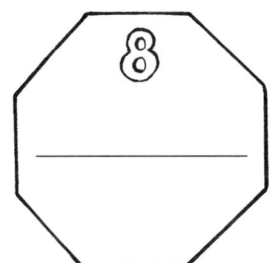 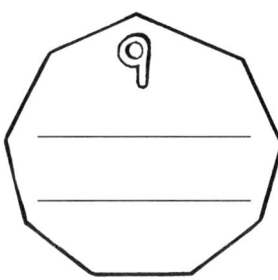

2. Which three words in the Spelling List are months of the year?

_____

_____

_____

3. How many sports events are in a heptathlon?

_____

4. Which word describes someone who is:

70 years old _____

80 years old _____

90 years old _____ ?

5. What is a group of seven musicians called?

_____

6. What is a group of eight musicians called?

_____

7. How many arms does an octopus have?

_____

Draw an octopus in the aquarium.

Dictation: Prefixes - 7, 8, 9

1. _____

_____

2. _____

_____

3. _____

_____

'There', 'their' and 'they're' are homophones. They are words that sound the same but have different spellings and meanings. Which one should be used to complete each sentence correctly?

1. In music there / their / they're are eight notes in an octave.
2. The couple have announced there / their / they're engagement. There / Their / They're getting married next September.
3. I congratulated my sisters on there / their / they're success in the heptathlon.
4. There / Their / They're are seven brothers in my class at school. There / Their / They're septuplets!
5. During November there / their / they're will be no concerts in the local park.
6. Did you know that octopuses have eight arms and three hearts? There / Their / They're really fascinating!
7. There / Their / They're are several septuagenerians among my grandfather's friends.
8. There / Their / They're old castle has four octagonal towers.

they're
they're
their
their
there
there

Parse the sentence and then write it on the wall.

The two small octopuses slept peacefully in their aquarium.

subject	verb	object
	transitive / intransitive	

Grammar 5 – Parts of Speech

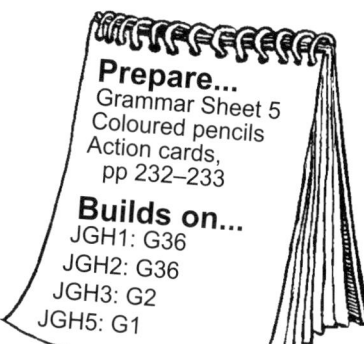

Prepare...
Grammar Sheet 5
Coloured pencils
Action cards,
pp 232–233

Builds on...
JGH1: G36
JGH2: G36
JGH3: G2
JGH5: G1

Aim: Revise all the parts of speech learnt so far (nouns, pronouns, adjectives, verbs, adverbs, prepositions and conjunctions; see pages 4 to 19) and introduce a new game to reinforce the learning.

Introduction: Briefly look at **Nouns**, which were revised in Grammar Lesson 4, and ask the children what other parts of speech they know: **Pronouns**: The small words that replace nouns, such as the personal pronouns (like 'I'/'me' and 'we'/'us') and possessive pronouns (for example, 'mine' and 'ours'); **Adjectives:** Words that describe nouns and pronouns (including possessive adjectives like 'my' and comparatives and superlatives like 'bigger' and 'biggest'); **Verbs:** Revised in Grammar Lesson 2, these are 'doing words' that always appear in a sentence and describe past, present and future actions; **Adverbs:** Words, commonly ending in ‹-ly›, that tell us more about how, where, when, how much or how often something happens. They mostly describe verbs, but can also modify other adverbs (as in 'really slowly') and adjectives (as in 'really happy'); **Prepositions:** Words that relate one noun or pronoun to another, such as 'under' and 'in'. (Such words can also be adverbs if they do not come before a noun or pronoun: for example, 'We went in'.) Prepositional phrases can also act as adverbs; **Conjunctions**: Words such as 'and', 'but', 'or', 'so' and 'because' that are used to join sentences, or parts of a sentence, to create longer, less repetitive sentences. Revise the action and colour for each part of speech, and remind the class that many words can act as different parts of speech, depending on how they are used. Write a sentence on the board and parse it with the class: We^P saw^V clowns^N and^C acrobats^N (in^Pre the circus^Adj tent^N)^Adv.

Main point: Knowing the parts of speech and being able to identify them in a sentence is fundamental to understanding grammar. This is why the children have regular parsing practice in their spelling lessons, underlining words in a particular colour to show how they are being used. Without this knowledge children would struggle to understand the complexities of sentence structure and could not, for example, identify the subject and object of a sentence, another regular activity in the spelling lessons (see Sentence Walls: pages 28 and 29). Such multisensory activities are accessible and visual ways to help children understand how language works, and another example is the game Grammar Action Sentences. This game can be played either by doing the grammar actions themselves or by using enlarged copies of the actions found on pages 232 and 233. The actions should be ordered in a sequence, following the pattern of a simple sentence: for example, this could be indefinite article / adjective / common noun / verb / adverb. The children call out possible words for each action and create a sentence, such as 'A small kitten purred happily'.

Grammar Sheet 5: The children write inside each of the outlined parts of speech in the appropriate colour *[black (nouns), pink (pronouns), blue (adjectives), red (verbs), orange (adverbs), green (prepositions), purple (conjunctions). 'Articles' could be done in pencil or in blue, as you prefer]*. They then write five sentences, thinking of appropriate words for each action. The action sequences reflect five different sentence patterns: 1. indefinite article / adjective / common noun / verb (present) / adverb, 2. indefinite article / adjective / adjective / common noun / verb (past), 3. pronoun / verb (future) / preposition / definite article / common noun, 4. proper noun / verb (past) / preposition / definite article / adjective / common noun, 5. proper noun / conjunction / proper noun / verb (present) / adverb.

Extension activity: Give the class new action sequences, using other sentence patterns. These can be made easily by copying, cutting and pasting the actions from the worksheet. Alternatively, the class can use the original sequences to write new sentences.

Rounding off: Go over the sheet/extension activity with the class, sharing their sentences.

Grammar Action Sentences

These rows of grammar actions represent five possible sentences. Look at the actions and think of suitable words to make each sentence. Then write your sentences underneath.

1. _____

_____

2. _____

_____

3. _____

_____

4. _____

_____

5. _____

_____

Spelling 6 – Numerical Prefix for 10: ‹dec-›

Prepare...
Spelling Sheets 6a/b
Coloured pencils

Builds on...
JGH2: G27
JGH3: G32
JGH4: S31-36
JGH5: S7-12
JGH6: S1-5

Revision: Ask the class to spell the number 'two' and the possessive adjectives 'its', 'our', 'your' and 'their', and to give the spellings and meanings of their homophones (see Spelling Lessons 1 to 5). Now discuss 'where' (a question word relating to place), 'wear' (a verb describing putting on things like clothes and shoes) and 'were' (part of the irregular verb 'to be'). Although 'were' is not strictly a homophone of 'where', their spellings are often confused. Write a sentence on the board and ask the class which spellings are needed to complete it: (Where) (were) you hoping to (wear) the dress? Repeat with some examples suggested by the class. Ask the children if they can remember any of the prefixes for words relating to the numbers four to nine.

Main point: English words relating to 'ten' often have the prefix ‹dec-›, as the Latin and Greek words for 'ten' are 'decem' and 'deka'. (The reason why September, October, November and December have their number prefixes is because they were the seventh, eighth, ninth and tenth months in the old Roman calendar.) Words starting with ‹cent-› and ‹milli-›, meaning 'a hundred' and 'a thousand', also come from Latin, but other number-related words like 'twice', 'twelfth', 'twentieth', 'forty' and 'hundred' have their roots in Old English.

Spelling list: Go through the list, discuss the meaning of each word, and ask the class to find and highlight the prefixes ‹dec-›, ‹cent-› and ‹milli-› when they appear. Point out other spelling features, such as the 'soft ‹c›' in ‹cent›, 'twice', 'December', 'decibel' and 'decimal', the /ool/ spelling in 'decima**l**', the ‹age› saying /ij/ at the end of 'percentage', and the ‹ion› saying /yoon/ after ‹ll› and silent ‹e› in both 'mill**ion**aire' and 'bill**ion**aire'. It is a good idea to blend and sound out the spelling words quickly every day with the class, using the 'say it as it sounds' strategy where appropriate (stressing the pure sound of any schwas, for example, as in 'dec**ag**on' and 'twent**i**eth'), or you could break down some of the words into prefix and root word.

Spelling Sheet 6a: The children split each word into syllables to help remember the spelling [1. dec/a/gon, 2. dec/ade, 3. twice, 4. for/ty, 5. hun/dred, 6. De/cem/ber, 7. twelfth, 8. twen/ti/eth, 9. per/cent, 10. cen/tu/ri/on, 11. dec/i/bel, 12. dec/i/mal, 13. per/cent/age, 14. mil/len/ni/um, 15. de/cath/lon, 16. mil/lion/aire, 17. bil/lion/aire, 18. de/cath/lete]. They then answer each question in the quiz [1. dec- (10); cent- (100); milli- (1,000), 2. December, 3. decathlon, 4. decathlete, 5. a hundred, 6. one hundred percent, 7. 0.75 (B), 8. a decade, 9. a millennium, 10. 1,000, 11. 1,000,000, 12. decibels, 13. twice; twelfth; twentieth].

Spelling Sheet 6b: The children complete each sentence by crossing out the wrong homophone. [The correct spellings are: 1. Where; were, 2. were, 3. wear, 4. where, 5. wear, 6. where, 7. were, 8. were]. Then they parse the sentence and complete the wall [Top: May–and–Daisy - are celebrating - birthday / Bottom: (blank) - today - their twentieth / Verb: transitive]. The 'and' can be bracketed with dotted lines to show it is not one of the subjects.

May^N and^C Daisy^N (are celebrating)^V their^Adj twentieth^Adj birthday^N today^Adv.

Noun^N (black), Verb^V (red), Pronoun^P (pink), Adjective^Adj (blue), Adverb^Adv (orange), Conjunction^C (purple), Preposition^Pre (green)

Dictation: (This can be done in the spelling lesson or at another time during the week.) Call out the sentences for the children to write down. In Sentence 2, remind them to use speech marks with the correct punctuation. 'December' and 'Miss Beech' are proper nouns and need initial capital letters.

1. A high percentage of tourists visit in December.
2. "Remember where to put the decimal point," said Miss Beech.
3. They celebrated the new millennium with hundreds of fireworks.

Spelling List 6

1. decagon

2. decade

3. twice

4. forty

5. hundred

6. December

7. twelfth

8. twentieth

9. percent

10. centurion

11. decibel

12. decimal

13. percentage

14. millennium

15. decathlon

16. millionaire

17. billionaire

18. decathlete

‹dec-› and more

Answer these questions, which are all related to the Spelling List.

1. What are the prefixes for these numbers?

   10 _____

   100 _____

   1,000 _____

2. Which word in the Spelling List is a month of the year? _____

3. Which of these sports competitions has the most events: the heptathlon, decathlon, pentathlon, biathlon or triathlon? _____

4. What do you call an athlete who takes part in a decathlon? _____

5. In Roman times, how many soldiers was a centurion in charge of? _____

6. How is 100% written in words?

   _____

7. Which of these is a decimal number?

   A. ¾   B. 0.75   C. 75%

8. What is a period of ten years called?

   _____

9. What is a period of a thousand years called?

   _____

10. How is one thousand written as a number?

    _____

11. How is one million written as a number?

    _____

12. Are units that measure the loudness of sound called 'decagons' or 'decibels'? _____

13. Which three words in the Spelling List belong to the same word family as 'two'?

    _____

Dictation: ‹**dec-**› and more

10
50%
30%
20%
7%
15%
38%
40%
½
50%
0.5
REDUCED BY 20%

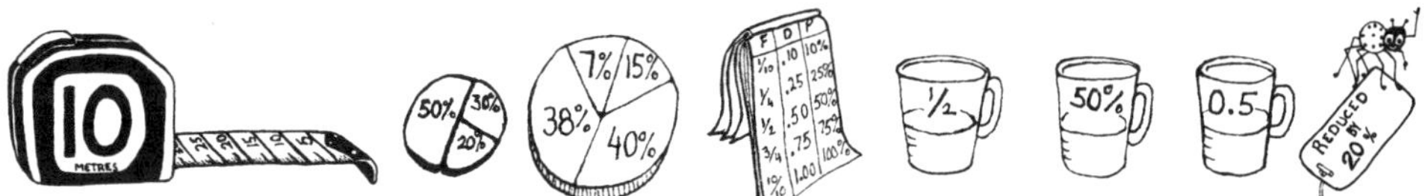

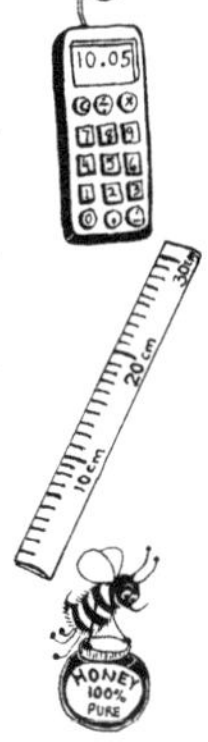

1. ____

   ____

2. ____

   ____

3. ____

   ____

'Where', 'wear' and 'were' are homophones. They are words that sound the same or similar, but have different spellings and meanings. Which one should be used to complete each sentence correctly?

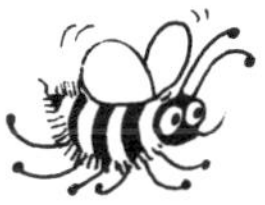

1. Where / Wear / Were | where / wear / were | the hundred gold coins found?
2. Prices | where / wear / were | reduced by forty percent in the sale.
3. The famous actress will never | where / wear / were | the same dress twice.
4. My family moved to the country, | where / wear / were | we lived for over a decade.
5. Her brother wants to | where / wear / were | a centurion's costume to the party.
6. We all tried to guess | where / wear / were | the millionaire would be staying this summer.
7. All the decathletes | where / wear / were | training hard.
8. You | where / wear / were | celebrating your granny's birthday on the twelfth of December.

where
where
wear
wear
were
were

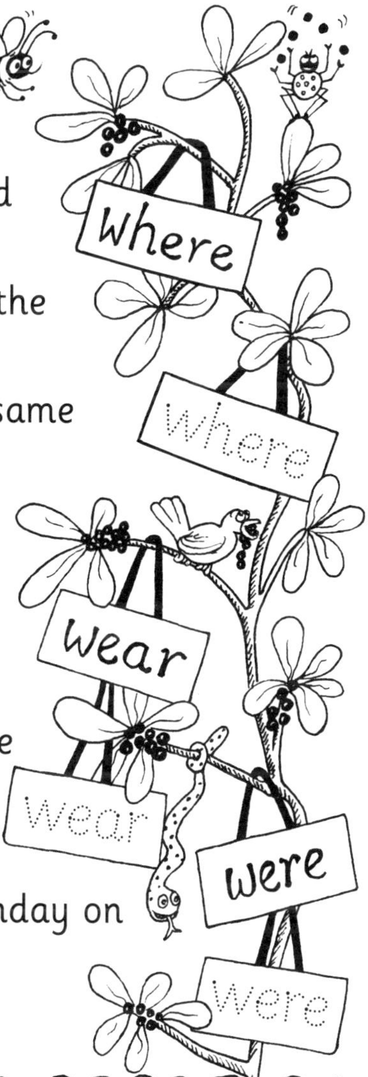

Parse the sentence and then write it on the wall.

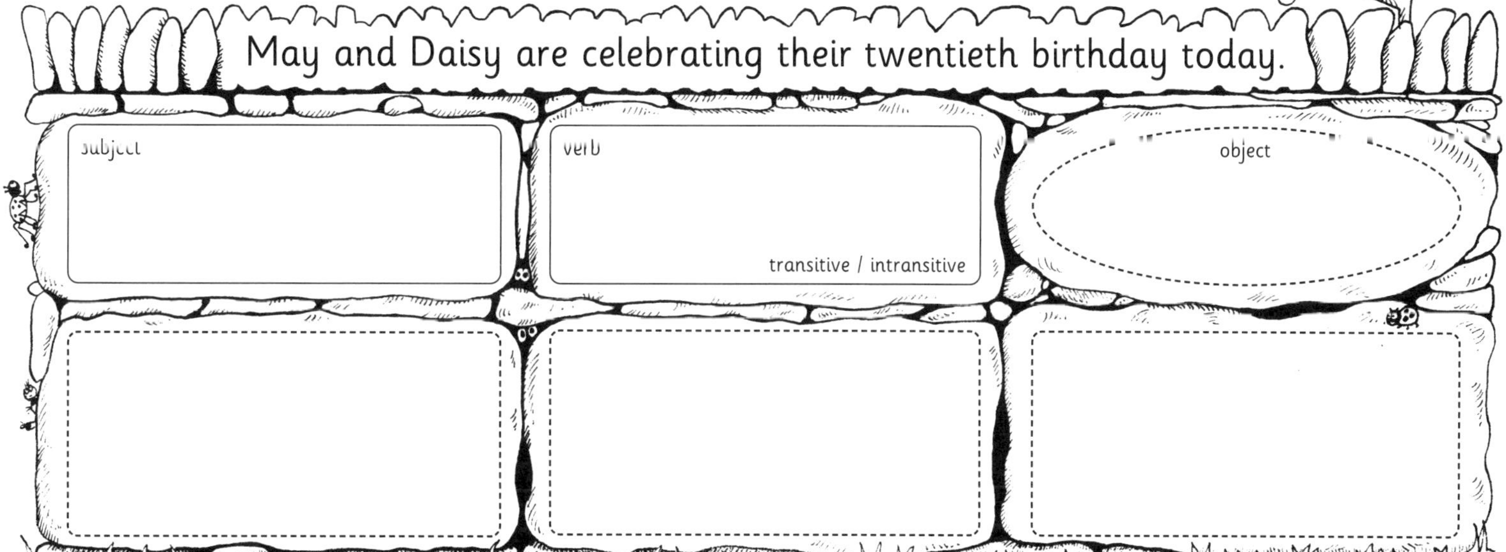

May and Daisy are celebrating their twentieth birthday today.
subject
verb
transitive / intransitive
object

Grammar 6 – Direct and Indirect Objects

Prepare...
Grammar Sheet 6
Red pencils

Builds on...
JGH3: G25-27, G35
JGH4: G3
JGH5: G3, G15-17

Aim: Develop the children's ability to identify the subject and object of a sentence when there is both a main and secondary object. Introduce the terms 'direct' and 'indirect' objects.

Introduction: Write 'Dan and Sam are cooking their evening meal' on the board and ask the children to identify the subject and object of the sentence. The children should ask themselves who or what is **doing** the verb action to find the subjects ('Dan' and 'Sam') and who or what is **receiving** the verb action to find the object (meal). Point out the two subjects and ask the children if they can remember what multiple subjects or objects are called *[compound]*. Also remind them that although we usually identify just the 'simple' subject or object (the noun or pronoun on its own), the whole noun phrase can be considered as such, so we could say that 'their evening meal' is the object. Ask some children to come up and draw a box around each of the subjects, with a small ‹s› in the corner, and a ring around the object, with a small ‹o› inside. Now rub out 'their evening meal' and ask if the remaining words still form a sentence. The children should recognise that they do, as they know that while a sentence always has a verb and subject, it does not necessarily need an object. Remind the children that verbs that do have an object are said to be 'transitive', because the verb sends its action to the object (the prefix ‹trans-› means 'across'), whereas those that do not are called 'intransitive' (the prefix ‹in-› means 'not'). Point out that in the first sentence the verb 'to cook' is transitive and in the second it is intransitive and many verbs can be both.

Main point: Now write 'Dan is cooking Jane a meal' on the board and ask the children to find the object of the sentence. Some of the children may say that Jane is the object because her name follows the verb (in English, the order of a sentence is often subject–verb–object), but if this were the case, Dan would be cooking Jane! Ask the class to consider carefully what is being cooked *[a meal]* and explain that there are in fact two objects in this sentence. They are not compound objects, because they are not equally important; instead, in sentences like this, there is a **direct object**, which receives the verb action, and an **indirect object**, <u>for whom</u> or <u>to whom</u> the verb action is done. To identify the indirect object here, the children need to think about who Dan is cooking for: he is cooking a meal <u>for Jane</u>. Draw a ring around 'meal' and put a small ‹o› inside, and then draw a ring around 'Jane'. Write some more examples on the board and discuss them with the class.

Grammar Sheet 6: The children find the subject, verb, and direct object in each sentence, drawing a box with a small ‹s› around the subject, underlining the verb in red, and putting a ring with a small ‹o› around the direct object *[1. Bill / sent / present, 2. girl / sang /song, 3. Aunt Jill / made / sandwiches, 4. He / gave / flowers, 5. I / wrote / letter, 6. Liz / threw / football, 7. Dad / bought / uniform, 8. Miss Beech / read / story, 9. We / cooked / meal, 10. Alex–Jo / showed / homework]*. They then identify the indirect object, deciding to whom or for whom the verb action is done, and draw a ring around it *[1. cousin, 2. granny, 3. us, 4. mother, 5. friend, 6. me, 7. Sam, 8. class, 9. guests, 10. Miss Beech]*. Finally, the children rewrite the bottom sentences so that they have indirect objects instead of prepositional phrases beginning with 'to' or 'for' *[11. They baked Meg a lovely cake, 12. Uncle Jim got his son a new tricycle, 13. The local farm sells the villagers fresh milk and eggs]*.

Extension activity: The children rewrite the first ten sentences, using prepositional phrases beginning with 'to' or 'for' instead of indirect objects.

Rounding off: Go over the sheet with the children, discussing their answers. Point out that sentences 1 to 10 follow the same order: subject–verb–indirect object–direct object. If they have done the extension activity, ask some children to read out a few of their sentences.

Direct and Indirect Objects

A sentence always has a **verb** and **subject** (the person or thing doing the verb action).
It may also have a **direct object** (the person or thing receiving the verb action).
A sentence with a direct object sometimes has an **indirect object**. This is
the person or thing **for whom** or **to whom** the verb action is done.

In each sentence, underline the verb in red and identify the subject, direct object
and indirect object.

1. Bill sent his cousin an expensive present.

2. The little girl sang her granny a song.

3. Aunt Jill made us some sandwiches.

4. He gave his mother some flowers.

5. I wrote my friend a long letter.

6. Liz threw me the old football.

7. Dad bought Sam a new uniform.

8. Miss Beech read her class a story.

9. We cooked our guests a tasty meal.

10. Alex and Jo showed Miss Beech their homework.

Rewrite each sentence so that it has an indirect object instead of a prepositional phrase.

11. They baked a lovely cake for Meg.

_____

_____

12. Uncle Jim got a new tricycle for his son.

_____

_____

13. The local farm sells fresh milk and eggs to the villagers.

_____

_____

Grammar Sheet 6 (JGH6)

Spelling 7 – ‹ei› and ‹eigh› for the /ai/ Sound

Prepare...
Spelling Sheets 7a/b
Large ‹ei› and ‹eigh›
word cards
Coloured pencils

Builds on...
JGH1: S14, S19
JGH2: S13, S31
JGH3: S2, S19

Revision: Write these words on the board and identify the number prefix in each one: **uni**form, **bi**cycle, **tri**angle, **quar**ter, **penta**thlon, **hexa**gon. Remind the class that these prefixes are related to Latin and Greek numbers. Ask the class to suggest more words with these prefixes or to call out other prefixes for the numbers one to six.

Main point: Revise some of the ways the /ai/ sound can be written, and write them on the board; the most common spellings are ‹ai›, ‹ay› and ‹a_e›, but the children will also know that the vowel ‹a› sometimes says its long vowel sound (as in 'apron' and 'pastry') and that some words, like 'reindeer' and 'eight', take the ‹ei› or ‹eigh› spellings. Other spelling patterns exist too, such as those found in words like 'gr**ea**t', 'th**ey**', 'ball**et**', 'f**ete**' and 'str**aigh**t' (all introduced in Spelling Lesson 17), so if they are called out, add them to the list. Ask the children to suggest some words for ‹ei› and ‹eigh›; write them on the board and then put them in alphabetical order with the class. Then ask five children to stand at the front, each holding a sheet of paper with an ‹ei› or ‹eigh› word printed on it. Ask them to put themselves into alphabetical order: beige, neigh, veil, vein, weight.

Spelling list: Go through the list, discuss the meaning of any unfamiliar words, and ask the class to find and highlight the ‹ei› or ‹eigh› spelling each time. Point out other spelling features, such as the 'silent ‹g›' digraph in 'rei**g**n', 'fei**g**n' and 'dei**g**n', the 'soft ‹g›' or /zh/ sound in 'beige', the way the ‹t› in ‹th› also says its own sound in 'eighth', the ‹le› saying /ool/ at the end of 'inveigle', and the ‹ur› spelling and 'soft ‹c›' in 'surveillance'. Also point out the homophones 'rein' and 'reign', the antonyms 'veil' and 'unveil', and the fact that 'feign' and 'feint' belong to the same word family ('to feign' means 'to pretend' and a 'feint' in boxing or fencing is a pretended attack). It is a good idea to blend and sound out the spelling words quickly every day with the class, using the 'say it as it sounds' strategy where appropriate (stressing the pure sound of any schwas, for example, as in 's**ur**veill**a**nce' and 'neighb**our**hood').

Spelling Sheet 7a: The children split each word into syllables to help remember the spelling [1. vein, 2. veil, 3. rein, 4. reign, 5. feint, 6. weigh, 7. weight, 8. beige, 9. feign, 10. eighth, 11. neigh, 12. un/veil, 13. freight, 14. in/vei/gle, 15. deign, 16. weight/lift/er, 17. sur/veil/lance, 18. neigh/bour/hood]. They then put the spelling words into alphabetical order [1. beige, 2. deign, 3. eighth, 4. feign, 5. feint, 6. freight, 7. inveigle, 8. neigh, 9. neighbourhood, 10. reign, 11. rein, 12. surveillance, 13. unveil, 14. veil, 15. vein, 16. weigh, 17. weight, 18. weightlifter].

Spelling Sheet 7b: The children write the meanings for each pair of homophones, using a dictionary to help them if needed. Then they parse the sentence and complete the wall [Top: baker - has weighed - ingredients / Bottom: The - precisely - the cake's/ Verb: transitive]. Possessive nouns always act as adjectives, so 'cake's' should be underlined in blue. The adverb 'precisely' is made by adding ‹-ly› to the adjective 'precise'.

The baker[N] (has weighed)[V] the cake's[Adj] ingredients[N] precisely[Adv].

Noun[N] (black), Verb[V] (red), Pronoun[P] (pink), Adjective[Adj] (blue), Adverb[Adv] (orange), Conjunction[C] (purple), Preposition[Pre] (green)

Dictation: (This can be done in the spelling lesson or at another time during the week.) Call out the sentences for the children to write down. Remind them to use the right spelling ('reins', not 'reigns') in Sentence 2 and speech marks with the correct punctuation in Sentence 3.

1. The bride wore her grandmother's veil.
2. The horses neighed and shook their reins.
3. "How much weight can they lift?" we wondered.

  ‹ei› ‹eigh›

Spelling List 7

Put the words in the Spelling List into alphabetical order.

1. vein

2. veil

3. rein

4. reign

5. feint

6. weigh

7. weight

8. beige

9. feign

10. eighth

11. neigh

12. unveil

13. freight

14. inveigle

15. deign

16. weightlifter

17. surveillance

18. neighbourhood

1. _____

2. _____

3. _____

4. _____

5. _____

6. _____

7. _____

8. _____

9. _____

10. _____

11. _____

12. _____

13. _____

14. _____

15. _____

16. _____

17. _____

18. _____

a b c d e f g h i j k l m n o p q r s t u v w x y z

Dictation: ‹ei› ‹eigh›

1. _____

_____

2. _____

_____

3. _____

_____

Write the meanings for these pairs of homophones. Use a dictionary if you need to check.

rein

reign

weigh

way

feint

faint

vein

vain

_____

_____

_____

_____

_____

_____

_____

_____

_____

_____

_____

_____

_____

_____

_____

_____

_____

Parse the sentence and then write it on the wall.

The baker has weighed the cake's ingredients precisely.

subject	verb	object
	transitive / intransitive	

Grammar 7 – Indirect Objects and Sentence Walls

Prepare...
Grammar Sheet 7
Red pencils

Builds on...
JGH5: G3, G15-16
JGH6: G6

Aim: Develop the children's ability to identify the indirect object in a sentence and put it into a sentence wall.

Introduction: Write this sentence on the board and parse it with the children: Sally^N offered^V her^{Adj} friend^N a cheese^{Adj} sandwich^N. Remind the class that a sentence always has a verb and subject and, if the verb is transitive, it will also have an object. We find the subject by asking who or what is doing the offering *[Sally]* and identify the object by asking what it is that Sally offered *[a cheese sandwich]*. Draw a box around 'Sally', with a small ‹s› in the corner, and a ring around 'sandwich', with a small ‹o› inside. Point out that although 'a cheese sandwich' can be considered the object, we only highlight the main noun or pronoun, which we call the 'simple' object. Now ask what role the friend is playing: (s)he is the person to whom Sally offered the sandwich. Remind the class that the verb action has either a direct or indirect effect on an object: the person (or thing) receiving the verb action is called the **direct object** and the person (or thing) <u>for whom</u> or <u>to whom</u> the verb action is done is called the **indirect object**. Draw a ring around 'friend' and explain that in this sentence the direct object is 'sandwich' and the indirect object is 'friend'.

Main point: Sentence walls allow us to organise a sentence visually so we can see at a glance what the main building blocks are and how they relate to each other. The familiar layout can be easily adapted for sentences with an indirect object to look like this:

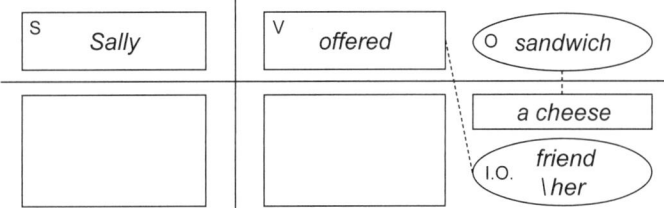

Draw the boxes on the board and show the children how to put the sentence into the wall. When the wall is complete, join the indirect object and its modifiers to the verb with a line. Then join the object to its modifiers in the same way.

Grammar Sheet 7: The children find the subject, verb, and direct object in each sentence, drawing a box with a small ‹s› around the subject, underlining the verb in red, and putting a ring with a small ‹o› around the direct object *[1. She/told/news, 2. father/sent/book, 3. Dad/read/story, 4. Aunt Jill–Sam/threw/rope, 5. cousin/made/dress, 6. He/wrote/poems, 7. Grandpa/bought/octopus, 8. grandparents/sang/lullaby, 9. centurion/gave/order, 10. twins/took/note, 11. I/knitted/hat–scarf, 12. Alex–Meg/showed/photos]*. They then identify the indirect object, deciding to whom or for whom the verb action is done, and draw a ring around it *[1. neighbours, 2. him, 3. children, 4. Liz, 5. me, 6. girlfriend, 7. baby, 8. babies, 9. soldiers, 10. mother, 11. Grandma, 12. Uncle Jim]*. Finally, they arrange the sentences on the wall, putting the subject, verb and direct object along the top (if the subject or object is compound, bracket 'and' with dots), and the words modifying them underneath, with the indirect object in the bottom right oval, joined to the verb with a line *[Top: as shown above; Bottom: 1. (blank) - (blank) - the exciting/neighbours (her), 2. Bill's - (blank) - an interesting/him, 3. (blank) - (blank) - a bedtime/children (the), 4. (blank) - (blank) - the/Liz, 5. My - (blank) - a beautiful/me, 6. (blank) - (blank) - some/girlfriend (his), 7. (blank) - (blank) - a toy/baby (the), 8. Their - (blank) - a/babies (the), 9. the - Firmly - an/soldiers (the), 10. The - immediately - the/mother (their), 11. (blank) - patiently - a beige/Grandma, 12. (blank) - Excitedly - the/Uncle Jim]*.

Extension activity: Ask the children to write some sentences of their own with a direct and indirect object.

Rounding off: Go over the sheet/extension activity with the class, discussing the answers.

Indirect Objects and Sentence Walls

In each sentence, underline the verb in red. Then identify the subject, direct object and indirect object. The indirect object is the person or thing **to whom** or **for whom** the verb action is done.

1. She told her neighbours the exciting news.

2. Bill's father sent him an interesting book.

3. Dad read the children a bedtime story.

4. Aunt Jill and Sam threw Liz the rope.

5. My cousin made me a beautiful dress.

6. He wrote his girlfriend some poems.

7. Grandpa bought the baby a toy octopus.

8. Their grandparents sang the babies a lullaby.

9. Firmly, the centurion gave the soldiers an order.

10. The twins immediately took their mother the note.

11. I patiently knitted Grandma a beige hat and scarf.

12. Excitedly, Alex and Meg showed Uncle Jim the photos.

Now cut up each sentence, or write it on pieces of paper, and arrange the words on the wall. Put the indirect object and anything that describes it in the same box, but put the indirect object first and the other words underneath, and join them with a diagonal line.

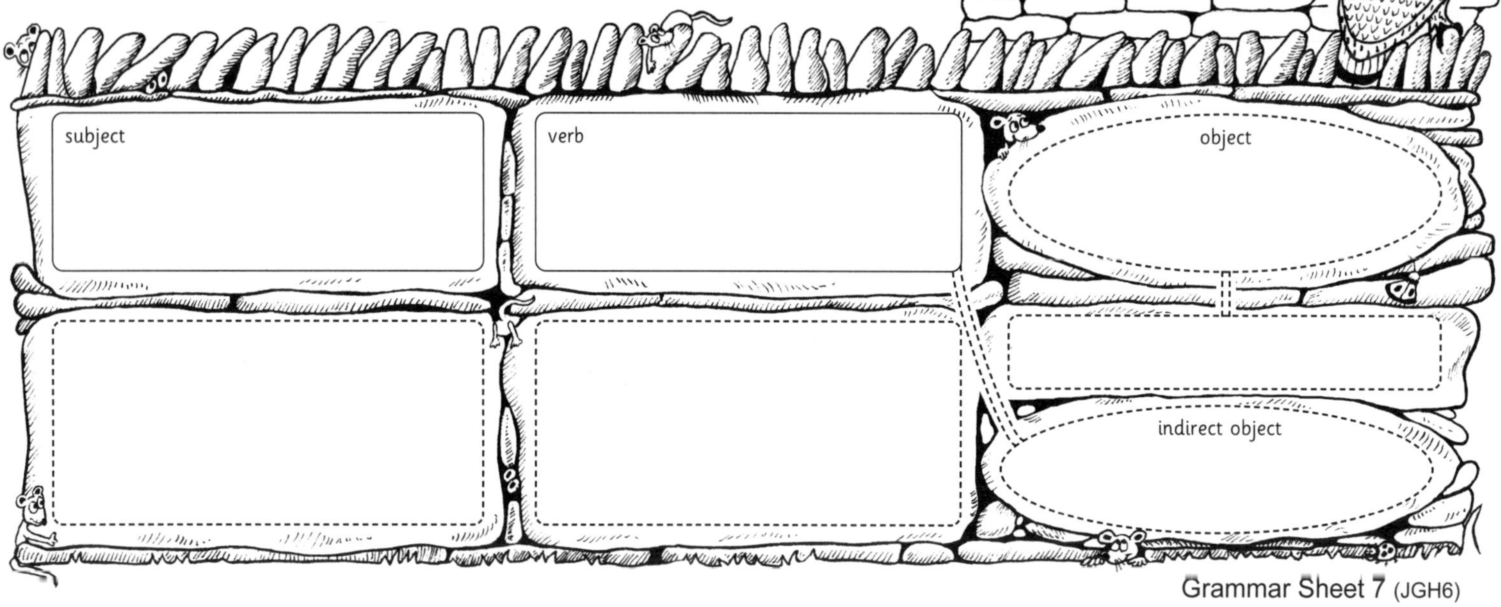

subject

verb

object

indirect object

Spelling 8 – ‹ei› and ‹ie› for the /ee/ Sound

Prepare...
Spelling Sheets 8a/b
Coloured pencils

Builds on...
JGH2: S31
JGH3: S3, S7, S20, S26
JGH6: S7

Revision: Write these words on the board and identify the number prefix in each one: **Sept**ember, **Oct**ober, **Novem**ber, **Dec**ember (the seventh, eighth, ninth and tenth months in the old Roman calendar). Ask the class to call out other prefixes for the numbers or suggest more words.

Main point: Probably the most well known, but most misunderstood, spelling rule in English is this: ‹i› before ‹e›, except after ‹c›. Many people find they cannot use the rule successfully, because it seems to have too many exceptions, like in 'weird', 'their' and 'height', or in words like 'vein' and 'weight', which the children learnt in the previous lesson. Write the words on the board, add 'niece' and 'ceiling', and discuss the different vowel sounds being made: /ear, air, ie, ai, ee/. Look at some more words from the spelling list and point out that the rule does work when you remember it like this: 'If you want to say /ee/, it's ‹i› before ‹e›, except after ‹c›'. There are a few exceptions, however, and these can be remembered as 'S**ei**ze n**ei**ther prot**ei**n nor caff**ei**ne'.

Spelling list: Go through the list, discuss the meaning of any unfamiliar words, and ask the class to find and highlight the ‹ie› or ‹cei› spelling each time. Point out other spelling features, such as the ‹k› in 'shriek' and 'handkerchief', the 'soft ‹g›' in 'siege' and 'hygiene', the 'soft ‹c›' in 'niece' and ‹cei› words, the ‹e› saying /i/ (or becoming neutral) in 'd**e**ceit', 'r**e**ceive', 'd**e**ceive', 'r**e**trieve' and 'r**e**prieve', the ‹ve› saying /v/ in words ending in ‹ieve› or ‹eive›, the ‹y› saying /ie/ in 'hygiene', the ‹n› saying /ng/ and silent ‹d› in 'handkerchief', and the prefix ‹in-›, suffix ‹-able› and ‹le› saying /ool/ in 'inconceivable'. It is a good idea to blend and sound out the spelling words quickly every day with the class, using the 'say it as it sounds' strategy where appropriate (stressing the pure sound of any schwas, for example, as in 'achi**e**ve' 'p**e**rceive', 'handk**e**rchief' and 'inc**o**nceiv**a**ble').

Spelling Sheet 8a: The children split each word into syllables to help remember the spelling *[1. shriek, 2. wield, 3. siege, 4. yield, 5. cei/ling, 6. fien/dish, 7. niece, 8. de/ceit, 9. re/ceive, 10. de/ceive, 11. a/chieve, 12. con/ceit/ed, 13. hy/giene, 14. re/trieve, 15. per/ceive, 16. re/prieve, 17. hand/ker/chief, 18. in/con/ceiv/a/ble]* and add the missing letters *[Top: yield, siege, wield; ceiling, shriek, fiendish; niece, receive, deceit; deceive, conceited, achieve; reprieve, perceive, retrieve; inconceivable, hygiene, handkerchief / Bottom: priest, shield, briefly; believable, conceivable; field, piece, thief; preconceived, deceitful; briefcase, relieved, chieftain]*.

Spelling Sheet 8b: The children write the numbers as words, replacing 'toughy ‹y›' with 'shy ‹i›' before adding the suffix *[thirtieth, fortieth, fiftieth, sixtieth, seventieth, eightieth, ninetieth]*, or by using a hyphen *[fifty-two, eighty-six, thirty-five, forty-eight]*. Then they parse the sentence and complete the wall *[Top: Mr Brown - will have bought - handkerchiefs / Bottom: (blank) - (blank) - some / Indirect Object: niece (his)/ Verb: transitive]*. 'Mr Brown' is a proper noun (black) and 'his' is a possessive adjective (blue) describing who the niece 'belongs' to. All parts of the verb should be underlined in red.

(Mr Brown)[N] (will have bought)[V] his[Adj] niece[N] some[Adj] handkerchiefs[N].

Noun[N] (black), Verb[V] (red), Pronoun[P] (pink), Adjective[Adj] (blue), Adverb[Adv] (orange), Conjunction[C] (purple), Preposition[Pre] (green)

Dictation: (This can be done in the spelling lesson or at another time during the week.) Call out the sentences for the children to write down. Remind them to use the right homophone ('vain', not 'vein') in Sentence 1 and speech marks with the correct punctuation in Sentence 2.

1. My niece is never vain or conceited.
2. "What a fiendish plan!" the reader exclaimed.
3. The knight wielded his sword many times in battle.

‹ei› and ‹ie› for /ee/

Spelling List 8

1. shriek
_____
2. wield
_____
3. siege
_____
4. yield
_____
5. ceiling
_____
6. fiendish
_____
7. niece
_____
8. deceit
_____
9. receive
_____
10. deceive
_____
11. achieve
_____
12. conceited
_____
13. hygiene
_____
14. retrieve
_____
15. perceive
_____
16. reprieve
_____
17. handkerchief
_____
18. inconceivable
_____

Add the missing letters – ‹ei› or ‹ie› – to complete the Spelling List words in the handkerchief. Remember, **if the spelling says /ee/, it is ‹i› before ‹e›, except after ‹c›.**

y___ld   s___ge   w___ld

c___ling   shr___k   f___ndish

n___ce   rec___ve   dec___t

dec___ve   conc___ted   ach___ve

repr___ve   perc___ve   retr___ve

inconc___vable   hyg___ne   handkerch___f

‹i› before ‹e›, except after ‹c›, if you want to say /ee/

These words are also missing ‹ei› or ‹ie›. Can you complete them?

pr___st   sh___ld   br___fly

bel___vable   conc___vable

f___ld   p___ce   th___f

preconc___ved   dec___tful

br___fcase   rel___ved   ch___ftain

Dictation: ‹ei› and ‹ie› for /ee/

1. _____
   _____
2. _____
   _____
3. _____
   _____

When we use numbers to order things, we usually add the suffix ‹-th› (except in 'first', 'second' and 'third'). If the number ends in ‹y›, we replace it with ‹i› and add the suffix ‹-eth›. Write these positional numbers as words.

20 = twenty   twent~~y~~ + i + eth   20th = twentieth

30th _____   40th _____

50th _____   60th _____

70th _____   80th _____

90th _____

When the numbers 21 to 99 are written as compound words, we use a hyphen. Write the numbers below as words.

52 _____   86 _____

35 _____   48 _____

Parse the sentence and then write it on the wall.

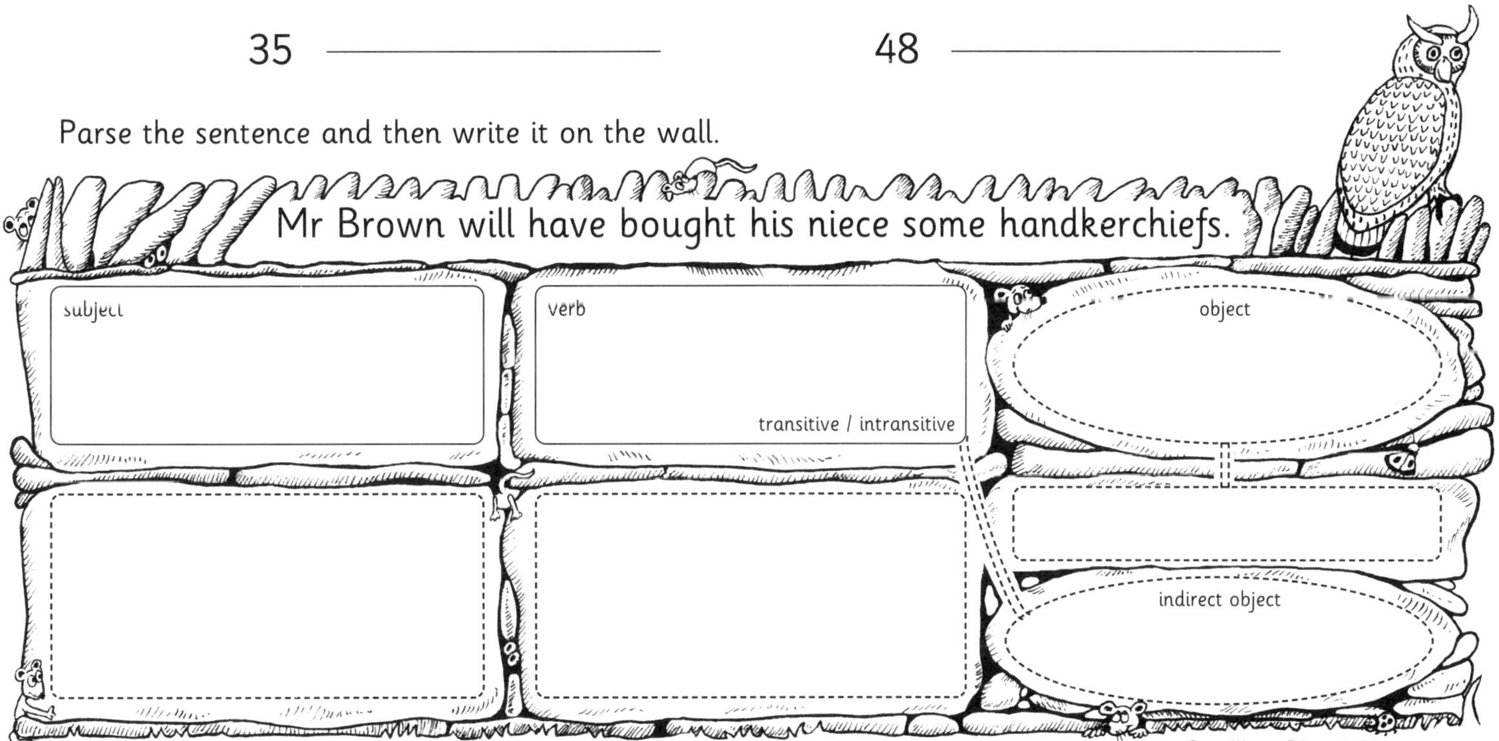

Mr Brown will have bought his niece some handkerchiefs.

subject	verb	object
	transitive / intransitive	
		indirect object

Grammar 8 – Linking Verbs

Prepare...
Grammar Sheet 8
Red pencils

Builds on...
JGH1: G14-18, G26
JGH2: G16-18, G21
JGH3: G5, G8-9, G17
JGH5: G4
JGH6: G2

Aim: Refine the children's understanding of verbs by introducing the idea that they are not all 'doing' words; some are better thought of as 'being' words, because they describe a state of being or change. These two types of verb are known as action verbs and linking verbs.

Introduction: 'To be' is one of the most common verbs in English, frequently used as a main verb and also as an auxiliary (helping to form the past, present and continuous tenses). It is also very irregular, at least in the simple past and present tenses, and has the 'tricky' past participle 'been'. Children can find it difficult to identify as a verb in a sentence, so conjugating the simple tenses with the class and doing the pronoun actions is particularly helpful:

Past	*Present*	*Future*
I was, you were,	I am, you are,	I shall be, you will be
he / she / it was, etc	he / she / it is, etc	he / she / it will be, etc

Main point: When the children are young, they are encouraged to think of verbs as 'doing' words: the verbs 'to run', 'to cook' and 'to sing' all name a particular action; however, some verbs, including 'to be', are better described as 'being' words, because they name a state of being or change. 'Being' verbs act differently in a sentence: they do not take a direct object, but instead often link the subject to a word or phrase (called the 'subject complement') that completes our understanding of it. For example, in 'The dog was really fierce', the verb ('was') links the subject 'dog' to the adjective 'fierce', which describes it; and in 'Jane is a farmer', the verb ('is') links the subject 'Jane' to the noun 'farmer', which identifies her. (Sentences like this are sometimes likened to an equation, with the verb as an equals sign: ‹=›). Write the sentences on the board and discuss them with the class, identifying the verb and subject each time and underlining 'fierce' in blue and 'farmer' in black. Then link the complement back to the subject with an arrow. Explain that verbs like this are known as 'linking' (or 'copular') verbs, while 'doing' verbs are more commonly called 'action' verbs. Other common linking verbs are 'to seem', 'to appear', 'to become', 'to remain', 'to look', 'to sound', 'to smell', 'to taste' and 'to feel'. However, most linking verbs can also act as action verbs, so care is needed when giving examples. Draw six boxes on the board and show the children how to put the two sentences into a 'wall'. Put the verb and subject complement on the same line in the verb box and separate them with a diagonal line. If the subject complement has a modifier, put that underneath in the usual way:

1. | ᵛ was \ fierce \ really | 2. | ᵛ is \ farmer \ a |

Grammar Sheet 8: The children find the verb 'to be' in each sentence, underline it in red, and then identify the subject, drawing a box with a small ‹s› around it. They then identify the subject complement, underlining it in the appropriate colour, and link it to the subject with an arrow. *[In subject/verb/complement order: 1. They/are being/naughty (blue), 2. ceiling/was/high (blue), 3. actors/were/conceited (blue), 4. children/had been/excited (blue), 5. handkerchiefs/are/present (black), 6. journey/has been/long (blue), 7. You/have been/ busy (blue), 8. We/will be/millionaires (black), 9. niece/is/doctor (black), 10. I/am/weightlifter (black)].* They then choose from the five verbs, all of which describe the senses, to complete the sentences *[11. smell, 12. feel, 13. look, 14. sound, 15. taste]*. Then they parse the sentence *[Hisᴬᵈʲ youngerᴬᵈʲ sistersᴺ areⱽ athletesᴺ]* and complete the wall *[Top: sisters - are\athletes - (blank) / Bottom: His younger - (blank) - (blank) / Verb: linking]*.

Extension activity: The children put some of Sentences 1 to 10 into sentence wall boxes.

Rounding off: Go over the sheet/extension activity with the class, discussing the answers.

Linking Verbs

Red

Some verbs are 'being' words rather than 'doing' words. They link the subject to its 'complement'. This is often a noun or pronoun that **identifies** the subject or an adjective that **describes** it. The most common linking verb is 'to be'.

In the sentences, underline each form of 'to be' in red and identify the subject. Then find the subject complement and underline it in either black (for a noun) or blue (for an adjective). Link each complement back to the subject with an arrow.

1. They are being very naughty.
2. The ceiling was incredibly high.
3. Both actors were rather conceited.
4. The children had been quite excited.
5. Those pretty handkerchiefs are a present.

6. The journey has been long.
7. You have been really busy.
8. We will be millionaires.
9. Our niece is a doctor.
10. I am a weightlifter.

Other verbs can be linking verbs too. Read the sentences below and decide which linking verb is needed to complete each one. What do these verbs have in common?

11. The flowers in the garden _____ sweet.
12. The rabbit's fur _____s soft and silky.
13. This evening you _____ tired but happy.
14. Her voice _____s quite young on the phone.
15. The sandwiches _____ better than they look.

taste smell sound look feel

Parse the sentence and then write it on the wall. Put the subject complement in the same box as the verb, on the same line, and separate them with a diagonal line.

His younger sisters are athletes.

subject	verb	object
	action / linking	

Spelling 9 – ‹ei›, ‹eigh›, ‹eir›

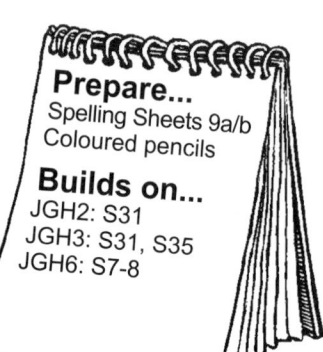

Prepare...
Spelling Sheets 9a/b
Coloured pencils

Builds on...
JGH2: S31
JGH3: S31, S35
JGH6: S7-8

Revision: Revise the spelling rule: 'If you want to say /ee/, it's ‹i› before ‹e›, except after ‹c›'. Write these words on the board and ask the class whether ‹ei› or ‹ie› is needed to complete them: ch(<u>ie</u>)f, f(<u>ie</u>)ld, c(<u>ei</u>)ling, th(<u>ie</u>)ves, p(<u>ie</u>)ce, dec(<u>ei</u>)ve, rec(<u>ei</u>)pt, br(<u>ie</u>)fcase.

Main point: Write the words 'veil' and 'eight' on the board in one column and 'receive' in another and remind the children that the spellings ‹ei› and ‹eigh› usually make the /ai/ sound, but ‹ei› can also make the /ee/ sound when it follows the letter ‹c›. Now write 'height' and 'feisty' in a third column and explain that ‹ei› and ‹eigh› can also make the sound /ie/. Then add 'their' and 'weird' in two new columns and explain that the ‹ei› in these words is actually part of the spelling pattern ‹eir›, which is one of the alternative spellings of both /air/ and /ear/. Finally, add the words 'counterfeit' and 'heifer' in two more columns and point out that ‹ei› occasionally makes an /i/ sound and can, on rare occasions, even make an /e/ sound.

Spelling list: Go through the list, discuss the meaning of any unfamiliar words, ask the class to find and highlight the ‹ei›, ‹eigh› or ‹eir› spelling each time and discuss the sound it is making. Point out other spelling features, such as the silent ‹h› in 'heir', 'heirloom' and 'Fahrenheit', the ‹ur› spelling of /er/ in 'surfeit' and the ‹ow› spelling of /ou/ in 'eiderdown', the 'silent ‹g›' digraph in 'foreign' and 'sovereign', the ‹s› saying **/s/** and <u>/z/</u> in '**seismic**', the ‹c› and ‹k› spellings in 'seismic' and 'kaleidoscope', and the capital F in 'Fahrenheit'. Point out that the ‹ei› in 'either' can say /ee/ or /ie/ and that 'sovereign' has only two syllables as the /er/ is not usually pronounced. It is a good idea to blend and sound out the spelling words quickly every day with the class, using the 'say it as it sounds' strategy where appropriate (stressing the pure sound of any schwas, for example, as in 'k**a**leid**o**scope').

Spelling Sheet 9a: The children split each word into syllables to help remember the spelling *[1. weir, 2. their, 3. heir, 4. weird, 5. for/feit, 6. ei/ther, 7. height, 8. sur/feit, 9. for/eign, 10. heif/er, 11. feist/y, 12. sove/reign, 13. seis/mic, 14. heir/loom, 15. ei/der/down, 16. coun/ter/feit, 17. ka/lei/do/scope, 18. Fahr/en/heit]*. They then find the spelling words in the word search and work out which one is missing *[Fahrenheit]*. Then they read each phrase and identify which of the three spelling words it is describing *[1. B, 2. B, 3. C]*.

Spelling Sheet 9b: The children add the missing letters in each word *[Top: w**ei**rd, h**eigh**t, th**eir**, w**eir**, f**ei**sty; Bottom: s**ei**smic, h**eir**loom, **ei**derdown, kal**ei**doscope, Fahrenh**ei**t]* and identify which sound they are making *[Activity 1: all say /ie/, except for 'their' and 'heirloom', which say /air/, and 'weird' and 'weir', which say /ear/. Activity 2: the ‹ei› in 'heifer' says /e/]*. Then they parse the sentence and complete the wall *[Top: sovereigns - were\counterfeit - (blank) / Bottom: The gold - (blank) - (blank) / Verb: linking]*. The verb 'were' links the adjective complement 'counterfeit' to the subject 'sovereigns' it is describing.

The gold[Adj] sovereigns[N] were[V] counterfeit[Adj].

Noun[N] (black), Verb[V] (red), Pronoun[P] (pink), Adjective[Adj] (blue), Adverb[Adv] (orange), Conjunction[C] (purple), Preposition[Pre] (green)

Dictation: (This can be done in the spelling lesson or at another time during the week.) Call out the sentences for the children to write down. Remind them to write the compound numbers correctly in Sentences 1 and 2 and to use speech marks with the correct punctuation in Sentence 3.

1. Their sovereign reigned for fifty-two years.
2. The farmer keeps eighty-two heifers in the field.
3. "What is your height and weight?" asked the nurse.

Spelling List 9

‹ei› ‹eigh› ‹eir›

Find the words from the Spelling List. Which one is missing?

1. weir

2. their

3. heir

4. weird

5. forfeit

6. either

7. height

8. surfeit

9. foreign

10. heifer

11. feisty

12. sovereign

13. seismic

14. heirloom

15. eiderdown

16. counterfeit

17. kaleidoscope

18. Fahrenheit

s	e	j	h	r	k	b	o	s	u	r	f	e	i	t
c	o	u	n	t	e	r	f	e	i	t	i	d	s	h
u	c	h	i	n	i	z	b	i	e	i	r	o	l	e
g	b	e	p	b	d	l	o	s	a	d	x	w	t	i
r	e	i	t	h	e	r	w	m	r	o	u	b	h	r
x	v	r	p	o	r	f	s	i	d	e	f	j	r	o
k	a	l	e	i	d	o	s	c	o	p	e	f	o	l
a	l	o	o	s	o	r	o	g	h	e	i	g	h	t
p	c	o	s	i	w	f	v	b	e	c	s	l	e	g
z	b	m	j	b	n	e	e	r	i	x	t	j	i	e
n	e	y	k	w	e	i	r	y	r	o	y	t	f	i
b	i	z	b	e	n	t	e	t	h	j	t	q	e	n
c	w	b	e	i	o	r	i	k	a	l	o	n	r	l
m	e	f	o	r	e	i	g	n	t	c	a	p	g	o
d	n	u	n	d	i	l	n	k	e	i	r	j	e	y

 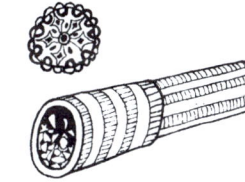  

Which of these spelling words match the description? Use a dictionary to help you, if necessary.

1. **a young cow that has not had a calf**
   A. surfeit
   B. heifer
   C. heirloom

2. **a scale of temperature in which water freezes at 32 degrees**
   A. surfeit
   B. Fahrenheit
   C. counterfeit

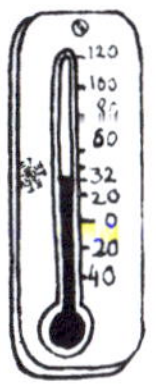

3. **a tube with mirrors and bits of coloured glass that makes patterns when it is turned**
   A. eiderdown
   B. sovereign
   C. kaleidoscope

Dictation: ‹ei› ‹eigh› ‹eir›

1. _____
   _____

2. _____
   _____

3. _____
   _____

The words below are missing ‹ei›, ‹eigh› or ‹eir›. Complete each one, decide which sound the missing letters make, and put each word in the correct column.

/air/	/ear/	/ie/
_____	_____	_____
_____	_____	_____
_____	_____	_____

w___d	h___t	th___	w___	f___sty
s___smic	h___loom	___derdown	kal___doscope	Fahrenh___t

In which of the following words does ‹ei› make an /e/ sound?

beige   either   ceiling   heifer

Parse the sentence and then write it on the wall.

The gold sovereigns were counterfeit.

subject	verb	object
	action / linking	

Grammar 9 – Prepositional Phrases Acting as Adverbs

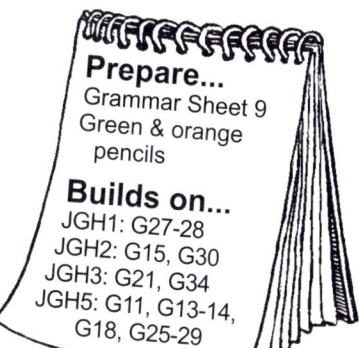

Prepare...
Grammar Sheet 9
Green & orange
pencils

Builds on...
JGH1: G27-28
JGH2: G15, G30
JGH3: G21, G34
JGH5: G11, G13-14,
G18, G25-29

Aim: Refine the children's understanding of how prepositional phrases can act as adverbs within a sentence and develop their ability to identify one when it comes at the beginning of a sentence.

Introduction: Remind the class that a phrase is a group of words that makes sense but has no verb and subject. Briefly revise prepositional phrases, which begin with a preposition and are often followed by a noun phrase or pronoun. Call out some prepositions and ask the class to turn them into prepositional phrases: for example, <u>at</u> the moment, <u>in</u> an hour, <u>above</u> the treetops, <u>on</u> the table, <u>after</u> the storm, <u>without</u> warning. Remind the class that prepositional phrases are often used as adverbs in sentences. Write a few examples on the board and discuss how each prepositional phrase gives us more information about where, when or how the verb is happening: I will go <u>in an hour</u> (when); the birds soared <u>above the treetops</u> (where); they left <u>without warning</u> (how). Ask some children to come up and parse the prepositional phrases, underlining the prepositions in green and putting orange brackets around each phrase.

Main point: Write 'Zack recently broke his arm' on the board and ask the children to identify the adverb in the sentence [*recently*]. Discuss with the class how we know that 'recently' is the adverb: it tells us more about when Zack broke his arm and, like a lot of adverbs, it is made by adding ‹-ly› to an adjective. Remind the class that even though adverbs often describe a verb, they do not always go next to it. Ask the children where else 'recently' could go in the sentence: it could be moved to the end (Zack broke his arm recently) or to the beginning, where the adverb is separated from the rest of the sentence with a comma (Recently, Zack broke his arm). Explain that when prepositional phrases act as adverbs, they too can be found in different parts of a sentence; they usually go immediately after an intransitive verb or towards the end, following an object or adverb, but they can also be found at the beginning of a sentence. Write 'I heard a strange noise in the middle of the night' on the board, and then write it again, with the prepositional phrase at the beginning: 'In the middle of the night, I heard a strange noise'. Point out that here, too, the phrase at the beginning is often followed by a comma, particularly if it is a long one, and discuss how the emphasis has subtly shifted to when the action takes place, creating a sense of expectation and drama. Try this with some other sentences, discussing the effect each time. Look again at the prepositional phrase '(<u>in</u> the middle) (<u>of</u> the night)' and point out that many longer phrases are created by putting two shorter prepositional phrases together.

Grammar Sheet 9: The children write inside the outlined word Prepositions in green and the word Adverbs in orange. They then identify the prepositional phrase that is acting as an adverb in each sentence, underlining the preposition in green and putting orange brackets around the phrase [1. <u>under</u> *the soft, warm eiderdown,* 2. <u>with</u> *a short, sharp shriek,* 3. <u>in</u> *the dark night sky,* 4. <u>between</u> *early December and late March,* 5. <u>among</u> *the rocks and seaweed].* Then they rewrite each sentence, putting the prepositional phrase at the beginning of the sentence, followed by a comma. Lastly, they read the prepositional phrases at the bottom of the sheet, think about what might happen next, and complete the sentences.

Extension activity: The children write some more sentences, using other prepositional phrases as adverbs. They can then swap their sentences with a partner and rewrite them so that the phrase appears at the beginning, followed by a comma.

Rounding off: Go over the sheet with the children, discussing their answers. If they have done the extension activity, ask some of the children to read out their sentences.

Prepositional
Phrases as Adverbs

Orange

Sometimes we put prepositional phrases at the beginning of a sentence to make our writing more interesting. Often a comma comes after the phrase, particularly if it is a long one. Identify the prepositional phrases below and then rewrite each sentence so that the phrase goes at the beginning. Remember to add the comma.

1. I slept peacefully (under the soft, warm eiderdown).
   _____
   _____

2. The owl flew off quickly with a short, sharp shriek.
   _____
   _____

3. We could see a billion stars in the dark night sky.
   _____
   _____

4. The gardens are closed between early December and late March.
   _____
   _____

5. The diver spotted a large octopus among the rocks and seaweed.
   _____
   _____

Prepositional phrases can often be put together to make a longer phrase. Read the ones below, and then think about what might happen next, before completing each sentence.

6. By the light of the moon, _____
   _____

7. From the top of the mountain, _____
   _____

8. At the bottom of the stairs, _____
   _____

9. During the long hot days of summer, _____
   _____

10. Below the tall trees in the forest, _____
    _____

Spelling 10 – ‹ci› for the /sh/ Sound

Prepare...
Spelling Sheets 10a/b
Coloured pencils

Builds on...
JGH2: S29-30
JGH5: S16, S26, S28

Revision: Write these words on the board and ask the class to identify the letters saying /sh/ in each one: man**si**on, pre**ss**ure, ini**ti**al, mi**ss**ion, spe**ci**al, ma**ch**ine, **s**ure, an**xi**ous. Apart from ‹ch›, which has French origins, words with these spellings usually come from Latin. Ask the children if they can think of other words with these spellings for /sh/.

Main point: Although it can be written in several different ways, /sh/ is most often spelt ‹ti› or ‹ci› in the middle of a longer word. These spellings can be combined with familiar suffixes to form words like sta**ti**on/suspi**ci**on, nego**ti**able/so**ci**able, ter**ti**ary/ benefi**ci**ary, pa**ti**ent/an**ci**ent, pa**ti**ence/cons**ci**ence, Egyp**ti**an/musi**ci**an, nego**ti**ation/ appre**ci**ation, nego**ti**ate/ appre**ci**ate, cau**ti**ous/deli**ci**ous and ini**ti**al/so**ci**al; the spelling depends on the word's original Latin root. All the words in the spelling list take the ‹ci› spelling.

Spelling list: Go through the list, discuss the meaning of any unfamiliar words, and ask the class to find and highlight the ‹ci› saying /sh/ each time. Point out other spelling features, such as the long vowel sound(s) in words like '**a**ncient' and 'sp**eci**es', the prefixes meaning 'not' in '**un**social', '**in**sufficient' and '**in**efficient', the /ool/ spellings in 'unsoci**al**', 'soci**ab**le', '(e)speci**al**ly' and 'multiraci**al**', the ‹s› saying /z/ in 'specie**s**', the suffix ‹-ly› in '(e)special**ly**', the prefix in '**multi**racial', the ‹e› saying /i/ in '(in)**e**fficient', '**e**specially', 'ben**e**ficiary' and '**e**xcruciating', the 'soft ‹c›' in 'cons**c**ien**c**e', and the ‹u› saying /oo/ in 'excr**u**ciating'. Point out that '(in)efficient' and '(in)sufficient' have a double ‹f›, while 'proficient' does not (as a result of the way certain prefixes behave when added to a root word in Latin). Also explain that the /sh/ in 'conscience' is actually made by ‹sci› (you could also compare it to 'science', where the 'silent letter' digraph ‹sc› says /s/). It is a good idea to blend and sound out the spelling words quickly every day with the class, using the 'say it as it sounds' strategy where appropriate (stressing the pure sound of any schwas, for example, as in 'anci**e**nt').

Spelling Sheet 10a: The children split each word into syllables to help remember the spelling *[1. an/cient, 2. un/so/cial, 3. spe/cies, 4. so/cia/ble, 5. spe/cial/ly, 6. mul/ti/ra/cial, 7. ef/fi/cient, 8. suf/fi/cient, 9. sus/pi/cion, 10. con/science, 11. pro/fi/cient, 12. es/pe/cial/ly, 13. ap/pre/ci/a/tion, 14. in/suf/fi/cient, 15. co/er/cion, 16. in/ef/fi/cient, 17. ben/e/fi/cia/ry, 18. ex/cru/ci/at/ing].* They then work out the answers to the crossword clues and write them in *[1. suspicion, 2. sociable, 3. proficient, 4. multiracial, 5. appreciation, 6. conscience, 7. sufficient, 8. excruciating, 9. beneficiary, 10. inefficient, 11. unsocial, 12. insufficient, 13. species, 14. ancient, 15. coercion, 16. especially].*

Spelling Sheet 10b: The children read the sentences and identify the action verb and linking verb in each pair *[1. action/linking, 2. linking/action, 3. linking/action, 4. linking/ action, 5. action/ linking].* Then they parse the sentence and complete the wall *[Top: assistant - is\efficient (extremely) - (blank) / Bottom: Her - (blank) - (blank) / Verb: linking].* The verb 'is' links the adjective complement 'efficient' to the subject 'assistant' it is describing.

Her[Adj] assistant[N] is[V] extremely[Adv] efficient[Adj].

Noun[N] (black), Verb[V] (red), Pronoun[P] (pink), Adjective[Adj] (blue), Adverb[Adv] (orange), Conjunction[C] (purple), Preposition[Pre] (green)

Dictation: (This can be done in the spelling lesson or at another time during the week.) Call out the sentences for the children to write down. Remind them to use speech marks with the correct punctuation in Sentence 2. The proper noun 'Jane' needs a capital letter.

1. The detective regarded everyone with suspicion.
2. "Is Jane a beneficiary of her mother's will?" we asked.
3. He had shown his appreciation for all their kindness.

Spelling List 10

 **‹ci› for /sh/**

Work out the answers to the clues and complete the crossword. All of the answers are words in the Spelling List.

1. ancient
_____

2. unsocial
_____

3. species
_____

4. sociable
_____

5. specially
_____

6. multiracial
_____

7. efficient
_____

8. sufficient
_____

9. suspicion
_____

10. conscience
_____

11. proficient
_____

12. especially
_____

13. appreciation
_____

14. insufficient
_____

15. coercion
_____

16. inefficient
_____

17. beneficiary
_____

18. excruciating
_____

1. a feeling that tells you not to trust someone
2. if you are this, you enjoy being with other people
3. able to do something well or with skill
4. involving several different races of people
5. a feeling of being grateful for something
6. a person's sense of what is right and wrong
7. as much as is needed; enough
8. extremely painful, embarrassing or boring
9. a person who receives something, for example land or money, from someone who has died
10. not using energy, money or time in the best way
11. not wanting to be with other people
12. the opposite of Clue 7
13. a group of similar animals or plants
14. very old; existing thousands of years ago
15. the use of force or threats to make someone do something (s)he does not want to do
16. much more than usual; particularly

Dictation: ‹ci› for /sh/

1. _____

_____

2. _____

_____

3. _____

_____

The verbs 'taste', 'smell', 'sound', 'look' and 'feel' can be linking verbs or action verbs. The pairs of sentences below show examples of both. Can you work out which is which?

1. The explorer is looking for a rare species of plant.   action · linking
   The eiderdown looked warm and cosy.   action · linking

2. The ancient books smell sweet and musty.   action · linking
   Would you like to smell the perfume?   action · linking

3. I always feel very sociable at parties.   action · linking
   Meg felt the warm sand beneath her feet.   action · linking

4. Anna's toothache sounds excruciating!   action · linking
   The driver sounded his horn as a warning.   action · linking

5. The chef tasted the tomato sauce.   action · linking
   The vegetable stew tasted especially nice today.   action · linking

Parse the sentence and then write it on the wall.

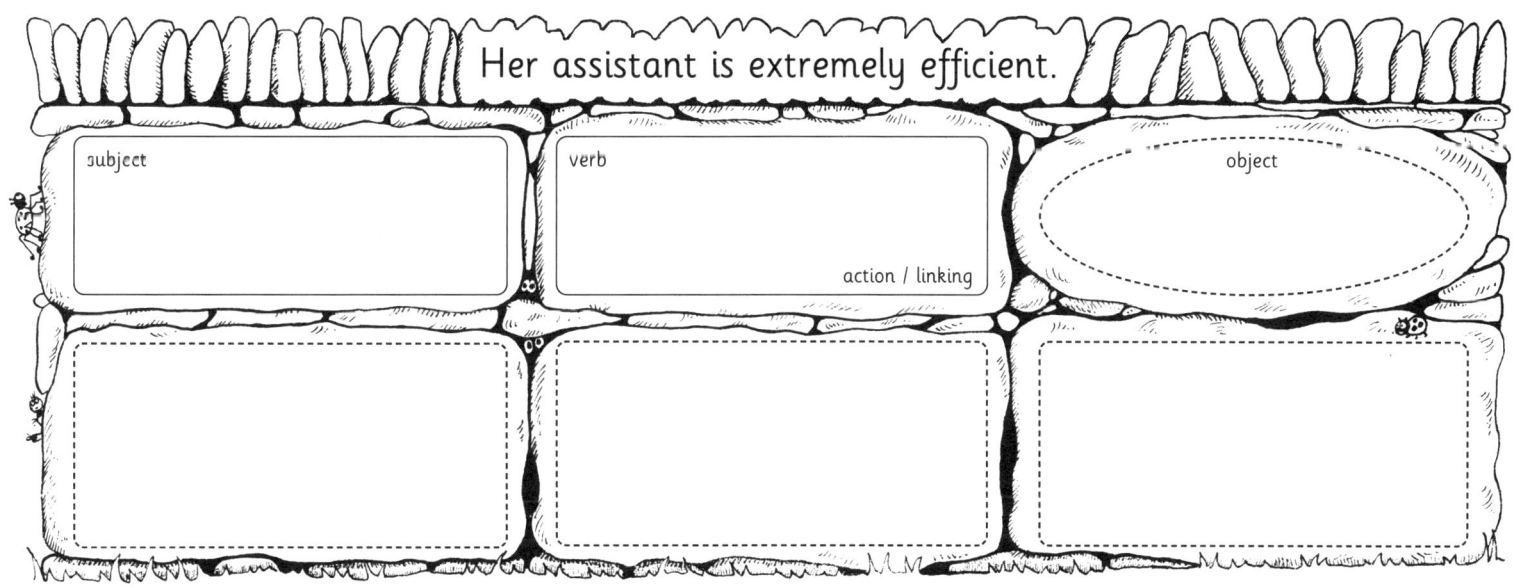

Her assistant is extremely efficient.

subject

verb

action / linking

object

Grammar 10 – Prepositional Phrases Acting as Adjectives

Prepare...
Grammar Sheet 10
Green, blue & orange pencils
Action/Comma Cards

Builds on...
JGH1: G21-22
JGH2: G9, G30
JGH5: G13-14,
G18, G23-24
JGH6: G9

Aim: Extend the children's understanding of prepositional phrases by introducing the idea that they can act as adjectives as well as adverbs.

Introduction: Write 'The birds were singing in the old oak tree' on the board and ask the children to identify the prepositional phrase [*in the old oak tree*]. Ask them what the phrase is doing [*it describes where the birds were singing, so it is acting as an adverb*], and ask a child to come and parse it, underlining the preposition 'in' in green and putting orange brackets around all the words in the phrase. Ask another child to come and rewrite the sentence so the prepositional phrase is at the beginning; remind the class that when we do this, we usually add a comma, especially after a long phrase [*In the old oak tree, the birds were singing*]. Give some children the action cards used in Grammar Lesson 5 and ask them to arrange themselves in the order of the first sentence: definite article / common noun / verb (past) / preposition / definite article / adjective / adjective / common noun. Then ask them to rearrange themselves so that the prepositional phrase goes at the beginning and ask another child to stand where the comma should go, holding a large 'comma' card.

Main point: Now write on the board 'The birds in the old oak tree were singing', and ask the class what the phrase is describing now. Explain that it is no longer describing the verb; instead, it is doing the job of an adjective, describing the birds by telling us **which ones** were singing. Similarly, in a sentence like 'The birds of prey were singing', the prepositional phrase tells us **what kind** of birds were singing. Write some noun phrases on the board and ask the children to identify the prepositional phrase in each one that is answering the question **which one?** or **what kind?** [*Possible examples include the boy (<u>in</u> the red coat), the handkerchief (<u>with</u> blue spots), a tube (<u>of</u> toothpaste), the plates (<u>on</u> the table)*]. Parse each one, underlining the preposition in green and putting blue brackets around all the words in the phrase. Look again at the first sentence and discuss how it would be put into a word wall, along with other examples:

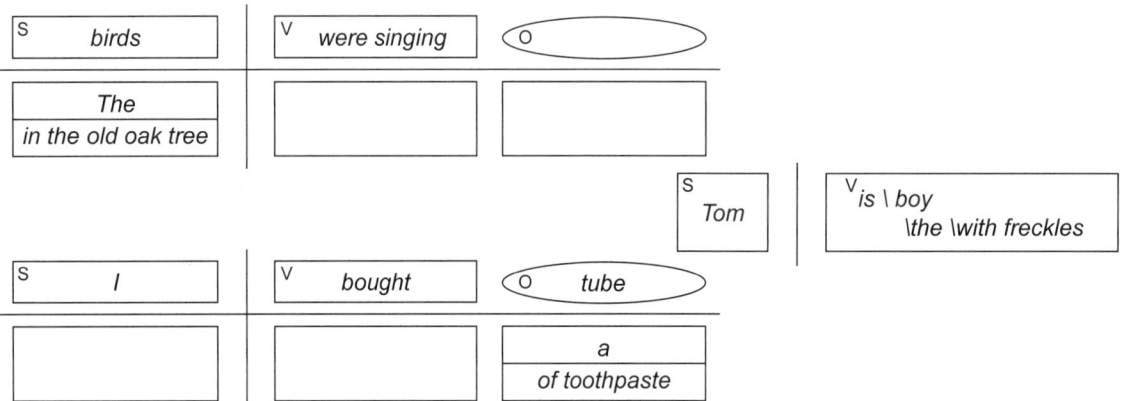

Grammar Sheet 10: The children write inside the outlined word Prepositions (green) and Adjectives (blue). They then identify the prepositional phrases acting as adjectives, underlining the preposition in green and putting blue brackets around each phrase [*1. <u>in</u> the field, 2. <u>of</u> chocolates, 3. <u>with</u> the kaleidoscope, 4. <u>after</u> October, 5. <u>of</u> perfume, 6. <u>on</u> the bed*], and answering each question in the way shown [*except answers 2 and 5: a box of chocolates/a bottle of perfume*]. Finally, they create eight long noun phrases by adding prepositional phrases of their own to four noun phrases and, similarly, their own noun phrases to four prepositional phrases.

Extension activity: The children put some of the sentences into sentence wall boxes.

Rounding off: Go over the sheet/extension activity with the class, discussing the answers.

Prepositional ✏ Blue
Phrases as Adjectives

Prepositional phrases can act as adjectives as well as adverbs. A prepositional phrase answers the question **Which one?** or **What kind?** when it is acting as an adjective.

Identify the prepositional phrases below. Underline the prepositions in green and put round brackets around each phrase, in blue. Then answer the questions to see how each phrase tells us more about the noun in bold.

1. The **horses** (in the field) were neighing loudly.
   Which horses were neighing loudly? _____ the ones in the field _____

2. I recently received a **box** of chocolates.
   What kind of box did I recently receive? _____

3. Anna is the **girl** with the kaleidoscope.
   Which girl is Anna? _____

4. November is the **month** after October.
   Which month is November? _____

5. She gave her niece a **bottle** of perfume.
   What kind of bottle did she give her niece? _____

6. The **eiderdown** on the bed is a family heirloom.
   Which eiderdown is a family heirloom? _____

Think of a prepositional phrase to complete each noun phrase and write it on the line.

7. the feisty heifer _____
8. the weird smell _____
9. the fiendish laughter _____
10. a pretty handkerchief _____

Think of four short noun phrases and write them on the lines. Then add a prepositional phrase to make each one longer.

near the park   inside the box
under the trees   up the road

11. _____

12. _____

13. _____

14. _____

Spelling 11 – ‹cious›

Prepare...
Spelling Sheets 11a/b
Coloured pencils

Builds on...
JGH5: S16, S25-26,
S27-28
JGH6: S10

Revision: Write these words on the board and ask the class to identify the letters saying /sh/ in each one: pen**si**on, rea**ss**ure, essen**ti**al, expre**ss**ion, offi**ci**al, **ch**ef, en**s**ure, obno**xi**ous. Apart from ‹ch›, which has French origins, words with these spellings usually come from Latin. Ask the children if they can think of other words with these spellings.

Main point: Write the words 'suspicious', 'ambitious' and 'anxious' on the board and remind the class that ‹-ous› is often preceded by /sh/, which can be spelt ‹ti›, ‹ci› and, very occasionally, ‹xi›. In this suffix, the ‹ou› has a neutral schwa sound, and so ‹tious›, ‹cious› and ‹xious› all say /shus/. This makes knowing which spelling to use difficult, so words like this have to be learnt. It helps to remember that the suffix ‹-ous› is found in adjectives that describe something as having the quality of the root (word): so 'suspicious' means 'full of suspicion', 'ambitious' means 'full of ambition' and 'anxious' means 'full of anxiety'. If the children already know the spelling of the root word, they can add the correct spelling of the suffix. All the words in the spelling list take the ‹ci› spelling.

Spelling list: Go through the list, discuss the meaning of any unfamiliar words, and ask the class to find and highlight the ‹cious› spelling each time. Point out other spelling features, such as the long vowel sound in words like 'gra**ci**ously' and 'atro**ci**ous', the ‹-ly› suffix in the adverbs 'graciously', 'viciously', 'suspiciously' and 'ferociously', the prefix in '**un**conscious', '**semi**-precious', '**pre**cocious' and '**sub**conscious', the ‹e› saying /i/ in 'tenacious' and 'precocious', and the ‹au› spelling in 'audacious' and 'auspicious'. Point out that – like 'conscience' in Spelling Lesson 10 – 'conscious', 'unconscious', 'luscious' and 'subconscious' belong to the small group of words where /sh/ is spelt ‹sci›. It is a good idea to blend and sound out the spelling words quickly every day with the class, using the 'say it as it sounds' strategy where appropriate (stressing the pure sound of any schwas, for example, as in 'm**a**licious').

Spelling Sheet 11a: The children split each word into syllables to help remember the spelling *[1. gra/cious/ly, 2. con/scious, 3. vi/cious/ly, 4. un/con/scious, 5. sem/i/ pre/cious, 6. sus/pi/cious/ly, 7. ma/li/cious, 8. a/tro/cious, 9. lus/cious, 10. vi/va/cious, 11. te/na/cious, 12. fe/ro/cious/ly, 13. au/da/cious, 14. aus/pi/cious, 15. of/fi/cious, 16. vo/ra/cious, 17. pre/co/cious, 18. sub/con/scious]*. They then unscramble the letters in the gemstones and add them to ‹cious› to make some of the spelling words *[semi-precious, viciously, graciously, unconscious, luscious, suspiciously, ferociously, tenacious, malicious, atrocious, precocious, voracious, subconscious, auspicious]*.

Spelling Sheet 11b: The children look up 'semi-precious' in the dictionary, check its meaning, and make as many words as they can with its letters. Then they parse the sentence and complete the wall *[Top: soup - tasted\delicious - (blank) / Bottom: The spiced pumpkin - (blank) - (blank) / Verb: linking]*. The verb 'tasted' links the adjective complement 'delicious' to the subject 'soup' it is describing.

The spiced[Adj] pumpkin[Adj] soup[N] tasted[V] delicious[Adj].

Noun[N] (black), Verb[V] (red), Pronoun[P] (pink), Adjective[Adj] (blue), Adverb[Adv] (orange), Conjunction[C] (purple), Preposition[Pre] (green)

Dictation: (This can be done in the spelling lesson or at another time during the week.) Call out the sentences for the children to write down. Remind them to use speech marks with the correct punctuation in Sentence 1. The proper noun 'Fred' needs a capital letter.

1. "What an atrocious song!" exclaimed Fred.
2. The fierce pack of wolves howled ferociously.
3. Her silver locket was decorated with semi-precious stones.

 **‹cious›**

Spelling List 11

1. graciously
   _____

2. conscious
   _____

3. viciously
   _____

4. unconscious
   _____

5. semi-precious
   _____

6. suspiciously
   _____

7. malicious
   _____

8. atrocious
   _____

9. luscious
   _____

10. vivacious
    _____

11. tenacious
    _____

12. ferociously
    _____

13. audacious
    _____

14. auspicious
    _____

15. officious
    _____

16. voracious
    _____

17. precocious
    _____

18. subconscious
    _____

Unscramble the letters in the gemstones and add them to ‹cious›
to make words from the Spelling List.

_____ cious

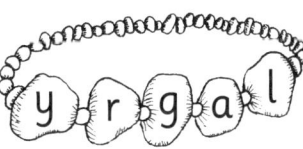

_____ cious _____

_____ cious

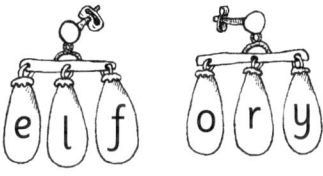

_____ cious _____

_____ cious

_____ cious

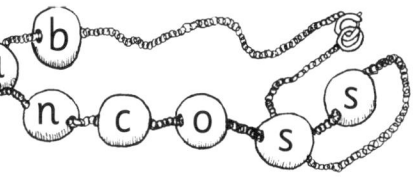

_____ cious

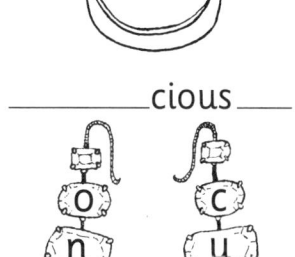

_____ cious _____

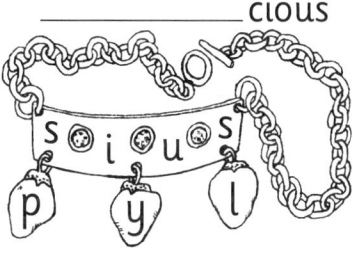

_____ cious

_____ cious

_____ cious

_____ cious

_____ cious

Dictation: ‹cious›

1. _____
   _____
2. _____
   _____
3. _____
   _____

Look this word up in the dictionary. See how many words you can make with its letters.

s e m i - p r e c i o u s

Parse the sentence and then write it on the wall.

The spiced pumpkin soup tasted delicious.

subject	verb	object
	action / linking	

Grammar 11 – Relative Clauses

Prepare...
Grammar Sheet 11
Pink, blue & orange pencils

Builds on...
JGH1: G10
JGH3: G27-28
JGH4: G30

Aim: Introduce relative clauses, which are a special kind of dependent (or 'subordinate') clause that starts with either a relative pronoun ('who', 'which', 'that', 'whom', 'whose') or relative adverb ('why', 'where', 'when').

Introduction: Write three simple sentences on the board and ask the children to identify the pronouns, underlining them in pink: <u>I</u> have a dog. The dog belongs to <u>me</u>. <u>It</u> is <u>mine</u>. Briefly revise personal and possessive pronouns (see pages 9 and 10) and point out that the personal pronoun 'I' (the subject) changes to 'me' when it becomes the object, and that the possessive pronoun 'mine' stands in for 'my dog'. Now write on the board 'I have a dog because I love animals' and remind the class that a long sentence often has more than one clause in it. Ask the children if they can remember what a clause is *[a group of words which makes sense and contains a subject and verb]* and discuss how the clause 'I have a dog' can stand alone as a simple sentence, whereas 'because I love animals' cannot, because it depends on the rest of the sentence for its meaning. Remind the children that the first kind of clause is called an 'independent' clause and the second one is called a 'dependent' or 'subordinate' clause.

Main point: Write these two noun phrases on the board and compare them: 'the girl in the green dress' and 'the girl who has a green dress'. The children should recognise that the first contains a prepositional phrase *[in the green dress]* which acts as an adjective to describe the girl; in the second, however, this job is done by 'who has a green dress', which is a special kind of dependent clause, known as a relative clause. It is dependent because it has a verb *[has]* and subject *[who]* but does not represent a complete thought, and it is relative because it starts with a pronoun that **relates** the clause to what it is describing. Underline the word 'who' in pink and explain that there are five main relative pronouns that can be used in this way: 'who', 'which', 'that', 'whom' and 'whose'. To describe people, we use 'who' for the subject of the clause and 'whom' for the object, but we only use 'which' to describe things; we can also use 'that' to describe either people or things and 'whose' to show possession. On the board, write some more examples of relative clauses describing nouns, and ask some children to underline the relative pronouns in pink and put blue brackets around each clause. Possible examples include 'the letter (<u>which</u> arrived this morning)', 'the music (<u>that</u> we like)', 'the friend (<u>whom</u> I often visit)', 'the writer (<u>whose</u> books you enjoy)'. Write three more noun phrases on the board and ask what is different about the relative clauses: 'the time (<u>when</u> I eat lunch)', 'the town (<u>where</u> you live)', 'the reason (<u>why</u> we were late)'. Point out that 'when', 'where' and 'why' are not pronouns but adverbs, and explain that they are usually used in everyday language to replace the more formal phrases 'in which', 'on which', 'at which' and 'for which'. Discuss which phrases are being replaced in the three examples *[at which, in which, for which]* and parse the clauses with the children, putting blue brackets around them and underlining the adverbs 'when', 'where' and 'why' in orange.

Grammar Sheet 11: The children write inside the outlined pronouns in pink and the outlined adverbs in orange. They then identify the relative clause acting as an adjective in each noun phrase, underlining the pronoun in pink and putting blue brackets around the clause *[1. <u>whom</u> I saw twice last year, 2. <u>that</u> he bought for his camera, 3. <u>whose</u> birthday is in September, 4. <u>which</u> they built in the twelfth century, 5. <u>who</u> won first prize in the competition]*. Finally, they rewrite the noun phrases, replacing each 'which' phrase in the relative clause with the correct adverb *[6. when, 7. where, 8. why, 9. where, 10. when, 11. why]*.

Extension activity: The children try parsing the relative clauses in the rewritten phrases (6 to 11), underlining the adverbs in orange and putting blue brackets around the clauses.

Rounding off: Go over the sheet/extension activity with the class, discussing the answers.

Relative Clauses

REMEMBER! A clause is a group of words that makes sense and has both a verb and a subject. Clauses that cannot stand alone as a simple sentence are called 'dependent' or 'subordinate' clauses.

Relative clauses are a special kind of **dependent** clause. They are 'relative' because they always start with a pronoun or adverb that relates the clause to what it is describing.

who   which   that   whom   whose   when   why   where

Relative clauses act as adjectives. Identify the ones below that are describing the nouns in bold. Underline the relative pronouns in pink and put round brackets around the clauses in blue.

1. the **doctor** (<u>whom</u> I saw twice last year)
2. the **tripod** that he bought for his camera
3. my **niece** whose birthday is in September
4. the **castle** which they built in the twelfth century
5. the **weightlifter** who won first prize in the competition

Some relative clauses start with 'where', 'when' and 'why'. These adverbs replace such phrases as 'in which', 'on which', 'at which' and 'for which', which are used in more formal language. Rewrite the noun phrases below, replacing the 'which' phrase with the correct adverb.

6. the day **on which** the triplets were born

   _____

7. the ancient city **in which** the treasure was found

   _____

8. the reason **for which** octopuses have eight tentacles

   _____

9. the museum **at which** we saw the foreign coins

   _____

10. the year **in which** she won the heptathlon

    _____

11. the reason **for which** triceratops had three horns

    _____

Spelling 12 – ‹-eous›

Prepare...
Spelling Sheets 12a/b
Coloured pencils

Builds on...
JGH5: S25–26
JGH6: S11

Revision: Write these adjectives on the board, identify the ‹-ious› suffix in each one, and discuss whether the ‹i› is spoken (either as /i/ or /ee/) or is part of the spelling for /sh/ or /j/: gra**cious**, infec**tious**, nox**ious**, relig**ious**, ser**ious**, obv**ious**, dub**ious**. Ask the children if they can think of other words with the ‹-ious› suffix.

Main point: Write the words 'hideous' and 'gorgeous' on the board and ask the class what they have in common. The children may recognise them as antonyms (words with opposite meanings), but they should also notice that these words are both adjectives in which the suffix ‹-ous› follows the letter ‹e›. The suffix ‹-eous› is a less common variant of ‹-ious›, and words with this spelling usually have Old French or Latin origins. Unlike the ‹i› in ‹-ious›, which is sometimes pronounced and sometimes not, the ‹e› in ‹-eous› is nearly always spoken, although the sound it makes is either /i/ or /ee/, not /e/. The main exception is when ‹e› is part of the 'soft ‹g›' spelling, as in 'gorgeous', 'outrageous', 'courageous' and 'advantageous'.

Spelling list: Go through the list, discuss the meaning of any unfamiliar words, and ask the class to find and highlight the ‹eous› spelling each time. Point out other spelling features, such as the schwa (neutral vowel sound) in ‹-ous›, the ‹igh› spelling of /ie/ and ‹te› saying /ch/ in 'righteous', the long vowel sound in words like 'outrageous' and 'erroneous', the ‹our› spelling of /er/ in 'courteous' and 'discourteous' (which are a pair of antonyms), the ‹e› saying /i/ in 'erroneous' and 'extraneous', the ‹au› spelling in 'nauseous' and the 'silent ‹c›' digraph in 'miscellaneous'. It is a good idea to blend and sound out the spelling words quickly every day with the class, using the 'say it as it sounds' strategy where appropriate (stressing the pure sound of any schwas, for example, as in 'adv**a**ntageous', 'misc**e**llaneous' and 'inst**a**ntaneous').

Spelling Sheet 12a: The children split each word into syllables to help remember the spelling *[1. hid/e/ous, 2. gor/geous, 3. pit/e/ous, 4. gas/e/ous, 5. right/eous, 6. out/ra/geous, 7. cou/ra/geous, 8. cour/te/ous, 9. boun/te/ous, 10. er/ro/ne/ous, 11. nau/se/ous, 12. ad/van/ta/geous, 13. ex/tra/ne/ous, 14. sim/ul/ta/ne/ous, 15. spon/ta/ne/ous, 16. mis/cel/la/ne/ous, 17. in/stan/ta/ne/ous, 18. dis/cour/te/ous].* Then they identify the correct meaning of 'bounteous' *[A]*, 'spontaneous' *[A]* and 'miscellaneous' *[C]*. Lastly, they write a noun phrase for each of the six spelling words shown and draw a picture to illustrate one of them.

Spelling Sheet 12b: The children write the adjective and adverb for each root word *[outrageous(ly), bounteous(ly), courteous(ly), erroneous(ly), piteous(ly), righteous(ly), instantaneous(ly), nauseous(ly), courageous(ly), advantageous(ly)].* Then they parse the sentence and complete the wall *[Top: heroes - received - medals / Bottom: The courageous - courteously - their / Verb: action].* 'Their' is a possessive adjective and should be underlined in blue. 'Courteously' is an adverb made by adding ‹-ly› to the adjective 'courteous'.

The courageous[Adj] heroes[N] received[V] their[Adj] medals[N] courteously[Adv].

Noun[N] (black), Verb[V] (red), Pronoun[P] (pink), Adjective[Adj] (blue), Adverb[Adv] (orange), Conjunction[C] (purple), Preposition[Pre] (green)

Dictation: (This can be done in the spelling lesson or at another time during the week.) Call out the sentences for the children to write down. Remind them to use speech marks with the correct punctuation in Sentence 1. Sentence 3 needs a question mark.

1. "What gorgeous flowers!" I exclaimed.
2. The smell of rotten eggs is nauseous.
3. Do you think it is an outrageous idea?

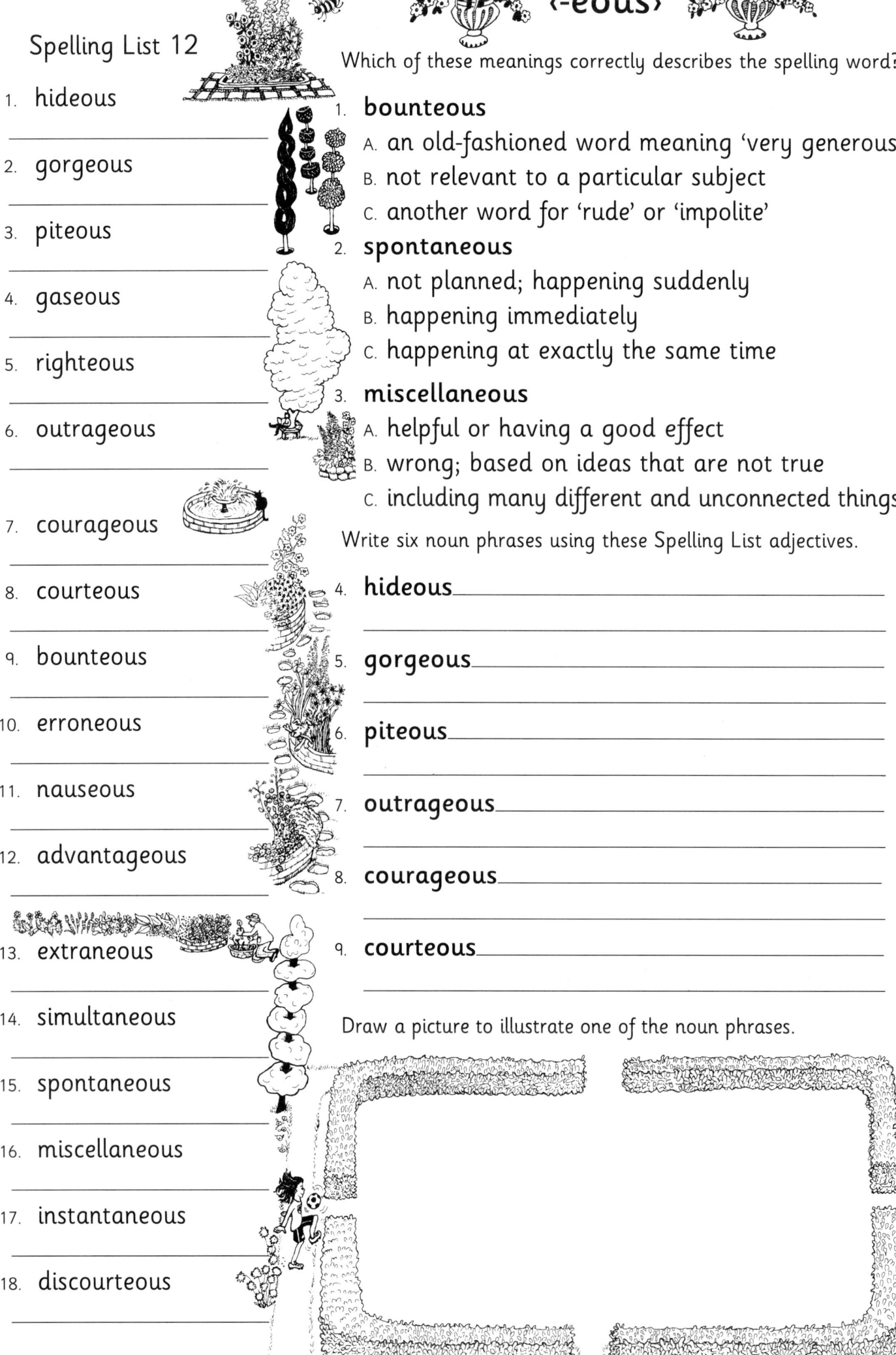

Spelling List 12

1. hideous

_____

2. gorgeous

_____

3. piteous

_____

4. gaseous

_____

5. righteous

_____

6. outrageous

_____

7. courageous

_____

8. courteous

_____

9. bounteous

_____

10. erroneous

_____

11. nauseous

_____

12. advantageous

_____

13. extraneous

_____

14. simultaneous

_____

15. spontaneous

_____

16. miscellaneous

_____

17. instantaneous

_____

18. discourteous

_____

‹-eous›

Which of these meanings correctly describes the spelling word?

1. **bounteous**
   A. an old-fashioned word meaning 'very generous'
   B. not relevant to a particular subject
   C. another word for 'rude' or 'impolite'

2. **spontaneous**
   A. not planned; happening suddenly
   B. happening immediately
   C. happening at exactly the same time

3. **miscellaneous**
   A. helpful or having a good effect
   B. wrong; based on ideas that are not true
   C. including many different and unconnected things

Write six noun phrases using these Spelling List adjectives.

4. **hideous**_____

_____

5. **gorgeous**_____

_____

6. **piteous**_____

_____

7. **outrageous**_____

_____

8. **courageous**_____

_____

9. **courteous**_____

_____

Draw a picture to illustrate one of the noun phrases.

Dictation: ‹-eous›

1. _____

_____

2. _____

_____

3. _____

_____

Write the adjective and adverb for each of these root words, adding the suffix(es) correctly.

Noun	Adjective ‹-eous›	Adverb ‹-ly›
outrage	_____	_____
bounty	_____	_____
court	_____	_____
error	_____	_____
pity	_____	_____
right	_____	_____
instant	_____	_____
nausea	_____	_____
courage	_____	_____
advantage	_____	_____

Parse the sentence and then write it on the wall.

The courageous heroes received their medals courteously.

subject

verb

object

action / linking

Grammar 12 – Relative Clauses in Sentences

Prepare...
Grammar Sheet 12
Pink & blue pencils

Builds on...
JGH1: G10
JGH3: G27-28
JGH4: G30
JGH5: G32
JGH6: G11

Aim: Develop the children's understanding of how relative clauses act as adjectives, either to give important information that helps us identify who or what is being described ('defining' clauses), or to add extra information that is interesting, but not essential ('non-defining' clauses).

Introduction: Briefly revise what the children have learnt about relative clauses so far. Relative clauses are a special kind of dependent clause, so they have a verb and subject, but do not represent a complete thought. They start with a relative pronoun ('who', 'which', 'that', 'whom', 'whose') or adverb ('where', 'when', 'why') that **relates** the clause to what it is describing. Call out the beginnings of some noun phrases and ask the class to complete the relative clauses: possible examples include 'the day (when...)', 'my friend (who...)', 'some trees (which...)', 'the house (that...)', 'a place (where...)', 'the actor (whom...)', 'an artist (whose...)'. Write the completed phrases on the board and ask some children to come and identify the relative clauses, underlining the pronouns in pink and adverbs in orange, and putting each clause in blue brackets.

Main point: Relative clauses cannot stand on their own as simple sentences. They act as adjectives, giving us more information about a noun or pronoun. When a relative clause is used in a sentence, the information it provides does one of two things: it either defines the noun, giving us the information we need to identify which person or thing is meant, or it provides some extra detail which, while interesting, could easily be left out. We call these two kinds of clauses **defining** and **non-defining** clauses. Write two sentences on the board and identify the relative clause in each one, underlining the pronoun in pink and putting blue brackets around the clause: 'She is the girl (who won the race).' 'Paris, (which is the capital of France), is a beautiful city'. Discuss them with the class and explain that in the first sentence, the relative clause defines which girl we are talking about: without it we would be left asking 'which girl?'; whereas in the second sentence, the clause tells us more about Paris, but it does not aim to help us understand 'which' Paris is being referred to. Point out that the non-defining clause is separated from the main clause by a pair of bracketing commas. These work in a similar way to parentheses, telling us that the information inside is extra information that could easily be removed without changing the sense. In our writing, it is important to know when to put commas in, because it will affect the meaning: for example, the sentence 'John is in the park where his friends are playing', tells us which park John is in (the one where his friends are playing); whereas 'John is in the park, where his friends are playing', tells us that John is in the park and his friends are also playing there. Point out that in this last example, the closing comma is not needed because the clause comes at the end of the sentence. Clauses starting with 'that' are always defining clauses and never have a comma.

Grammar Sheet 12: The children identify the defining clauses, underlining the pronoun in pink and putting blue brackets around the clause [1. who owns a blue bicycle, 2. which escaped from the zoo, 3. whose ceiling had collapsed, 4. whom you like, 5. that my niece is baking]. They then answer each question in the way shown. Then they rewrite the next set of sentences, adding in the extra information given and putting bracketing commas around each non-defining clause [6. My dad, who loves gardening, especially likes roses; 7. I had some semi-precious stones, which my sister gave me; 8. His friend, whose name is Tom, is rather unsocial; 9. They would like to visit Rome, where their cousins live; 10. Jenny, whom they met forty years ago, is coming to stay].

Extension activity: The children write some sentences of their own with defining or non-defining relative clauses.

Rounding off: Go over the sheet/extension activity with the class, discussing the answers.

Relative Clauses in Sentences

There are two main kinds of relative clause. The way a clause is used in a sentence determines which kind it is.

Defining clauses give us important information that helps us identify the particular person or thing that we are talking about.

Without them, the meaning of the sentence would be quite different.

essential information = **defining** clause

If a clause starts with 'that' it is always a **defining** clause.

Identify the defining clauses below. Underline the pronouns in pink and put round brackets around each clause in blue. Then answer the questions to see how each clause helps us to identify the noun in bold.

1. We saw the **woman** (<u>who</u> owns a blue bicycle) in the park.
   Which woman did we see in the park? _the one who owns a blue bicycle_

2. They have caught the ferocious **lion** which escaped from the zoo.
   Which ferocious lion have they caught? _____

3. They rescued the **man** whose ceiling had collapsed.
   Which man did they rescue? _____

4. The **author** whom you like has written a new trilogy.
   Which author has written a new trilogy? _____

5. The **pie** that my niece is baking smells delicious.
   Which pie smells delicious? _____

Non-defining clauses give us some extra information that could just as easily be left out.

We separate them from the rest of the sentence with commas to show that they are not essential.

extra information = **non-defining** clause

Rewrite each sentence, adding the extra information about the noun in bold. Put commas around the non-defining clause, unless it is at the end of the sentence, when only the first comma is needed.

6. My **dad** especially likes roses.   who loves gardening
   _____

7. I had some semi-precious **stones**.   which my sister gave me
   _____

8. His **friend** is rather unsocial.   whose name is Tom
   _____

9. They would like to visit **Rome.**   where their cousins live
   _____

10. **Jenny** is coming to stay.   whom they met forty years ago
    _____

Spelling 13 – Double Letters

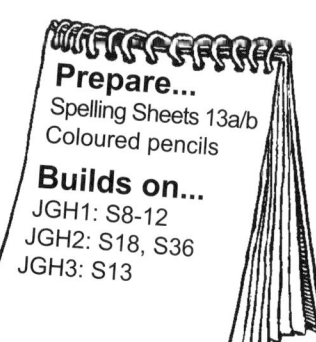

Prepare...
Spelling Sheets 13a/b
Coloured pencils

Builds on...
JGH1: S8-12
JGH2: S18, S36
JGH3: S13

Revision: Write the words 'fell', 'back', 'hopped' and 'nibble' on the board, underline the double letters, and then compare them to 'feel', 'bark', 'hoped' and 'nimble'. Revise the rules for consonant doubling, when two letters form a 'wall', either to end a short word with a short vowel sound (if the final letter is ‹f›, ‹l›, ‹s› or ‹z›) or to stop the 'magic' of one vowel changing the short, stressed sound of another (see pages 38 and 39).

Main point: The rule for consonant doubling is very reliable when adding a suffix that starts with a vowel (as in 'equi**pp**ed' and 'progra**mm**ed') but elsewhere in a word, it can be dependent on other factors like word meaning or origin. For example, some words with a Latin root have a prefix like ‹sub-› or ‹ad-›, which adapts its final consonant to the first letter of the stem, as in 'suppose' (from 'sup' + 'ponere'), 'address' (from 'ad' + 'directus'), 'aggressive' (from 'aggression': 'ag' + 'gredi') and 'apparent' (from 'appear': 'ap' + 'parere'). This makes spelling difficult and so time must be spent looking at words and noting when double letters appear.

Spelling list: Go through the list, discuss the meaning of any unfamiliar words, and ask the class to find and highlight the double letters in each word. Point out other spelling features, such as ‹s› saying **/s/** and _/z/_ in '**s**uppo_s_e', the ‹ch› in 'attached' (‹tch› usually follows a short vowel sound), the ‹ee› in 'committee', the ‹e› saying /i/ in '**e**quipped', '**e**mbarrass' and 'corr**e**spond', the vowel saying its long sound in 'pr**o**grammed', 'comm**u**nity' and 'comm**u**nicate', the ‹ive› saying /iv/ in 'aggress**ive**', the different spellings of /shun/ in 'posse**ssion**' and 'interrup**tion**', the prefixes in '**inter**ruption', '**ex**aggerate' and '**re**commend', and the ‹ex› saying /igz/ and 'soft ‹g›' in 'exaggerate'. It is a good idea to blend and sound out the spelling words quickly every day with the class, using the 'say it as it sounds' strategy where appropriate (stressing the pure sound of any schwas, for example, as in '**a**rrive' and '**a**ppar**e**nt').

Spelling Sheet 13a: The children split each word into syllables to help remember the spelling *[1. ad/dress, 2. ar/rive 3. sup/pose, 4. at/tached, 5. com/mit/tee, 6. e/quipped, 7. pro/grammed, 8. ag/gres/sive, 9. ap/par/ent, 10. har/ass, 11. pos/ses/sion, 12. com/mu/ni/ ty, 13. in/ter/rup/tion, 14. com/mu/ni/cate, 15. em/bar/rass, 16. ex/ag/ge/rate, 17. rec/om/mend, 18. cor/re/spond]*. They then find the spelling words in the word search, and identify the synonym for each group of words *[1. A, 2. B, 3. B, 4. C]*.

Spelling Sheet 13b: The children identify the words acting as adjectives and decide if they are prepositional phrases or relative clauses *[1. why we were late (clause), 2. about ancient Egypt (phrase), 3. above the fireplace (phrase), 4. which I lost today (clause), 5. from her niece and nephew (phrase), 6. that something is wrong (clause), 7. in the middle of the night (phrase), 8. who sang at the concert (clause)]*. Then they parse the sentence and complete the wall *[Top: dog - was\aggressive (very) - (blank) / Bottom: The/in the park - (blank) - (blank) / Verb: linking]*. The verb 'was' links the adjective complement 'aggressive' to the subject 'dog' it is describing. 'In the park' is a prepositional phrase describing 'dog', so it needs blue brackets.

The dog[N] (in[Pre] the park[N])[Adj] was[V] very[Adv] aggressive[Adj].

Noun[N] (black), Verb[V] (red), Pronoun[P] (pink), Adjective[Adj] (blue), Adverb[Adv] (orange), Conjunction[C] (purple), Preposition[Pre] (green)

Dictation: (This can be done in the spelling lesson or at another time during the week.) Call out the sentences for the children to write down. Remind them to use speech marks with the correct punctuation in Sentence 2. 'Sam' is a proper noun and needs a capital letter.

1. We were supposed to arrive before dinner.
2. "I was so embarrassed!" exclaimed Sam.
3. There were no interruptions during the lesson.

Double Letters

Spelling List 13

1. address
2. arrive
3. suppose
4. attached
5. committee
6. equipped
7. programmed
8. aggressive
9. apparent
10. harass
11. possession
12. community
13. interruption
14. communicate
15. embarrass
16. exaggerate
17. recommend
18. correspond

Find the words from the Spelling List.

s	x	a	g	g	r	e	c	h	a	r	a	s	s	t
u	p	o	s	s	e	s	c	i	r	r	o	l	e	t
p	t	h	e	n	p	r	o	g	r	a	m	m	e	d
p	e	a	s	e	c	o	m	m	i	t	t	e	e	e
o	e	r	u	h	d	l	m	s	v	t	x	e	q	x
s	x	r	p	o	e	r	u	m	e	a	b	b	u	r
e	a	p	p	a	r	e	n	t	d	c	c	p	i	r
a	g	g	r	e	s	s	i	v	e	h	o	r	p	e
d	g	h	a	t	t	a	c	g	h	e	m	o	p	c
d	e	m	b	a	r	r	a	s	s	d	m	g	e	o
r	r	a	d	d	r	e	t	r	i	x	u	r	d	m
e	a	z	c	o	r	r	e	s	p	o	n	d	f	m
s	t	b	e	p	o	s	s	e	s	s	i	o	n	e
s	e	f	i	n	t	e	r	r	u	p	t	i	o	n
c	o	m	m	i	t	y	a	t	t	a	y	h	e	d

Which is the correct synonym for each group of words?
Use a thesaurus to help you, if necessary.

1. **obvious, clear, supposed**
   A. apparent
   B. attached
   C. programmed

2. **think, guess, assume**
   A. harass
   B. suppose
   C. exaggerate

3. **suggest, nominate, advise**
   A. correspond
   B. recommend
   C. communicate

4. **group, neighbourhood, citizens**
   A. committee
   B. address
   C. community

Dictation: double letters

1. _____

_____

2. _____

_____

3. _____

_____

Find the words describing the nouns in bold and put blue brackets around them. To do this, ask the question 'Which reason/book/mirror?' etc. Then decide whether they are prepositional phrases or relative clauses. To help you, think about whether they start with a preposition or a relative pronoun (or adverb), and remember that a clause has a verb and subject, but a phrase does not.

1. the **reason** why we were late   prepositional phrase · relative clause

2. a **book** about ancient Egypt   prepositional phrase · relative clause

3. the **mirror** above the fireplace   prepositional phrase · relative clause

4. the **handkerchief** which I lost today   prepositional phrase · relative clause

5. a **postcard** from her niece and nephew   prepositional phrase · relative clause

6. a **suspicion** that something is wrong   prepositional phrase · relative clause

7. the **storm** in the middle of the night   prepositional phrase · relative clause

8. the **trio** who sang at the concert   prepositional phrase · relative clause

Parse the sentence and then write it on the wall.

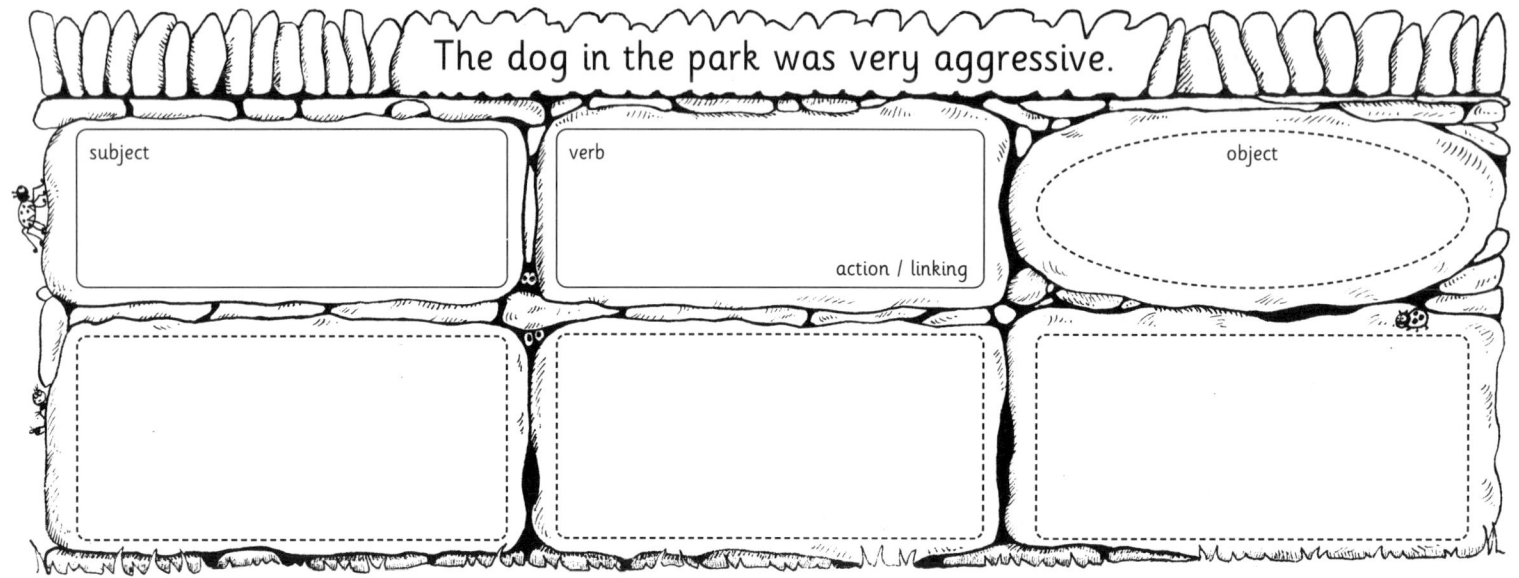

The dog in the park was very aggressive.

subject	verb	object
	action / linking	

Grammar 13 – Coordinating Conjunctions

Prepare...
Grammar Sheet 13
Purple pencils
Action Cards

Builds on...
JGH2: G23
JGH4: G27

Aim: Refine the children's understanding of the conjunctions '**for**', '**and**', '**nor**', '**but**', '**or**', '**yet**' and '**so**', which join together words, phrases or clauses of equal importance. Explain that they are called coordinating conjunctions and can be remembered by the acronym FANBOYS.

Introduction: Briefly revise conjunctions with the class. Conjunctions are the (usually) small words that join parts of a sentence together, such as 'or', 'but' and 'so'. Ask the children to think of other conjunctions, such as 'because', 'and', 'yet', 'if' and 'while', and how they would put them into sentences. Write some of the suggestions on the board and underline the conjunctions in purple. Parse one of the simpler sentences to create a grammar action sentence, using the action cards. Ask the class to call out different words each time to make a new sentence: for example, with the sequence pronoun / verb / conjunction / pronoun / verb, the class could create sentences like 'He skips and she jumps', 'I shall go but you will stay', 'We talked while we waited'. Remind them that many conjunctions can be used to join an independent clause to a dependent (or 'subordinate') one, but there is a small group of conjunctions – 'for', 'and', 'nor', 'but', 'or', 'yet' and 'so' – which join independent clauses (also known as simple sentences) to form compound sentences.

Main point: Using conjunctions in compound sentences helps us avoid having lots of short, repetitive sentences in our writing; it creates a natural flow and helps us digest the information more easily. The conjunctions can do this in other ways too. Instead of writing 'Joe put on his coat. Joe put on his scarf. Jess put on her coat. Jess put on her scarf', we are much more likely to write 'Joe <u>and</u> Jess put on their coats <u>and</u> scarves', combining everything in one sentence and using compound subjects and objects joined by 'and'. Similarly, we could shorten a compound sentence like 'Did you leave your book at home, <u>or</u> did you leave it in the car?' to 'Did you leave your book at home <u>or</u> in the car?' Discuss these examples with the class and look at how the conjunctions can join words *[Joe/Jess, coats/scarves]*, phrases *[at home/in the car]* and clauses *[did you leave your book at home/did you leave it in the car]*. Point out that the joined parts are equally important: Jess is just as much the subject of the sentence as Joe, and the book is as likely to be at home as in the car. The conjunctions that join words, phrases and clauses of equal importance are called **coordinating** conjunctions and they can be remembered by the acronym FANBOYS. These conjunctions always go between the parts they are joining and, like other conjunctions, they express meaning: 'and' simply tells us that more information is being added, 'or' provides an alternative, 'so' shows us the consequences, and the information following 'but' and 'yet' provides a general *[but]* or strong *[yet]* contrast. Two other conjunctions are less commonly used: 'for' introduces further information as an explanation, and 'nor' excludes more information. Explain that in a compound sentence using 'nor', the verb in the first clause is always negative and the one in the second clause always goes before the subject, as in 'I am <u>not</u> tired, nor <u>am I</u> hungry'. 'And', 'nor', 'but' and 'or' are also used in pairs of correlative conjunctions, as in 'I am <u>neither</u> tired <u>nor</u> hungry', but the children can learn about this when they are older.

Grammar Sheet 13: The children write inside the outlined word Conjunctions, using a purple pencil. They then match each one to its correct function *[see Main Point]*. Finally, they read the sentences and decide which of the coordinating conjunctions is needed each time to complete them *[1. or, 2. so, 3. nor, 4. or, 5. but, 6. and, 7. for, 8. nor, 9. yet, 10. and, 11. yet, 12. so, 13. for, 14. but]*.

Extension activity: The children write a phrase or sentence for each of the conjunctions.

Rounding off: Go over the sheet with the children, checking their answers. If they have done the extension activity, ask some of them to read out their phrases and sentences.

Coordinating Conjunctions

Coordinating conjunctions join words, phrases or clauses of equal importance within a sentence. It is important to use the right one to show the relationship between the joined parts. Match each of the conjunctions below with its correct function.

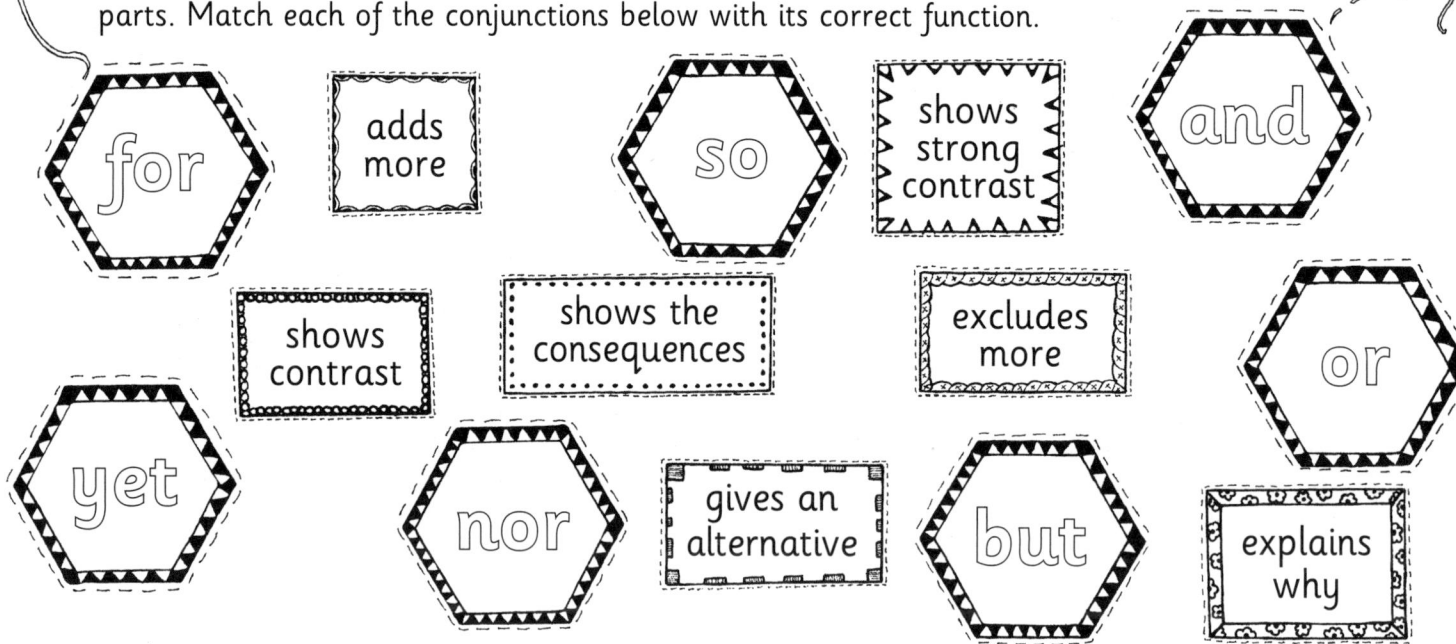

for — adds more — so — shows strong contrast — and

shows contrast — shows the consequences — excludes more — or

yet — nor — gives an alternative — but — explains why

Write in the correct coordinating conjunction to complete each sentence correctly.

1. Is the patient conscious _____ unconscious?
2. The tie was hideous _____ my dad never wore it.
3. His latest book was not well-written, _____ was it especially interesting.
4. Who is the eldest, your niece _____ your nephew?
5. I tried two kinds of shampoo _____ I did not like either of them.
6. For my birthday I got a gorgeous necklace _____ a matching pair of earrings.
7. They spent many years in jail, _____ their crimes were truly malicious.
8. The ancient castle is not in France, _____ is it in Spain.
9. The weather was atrocious, and _____ they insisted on going for a walk.
10. Those luscious blackberries were sweet _____ very juicy.
11. It was an outrageous lie and _____ they still believed him.
12. The money was counterfeit _____ they called the police.
13. The knight was famous throughout the land, _____ he was courageous in battle.
14. It seemed like a spontaneous decision, _____ I had thought about it very carefully.

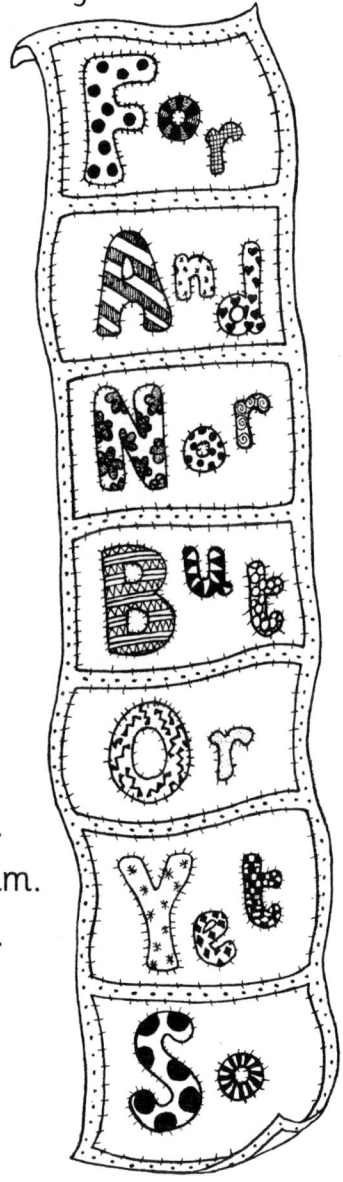

For And Nor But Or Yet So

Spelling 14 – ‹cc› for the /k/ Sound

Prepare...
Spelling Sheets 14a/b
Coloured pencils

Builds on...
JGH1: S11
JGH2: S12, S18
JGH6: S13

Revision: Write these words on the board, putting only one consonant letter where there should be two: adres, arive, embaras, interuption, atached, supose, posesion, recomend. Discuss which letters are missing and then ask the children to put the words into sentences.

Main point: Revise the main ways the /k/ sound can be written; ‹c›, ‹k› and ‹ck› are the most common, but ‹ch› and ‹que› are also used in words with Greek or French origins (see Spelling Lesson 31). The letter ‹c› can be used for /k/ anywhere in a word, except before ‹e›, ‹i› or ‹y›; then it becomes a 'soft ‹c›' and says /s/, so words like 'kept', 'kitten' and 'sky' are written with a ‹k›. We also tend to use ‹k› after a long vowel sound and ‹c› after a short one (as in 'oak' and 'act'). This makes ‹c› subject to the doubling rule; it becomes ‹ck› at the end of short words like 'stick' (and keeps this spelling when a suffix is added) but it is written as ‹cc› in longer words without a suffix, such as 'hiccup', 'soccer' and 'raccoon'. The word 'soccer' is rather unusual, as ‹cc› before ‹e› usually says /ks/, as in 'accept'.

Spelling list: Go through the list, discuss the meaning of any unfamiliar words, and ask the class to find and highlight the ‹cc› spelling each time. Point out that the spelling always follows a short vowel and discuss other spelling features, such as the ‹ur› spelling of /er/ in 'occur', the ‹i› saying /ee/ at the end of 'broccoli', the ‹y› saying /ie/ in 'occupy', the vowel saying its long sound in 'piccolo' and 'occasionally', the ‹eer› spelling of /ear/ in 'buccaneer', and the ‹sion› saying /zhun/ and suffixes ‹-al› and ‹-ly› in 'occasionally'. It is a good idea to blend and sound out the spelling words quickly every day with the class, using the 'say it as it sounds' strategy where appropriate (stressing the pure sound of any schwas, for example, as in '**o**ccur' and 'accur**ate**').

Spelling Sheet 14a: The children split each word into syllables to help remember the spelling *[1. hic/cup, 2. oc/cur, 3. ac/claim, 4. ac/count, 5. rac/coon, 6. soc/cer, 7. broc/co/li, 8. moc/ca/sin, 9. oc/cu/py, 10. ac/cord/ing, 11. ac/cu/rate, 12. ac/com/plish, 13. pic/co/lo, 14. buc/ca/neer, 15. oc/ca/sion/al/ly, 16. ac/com/mo/date, 17. ac/com/pa/ny, 18. ac/cor/di/on].* They then write sentences for the first six spelling words and draw pictures of the words in the leaves.

Spelling Sheet 14b: The children match the independent clauses and join them together with a coordinating conjunction to make a compound sentence *[It was Tom's eighth birthday <u>so</u> we bought him a present, The sofa is not especially big <u>nor</u> is it very comfortable, Unicorns are mythical animals <u>yet</u> some people believe in them, Are we going in September <u>or</u> should we wait until October?, Dad collects foreign stamps <u>but</u> he has never been abroad, Grandma made a chocolate cake <u>and</u> the children decorated it, The princess was loved by everyone <u>for</u> she was kind and gracious].* Then they parse the sentence and complete the wall *[Top: raccoons - were eating - broccoli / Bottom: The/under the house - (blank) - our / Verb: action].* 'Under the house' is a prepositional phrase describing 'raccoons', so it needs blue brackets.

The raccoons[N] (under[Pre] the house[N])[Adj] (were eating)[V] our[Adj] broccoli[N].

Noun[N] (black), Verb[V] (red), Pronoun[P] (pink), Adjective[Adj] (blue), Adverb[Adv] (orange), Conjunction[C] (purple), Preposition[Pre] (green)

Dictation: (This can be done in the spelling lesson or at another time during the week.) Call out the sentences for the children to write down. Remind them to use speech marks with the correct punctuation in Sentence 1. 'Ken' and 'Jill' are proper nouns and need capital letters.

1. "Is that clock accurate?" asked Ken.
2. Jill plays the piccolo in the orchestra.
3. I have a comfortable pair of moccasins.

‹cc› for /k/

1. hiccup
2. occur
3. acclaim
4. account
5. raccoon
6. soccer
7. broccoli
8. moccasin
9. occupy
10. according
11. accurate
12. accomplish
13. piccolo
14. buccaneer
15. occasionally
16. accommodate
17. accompany
18. accordion

Write a sentence for each of the spelling words numbered below.

1. _____

2. _____

3. _____

4. _____

5. _____

6. _____

Draw a picture to illustrate each word.

raccoon

piccolo

broccoli

buccaneer

Dictation: ‹cc› for /k/

1. _____

_____

2. _____

_____

3. _____

_____

Match the independent clauses and join them together with a coordinating conjunction to make a compound sentence.

It was Tom's eighth birthday •

The sofa is not especially big •

Unicorns are mythical animals •

Are we going in September •

Dad collects foreign stamps •

Grandma made a chocolate cake •

The princess was loved by everyone •

For
And
Nor
But
Or
Yet
So

• some people believe in them.

• she was kind and gracious.

• should we wait until October?

• we bought him a present.

• the children decorated it.

• he has never been abroad.

• is it very comfortable.

Parse the sentence and then write it on the wall.

The raccoons under the house were eating our broccoli.

subject	verb	object
	action / linking	

Grammar 14 – Semicolons and Compound Sentences

Prepare...
Grammar Sheet 14
Coloured pencils

Builds on...
JGH4: G27, G30
JGH6: G13

Aim: Extend the children's knowledge of punctuation. Introduce them to the semicolon and explain that, like a coordinating conjunction, it can be used to join independent clauses in a compound sentence.

Introduction: Briefly revise sentences with the children. Remind them that all sentences must make sense, start with a capital letter, contain a verb and subject, and end with a full stop, question mark or exclamation mark. (If the words make sense but there is no verb and subject, it is a phrase.) A simple sentence has one verb and subject (including compound subjects and verbs), while a compound sentence has two or more simple sentences (also known as independent clauses) that are joined by a coordinating conjunction ('for', 'and', 'nor', 'but', 'or', 'yet' and 'so'). Write 'I stayed at home but you went out' on the board and discuss this compound sentence with the class; underline the conjunction 'but' in purple and the verbs 'stayed' and 'went' in red, and put a box with a small ‹s› in the corner around the subjects 'I' and 'you'. On the board, write a compound sentence for each of the other conjunctions, and look at how they express meaning: 'for' explains why, 'and' adds more information, 'nor' excludes more information, 'but' shows contrast, 'or' gives an alternative, 'yet' shows strong contrast, and 'so' shows the consequences.

Main point: Remind the children that we often use compound sentences to create a natural flow in our writing. Joining sentences together with a coordinating conjunction allows us to show a connection between ideas: adding or excluding information, giving a choice or an explanation, providing a contrast, or showing the consequences. Sometimes this connection is so obvious that we do not need to use the conjunction at all; instead we can join two closely related sentences with a punctuation mark called a **semicolon**. The semicolon looks similar to a colon but has a comma-like mark rather than a bottom dot. Like the colon, it marks a longer pause than a comma, but a shorter one than a full stop, and it indicates a connection between the two parts without interrupting the flow. Write a pair of closely related sentences on the board: 'It is raining' and 'The grass is wet'. Discuss how these sentences could be rewritten as a compound sentence, either with one of the conjunctions 'and' or 'so', or by using a semicolon. Ask a child to come up and do this with 'and'. Make sure (s)he removes the full stop at the end of the first sentence and removes the capital in 'The'. Now ask another child to come up and rewrite the compound sentence, replacing 'and' with a semicolon. Now write some compound sentences with semicolons on the board and discuss which conjunctions could be used instead.

Grammar Sheet 14: The children write inside the outlined semicolon ‹ ; › and then write one in each patchwork piece, using a different colour each time. They then rewrite the compound sentences, replacing the conjunction with a semicolon [1. *She arrived early; her friends were late, 2. Tom weighed the sugar; Sue beat the eggs, 3. It was a costume party; I went as a Roman centurion, 4. Go equipped with warm clothes; it will be very cold, 5. We highly recommended the steak; they chose the fish*]. Then they join each pair of simple sentences with a semicolon to make a compound sentence [6. *I had lost the address; I could not find the house, 7. The old lady was very poor; she had few possessions, 8. No one was hurt; the fire had been greatly exaggerated*]. Finally, they write a compound sentence of their own, joining the two clauses with a semicolon.

Extension activity: The children write more compound sentences with semicolons, swap them with a partner, and think of coordinating conjunctions that can be used in their place.

Rounding off: Go over the sheet with the children, checking their answers. If they have done the extension activity, ask some of them to read out their answers.

Semicolons and Compound Sentences

A semicolon marks the place where we should pause in speaking. Like the colon, it has a longer pause than a comma, but a shorter one than a full stop. Write a semicolon in each patchwork piece, using a different colour each time.

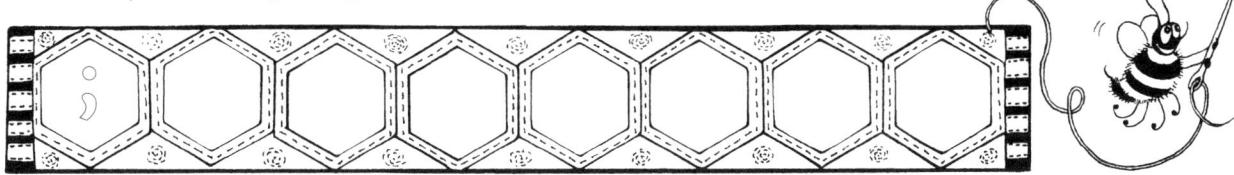

To help our writing flow better, we often join short simple sentences together to make a compound sentence. Usually we use coordinating conjunctions to do this, but when the sentences are closely related we can use a semicolon instead.

Underline each coordinating conjunction in purple, and then rewrite the compound sentences using a semicolon.

1. She arrived early but her friends were late.

    _____

2. Tom weighed the sugar and Sue beat the eggs.

    _____

3. It was a costume party, so I went as a Roman centurion.

    _____

4. Go equipped with warm clothes, for it will be very cold.

    _____

5. We highly recommended the steak, yet they chose the fish.

    _____

Join each pair of simple sentences with a semicolon to make a compound sentence.

6. I had lost the address. I could not find the house.

    _____

7. The old lady was very poor. She had few possessions.

    _____

8. No one was hurt. The fire had been greatly exaggerated.

    _____

Write a compound sentence of your own, using a semicolon.

9. _____

    _____

Spelling 15 – Doubling Rule for ‹fer›

Prepare...
Spelling Sheets 15a/b
Coloured pencils

Builds on...
JGH1: S8-12
JGH2: S18, S36
JGH3: S13
JGH6: S13-14

Revision: Write these words on the board, putting only one consonant letter where there should be two: programed, comunity, comitee, exagerate, hicup, ocupy, acompany, ocasion. Discuss which letters are missing and then ask the children to put the words into sentences.

Main point: If we stress a syllable, we say it slightly louder to give it more emphasis and to keep the vowel sound pure. Stress is an important feature of the consonant doubling rule. Words like 'grabbed', 'wedding', 'biggest', 'hotter' and 'funny' have a double consonant because this stops the vowel in the suffix influencing the short stressed vowel in the root word; other words do not, either because the vowel in the root word is unstressed ('opened') or long ('reading') or because two consonants already form a wall between the vowels ('helper'). The main exception to this rule are words like 'travelling' and 'pedalled' which double the ‹l›, even though it follows a schwa. Verbs ending in ‹fer› follow the rule in the usual way: we write 'referral' when the ‹fer› is stressed, but 'reference' when it is not. The main exception is the word 'transferable', which has a stressed ‹fer› but only one ‹r›.

Spelling list: Go through the list, discuss the meaning of any unfamiliar words, and ask the class to find and highlight the ‹fer› spelling each time. If the word has a suffix, ask the children where the stress is, and point out how the ‹r› is doubled if ‹fer› is stressed. Point out other spelling features, such as the ‹e› saying /i/ in 'refer', 'referral', 'prefer', 'preferred', 'defer' and 'deferred', the ‹al› spelling of /ool/ in 'referral', and the ‹-ence› suffix with a 'soft ‹c›' in the abstract nouns 'conference', 'deference', 'inference' and 'reference'. Remind the children about the prefixes ‹re-›, ‹trans-›, ‹pre-› and ‹de-›, and discuss how they add meaning to the words. It is a good idea to blend and sound out the spelling words quickly every day with the class, using the 'say it as it sounds' strategy where appropriate.

Spelling Sheet 15a: The children split each word into syllables to help remember the spelling *[1. re/fer, 2. re/fer/ral, 3. in/fer, 4. in/ferred, 5. trans/fer, 6. trans/fer/ring, 7. pre/fer, 8. pre/ferred, 9. de/fer, 10. de/ferred, 11. con/fer, 12. con/fer/ring, 13. of/fer, 14. of/fered, 15. con/fer/ence, 16. def/er/ence, 17. in/fer/ence, 18. ref/er/ence]*. They then write the meaning for each root word, using a dictionary if needed, and add the suffixes; they should double the ‹r› each time, except when ‹fer› is not stressed *[conference, deference, preference, offered, offering]*. Lastly, they look at the words in the sacks and identify the prefixes in the spelling words that have these meanings *[Right to left: ‹re-›, ‹de-›, ‹trans-›, ‹pre-›]*.

Spelling Sheet 15b: The children complete each sentence by making a list, using commas to separate the items. They then look at the lists below, which have items with commas, and write a semicolon in each box to separate them. Then they parse the sentence and complete the wall *[Top: bank - transferred - money / Bottom: The - to their account - the / Verb: action]*. 'To their account' is a prepositional phrase acting as an adverb, so orange brackets can be put around it.

The bank[N] transferred[V] the money[N] (to[Pre] their[Adj] account[N])[Adv].

Noun[N] (black), Verb[V] (red), Pronoun[P] (pink), Adjective[Adj] (blue), Adverb[Adv] (orange), Conjunction[C] (purple), Preposition[Pre] (green)

Dictation: (This can be done in the spelling lesson or at another time during the week.) Call out the sentences for the children to write down. Remind them to use speech marks with the correct punctuation in Sentence 3. 'Miss Beech' is a proper noun with initial capital letters.

1. The police are offering a reward for any information.
2. My friends preferred tennis and swimming to soccer.
3. "I will be at the conference next week," said Miss Beech.

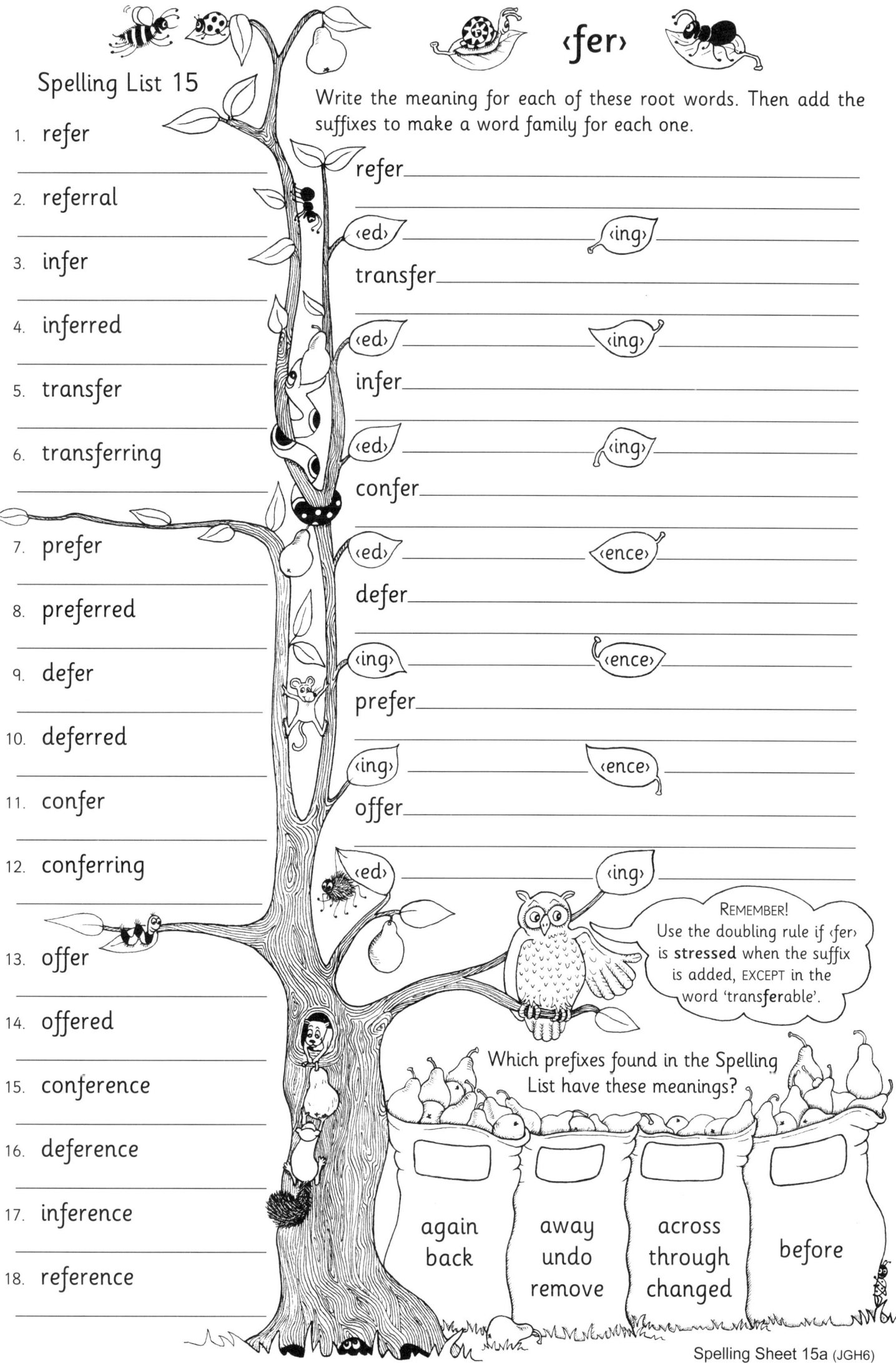

‹fer›

Spelling List 15

1. refer
2. referral
3. infer
4. inferred
5. transfer
6. transferring
7. prefer
8. preferred
9. defer
10. deferred
11. confer
12. conferring
13. offer
14. offered
15. conference
16. deference
17. inference
18. reference

Write the meaning for each of these root words. Then add the suffixes to make a word family for each one.

refer

‹ed›   ‹ing›

transfer

‹ed›   ‹ing›

infer

‹ed›   ‹ing›

confer

‹ed›   ‹ence›

defer

‹ing›   ‹ence›

prefer

‹ing›   ‹ence›

offer

‹ed›   ‹ing›

REMEMBER!
Use the doubling rule if ‹fer› is **stressed** when the suffix is added, EXCEPT in the word 'trans**fer**able'.

Which prefixes found in the Spelling List have these meanings?

again back | away undo remove | across through changed | before

Spelling Sheet 15a (JGH6)

Dictation: ‹fer›

1. _____

_____

2. _____

_____

3. _____

_____

Complete these sentences by making a list. Remember to use a comma to separate each item, except for the last two, which should be separated by 'and' instead.

1. On my walk I saw _____

_____

2. At the restaurant, the family ordered _____

_____

Sometimes, an item in a list already has a comma, such as 'a big, comfy chair' or 'a small, low table'. When this happens, you can use a semicolon instead of a comma to separate all the items. Look at the lists below and add the semicolons to make them more understandable.

3. For his birthday, Dad got some socks, gloves and slippers ☐ a warm, waterproof jacket ☐ and a black, green and gold mountain bike.

4. In Sam's lunchbox, there is a cheese, lettuce and tomato sandwich ☐ some raisins, nuts and pumpkin seeds ☐ and a red, shiny apple.

5. The singers in the concert are Marco from Rome, Italy ☐ Kimi from Tokyo, Japan ☐ Nate from Darwin, Australia ☐ and Miriam from Luxor, Egypt.

Parse the sentence and then write it on the wall.

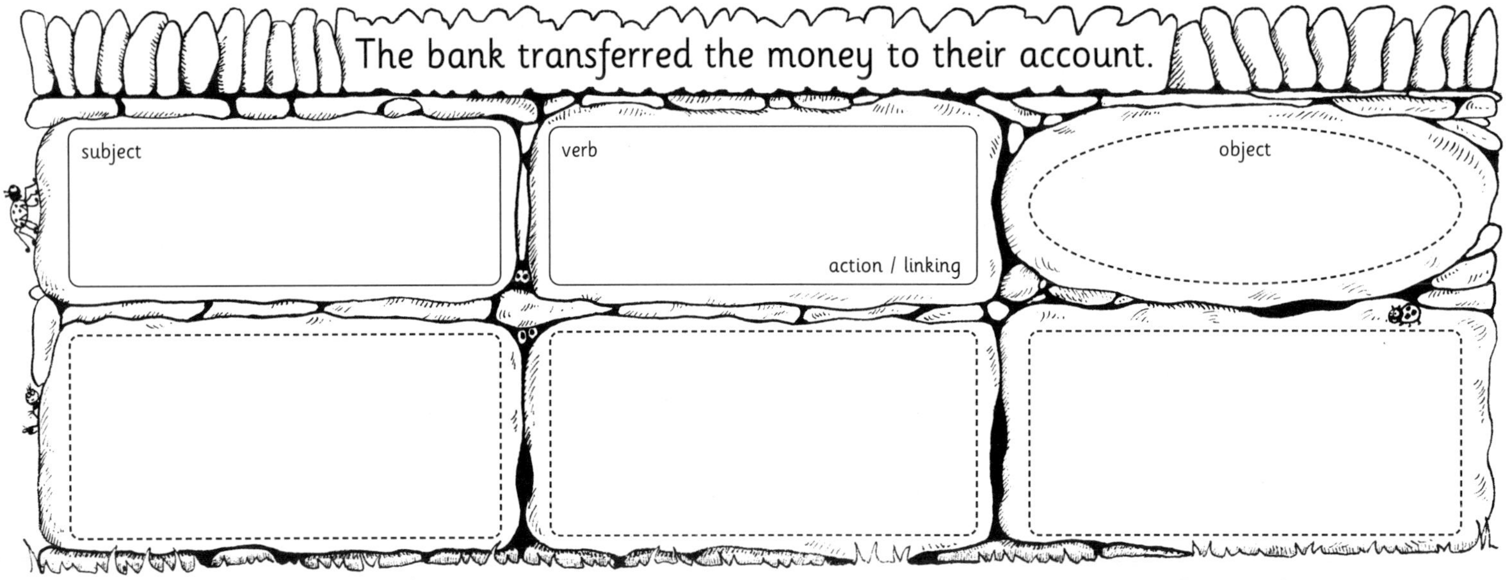

The bank transferred the money to their account.

subject	verb	object
	action / linking	

Grammar 15 – Colons in Sentences

Prepare...
Grammar Sheet 15
Coloured pencils

Builds on...
JGH5: G31
JGH6: G14

Aim: Extend the children's understanding of colons. Demonstrate that, as well as introducing a list of bullet points, a colon can be used in sentences to introduce things like a list of examples, a single idea or an explanation.

Introduction: Remind the class that punctuation helps us make sense of the words we use. A comma in the wrong place or a missing apostrophe can make our writing confusing or significantly change the meaning. Briefly revise the punctuation marks that the children know and discuss when they might be used. These include full stops, question marks, exclamation marks, commas, apostrophes, speech marks, hyphens, parentheses and semicolons (see Introduction, pages 23 to 27). On the board, write 'On the farm there were cows, sheep, goats and chickens' and discuss how commas can be used to separate the items in a list. Then show how the same list could be presented as bullet points for a presentation or report. Point out the differences, reminding the children that a vertical list always has an introduction that ends in a colon and does not have 'and' or 'or' before the final item.

Main point: Lists like the one above are very straightforward and only need commas to punctuate them in a sentence. Other lists, however, need more of an introduction, usually because they are very long or require more emphasis. On the board, write 'In our kitchen there are many things', without any punctuation. Ask the class what goes next and discuss how a full stop can be added, as the words form an independent clause or simple sentence. Another option is to expand the sentence by adding a list of what is in the kitchen. Explain that one way to do this is to add a colon, so the words become an introduction for the list. Add the colon, discuss what might be in the kitchen, and ask some children to come and make a long list to complete the sentence. Now write: 'In our kitchen there are five pans: a large frying pan, a small frying pan and three saucepans'. This list is not particularly long, but the introduction and colon tell us to expect two things: that there will be more information about the pans and that this information is important. Now write: 'There is only one thing wrong with our kitchen: it is too small'. Here there is no list at all, only a single idea, but the words and colon in the first clause are acting in the same way as before, introducing some more information and emphasising its importance. Here the information clarifies or identifies what 'the one thing' is, but it could also be an explanation or a set of examples. Tell the children that a colon can be thought of as a little fanfare, announcing the arrival of some important information. Write some more examples on the board and point out that the words before a colon always form an independent clause. This means a colon should never separate a verb from its object or complement (so we would never write 'I bought: eggs, milk and bread').

Grammar Sheet 15: The children write inside the outlined colon ⟨ ⟩ and then write one in each musical note, using a different colour each time. They then expand the sentences, adding a list of appropriate items each time, introduced by a colon. Remind the children to punctuate each list properly with commas and to move the full stop to the end. Then they decide whether Sentences 4 to 8 are using the colon correctly, putting ✓ in the banner for 'yes' *[Sentences 5, 7 and 8] or ✗ for 'no' [Sentences 4 and 6].* They then rewrite the incorrect sentences, making sure that the words in front of the colon can stand alone as a simple sentence *[For example, the first part could be rewritten as 'At the zoo I saw these creatures:' (Sentence 4) and 'Alex can play several instruments, including these:' (Sentence 6)].*

Extension activity: The children write some introductory sentences and swap them with a partner. They then expand each sentence by adding a list of items introduced by a colon.

Rounding off: Go over the sheet with the children, checking their answers. If they have done the extension activity, ask some of them to read out their lists.

Colons in Sentences

As well as introducing a list of bullet points, colons can also be used in sentences. We use a colon in our writing to introduce things like a **list of examples**, a **single idea** or an **explanation.** Write colons in the musical notes below, using a different colour each time.

Expand these sentences, using a colon to introduce a different list of examples each time.

1. We need to take the following items on our trip.

   _____

   _____

2. They sell many things at the market.

   _____

   _____

3. I bought these ingredients for the cake.

   _____

   _____

Identify which two sentences below are incorrect and rewrite them so that the colon is used properly.

REMEMBER! In a sentence, a colon is only used after an independent clause, and it never separates a verb from either its object or its complement.

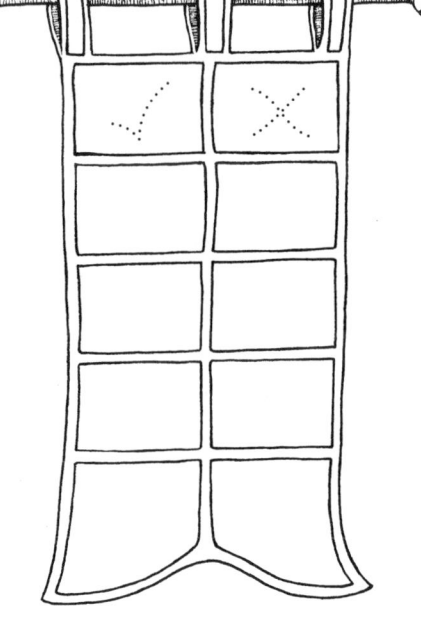

4. At the zoo I saw: raccoons, beavers, turtles, bears and many other animals.

5. There is an important reason to eat broccoli: it is extremely good for you.

6. Alex can play several instruments, including: the piccolo, the piano and the accordion.

7. Dad quickly poured me a glass of water: I had started to hiccup and could not stop.

8. Strange things occurred that night: clocks stopped, the mirror cracked and the owls shrieked loudly.

9. _____

   _____

10. _____

    _____

Spelling 16 – Spellings for the Long /oo/ Sound

Prepare...
Spelling Sheets 16a/b
Coloured pencils

Builds on...
JGH1: S17, S24
JGH3: S6, S24
JGH4: S15

Revision: Ask the children to suggest words that follow the spelling rule: 'If you want to say /ee/, it's ‹i› before ‹e›, except after ‹c›'. Write the following words on the board and ask the class to identify the sound that the ‹ei›, ‹eir› or ‹eigh› is making in each one: v**ei**l /ai/, rec**ei**ve /ee/, w**ei**rd /ear/, th**eir** /air/, f**ei**sty /ie/, counterf**ei**t /i/, h**ei**fer /e/, **eigh**th /ai/.

Main point: Revise the main ways the long /oo/ sound can be written and write them on the board; when the children are young, /oo/ is introduced as one of the sounds made by ‹oo›, as in 'moon', but they soon learn that it can also be represented by the /ue/ spellings, as in 'bl**ue**', 'J**u**ne', 'gr**ew**' and 'fl**u**'. Explain that there are other spelling patterns which are much less common, but which the children will know. Write the words 'fr**ui**t', 's**ou**p', 'sh**oe**' and 'm**o**vie' on the board and discuss which letters are making the /oo/ sound. See if the class can think of other words using these spellings and add them to the board. In Spelling Lesson 25, the children will be reminded that long /oo/ can also be written as ‹ough›, but this is a rare spelling and they are likely to come across it only in variations of the word 'through'.

Spelling list: Go through the list, discuss the meaning of any unfamiliar words, and ask the class to find and highlight the long /oo/ spelling each time. Point out other spelling features, such as the ‹ie› saying /ee/ in 'movie', the ‹ve› saying /v/ in 'prove', 'disapprove' and 'improvement', the ‹te› saying /t/ in 'route', the 'soft ‹c›' in 'juice', the ‹se› saying /z/ in 'bruise', the ‹e› saying /i/ in 'recruit' and 'removal', the prefix in '**re**cruit', '**re**moval', '**dis**approve' and '**im**provement', and the suffix in 'remov**al**', 'approv**al**' and 'improve**ment**'. It is a good idea to blend and sound out the spelling words quickly every day with the class, using the 'say it as it sounds' strategy where appropriate (stressing the pure sound of any schwas, for example, as in 'c**a**noe' and 'dis**a**pprove').

Spelling Sheet 16a: The children split each word into syllables to help remember the spelling *[1. fruit, 2. suit, 3. soup, 4. youth, 5. mov/ie, 6. prove, 7. shoe, 8. route, 9. ca/noe, 10. group, 11. juice, 12. bruise, 13. wound, 14. re/cruit, 15. re/mov/al, 16. ap/prov/al, 17. dis/ap/prove, 18. im/prove/ment].* They then write sentences for the first twelve spelling words.

Spelling Sheet 16b: The children write the name for each fruit *[Top: apple, banana, pear; Middle: watermelon, pineapple, orange; Bottom: grape, cherry, strawberry].* Then they parse the sentence and complete the wall *[Top: brother - showed - knee / Bottom: Robert's little -(blank) - his bruised / Indirect Object: nurse (the) / Verb: action].* 'Robert's' should be under-lined in blue, as possessive nouns always act as adjectives.

Robert's^{Adj} little^{Adj} brother^N showed^V the nurse^N his^{Adj} bruised^{Adj} knee^N.

Noun^N (black), Verb^V (red), Pronoun^P (pink), Adjective^{Adj} (blue), Adverb^{Adv} (orange), Conjunction^C (purple), Preposition^{Pre} (green)

Dictation: (This can be done in the spelling lesson or at another time during the week.) Call out the sentences for the children to write down. Remind them to use speech marks with the correct punctuation in Sentence 3. 'Jill' is a proper noun and needs a capital letter.

1. I lost my shoe as I got out of the canoe.
2. The movie tells the story of a wounded soldier.
3. "I can prove that you stole the suit!" exclaimed Jill.

Long /oo/ Spellings

Write a sentence for each of these spelling words.

1. fruit
2. suit
3. soup
4. youth
5. movie
6. prove
7. shoe
8. route
9. canoe
10. group
11. juice
12. bruise
13. wound
14. recruit
15. removal
16. approval
17. disapprove
18. improvement

soup _____

fruit _____

movie _____

youth _____

prove _____

suit _____

bruise _____

group _____

shoe _____

juice _____

route _____

canoe _____

Dictation: long /oo/

1. _____

_____

2. _____

_____

3. _____

_____

Write the name for each fruit. Some can be made into fruit juice – which juice do you like best?

_____   _____   _____

_____   _____   _____

_____   _____   _____

Parse the sentence and then write it on the wall.

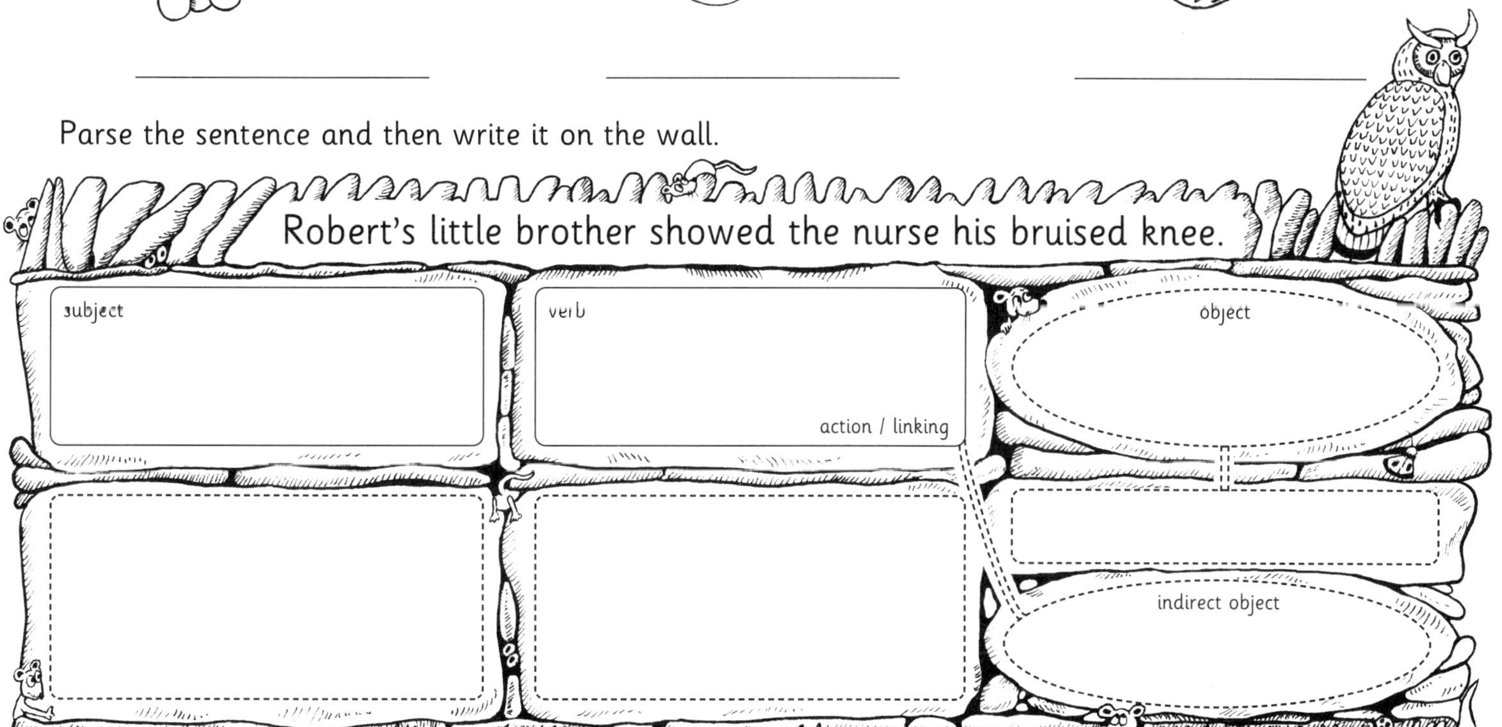

Robert's little brother showed the nurse his bruised knee.

subject	verb	object
	action / linking	
		indirect object

Grammar 16 – Subordinating Conjunctions

Prepare...
Grammar Sheet 16
Purple & red pencils

Builds on...
JGH2: G23
JGH4: G27, G30
JGH6: G11-13

Aim: Reinforce the children's knowledge of conjunctions. Explain that those which are used to join a 'main' or 'independent' clause to a 'subordinate' or 'dependent' one are called subordinating conjunctions.

Introduction: Briefly revise the coordinating conjunctions ('for', 'and', 'nor', 'but', 'or', 'yet' and 'so'), which are used to join words, phrases and clauses of equal importance and can be remembered by the acronym FANBOYS. These conjunctions always go between the parts they are joining and, like other conjunctions, they express meaning, explaining why ('for'), adding or excluding more information ('and'/'nor'), showing a general or strong contrast ('but'/'yet'), giving an alternative ('or'), or showing the consequences ('so'). Coordinating conjunctions can be used to join two independent clauses in a compound sentence: for example, 'I read a book and you wrote a story'. Write this sentence on the board and identify the two clauses, underlining 'and' first in purple, and then asking the class to identify the subject and verb on either side of the conjunction [I read/you wrote].

Main point: Remind the class that not all clauses are independent; some have a subject and verb but cannot stand alone as a simple sentence. These are called 'dependent' clauses because they depend on more information for their meaning. Write two examples on the board: 'which I found in my pocket' and 'when the sun shines'. Identify the subject and verb in each clause [I found/sun shines] and discuss how they are dependent because we are left to wonder what was found in the pocket and what happens when the sun shines. Remind the class that the first example is a special kind of dependent clause, more commonly known as a relative clause. This is because it starts with a relative pronoun ('which') that relates the clause to what it is describing. However, most dependent clauses are like the second example and start with a **subordinating** conjunction, so called because it joins a main clause to a subordinate one. Remind the class that the prefix ‹sub-› means 'below' or 'under' and so 'subordinate' means 'ranked/ordered below'. Explain that a subordinating conjunction, unlike a coordinating one, is part of the clause itself. We can see this by putting the clause into a sentence, such as 'We play outside when the sun shines'. If we wanted to put the clause at the beginning of the sentence, we would also have to move the conjunction because it is part of the clause: 'When the sun shines, we play outside'. (In Grammar Lesson 19 the children will learn that dependent clauses can be moved in this way because they are acting as adverbs.) Point out that we cannot do this in a compound sentence: for example, we would never write 'And you wrote a story, I read a book'. Call out some subordinating conjunctions, such as 'if', 'because', 'although', 'unless', 'while' and 'wherever', and ask the children to put them into subordinate clauses.

Grammar Sheet 16: The children write inside the outlined word Conjunctions, using a purple pencil. They then parse each subordinate clause, underlining the subordinate conjunction in purple, drawing a box with a small ‹s› around the subject and underlining the verb in red [1. because / they / offered, 2. whereas / Ben / preferred, 3. while / you / are painting, 4. although / she / had, 5. whether / you / call, 6. unless / you / accompany, 7. until / we / achieve, 8. when / horses / neigh, 9. once / we / have arrived, 10. if / I / embarrassed]. They then match each main clause to the correct subordinate clause, writing it on the line and adding a full stop to complete each sentence [11 and 5; 12 and 1; 13 and 10; 14 and 7; 15 and 2; 16 and 3; 17 and 4; 18 and 9; 19 and 6; 20 and 8].

Extension activity: Write on the board the subordinate clauses that the class thought of earlier and ask the children to put them into sentences.

Rounding off: Go over the sheet/extension activity with the class, discussing the answers.

Subordinating Conjunctions

Unlike coordinating conjunctions, which join together clauses of equal importance, a **subordinating conjunction** joins the 'main' or 'independent' clause in a sentence to a less important 'subordinate' or 'dependent' one.

A subordinate clause starts with a subordinating conjunction and always contains a verb and subject. In each clause below, underline the conjunction in purple and the verb in red, and identify the subject.

1. because they offered to help
2. whereas Ben preferred chocolate
3. while you are painting the ceiling
4. although she had some interruptions
5. whether you call it soccer or football
6. unless you accompany me
7. until we achieve our goal
8. when the horses neigh
9. once we have arrived
10. if I embarrassed you

Complete these sentences by matching each subordinate clause above to the correct main clause below.

11. It is the same game _____

12. I thanked my friends _____

13. I am really sorry _____

14. We will not give up _____

15. His sisters loved ice cream _____

16. I will be holding the ladder _____

17. Sam finished her work _____

18. We can unpack our things _____

19. Miss Beech says I cannot go _____

20. The donkeys often bray _____

Spelling 17 – Spellings for the /ai/ Sound

Prepare...
Spelling Sheets 17a/b
Coloured pencils

Builds on...
JGH1: S14, S19
JGH2: S13, S31
JGH3: S2, S19
JGH6: S7

Revision: Write these words on the board and ask the class to identify the letters saying /ai/ in each one: expl**ai**n, **A**pril, Thursd**ay**, decor**a**te, b**ei**ge, n**eigh**. Ask the class to suggest other words with these spellings.

Main point: Other spelling patterns exist for the /ai/ sound, besides the more common ones. It can be written as ‹ey›, usually at the end of words like 'they', 'obey' and 'prey', or as ‹et› in words with a French origin, such as 'ballet', 'sorbet' and 'cabaret'. There are only three common words with the ‹ea› spelling, which can be remembered as 'Let's break for a great big steak', while the spellings in 'fete' and 'straight' are much rarer. See if the children can think of other words with these spellings and write them on the board.

Spelling list: Go through the list, discuss the meaning of any unfamiliar words, and ask the class to find and highlight the /ai/ spelling each time. Point out other spelling features, such as the ‹k› spelling after the long vowel in 'break' and 'steak', the double letters in 'ballet' and 'buffet', the different spellings of /ai/ in 'heyday', the ‹o› saying its long vowel sound in 'obey', the ‹ch› saying /sh/ in 'sachet', the ‹ou› spelling for the different vowel sounds in 'bouquet' and 'gourmet', the ‹qu› saying /k/ in 'bouquet', and the ‹ur› spelling of /er/ in 'survey'. Discuss how the words 'prey', 'break', 'great' and 'steak' have the homophones 'pray', 'brake', 'grate' and 'stake' and point out that here 'buffet' is a noun, but when it is pronounced /bufit/ it is a verb with a totally different meaning. Ask the class what words that look the same but sound different and have different meanings are called [*heteronyms*]. It is a good idea to blend and sound out the spelling words quickly every day with the class, using the 'say it as it sounds' strategy where appropriate (stressing the pure sound of any schwas, for example, as in '**c**onvey' and 'cab**a**ret').

Spelling Sheet 17a: The children split each word into syllables to help remember the spelling [*1. they, 2. prey, 3. break, 4. great, 5. steak, 6. bal/let, 7. hey/day, 8. fete, 9. buf/fet, 10. con/vey, 11. o/bey, 12. sor/bet, 13. sach/et, 14. straight, 15. bou/quet, 16. gour/met, 17. sur/vey, 18. cab/a/ret*] and write in the missing letters [*Top: ob**ey**, st**ea**k, pr**ey**; buff**et**, surv**ey**, ball**et** / Middle: gourm**et**, cabar**et**; h**ey**day, bouqu**et** / Bottom: br**ea**k, th**ey**, gr**ea**t; sach**et**, conv**ey**, sorb**et***]. They then sort the spelling list words, according to their /ai/ spelling [*‹ea›: break, great, steak; ‹et›: ballet, buffet, sorbet, sachet, bouquet, gourmet, cabaret; ‹ey›: they, prey, heyday, convey, obey, survey*] and identify the missing words [*fete, straight*].

Spelling Sheet 17b: The children write the meanings for each pair of homophones, using a dictionary to help them if needed. Then they parse the sentence and complete the wall [*Top: dancer - received - bouquet / Bottom: The great ballet - (blank) - a huge/of lilies / Verb: action*]. 'Ballet' is a noun acting as an adjective and should be underlined in blue. The prepositional phrase 'of lilies' describes the bouquet, so blue brackets can be put around it.

The great[Adj] ballet[Adj] dancer[N] received[V] a huge[Adj] bouquet[N] (of[Pre] lilies[N])[Adj].

Noun[N] (black), Verb[V] (red), Pronoun[P] (pink), Adjective[Adj] (blue), Adverb[Adv] (orange), Conjunction[C] (purple), Preposition[Pre] (green)

Dictation: (This can be done in the spelling lesson or at another time during the week.) Call out the sentences for the children to write down. Sentence 1 starts with a prepositional phrase, which is often separated from the rest of the sentence by a comma. Remind the children to use speech marks with the correct punctuation in Sentence 2.

1. In its heyday, it was a great place for a weekend break.
2. "The dog obeyed my command straight away!" I exclaimed.
3. She had a big steak and lemon sorbet at the gourmet restaurant.

/ai/ Spellings

Spelling List 17

1. they
_____
2. prey
_____
3. break
_____
4. great
_____
5. steak
_____
6. ballet
_____
7. heyday
_____
8. fete
_____
9. buffet
_____
10. convey
_____
11. obey
_____
12. sorbet
_____
13. sachet
_____
14. straight
_____
15. bouquet
_____
16. gourmet
_____
17. survey
_____
18. cabaret
_____

Add the missing letters for /ai/ – ‹ey›, ‹ea› or ‹et› – to complete these Spelling List words.

ob____   st____k   pr____

buff____   surv____   ball____

gourm____   cabar____

h____day   bouqu____

br____k   th____   gr____t

sach____   conv____   sorb____

‹ea›
‹et›
‹ey›

Sort the Spelling List words into their spelling groups. This leaves two that have unusual spellings for /ai/. Which words are they?

_____   _____

Dictation: /ai/

1. _____
   _____

2. _____
   _____

3. _____
   _____

Write the meanings for these pairs of homophones. Use a dictionary if you need to check.

steak

stake

great

grate

break

brake

prey

pray

Parse the sentence and then write it on the wall.

The great ballet dancer received a huge bouquet of lilies.

subject	verb	object
	action / linking	

Grammar 17 – Complex Sentences

Prepare...
Grammar Sheet 17
Purple & red pencils

Builds on...
JGH2: G23
JGH4: G27, G30
JGH6: G11-14, G16

Aim: Introduce the term 'complex sentence' to describe a sentence with a main clause and a subordinate one. Explain that the main clause always has the important information, while the subordinate one tells us more about it, describing, for example, when, where or why it happened.

Introduction: Briefly revise clauses with the class. A clause is a group of words that makes sense and contains a subject and verb. If it can stand alone as a simple sentence, it is called an 'independent' or 'main' clause, but if it depends on more information for its meaning, it is called a 'dependent' or 'subordinate' one. Relative clauses, which are a special kind of dependent clause, begin with a relative pronoun ('who', 'which', 'that', 'whom', 'whose') or adverb ('where', 'when', 'why') that relates the clause to what it is describing; however, most dependent clauses start with a subordinating conjunction, so called because it tells us that the clause it belongs to is 'ranked below' the main clause in terms of importance. Call out some subordinating conjunctions, such as 'if', 'because', 'although', 'unless', 'while' and 'wherever', and ask the children to put them into sentences.

Main point: Ask the children what kinds of sentence they know; they should be able to name **simple** sentences, which have only one (independent) clause, and also **compound** sentences, where two independent clauses are joined together with either a coordinating conjunction or a semicolon. Point out that they know another type of sentence: one which has both an independent clause and a dependent clause. Explain that this is called a **complex** sentence and it can usually be written by starting with either clause (but not when there is a relative clause). Also explain that when the dependent clause comes first we separate the clauses with a comma. Show this on the board, using some of the sentences suggested earlier by the class, and identify which clause is which each time. Ask some children to come up and put square brackets around the independent clauses. Point out that these always contain the most important information, which is why they are called main clauses. The dependent clauses, which provide extra information that cannot be used alone, are not so important and this is why they are described as subordinate. Look at the examples on the board and discuss what each subordinate clause is telling us about the main clause. Some explain it (using conjunctions like 'because', 'since' and 'as'), some provide a contrast to it (with conjunctions like 'though', 'while' and 'although'), and others make the clause conditional (using 'if' and 'unless'). Many indicate time (with 'as', 'while', 'when', 'after', 'before', 'until', 'since' and 'whenever') and a few indicate place (with 'where', 'wherever' and 'everywhere').

Grammar Sheet 17: The children look at the two clauses in each sentence and draw a box with a small ‹s› around the subjects and underline the verbs in red [1. Ted drank/he finished, 2. I will clean/I go, 3. Granny hummed/she stirred, 4. We eat/we go, 5. route was/they went, 6. Dad has worn/he bought]. They then put square brackets around the main clause and underline the conjunction at the beginning of the subordinate clause in purple: 1. [Ted drank some fruit juice] <u>after</u> he finished his toast, 2. [I will clean my shoes] <u>before</u> I go to school, 3. [Granny hummed a tune] <u>as</u> she stirred the soup, 4. [We always eat popcorn] <u>whenever</u> we go to the movies, 5. [The route was hard and dangerous] <u>wherever</u> they went, 6. [Dad has worn the suit twice] <u>since</u> he bought it]. They then rewrite the sentences, putting the subordinate clause first. They should remember to add the comma and make sure that the main clause no longer starts with a capital letter (unless it is a proper noun).

Extension activity: The children look at each sentence on Grammar Sheet 17 and think about what kind of extra information the subordinate clause is giving (all the sentences say something about when the main clause happens, except for Sentence 5, which says where).

Rounding off: Go over the sheet/extension activity with the class, discussing the answers.

Complex Sentences

A sentence with an independent clause and a subordinate clause is called a **complex** sentence.

The **main** or 'independent' clause has the important information we need to know about something.

The **subordinate** or 'dependent' clause provides extra detail, such as telling us more about when, where or why it happened.

Remember that subordinate clauses always start with a **subordinating conjunction**.

main clause + subordinate clause = complex sentence

Identify the main clause and subordinate clause in each sentence. Start by identifying the verb and subject in each clause. Then put square brackets around the main clause to show that this part of the sentence is the most important, and underline the conjunction belonging to the subordinate clause in purple.

1. [Ted drank some fruit juice] after he finished his toast.

2. I will clean my shoes before I go to school.

3. Granny hummed a tune as she stirred the soup.

4. We always eat popcorn whenever we go to the movies.

5. The route was hard and dangerous wherever they went.

6. Dad has worn the suit twice since he bought it.

subordinate clause + comma + main clause = complex sentence

We can change the rhythm of our writing and make it more interesting by putting the subordinate clause at the beginning of the sentence. When we do this, we separate the two clauses with a comma. Rewrite the sentences above in this way.

7. _____

8. _____

9. _____

10. _____

11. _____

12. _____

Spelling 18 – 'Silent ‹h›' Digraphs

Prepare...
Spelling Sheets 18a/b
Coloured pencils

Builds on...
JGH2: S1-4, S25-26
JGH3: S33
JGH4: S16, S19-20

Revision: Write these words on the board, and ask the children to find the silent letter in each one: plum**b**er, **w**riting, **k**nuckle, r**h**ythmic, **w**holesome, s**c**issors, si**g**npost, sand**c**astle. Ask the children if they can think of other words that have silent letters.

Main point: Remind the class that a silent letter often goes with a particular consonant to form a 'silent letter' digraph. Common pairings include ‹mb›, ‹wr›, ‹kn›, ‹rh›, ‹wh›, ‹sc›, ‹gn› and ‹st›. As we can see from ‹wh› and ‹wr›, sometimes the same silent letter can be used in different digraphs. This is particularly true of silent ‹h›, which is often paired with ‹r› but is also found with ‹w› and ‹g› in words like '<u>wh</u>isper' and '<u>gh</u>ostly'. There are less common 'silent ‹h›' digraphs too, such as ‹kh› and ‹dh› which – like ‹rh› – are found in words that have been borrowed from other languages. For example, words like 'khaki', 'Buddhism' and 'jodhpurs' come from India: 'khaki' means 'dust-coloured' in Urdu, 'Buddha' means 'enlightened' in Sanskrit and a pair of jodhpurs takes its name from the Indian city of Jodhpur; other words come from Arabic ('sheikh') and Egyptian ('ankh'), while ‹rh› words come from Greek.

Spelling list: Go through the list, discuss the meaning of any unfamiliar words, and ask the class to find and highlight the 'silent ‹h›' digraph each time. Point out other spelling features, such as the initial capital letter in the proper nouns 'Sikh' and 'Buddhism', the ‹i› saying /ee/ in 'Sikh', 'khaki' and 'dhoti', the ‹n› saying /ng/ in 'ankh', the way 'magic ‹e›' influences ‹y› to say /ie/ in 'rh**y**me' (whereas in 'rh**y**thm', 'rh**y**thmically' and 'g**y**mkhana' it says /i/), the ‹u› spelling in 'Buddhism', 'rhubarb' and 'sadhu', the vowel making its long sound in 'rh**i**no', 'dh**o**ti' and 'rh**i**noceros', the ‹ur› in 'jodhpurs', the ‹ei› saying /ai/ or /ee/ in 'sheikh', the 'soft ‹g›' in 'gymkhana' and 'soft ‹c›' in 'rhinoceros', and the ‹eu› saying /oo/ in 'rheumatism'. It is a good idea to blend and sound out the spelling words quickly every day with the class, using the 'say it as it sounds' strategy where appropriate (stressing the pure sound of any schwas, for example, as in 'rhinoc**e**ros').

Spelling Sheet 18a: The children split each word into syllables to help remember the spelling *[1. Sikh, 2. ankh, 3. kha/ki, 4. rhyme, 5. rhyth/m, 6. Bud/dhis/m, 7. rhi/no, 8. jodh/purs, 9. rhu/barb, 10. rhom/bus, 11. rhap/so/dy, 12. sheikh, 13. dho/ti, 14. sa/dhu, 15. gym/kha/na, 16. rhi/noc/er/os, 17. rheu/ma/tis/m, 18. rhyth/mi/cal/ly].* They then work out the answers to the crossword clues and write them in *[1. ankh, 2. rhythmically, 3. Buddhism, 4. rhythm, 5. gymkhana, 6. Sikh, 7. rheumatism, 8. sheikh, 9. dhoti, 10. rhombus, 11. sadhu, 12. khaki, 13. rhyme, 14. jodhpurs, 15. rhapsody, 16. rhubarb, 17. rhino, 18. rhinoceros].*

Spelling Sheet 18b: The children write rhyming words and use some of them in a short poem. Then they parse the sentence and complete the wall *[Top: Dad - has bought - shorts / Bottom: (blank) - (blank) - the khaki/with the big pockets / Verb: action].* 'With the big pockets' is a prepositional phrase describing the shorts, so blue brackets can be put around it.

Dad^N (has bought)^V the khaki^Adj shorts^N (with^Pre the big^Adj pockets^N)^Adj.

Noun^N (black), Verb^V (red), Pronoun^P (pink), Adjective^Adj (blue), Adverb^Adv (orange), Conjunction^C (purple), Preposition^Pre (green)

Dictation: (This can be done in the spelling lesson or at another time during the week.) Call out the sentences for the children to write down. Remind them to use speech marks with the correct punctuation in Sentence 1. 'Egypt' is a proper noun and needs a capital letter.

1. "Can I wear my jodhpurs to the gymkhana?" she asked.
2. My book on ancient Egypt has a great picture of an ankh.
3. Our grandfather showed us the best way to grow rhubarb.

Spelling List 18

1. Sikh
2. ankh
3. khaki
4. rhyme
5. rhythm
6. Buddhism
7. rhino
8. jodhpurs
9. rhubarb
10. rhombus
11. rhapsody
12. sheikh
13. dhoti
14. sadhu
15. gymkhana
16. rhinoceros
17. rheumatism
18. rhythmically

Work out the answers to the clues and complete the crossword. All of the answers are words in the Spelling List.

1. an ancient Egyptian symbol, meaning 'life'
2. music and dance can be performed in this way
3. a religion, originally from east and central Asia
4. a strong pattern of sounds or movements that is repeated regularly
5. a day of horse racing and jumping competitions
6. a member of a religious group, founded in India
7. a disease that makes your joints stiff and painful
8. an Arab prince, ruler or chief
9. a traditional Indian garment, worn by men
10. a shape like a square but with sloping sides
11. a Hindu holy man who lives a very simple life
12. a light shade of yellow-brown or green-brown
13. another word for a short poem or verse
14. special trousers sometimes worn when riding horses
15. a piece of classical music expressing great emotion
16. thick red plant stems that can be cooked and eaten
17. a shorter way of saying Clue 18
18. a very big animal with one or two horns on its nose

Dictation: silent ‹h›

1. _____
   _____
2. _____
   _____
3. _____
   _____

Can you think of any words that rhyme with the ones below? Write an example for each one.

sheikh	suit	prey	arrive
acclaim	confer	canoe	rhyme
preferred	address	straight	buccaneer

Now try writing a short poem using some of these rhyming words.

Parse the sentence and then write it on the wall.

Dad has bought the khaki shorts with the big pockets.

subject	verb	object
	action / linking	

Grammar 18 – Simple, Compound and Complex Sentences

Prepare...
Grammar Sheet 18
Purple pencils

Builds on...
JGH2: G23
JGH4: G27, G30
JGH6: G11-14,
G16-G17

Aim: Reinforce the children's understanding of sentences, and enable them to recognise simple, compound and complex sentences more easily.

Introduction: Remind the class that several things are needed to make a group of words a sentence. A sentence must make sense, start with a capital letter, contain a verb and subject, and end with a full stop, question mark or exclamation mark. Write 'a chocolate cake' on the board and ask if this is a sentence. Although the words make sense, there is no verb or subject. Instead, all the words describe (or 'modify') the noun 'cake' and so we can identify them as a noun phrase. Now expand the phrase, adding a verb and subject to make it a sentence: for example, 'Tom made a chocolate cake'. Underline the verb *[made]* in red and ask the children to identify the subject *[Tom]* and object *[cake]*. Remind them that the subject does the verb action and the object (if there is one) receives the verb action. Now add the word 'Anna' after the verb and ask the class what this word is doing. Anna is the person <u>for whom</u> Tom made the cake, so she is the indirect object. Another thing that a sentence must have is at least one clause. Ask the children what the different clauses are called *['independent' or 'main' clauses, 'dependent' or 'subordinate' clauses, and relative clauses]*. Remind them that a sentence can be called simple, compound or complex, depending on which clauses are used and how many there are.

Main point: It is important to use different kinds of sentences in our writing to provide variety and interest. Write on the board 'Tom made a chocolate birthday cake for his friend Anna', and ask the class what kind of sentence it is. There is only one verb *[made]* with a subject *[Tom]* so the words form an independent clause which, when used on its own, is known as a **simple** sentence. Now write 'It is Anna's birthday, so Tom made her a chocolate cake' and discuss what kind of sentence this is. There are two clauses *[It is Anna's birthday/ Tom made her a chocolate cake]* joined by a coordinating conjunction, 'so'. Both are equally important and could stand alone as simple sentences, but together they form a **compound** sentence. Now write 'Tom made Anna a chocolate cake because it is her birthday'. Again, there are two clauses and a conjunction, but this time the clause 'because it is her birthday' is subordinate, or 'ranked below' the main clause, making this a **complex** sentence. Remind the class that most subordinate clauses start with a subordinating conjunction and can go at the start of the sentence; however, relative clauses (which are a special kind of subordinate clause) start with a pronoun or an adverb and do not work in this way.

Grammar Sheet 18: In each sentence, the children underline the conjunction in purple and put square brackets around any independent clauses, before deciding what kind of sentence it is: *1. [You are wrong]* <u>and</u> *[I can prove it]* COMPOUND, *2. [It was a cold day]* <u>so</u> *[Grandma made some soup]* COMPOUND, *3. [The children paddled their canoes down the river]* SIMPLE, *4. [They took umbrellas]* <u>because</u> *it was raining* COMPLEX, *5. [I am really tired now]* <u>but</u> *[I had a great time]* COMPOUND, *6. [The dog obeyed]* <u>whenever</u> *Jack said, "Sit"* COMPLEX, *7. [Uncle Jim loves steak with mashed potatoes]* SIMPLE, *8. [Joe likes ice cream,]* <u>yet</u> *[he has never tried sorbet]* COMPOUND, *9. [Do you want fruit]* <u>or</u> *[would you prefer chocolate?]* COMPOUND, *10. [Sally bruised her knee]* <u>when</u> *she fell off her bike* COMPLEX, *11. [The new gourmet restaurant is very expensive]* SIMPLE, *12. [Both the twins are doing ballet this year]* SIMPLE, *13. [I went straight home]* <u>before</u> *it got dark* COMPLEX, *14. [You will be in trouble]* <u>if</u> *you break anything* COMPLEX, *15. [We gave Sue a bouquet of flowers for her birthday]* SIMPLE.

Extension activity: The children write three sentences: one simple, one compound and one complex. They then swap sentences with a partner and identify which kinds they are.

Rounding off: Go over the sheet/extension activity with the class, discussing the answers.

Simple, Compound and Complex Sentences

A **simple** sentence (or 'independent clause') has a verb and a subject. It expresses a complete thought.
A **compound** sentence has two independent clauses, joined by a coordinating conjunction or a semicolon.
A **complex** sentence has a main (or 'independent') clause, plus a subordinate (or 'dependent') clause that starts with a subordinating conjunction or with a relative pronoun or adverb.

Are these sentences simple, compound or complex? Underline any conjunctions in purple, and put square brackets around the independent clauses. Then circle the answer you think is correct.

REMEMBER! If there is only an independent clause, circle 'simple'.

If there are two clauses joined by one of the FANBOYS conjunctions (for, and, nor, but, or, yet, so), circle 'compound'.

If there are two clauses and the one starting with the conjunction can be moved to the beginning of the sentence, circle 'complex'.

1. You are wrong and I can prove it.   simple · compound · complex

2. It was a cold day so Grandma made some soup.   simple · compound · complex

3. The children paddled their canoes down the river.   simple · compound · complex

4. They took umbrellas because it was raining.   simple · compound · complex

5. I am really tired now but I had a great time.   simple · compound · complex

6. The dog obeyed whenever Jack said, "Sit".   simple · compound · complex

7. Uncle Jim loves steak with mashed potatoes.   simple · compound · complex

8. Joe likes ice cream, yet he has never tried sorbet.   simple · compound · complex

9. Do you want fruit or would you prefer chocolate?   simple · compound · complex

10. Sally bruised her knee when she fell off her bike.   simple · compound · complex

11. The new gourmet restaurant is very expensive.   simple · compound · complex

12. Both the twins are doing ballet this year.   simple · compound · complex

13. I went straight home before it got dark.   simple · compound · complex

14. You will be in trouble if you break anything.   simple · compound · complex

15. We gave Sue a bouquet of flowers for her birthday.   simple · compound · complex

Grammar Sheet 18 (JGH6)

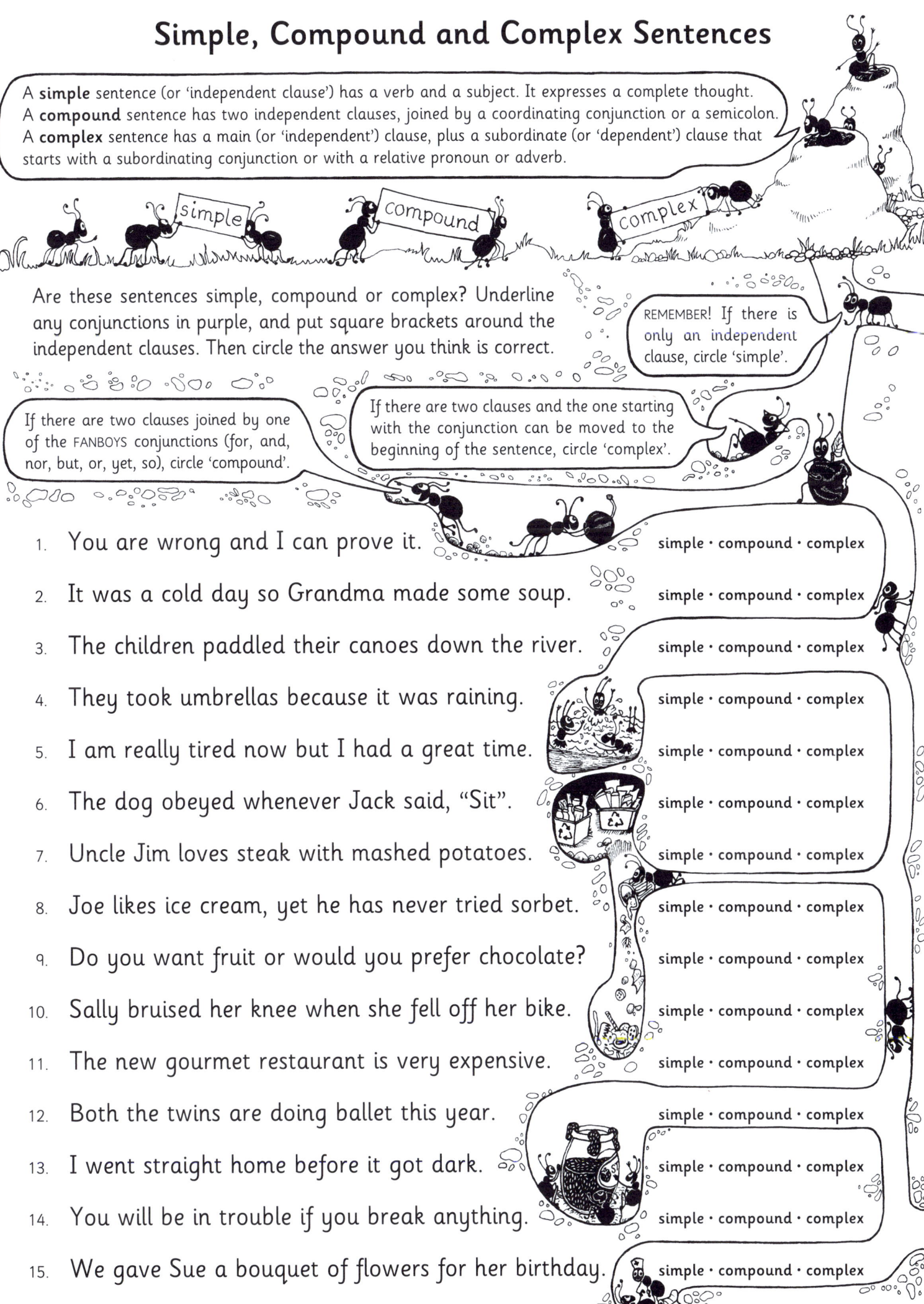

Spelling 19 – Spellings for the /t/ Sound

Prepare...
Spelling Sheets 19a/b
Coloured pencils
Builds on...
JGH2: S1-4, S25-26
JGH3: S33
JGH4: S16, S19-20
JGH6: S18

Revision: Write these words on the board, and ask the children to find the 'silent ‹h›' digraph in each one: din**gh**y, shei**kh**, **rh**ino, jo**dh**purs, **wh**eel, **rh**ombus, **kh**aki, Bud**dh**ism. Ask the children if they can think of other words that have a 'silent ‹h›' digraph.

Main point: The letter ‹t› is often paired with different silent letters to make the /t/ sound in words with a foreign origin. Common pairings include ‹**bt**›, ‹**te**›, ‹**tte**› and ‹**th**›. The 'silent letter' digraph ‹**bt**› is found in words with a Latin origin, as are some words ending in ‹**te**› (although others are Germanic). The ‹**tte**› spelling is found in words borrowed from French and usually indicates a smaller version of the root word, so a rosette is a small rose and a statuette is a small statue. (The word 'silhouette' is named after the French author and politician Étienne de Silhouette). The ‹**th**› digraph often appears in proper nouns, such as 'Es**th**er', '**Th**omas', '**Th**ailand' and 'the **Th**ames'. There is also a highly unusual spelling for /t/, which is the ‹**cht**› found in 'yacht'. This derives from 'jaghtschip', the Dutch word for a fast pirate ship.

Spelling list: Go through the list, discuss the meaning of any unfamiliar words, and ask the class to find and highlight the 'silent letter' digraph (or trigraph) saying /t/ each time. Point out other spelling features, such as the vowel making its long sound in 'p**a**ste', 'b**a**ste', 'r**o**sette' and 'f**a**vourite', the way 'magic ‹e›' influences ‹y› to say /ie/ in 'th**y**me', the initial capital letter in the proper noun 'Thailand' and its ‹ai› saying /ie/, the ‹a› saying /o/ in 'yacht', the ‹le› saying /ool/ at the end of 'subt**le**' and 'redoubt**le**', the ‹s› saying /z/ in 'ro**s**ette', the ‹e› saying /i/ in 'pal**e**tte' and 'r**e**doubtable', the ‹ui› saying /wee/ in 's**ui**te', the silent letters in 'baguette' and 'silhouette', the ‹u› and ‹ou› saying /oo/ in 'br**u**nette' and 'silh**ou**ette', and the suffix in 'redoubt**able**'. It is a good idea to blend and sound out the spelling words quickly every day with the class, using the 'say it as it sounds' strategy where appropriate (stressing the pure sound of any schwas, for example, as in 'def**i**nite', 'fav**ou**rite' and 'redoubt**able**').

Spelling Sheet 19a: The children split each word into syllables to help remember the spelling *[1. debt, 2. doubt, 3. paste, 4. baste, 5. thyme, 6. Thai/land, 7. yacht, 8. sub/tle, 9. ro/sette, 10. pal/ette, 11. def/i/nite, 12. fa/vour/ite, 13. suite, 14. ba/guette, 15. stat/u/ette, 16. bru/nette, 17. sil/hou/ette, 18. re/doubt/a/ble]*. They then write the meanings for the spelling words shown, using a dictionary if needed. Finally, they draw a picture for each of the words shown under the four easels.

Spelling Sheet 19b: The children think of a main clause to go with each subordinate clause and write it down. (They should add a comma after the subordinate clause if it is at the beginning.) They then decide whether the subordinate clause explains or provides a contrast to the main clause, states a condition of it, or places it in a particular time *[1. says when, 2. contrasts, 3. makes conditional, 4. explains]*. Then they parse the sentence and complete the wall *[Top: chef - had basted - potatoes / Bottom: The - definitely - the roast / Verb: action]*.

The chef^N had definitely^Adv basted^V the roast^Adj potatoes^N.

Noun^N (black), Verb^V (red), Pronoun^P (pink), Adjective^Adj (blue), Adverb^Adv (orange), Conjunction^C (purple), Preposition^Pre (green)

Dictation: (This can be done in the spelling lesson or at another time during the week.) Call out the sentences for the children to write down. Remind them to use speech marks with the correct punctuation in Sentence 3. 'Granny' is a proper noun and needs a capital letter.

1. Granny grows mint and thyme in her herb garden.
2. The winner of the talent show got a golden statuette.
3. "Would you like a cheese and tomato baguette?" I asked.

Spelling List 19

1. debt
   _____
2. doubt
   _____
3. paste
   _____
4. baste
   _____
5. thyme
   _____
6. Thailand
   _____
7. yacht
   _____
8. subtle
   _____
9. rosette
   _____
10. palette
    _____
11. definite
    _____
12. favourite
    _____
13. suite
    _____
14. baguette
    _____
15. statuette
    _____
16. brunette
    _____
17. silhouette
    _____
18. redoubtable
    _____

Spellings for /t/

Write the meaning for each of these spelling words.

1. debt _____
   _____
2. doubt _____
   _____
3. paste _____
   _____
4. thyme _____
   _____
5. Thailand _____
   _____
6. palette _____
   _____
7. brunette _____
   _____
8. silhouette _____
   _____

Draw a picture to illustrate each word.

yacht

rosette

baguette

statuette

Dictation: /t/

1. _____
   _____
2. _____
   _____
3. _____
   _____

Think of a main clause to go with each subordinate clause to make a complex sentence. Write the sentence down and remember to add a comma after the subordinate clause if it goes at the beginning. What does the subordinate clause tell us about the main clause?

1. after our trip to Thailand

   _____
   _____

   explains · contrasts · makes conditional · says when

2. although I had some doubts

   _____
   _____

   explains · contrasts · makes conditional · says when

3. unless you pay your debts

   _____
   _____

   explains · contrasts · makes conditional · says when

4. because the yacht was very fast

   _____
   _____

   explains · contrasts · makes conditional · says when

Parse the sentence and then write it on the wall.

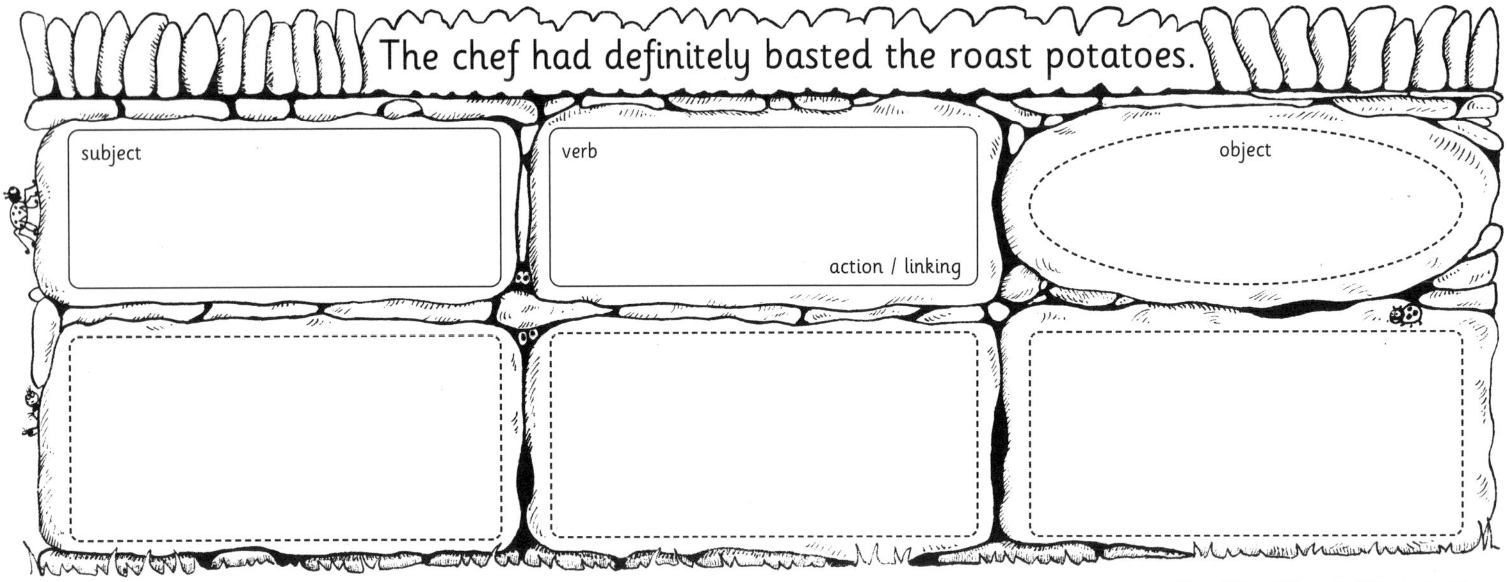

The chef had definitely basted the roast potatoes.

subject	verb	object
	action / linking	

Grammar 19 – Adverbials

Prepare...
Grammar Sheet 19
Orange pencils
Action cards

Builds on...
JGH1: G27-G28
JGH2: G15; JGH3: G21
JGH4: G29; JGH5: G11,
G14, G18, G25,
G26-G29; JGH6: G16

Aim: Introduce the term 'adverbial', which is used to describe any word, phrase or clause that acts as an adverb in a sentence. An adverbial placed at the beginning of a sentence is called a 'fronted' adverbial, and it is usually separated from the rest of the sentence by a comma.

Introduction: On the board, write the adverbs 'loudly', 'here', 'today' and 'sometimes'. Give out some action cards and ask the children to stand in the following order: definite article / noun / verb / adverb. Ask the class to think of a sentence for each adverb, using this sequence *[possible examples are 'The baby is crying loudly', 'The family moved here', 'The sale ends today', 'The boys argue sometimes']* and discuss how each adverb tells us more about how *[loudly]*, where *[here]*, when *[today]* or how often *[sometimes]* the verb is done. Also remind the class that some adverbs tell us how much or to what extent the verb is done, as in 'The plan almost worked'. Discuss how most adverbs can go in several different positions, but ones like 'almost' always go between the subject and verb or after the auxiliary verb (The plan <u>had</u> almost <u>worked</u>). Remind the class that some adverbs like 'really', 'very' and 'too' can also describe adverbs and adjectives.

Main point: With the class, parse one of the earlier sentences and put it into sentence wall boxes on the board (see pages 28 and 29 of the Introduction): for example, 'The family[N] moved[V] here[Adv] *[Top: family - moved - (blank) / Bottom: The - here - (blank)]*. Remind the children that 'here' goes in the box underneath the verb because it is an adverb telling us more about <u>where</u> the family moved. Ask them what else can go in this box *[prepositional phrases acting as adverbs]* and replace 'here' with 'in a hurry' on the sentence wall. Point out that if we parsed the new sentence, we would put orange brackets around this phrase because it tells us more about <u>how</u> the family moved. Now write 'The family moved because the house was too small' on the board. Identify the two clauses in this complex sentence and discuss what the subordinate clause tells us about the verb in the main clause *[it tells us <u>why</u> the family moved]*. Put orange brackets around 'because the house was too small' and write it in the box under the verb in the sentence wall. Explain that any word, phrase or clause that acts as an adverb in a sentence is called an **adverbial**. Adverbials tell us more about the main verb (and also sometimes about the whole sentence), such as how, where, when or why it happened. The most common adverbials are adverbs, noun phrases, prepositional phrases and subordinate clauses. Adverbial noun phrases express time, telling us when *[next Sunday, this month, tomorrow afternoon]*, how often *[every week, each year]*, or how long *[all day, the whole time]* something happens. Write 'The family moved last week' on the board and put orange brackets around 'last week'. Then put the sentence into the Wall, with the noun phrase in the box under the verb. Tell the class that when adverbials go at the start of a sentence, they are called **fronted adverbials**, which we usually follow with a comma.

Grammar Sheet 19: The children write inside the outlined word Adverbs, using an orange pencil. They then find the adverbial in each sentence, put orange brackets around it, and decide what it is telling them about the verb *[1. because I had the hiccups (WHY), 2. carefully (HOW), 3. on Tuesday (WHEN), 4. in silence (HOW), 5. wherever he goes (WHERE), 6. next month (WHEN), 7. in her hands (WHERE), 0. last year (WHEN), 9. at the beach (WHERE), 10. for my birthday (WHY), 11. rhythmically (HOW), 12. when we were young (WHEN)]*. They then rewrite six of the sentences so each has a fronted adverbial, separated from the rest of the sentence with a comma.

Extension activity: Write some adverbials on the board, such as 'across the room', 'as it was late', 'this morning' and 'suddenly' for the children to put into sentences. Remind the children that if they use a fronted adverbial, they must follow it with a comma.

Rounding off: Go over the sheet/extension activity with the class, discussing the answers.

Adverbials

An **adverbial** is any word, phrase or clause that acts as an adverb in a sentence. The most common adverbials are adverbs, noun phrases, prepositional phrases and subordinate clauses. They tell us more about, for example, **where, when, how** or **why** the verb is happening.

Identify the adverbial in each sentence and put orange brackets around it. Then decide what the adverbial is telling us about the verb.

1. I drank some water (because I had the hiccups).   How? · Where? · When? · Why?

2. Tom carefully drew a square and a rhombus.   How? · Where? · When? · Why?

3. They had rhubarb and custard on Tuesday.   How? · Where? · When? · Why?

4. The hungry wolf hunted its prey in silence.   How? · Where? · When? · Why?

5. Grandpa wears a suit wherever he goes.   How? · Where? · When? · Why?

6. There will be a gymkhana next month.   How? · Where? · When? · Why?

7. Grandma has rheumatism in her hands.   How? · Where? · When? · Why?

8. The zoo received a white rhino last year.   How? · Where? · When? · Why?

9. Anna wore her khaki shorts at the beach.   How? · Where? · When? · Why?

10. I got some new moccasins for my birthday.   How? · Where? · When? · Why?

11. The little brown crickets chirped rhythmically.   How? · Where? · When? · Why?

12. We loved nursery rhymes when we were young.   How? · Where? · When? · Why?

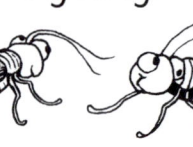

An adverbial that begins a sentence is called a **fronted adverbial.** We usually use a comma to separate a fronted adverbial from the rest of the sentence. Choose six of the sentences above and rewrite them so the adverbial is at the beginning, followed by a comma.

13. _____

14. _____

15. _____

16. _____

17. _____

18. _____

Spelling 20 – Spellings for the /**m**/ Sound

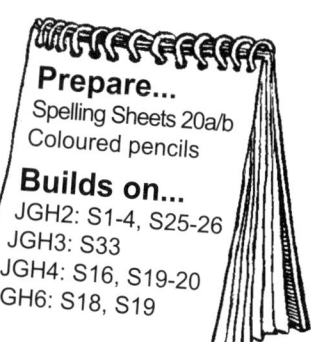

Prepare...
Spelling Sheets 20a/b
Coloured pencils

Builds on...
JGH2: S1-4, S25-26
JGH3: S33
JGH4: S16, S19-20
JGH6: S18, S19

Revision: Write these words on the board, and ask the children to identify the 'silent letter' digraph (or trigraph) saying /t/ in each one: dou<u>bt</u>, ya<u>cht</u>, pas<u>te</u>, su<u>bt</u>le, pale<u>tte</u>, sui<u>te</u>, brune<u>tte</u>, <u>th</u>yme. Ask the children if they can think of other words that have these spellings.

Main point: The letter ‹m› is often paired with different silent letters to make the /m/ sound. Common pairings include ‹mb›, ‹me› and ‹mn›. The 'silent letter' digraphs ‹mb› and ‹me› are found in words derived from Old and Middle English, some of which (such as 'tomb' and 'bomb') go further back to Latin and Greek, as do the words ending in ‹mn›. There is also a rarer spelling of /m/, sometimes used in British English, which is found in words like 'gra<u>mme</u>' and 'progra<u>mme</u>'. These words come from Latin and Greek via French and have kept the French spelling. They can also be spelt 'gram' and 'program'.

Spelling list: Go through the list, discuss the meaning of any unfamiliar words, and ask the class to find and highlight the 'silent letter' digraph saying /m/ each time. Point out other spelling features, such as the ‹o› saying /u/ in 'c**o**me', 's**o**me', 'inc**o**me', 'outc**o**me' and 'honeyc**o**mb', the ‹y› saying /i/ in 'hymn', the ‹au› spelling in 'autumn', the silent ‹d› in 'handsome', the ‹o› saying /oo/ in 't**o**mbstone' and the ‹ey› saying /ee/ and ‹o› saying its long vowel sound in 'honeyc**o**mb'. It is a good idea to blend and sound out the spelling words quickly every day with the class, using the 'say it as it sounds' strategy where appropriate (stressing the pure sound of any schwas, for example, as in 'welc**o**me' and 'sol**e**mn').

Spelling Sheet 20a: The children split each word into syllables to help remember the spelling *[1. numb, 2. bomb, 3. come, 4. some, 5. hymn, 6. au/tumn, 7. wel/come, 8. col/umn, 9. dumb, 10. sol/emn, 11. con/demn, 12. grue/some, 13. in/come, 14. out/come, 15. hand/some, 16. thumb/nail, 17. tomb/stone, 18. hon/ey/comb]*. They then write a sentence for each of the spelling words shown, using a dictionary to check the meaning if needed. Finally, they find the compound words in the spelling list *['income', 'outcome', 'thumbnail', 'tombstone', 'honeycomb']* and write three of them in the compound birds, putting the first part of the word in the bird's body and the second part in the tail. 'Handsome' is not really a compound word as ‹-some› is a suffix added to words to make adjectives.

Spelling Sheet 20b: The children think of an antonym and a synonym for each word. *[Possible answers include: pleasant, lovely/ghastly, hideous (gruesome); trust, believe/ distrust, suspect (doubt); tiny, ordinary, unpleasant/enormous, magnificent, enjoyable (great); unpleasant, discouraging, unpopular/pleasing, encouraging, desirable (welcome); leave, depart, retreat/ approach, arrive, reach (come); wrong, incorrect/correct, exact (accurate); carefree, lively/serious, stern (solemn); ugly, hideous/attractive, gorgeous (handsome)].* Then they parse the sentence and complete the wall *[Top: committee - gave - welcome / Bottom: The - (blank) - a courteous / Indirect Object: musicians (the) / Verb: action].*

The committee^N gave^V the musicians^N a courteous^Adj welcome^N.

Noun^N (black), Verb^V (red), Pronoun^P (pink), Adjective^Adj (blue), Adverb^Adv (orange), Conjunction^C (purple), Preposition^Pre (green)

Dictation: (This can be done in the spelling lesson or at another time during the week.) Call out the sentences for the children to write down. Remind them to use speech marks with the correct punctuation in Sentence 2. 'Roman' is a proper adjective and needs a capital letter.

1. The Roman temple had handsome marble columns.
2. "Come and try some lovely honeycomb," called the lady.
3. The gruesome monsters appeared among the tombstones.

Spellings for /m/

Spelling List 20

1. numb
2. bomb
3. come
4. some
5. hymn
6. autumn
7. welcome
8. column
9. dumb
10. solemn
11. condemn
12. gruesome
13. income
14. outcome
15. handsome
16. thumbnail
17. tombstone
18. honeycomb

Write a sentence for each of these spelling words.

numb _____

_____

hymn _____

_____

welcome _____

_____

column _____

_____

solemn _____

_____

condemn _____

_____

gruesome _____

_____

handsome _____

_____

honeycomb _____

_____

Can you find the compound words in the Spelling List?
Write three of them in the birds below.

Spelling Sheet 20a (JIGH6)

Dictation: /m/

1. _____

_____

2. _____

_____

3. _____

_____

Think of an antonym and a synonym for each word.

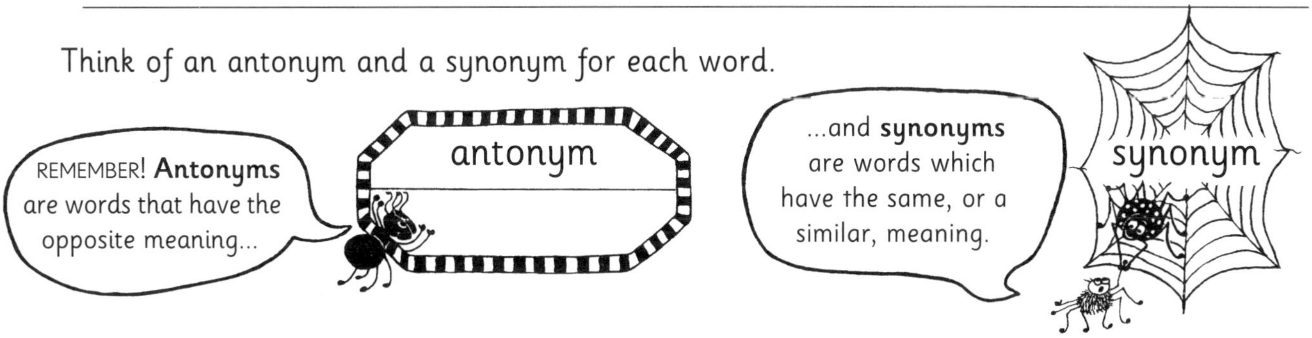

antonym

REMEMBER! **Antonyms** are words that have the opposite meaning...

...and **synonyms** are words which have the same, or a similar, meaning.

synonym

gruesome _____ _____

doubt _____ _____

great _____ _____

welcome _____ _____

come _____ _____

accurate _____ _____

solemn _____ _____

handsome _____ _____

Parse the sentence and then write it on the wall.

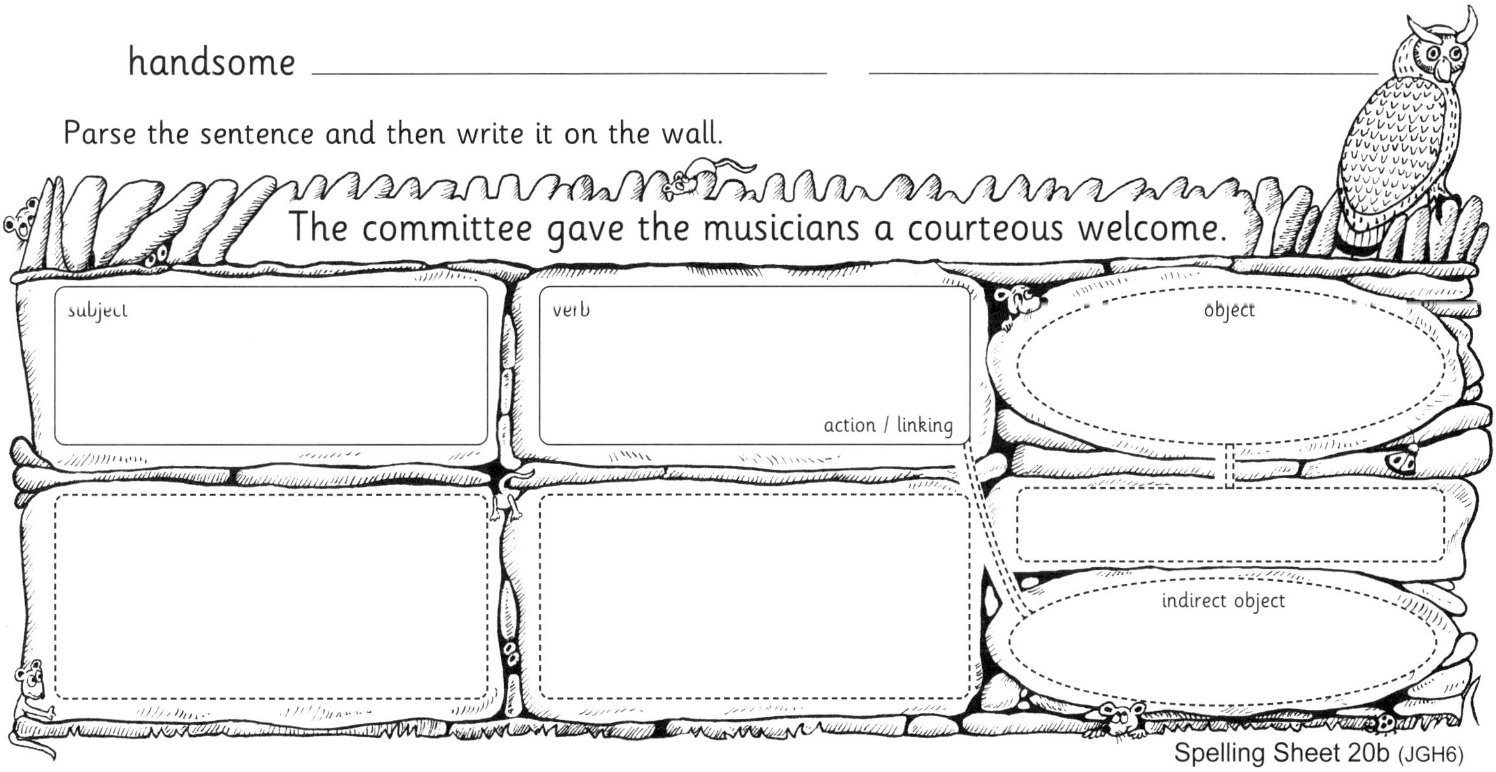

The committee gave the musicians a courteous welcome.

subject	verb	object
	action / linking	
		indirect object

Grammar 20 – Past Participles as Adjectives

Prepare...
Grammar Sheet 20
Blue & black pencils
(Dictionaries)

Builds on...
JGH1: G16-17
JGH2: G32
JGH3: G7-9, G17
JGH4: G11
JGH5: G6-7, G9

Aim: Refine the children's knowledge of participles, and develop their awareness that past participles, like present participles, can act as adjectives in a sentence.

Introduction: Remind the class that present participles (used in the continuous tenses) are completely regular, but past participles (used in the perfect tenses) can be regular or irregular, depending on the verb. If a verb is regular, its past participle is formed in the same way as the simple past tense, by adding the suffix ‹-ed›, but if the verb is irregular, the past participle can be formed in a variety of ways. Write the verbs 'climb', 'paste', 'slip', 'play' and 'hurry' on the board and discuss the spelling rules that are applied when making the past participles 'climbed', 'pasted', 'slipped', 'played' and 'hurried' (see pages 39 and 40). Then look at two common patterns for irregular verbs: 'ring/rang/rung' (where a change in vowel letter indicates a change in tense) and 'fall/fell/fallen' (where the vowel letter changes in the past tense, but the past participle is formed by adding ‹-n› or ‹-en› to the root verb). Ask the class to put some of these verbs into the perfect tenses *[for example: He has climbed the mountain three times; Someone will have rung the doorbell; Several people had slipped and fallen on the ice].*

Main point: As well as being used in the continuous and perfect tenses, participles can also be used as adjectives. Call out some present participles, ask the children to put each one into a noun phrase and write them on the board *[possible examples include: a crawling crab, the missing button, an annoying whine, a burning match, their flashing swords, some floating petals, a marching band].* Now do the same with some past participles *[examples include: piles of fallen leaves, a worried look, the hidden cave, two sliced onions, three beaten eggs, buried treasure, some stolen cars].* Look at some of the examples and compare the way that present and past participles act as adjectives. Explain that when present participles act as adjectives, they indicate an action that is still happening or that happens regularly, so that a missing button stays missing until it is found, and a marching band usually marches along as it plays. The action described is also usually done by the head noun (the main person or thing in the phrase). Past participles, however, usually indicate an action that has already happened and that is often done to the head noun, so the onions have already been sliced by someone and the treasure has already been buried by somebody. Past and present participles also differ when they concern feelings: for example, a story might be 'boring', 'interesting' or 'frightening' and we, in turn, can be 'bored', 'interested' or 'frightened' by the story. The present participles describe the thing that makes us feel a certain way and the past participles describe the way it makes us feel.

Grammar Sheet 20: The children write inside the outlined word Adjectives, using a blue pencil. They then write down the past participles *[broken, fried, frozen, torn, boiled, stolen],* applying the spelling rules for adding ‹-ed› and using a dictionary, if needed, to check any irregular verbs. Then they use the past participles to complete six sentences, deciding which adjective goes where *[1. fried, 2. broken, 3. torn, 4. stolen, 5. boiled, 6. frozen].* They should also underline these words in blue and the nouns they are describing in black. Finally, the children complete eight noun phrases by deciding what the past participles could be describing and expand four of them into sentences.

Extension activity: Write the verbs 'to freeze', 'to boil', 'to beat', 'to fall', 'to tire' and 'to terrify' on the board and ask the children to write down their present and past participles. They then use them as adjectives in some noun phrases or sentences.

Rounding off: Go over the sheet with the children, discussing their answers. If they have done the extension activity, ask some children to read out their sentences or phrases.

Past Participles as Adjectives

Some past participles are made by adding ‹-ed› to a regular verb, but many are irregular and have to be learnt. Look at the verbs below and write down the past participle for each one. If you are not sure, use a dictionary to help you.

to break   to fry   to freeze   to tear   to boil   to steal

_____ _____   _____ _____   _____ _____

Like present participles, past participles can be used as adjectives, as in 'the **fallen** tree'. Use your answers above to fill in the missing adjectives. Underline each adjective in blue and the noun it is describing in black.

1. He likes _____ onions with his steak.

2. One of my mother's shoes has a _____ heel.

3. Could you mend my _____ shirt straight away?

4. There is no doubt that the thieves hid the _____ money.

5. Dad mashed the _____ potatoes and cooked some broccoli.

6. Sorbet is a _____ dessert made from fruit juice, sugar and water.

What nouns could these past participles be describing?

the closed _____   the melted _____

an abandoned _____   a cracked _____

a knitted _____   the wrinkled _____

the chopped _____   the folded _____

Choose four of the noun phrases above and put them into sentences.

7. _____

_____

8. _____

_____

9. _____

_____

10. _____

_____

Spelling 21 – 'Silent ‹p›' Digraphs

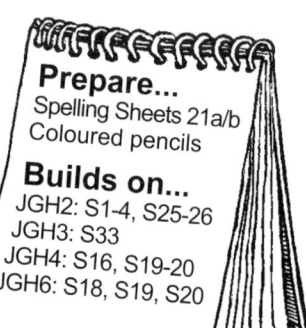

Revision: Write these words on the board, and ask the children to find the 'silent letter' digraph in each one: cli**mb**, aweso**me**, hy**mn**book, beco**me**, sole**mn**ly, cru**mb**, overco**me**, co**mb**. Ask the children if they can think of other words that have a 'silent letter' digraph that says /m/.

Main point: Remind the class that a silent letter often goes with a particular consonant to form a 'silent letter' digraph, such as ‹mb›, ‹wr›, ‹kn›, ‹rh›, ‹wh›, ‹sc›, ‹gn› and ‹st›. Sometimes, the same silent letter can be used in different digraphs: for example, silent ‹p› is often paired with ‹s›, ‹t› or ‹n› in words like '**p**salm', 'attem**p**t' and '**p**neumonia'. Words with these spellings are usually derived from other languages: ‹ps› and ‹pn› come from Greek, while ‹pt› comes from Latin.

Spelling list: Go through the list, discuss the meaning of any unfamiliar words, and ask the class to find and highlight the 'silent ‹p›' digraph each time. Point out other spelling features, such as the ‹al› saying /ar/ in 'psalm', the ‹y› saying /ie/ and the ‹ch› spelling of /k/ in 'psyche', 'psychiatry', 'psychology', 'psychiatrist' and 'psychological', the vowel saying its long sound in 'psych**e**', 'pseud**o**', 'pneum**o**nia', 'psych**i**atry', 'psych**i**atrist', 'ps**o**riasis' and 'ps**i**', the ‹eu› saying /ue/ in 'pseudo', 'pneumonia', 'pneumatic' and 'pseudonym', the ‹e› saying /i/, 'soft ‹c›' and ‹ei› saying /ee/ in 'receipt', the suffix in 'pneum**atic**', 'psych**ology**', 'psychiat**rist**' and 'psycholog**ical**', the ‹y› saying /ee/ at the end of 'psychiatry' and 'psychology', the 'soft ‹g›' in 'psychology' and 'psychological', and the ‹y› saying /i/ in 'pterodactyl' and 'pseudonym'. It is a good idea to blend and sound out the spelling words quickly every day with the class, using the 'say it as it sounds' strategy where appropriate (stressing the pure sound of any schwas, for example, as in '**a**ttempt and 'psychol**o**gy').

Spelling Sheet 21a: The children split each word into syllables to help remember the spelling *[1. psalm, 2. psy/che, 3. pseu/do, 4. tempt, 5. prompt, 6. at/tempt, 7. re/ceipt, 8. pneu/mo/ni/a, 9. pneu/mat/ic, 10. psy/chi/a/try, 11. psy/chol/o/gy, 12. pter/o/dac/tyl, 13. psy/chi/a/trist, 14. pseu/do/nym, 15. ptar/mi/gan, 16. pso/ri/a/sis, 17. psi, 18. psy/cho/log/i/cal].* They then put the spelling words into alphabetical order *[1. attempt, 2. pneumatic, 3. pneumonia, 4. prompt, 5. psalm, 6. pseudo, 7. pseudonym, 8. psi, 9. psoriasis, 10. psyche, 11. psychiatrist, 12. psychiatry, 13. psychological, 14. psychology, 15. ptarmigan, 16. pterodactyl, 17. receipt, 18. tempt].*

Spelling Sheet 21b: The children look up the word 'psychological' in the dictionary to check its meaning and make as many other words as they can with its letters. Then they parse the sentence and complete the wall *[Top: psoriasis - looked\sore (rather) - (blank) / Bottom: The/on the patient's arm - (blank) - (blank) / Verb: linking].* The verb 'looked' links the adjective complement 'sore' to the subject 'psoriasis' it is describing. 'On the patient's arm' is a prepositional phrase describing 'psoriasis', so it needs blue brackets.

The psoriasis[N] (on[Pre] the patient's[Adj] arm[N])[Adj] looked[V] rather[Adv] sore[Adj].

Noun[N] (black), Verb[V] (red), Pronoun[P] (pink), Adjective[Adj] (blue), Adverb[Adv] (orange), Conjunction[C] (purple), Preposition[Pre] (green)

Dictation: (This can be done in the spelling lesson or at another time during the week.) Call out the sentences for the children to write down. Remind them to use speech marks with the correct punctuation in Sentence 1. 'Miss Beech' is a proper noun and needs capital letters.

1. "A psalm is a hymn of praise," explained Miss Beech.
2. The psychiatrist will attempt some psychological tests.
3. The doctor had some doubts that the man had pneumonia.

'Silent ‹p› Digraphs'

Spelling List 21

1. psalm
2. psyche
3. pseudo
4. tempt
5. prompt
6. attempt
7. receipt
8. pneumonia
9. pneumatic
10. psychiatry
11. psychology
12. pterodactyl
13. psychiatrist
14. pseudonym
15. ptarmigan
16. psoriasis
17. psi
18. psychological

α β γ δ ε ζ η θ ι κ λ μ ν ξ ο π ρ σ τ υ φ χ ψ ω

Put the words in the Spelling List into alphabetical order.

1. _____
2. _____
3. _____
4. _____
5. _____
6. _____
7. _____
8. _____
9. _____
10. _____
11. _____
12. _____
13. _____
14. _____
15. _____
16. _____
17. _____
18. _____

a b c d e f g h i j k l m n o p q r s t u v w x y z

Dictation: silent ‹p›

αβγδεζηθικλμνξοπρστυφχψω

1. _____

_____

2. _____

_____

3. _____

_____

Check what this word means and see how many other words you can make with its letters.

p s y c h o l o g i c a l

Parse the sentence and then write it on the wall.

The psoriasis on the patient's arm looked rather sore.

subject

verb

action / linking

object

Grammar 21 – The Active and Passive Voice

Prepare...
Grammar Sheet 21
Red pencils

Builds on...
JGH3: G25-27, G35
JGH4: G3,
JGH5: G15-17
JGH6: G6-7

Aim: Introduce the idea that a sentence can be written in either an active or a passive voice. When the subject of the sentence **does** the verb action, we are writing in the active voice, but if the subject **receives** the verb action, we are writing in the passive voice.

Introduction: Remind the class that a sentence always has a verb and subject and, if the verb is transitive, it will also have an object. Discuss how the subject and object are identified by deciding who or what is **doing** the verb action *[the subject]* and who or what is **receiving** it *[the object].* Point out that sometimes the subject or object is compound, and that most 'simple' subjects and objects are part of a longer noun phrase. Also remind the class that the verb action has either a direct or an indirect effect on an object: the person or thing receiving the verb action is called the **direct object** and the person or thing <u>for whom</u> or <u>to whom</u> the verb action is done is called the **indirect object**. Write 'Granny and Grandpa sent their eldest grandchildren cards and presents' on the board and discuss it with the class. Point out the transitive verb 'sent'; the compound subjects *[Granny/Grandpa]* and direct objects *[cards/presents];* and the indirect object *[grandchildren]*, which is part of a longer noun phrase *[their eldest grandchildren].*

Main point: Not all sentences have a subject that performs the verb action. Sometimes the 'doer' of the verb is not known, or is considered less important, so the focus is put on the person or thing that receives the verb action instead. Write on the board 'The cars were stolen by the thieves last night' and ask the children to find the subject of the sentence. They will probably identify it correctly, because 'cars' appears before the verb and is the main focus of the sentence. However, they may also recognise that this subject is unusual, because it is not doing the stealing. Instead, the 'doer' or 'agent' of the verb action appears in the prepositional phrase 'by the thieves', which comes after the verb. In fact, this phrase could be removed and the sentence would still make sense. Explain that when the subject of a sentence is actively doing the verb, we say it is written in the **active voice**, but when the subject is passive and receives the verb action, it is written in the **passive voice**. Write some more examples on the board, such as 'The thieves have been arrested', 'Our bikes are kept in the garage', 'The cake was baked by Sue yesterday' and 'The fence will be painted today', and identify the verb and subject each time, along with the agent, if there is one. Look at the verb in each sentence and point out that it is formed in a special way in the passive voice, using the verb 'to be' as an auxiliary with the past participle of the main verb.

Grammar Sheet 21: The children write inside the outlined word 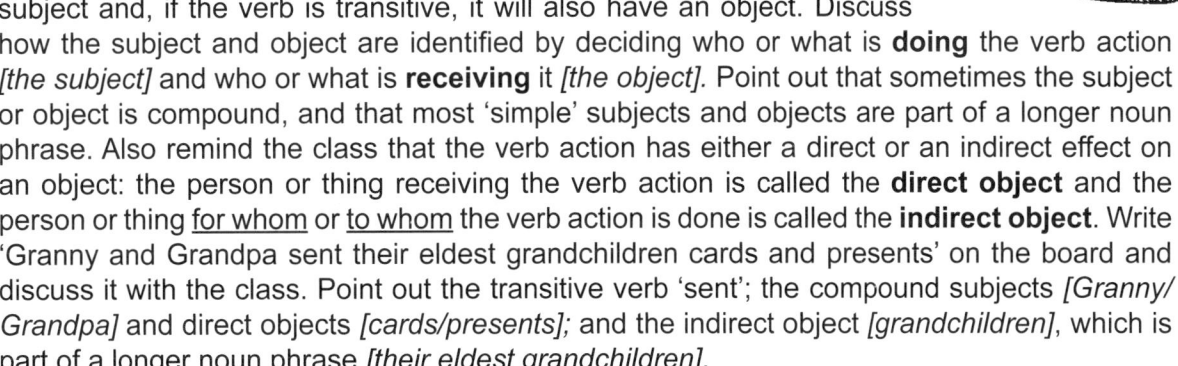 Verbs, using a red pencil. They then look at each pair of sentences and decide which is written in the active voice and which is written in the passive *[1. passive (yacht <u>was sailed</u>)/active (crew <u>sailed</u>), 2. active (Bees <u>store</u>)/passive (Honey <u>is stored</u>), 3. active (We <u>welcomed</u>)/passive (guests <u>were welcomed</u>), 4. passive (seeds <u>will be planted</u>/active (gardener <u>will plant</u>)].* They then look at each sentence below, identify the verb and subject, and decide whether it is written in the active or passive voice *[5. passive (hymn <u>was sung</u>), 6. active (Sam <u>bruised</u>), 7. active (Rhinos <u>come</u>), 8. passive (chicken <u>was basted</u>), 9. active (leaves <u>fell</u>), 10. passive (roselle <u>was awarded</u>), 11. passive (toothpaste <u>is kept</u>), 12. active (Lucy <u>went</u>), 13. passive (baguettes <u>are made</u>), 14. active (Granny <u>gave</u>)].*

Extension activity: The children put some passive sentences from Grammar Sheet 21 into six sentence wall boxes on the back of their sheet: for example, 'The yacht was sailed by the crew' *[Top: yacht - was sailed - (blank) / Bottom: The - by the crew - (blank)].*

Rounding off: Go over the sheet with the children, discussing their answers. If they have done the extension activity, make sure they have filled in the six boxes correctly.

Red

Verbs

The Active and Passive Voice

When the subject of a sentence is doing the verb action, we are writing in the **active** voice.

subject **doing** verb action (+ object) = **active** voice
subject **receiving** verb action (+ 'by' + agent) = **passive** voice

When we do not know who is doing the verb action, or we think that the object is more important, we can rewrite the sentence in the **passive** voice.

We do this by turning the object into the subject and by using the verb 'to be' with the past participle.

Decide which of the sentences in each pair is written in the active voice and which is written in the passive. Start by identifying the verb and subject. Then think about whether the subject is doing the verb action or receiving it.

1. The yacht was sailed by the crew.   active · passive
    The crew sailed the yacht.   active · passive

2. Bees store honey in a honeycomb.   active · passive
    Honey is stored in a honeycomb.   active · passive

3. We welcomed our guests to the party.   active · passive
    Our guests were welcomed to the party.   active · passive

4. Some seeds will be planted by the gardener.   active · passive
    The gardener will plant some seeds.   active · passive

Are these sentences active or passive? Identify the verb and subject in each one and circle the answer you think is correct.

5. A hymn was sung by the choir.   active · passive
6. Sam bruised his knee in the park.   active · passive
7. Rhinos come from Africa and Asia.   active · passive
8. The chicken was basted by the cook.   active · passive
9. The autumn leaves fell to the ground.   active · passive
10. A rosette was awarded to the winner.   active · passive
11. The toothpaste is kept in the bathroom.   active · passive
12. Lucy went to the gymkhana last Saturday.   active · passive
13. The baguettes are made early in the morning.   active · passive
14. Granny gave Anna some jodhpurs for her birthday.   active · passive

Spelling 22 – ‹ui› and ‹u› for the /i/ Sound

Prepare...
Spelling Sheets 22a/b
Coloured pencils

Builds on...
JGH1: S7
JGH3: S27

Revision: Write these words on the board, and ask the children to find the 'silent ‹p›' digraph in each one: <u>p</u>neumonia, <u>p</u>salm, recei<u>p</u>t, <u>p</u>syche, prom<u>p</u>t, <u>p</u>neumatic, <u>p</u>seudo, <u>p</u>tarmigan. Ask the children if they can think of other words that have a 'silent ‹p›' digraph.

Main point: The short vowel sound /i/ is usually represented by the letter ‹i›, although sometimes it is spelt ‹y› (as in 'hymn' and 'rhythm') and occasionally ‹e› (as in 'pretty' and 'English'). There are two less common spellings: ‹u›, as in 'busy', and – as a 'silent letter' digraph – ‹ui›, as in 'building'. These spellings are usually found in words originating from Old English, such as 'busy' and 'build', or Middle English (via Old French and based on Latin), such as 'biscuit', 'lettuce', 'minute' and 'circuit'. The word 'cuisine' is borrowed directly from French and so the ‹u› is not silent, but rather makes a /w/ sound, followed by the /i/.

Spelling list: Go through the list, discuss the meaning of any unfamiliar words, and ask the class to find and highlight the ‹ui› or ‹u› saying /i/ each time. Point out other spelling features, such as the ‹s› saying /z/ in 'busy', 'busily', 'cuisine', 'business', 'busybody' and 'businesslike', the ‹y› saying /ee/ in 'busy', 'busily', 'busybody' and 'bodybuilder', the suffix in 'busi**ly**', '(body) build**er**', '(out)build**ing**' and 'busi**ness**(like)', the prefix in '**re**built', the 'soft ‹c›' in 'lettuce' and 'circuit', the ‹te› saying /t/ in 'minute', the ‹i› saying /ee/ and ‹ne› saying /n/ in 'cuisine', the silent ‹i› in 'business(like)', the compound words 'built-in' (with its hyphen), 'busybody', 'outbuilding' and 'bodybuilder', and the ‹ir› spelling of /er/ in 'circuit'. It is a good idea to blend and sound out the spelling words quickly every day with the class, using the 'say it as it sounds' strategy where appropriate (stressing the pure sound of any schwas, for example, as in 'busin**e**ss').

Spelling Sheet 22a: The children split each word into syllables to help remember the spelling *[1. build, 2. built, 3. bus/y, 4. bus/i/ly, 5. bis/cuit, 6. re/built, 7. let/tuce, 8. min/ute, 9. build/er, 10. build/ing, 11. cui/sine, 12. busi/ness, 13. built-/in, 14. cir/cuit, 15. bus/y/bod/y, 16. busi/ness/like, 17. out/build/ing, 18. bod/y/build/er]* and then find the eighteen spelling words in the word search. They then identify the four spelling words that are in the same word family as 'busy' *[busily, business, busybody, businesslike]*.

Spelling Sheet 22b: The children look at the adjective 'busy' and write its comparative *[busier]* and superlative *[busiest]* in the elephants. They then write the comparative and superlative for each of the other adjectives *[straighter/straightest, subtler/subtlest, number/ numbest, greater/ greatest, feistier/feistiest, weirder/weirdest, prompter/promptest, handsomer/handsomest]*. Then they parse the sentence and complete the wall *[Top: buildings - were built - (blank) / Bottom: The ancient - in the twelfth century - (blank) / Verb: passive]*. The passive verb uses the auxiliary 'were' with the irregular past participle 'built'. 'In the twelfth century' is a prepositional phrase acting as an adverb, so it needs orange brackets.

The ancient[Adj] buildings[N] (were built)[V] (in[Pre] the twelfth[Adj] century[N])[Adv].

Noun[N] (black), Verb[V] (red), Pronoun[P] (pink), Adjective[Adj] (blue), Adverb[Adv] (orange), Conjunction[C] (purple), Preposition[Pre] (green)

Dictation: (This can be done in the spelling lesson or at another time during the week.) Call out the sentences for the children to write down. Remind them to use speech marks with the correct punctuation in Sentence 3. 'Dad' is a proper noun and needs a capital letter.

1. The rabbit was busily munching a juicy lettuce.
2. The bodybuilder was flexing his huge muscles.
3. "The biscuits will be ready in five minutes," said Dad.

‹ui› and ‹u› for /i/

Spelling List 22

1. build
2. built
3. busy
4. busily
5. biscuit
6. rebuilt
7. lettuce
8. minute
9. builder
10. building
11. cuisine
12. business
13. built-in
14. circuit
15. busybody
16. businesslike
17. outbuilding
18. bodybuilder

Find the words from the Spelling List.

c	l	a	b	i	s	c	i	r	c	u	b	o	d	p
r	e	b	u	z	j	b	o	i	r	b	u	s	y	c
u	t	c	s	u	i	u	n	g	r	c	i	m	o	i
i	t	u	i	s	n	s	y	b	u	i	l	d	e	r
b	u	i	l	d	e	i	t	o	v	r	d	e	t	e
u	c	s	y	n	s	n	b	d	o	c	i	b	m	b
s	e	i	k	o	s	e	u	y	d	u	n	r	i	u
y	d	n	c	u	r	s	i	b	m	i	g	p	n	i
b	i	e	j	b	i	s	c	u	i	t	m	o	u	l
o	u	t	b	u	i	l	d	i	n	g	a	h	c	t
d	g	d	u	i	d	i	t	l	u	c	e	f	i	m
y	q	u	s	l	y	k	x	d	t	i	n	g	r	l
s	t	e	i	t	b	e	n	e	e	n	e	s	s	i
c	i	r	b	i	u	i	l	r	b	u	i	l	t	k
b	u	s	i	n	e	s	s	t	l	e	t	t	u	a

Find the words in the Spelling List that are related to 'busy' and write them in the word family tree.

busy

Spelling Sheet 22a (JGH6)

Dictation: ‹ui› and ‹u› for /i/

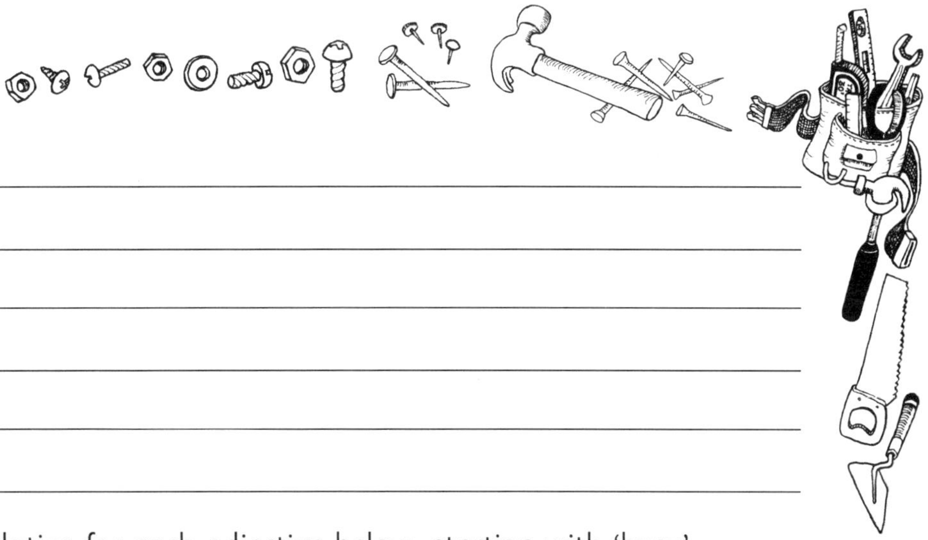

1. _____
   _____
2. _____
   _____
3. _____
   _____

Write the comparative and superlative for each adjective below, starting with 'busy'.

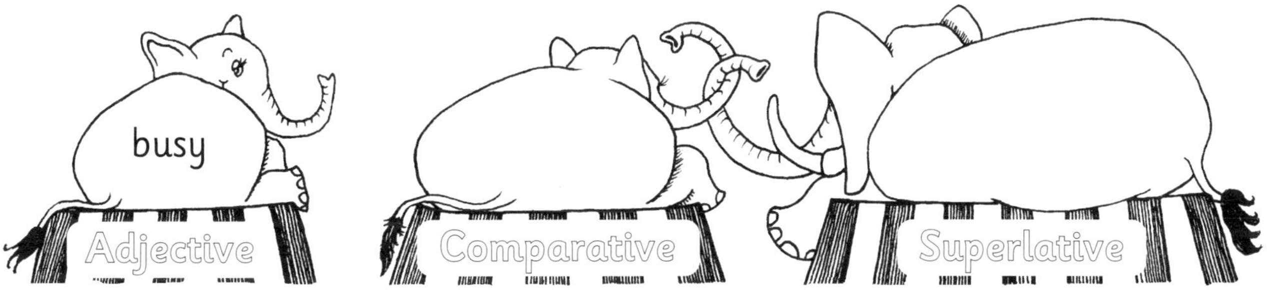

busy

Adjective | Comparative | Superlative

straight _____ _____

subtle _____ _____

numb _____ _____

great _____ _____

feisty _____ _____

weird _____ _____

prompt _____ _____

handsome _____ _____

Parse the sentence and then write it on the wall.

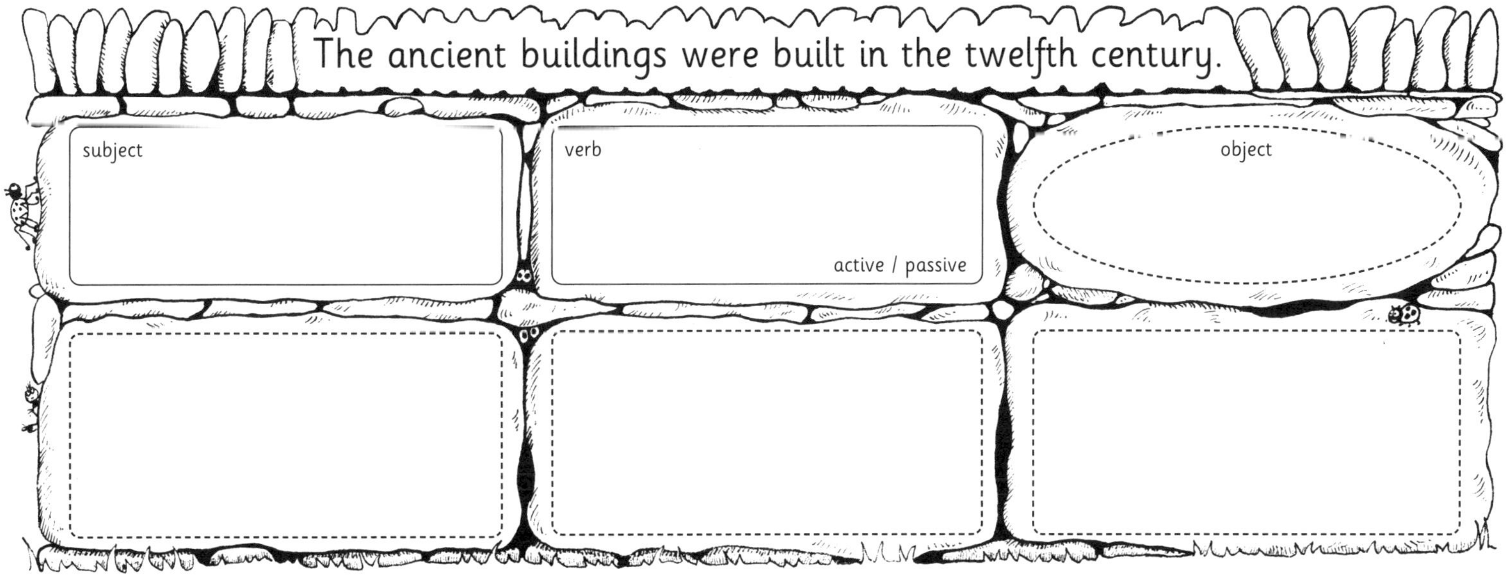

The ancient buildings were built in the twelfth century.

subject

verb

object

active / passive

Grammar 22 – The Passive Voice

Prepare...
Grammar Sheet 22
Red pencils

Builds on...
JGH3: G25-27, G35
JGH4: G3,
JGH5: G15-17
JGH6: G6-7, G21

Aim: Reinforce the children's understanding of sentences that are written in the passive voice, and develop their ability to rewrite them in the active voice, turning the agent back into the subject.

Introduction: Remind the children that not all sentences are written in the active voice (when the subject is doing the verb action); sometimes, the subject is the person or thing who receives the verb action, and this is called the passive voice. Write on the board, 'Granny's lettuces are being eaten by a rabbit' and discuss whether it is written in the active or passive voice. The subject 'lettuces' receives the action of the verb 'to eat', while the actual 'doer' of the verb (rabbit) appears as an agent in a prepositional phrase; also, the verb has an auxiliary ('are being', which is the present continuous of the verb 'to be') followed by the past participle 'eaten'; all this tells us that it is written in the passive voice. Discuss how writing it in the passive voice has put the main focus on the lettuces, rather than the rabbit, and remind the children that sometimes we do not know who is performing the action of the verb or might consider the information less important or even irrelevant. Underline the verb 'are being eaten' in red, and draw boxes around the subject 'lettuces' and agent 'rabbit', with a small ‹s› and ‹a› in the corner, respectively.

Main point: We usually use the active voice in our writing as it is generally considered to have a more direct and powerful effect on the reader. However, there are times when the passive is more appropriate, so the children have to be able to write in both voices. Ask the children how they would write the sentence on the board in the active voice. Remind them that, in the active voice, the subject of the verb is the 'doer' of the verb action, so they must turn the agent 'rabbit' back into the subject. Write 'A rabbit' on the board and then ask the children what form of the verb 'to eat' should follow. Explain that they need to use the same tense in the active as in the passive, and must make sure that the verb agrees with the subject. Remind the children that the verb 'to be' is in the present continuous and ask them what the present continuous of 'to eat' is *[am/are/is eating]*. As the subject is 'rabbit', the verb that follows must be in the third person singular, so add 'is eating' to the board, along with 'Granny's lettuces', to make the sentence 'A rabbit is eating Granny's lettuces'. Compare the two sentences and ask what role 'lettuces' plays in both sentences *[it is the subject in the passive voice and the direct object in the active voice]*. Point out that the auxiliary verb 'to be' is in the third person plural in the passive, but that it is in the third person singular in the active.

Grammar Sheet 22: The children write inside the outlined word Verbs, using a red pencil. They then look at the sentences and identify the subject, verb and agent in each one, underlining the verb in red and drawing a box around the subject and agent, with either a small ‹s› or ‹a› in the corner *[1. palette/was used/painter, 2. bouquet/was made/cousin, 3. statuette/was bought/friend, 4. horse/was sold/farmer, 5. temple/was supported/columns]*. They then rewrite the sentences in the active voice *[1. (as shown), 2. My cousin made the bride's bouquet, 3. Her friend bought the bronze statuette, 4. The farmer sold the handsome brown horse, 5. Many columns supported the ancient Greek temple]*. Lastly, the children identify the correct form of the auxiliary verb 'to be' to complete each sentence *[6. is being (painted), 7. are (visited), 8. was (interrupted), 9. have been (wounded), 10. was being (tempted)]*.

Extension activity: The children put some passive sentences from Grammar Sheet 22 into six sentence wall boxes on the back of their sheet: for example, 'An old palette was used by the painter' *[Top: palette - was used - (blank) / Bottom: An old - by the painter - (blank)]*.

Rounding off: Go over the sheet with the children, discussing their answers. If they have done the extension activity, ask the children to write some of their answers on the board.

Verbs — Red

The Passive Voice

REMEMBER! When we write in the passive voice, the 'receiver' of the verb action becomes the **subject** and the 'doer' of the verb (if it is known) becomes the **agent**.

In each sentence, underline the verb in red and draw boxes around the subject and agent, putting either a small ‹s› (for 'subject') or a small ‹a› (for 'agent') in the corner. Then rewrite the sentences in the active voice, turning the agent back into the subject.

1. An old ⟦palette⟧(s) <u>was used</u> by the ⟦painter⟧(a)

   The painter used an old palette.

2. The bride's bouquet was made by my cousin.

   _____

3. The bronze statuette was bought by her friend.

   _____

4. The handsome brown horse was sold by the farmer.

   _____

5. The ancient Greek temple was supported by many columns.

   _____

The sentences below are written first in the active voice and then in the passive. Choose the correct form of 'to be' each time to complete the passive sentence.

6. We **are painting** the ceiling.

   The ceiling ⟦ am being / are being / (is being) ⟧ painted by us.

7. Grandpa **visits** us twice a week.

   We ⟦ am / are / is ⟧ visited by Grandpa twice a week.

8. A loud noise **interrupted** the conference.

   The conference ⟦ was / were ⟧ interrupted by a loud noise.

9. A grizzly bear **has wounded** two ramblers.

   Two ramblers ⟦ have been / has been ⟧ wounded by a grizzly bear.

10. The chocolate chip cookies **were tempting** me.

    I ⟦ was being / were being ⟧ tempted by the chocolate chip cookies.

Grammar Sheet 22 (JGH6)

Spelling 23 – ‹gh›, ‹gue›

Prepare...
Spelling Sheets 23a/b
Coloured pencils

Builds on...
JGH3: S34
JGH4: S16

Revision: Write these words on the board and ask the class to identify the ‹u› or 'silent letter' digraph saying /i/ in each one: b**u**sy, bisc**ui**t, min**u**te, b**ui**lder, lett**u**ce, circ**ui**t, b**u**siness, c**ui**sine. (As 'cuisine' is borrowed directly from French, the ‹u› is not silent, but says /w/). Ask the children if they can think of other words with these spellings for /i/.

Main point: The ‹gh› spelling is used in several ways in English. It is found in some vowel-sound spellings, as in 'h<u>igh</u>', 'h<u>eigh</u>t', '<u>eigh</u>t', 'c<u>augh</u>t' and 'b<u>ough</u>t' (the other pronunciations of ‹ough› are taught in Spelling 25). It also says /f/ in words like 'tou**gh**' and 'lau**gh**' and – as a 'silent ‹h›' digraph – it says /g/ in words like '<u>gh</u>ost'. Words with this 'silent letter' digraph are often Germanic in origin, although 'spaghetti' is borrowed from Italian, 'ghoul' comes from Arabic and 'dinghy' is from Hindi. As well as ‹g› and ‹gh›, another spelling of the /g/ sound is ‹gue›, as in 'vague' and 'intrigue', although ‹gue› also makes the /ng/ sound when it is preceded by ‹n›, as in 'meringue'. This spelling is usually found in words that come from Latin via French, except for 'tongue', which is Germanic in origin.

Spelling list: Go through the list, discuss the meaning of any unfamiliar words, and ask the class to find and highlight the ‹gh› or ‹gue› spelling each time. Point out other spelling features, such as the way the ‹g› in 'dinghy' helps say /ng/, but sometimes also makes its own sound (depending on how it is said), the ‹y› saying /ee/ at the end of 'dinghy', 'ghastly' and 'ghoulishly', the vowel saying its long sound in 'r**o**gue', 'pl**a**gue', 'v**a**gue', 'gh**o**stwriter', 'd**i**alogue' and 'pr**o**logue', the ‹ea› in 'l**ea**gue' and 'coll**ea**gue', the suffix in 'ghast**ly**', 'ghostwrit**er**' and 'ghoulish**ly**', the ‹i› saying /a/ in 'meringue', the ‹i› saying /ee/ in 'intrigue', 'fatigue' and 'spaghetti', the ‹o› saying /u/ in 'tongue', the 'silent letter' digraph in 'ghost**w**riter', and the ‹ou› saying /oo/ in 'ghoulishly'. It is a good idea to blend and sound out the spelling words quickly every day with the class, using the 'say it as it sounds' strategy where appropriate (stressing the pure sound of any schwas, for example, as in 'm**e**ringue' and 'f**a**tigue').

Spelling Sheet 23a: The children split each word into syllables to help remember the spelling *[1. din/ghy, 2. rogue, 3. plague, 4. vague, 5. league, 6. ghast/ly, 7. me/ringue, 8. in/trigue, 9. tongue, 10. fa/tigue, 11. spa/ghet/ti, 12. ghost/writ/er, 13. col/league, 14. di/a/logue, 15. pro/logue, 16. ep/i/logue, 17. ha/rangue, 18. ghoul/ish/ly].* They then unscramble the letters in the meringues to make the first twelve spelling words *[ghastly, rogue, meringue, dinghy, tongue, vague, fatigue, league, plague, intrigue, spaghetti, ghostwriter].*

Spelling Sheet 23b: In each sentence, the children identify the verb and subject and then decide whether it is written in the active or passive voice *[1. passive/active, 2. passive/ active, 3. active/passive, 4. active/passive, 5. passive/active, 6. active/passive].* Then they parse the sentence and complete the wall *[Top: dinghy - was rebuilt - (blank) / Bottom: The old wooden - by Zack and his dad - (blank) / Verb: passive].* The passive verb uses the auxiliary 'was' with the irregular past participle 'rebuilt'.

The old^{Adj} wooden^{Adj} dinghy^N (was rebuilt)^V (by^{Pre} Zack^N and^C his^{Adj} dad^N)^{Adv}.

Noun^N (black), Verb^V (red), Pronoun^P (pink), Adjective^{Adj} (blue), Adverb^{Adv} (orange), Conjunction^C (purple), Preposition^{Pre} (green)

Dictation: (This can be done in the spelling lesson or at another time during the week.) Call out the sentences for the children to write down. Remind them to use speech marks with the correct punctuation in Sentence 2. 'Italian' is a proper adjective and needs a capital letter.

1. Spaghetti is an extremely popular pasta in Italian cuisine.
2. "A good meringue should melt on the tongue," said the chef.
3. The ghostwriter added a prologue and an epilogue to the story.

  ‹gh› ‹gue›

Spelling List 23

Unscramble the letters in the meringues to make words 1 to 12 from the Spelling List.

1. dinghy

_____

2. rogue

_____

3. plague

_____

4. vague

_____

5. league

_____

6. ghastly

_____

7. meringue

_____

8. intrigue

_____

9. tongue

_____

10. fatigue

_____

11. spaghetti

_____

12. ghostwriter

_____

13. colleague

_____

14. dialogue

_____

15. prologue

_____

16. epilogue

_____

17. harangue

_____

18. ghoulishly

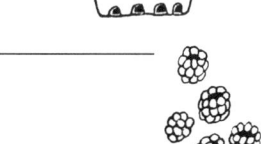

  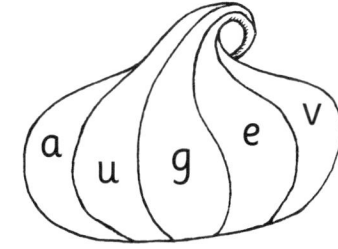

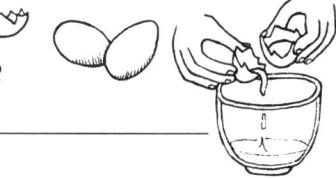  

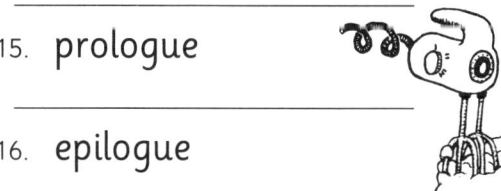  

Spelling Sheet 23a (JGH6)

Dictation: ‹gh› ‹gue›

1. _____

_____

2. _____

_____

3. _____

_____

Which sentence in each pair is written in the active voice and which is written in the passive? Start by identifying the verb and subject. Then think about whether the subject is doing the verb action or receiving it.

1. The brick wall has been completed by the busy builders.   active · passive
   The busy builders have completed the brick wall.   active · passive

2. A pterodactyl fossil was discovered by the local farmer.   active · passive
   The local farmer discovered a pterodactyl fossil.   active · passive

3. Arthur grows the best rhubarb in the village.   active · passive
   The best rhubarb in the village is grown by Arthur.   active · passive

4. The handsome stranger intrigued my friends.   active · passive
   My friends were intrigued by the handsome stranger.   active · passive

5. The dialogue for the play is being learnt by the actors.   active · passive
   The actors are learning the dialogue for the play.   active · passive

6. Granny will make a delicious lemon meringue pie.   active · passive
   A delicious lemon meringue pie will be made by Granny.   active · passive

Parse the sentence and then write it on the wall.

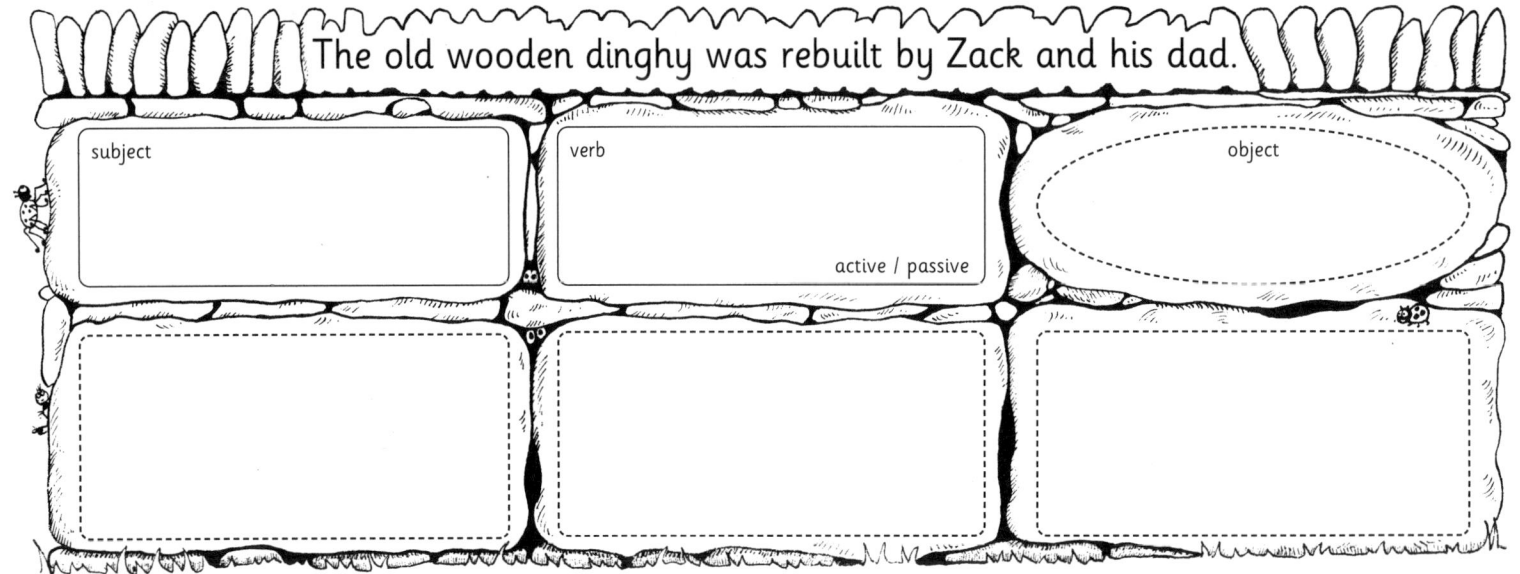

The old wooden dinghy was rebuilt by Zack and his dad.

subject   verb   object
                        active / passive

Grammar 23 – Gerunds

Prepare...
Grammar Sheet 23
Red & black pencils

Builds on...
JGH1: G5-6, G20
JGH2: G8, G32
JGH3: G7-10, G17
JGH4: G8-11, G29
JGH5: G4, G10
JGH6: G2, G4

Aim: Introduce gerunds, which are a special kind of noun, made by adding ‹-ing› to a verb. Rather than people or objects, gerunds name activities like 'reading' or 'camping', and they function like other nouns in a sentence, acting as the subject, object or complement, for example.

Introduction: Remind the class that the suffix ‹-ing› is added to verbs to make the present participle. Call out the verbs 'to fish', 'to skate', 'to lie', 'to jog', 'to cry' and 'to sway' and ask the children to use the present participle of each one in a sentence. Write their suggestions on the board, revising the spelling rules applied to make 'fishing', 'skating', 'lying', 'jogging', 'crying' and 'swaying' (see pages 39 and 40). Then discuss whether the participle is being used, along with the auxiliary 'to be', to form the continuous tenses (as in 'The children <u>were fishing</u> on the lake'), or whether it is acting as an adjective (as in 'the <u>swaying</u> branches of the tree').

Main point: Now write the sentence 'They were enjoying the singing' on the board. Identify the ‹-ing› words, 'enjoying' and 'singing', and discuss what each word is doing in the sentence. The children should be able to identify 'enjoying' as the present participle used with the auxiliary 'were' to form the past continuous of the verb 'to enjoy'. However, the word 'singing' is not a participle, as it is not acting as a verb or as an adjective. Ask the children 'Who or what were enjoying the singing?' to find the subject of the sentence *[They]* and 'They were enjoying what?' to find the direct object of the sentence *[the singing]*. Remind the children that the object of a sentence is usually a noun or pronoun and that words that can have 'the' in front of them are usually nouns, so 'singing' in this sentence is acting as a noun. Explain that nouns that are formed in this way are called 'gerunds' and instead of naming people or objects, they name activities. Gerunds act in the same way as other nouns in a sentence, so they can be the subject or object of a sentence, or a subject complement following a linking verb, for example. Write the following sentences on the board and ask the children what role the gerund is playing in each one: '<u>Smiling</u> makes me happy' *[subject]*, 'We love <u>jogging</u>' *[object]*, 'My best subject is <u>reading</u>' *[complement]*. Also point out that a gerund, like other nouns, can be used with adjectives, including articles and other determiners, to make a noun phrase, such as 'her baby's loud <u>crying</u>', or 'the rhythmic <u>swaying</u> of the branches'. Gerunds can also be used in gerund phrases, where the whole phrase acts, for example, as the subject, object or complement, as in '<u>Learning to swim</u> is an important skill', 'I like <u>playing the guitar</u>', or 'Her new pastime is <u>collecting stamps</u>', but the children can learn more about this when they are older.

Grammar Sheet 23: The children write inside the outlined word Nouns, using a black pencil. Then they complete the activity badges by drawing pictures to represent the gerunds 'swimming', 'cooking' and 'reading', by labelling the middle badges correctly *[dancing, painting, camping]*, and by choosing three other activities to label and illustrate. They then read the sentences and underline each verb in red and gerund in black, before answering each question and deciding whether the gerund is acting as a subject, object or complement *[1. do (verb) weightlifting (object), 2. is (verb) canoeing (complement), 3. Building (subject) will start (verb), 4. was (verb) singing (complement), 5. hiccuping (subject) annoyed (verb), 6. heard (verb) neighing (object)]*.

Extension activity: Write the following verbs on the board and ask the children to make some of them into gerunds and use them in a sentence: to walk, to bake, to dig, to fly, to draw, to drive, to knit, to study, to sail, to hike, to run, to play, to work, to race, to chat, to bully.

Rounding off: Go over the sheet with the children, discussing their answers. If they have done the extension activity, ask some children to read out their sentences.

Gerunds

Gerunds are a special kind of **noun** made by adding ‹-ing› to a verb. Instead of naming people or objects, they name **activities** like 'fishing' and 'skating'. Although gerunds look the same as present participles, they are used differently in a sentence.

Complete these activity badges by filling in the missing pictures and gerunds. Then think of some more activities to draw and label.

swimming

cooking

reading

In each sentence, underline the verb in red and the gerund in black. Then write the gerund on the line to answer the question below. Finally, decide whether the gerund is acting as the subject, object or subject complement.

1. They do weightlifting at the gym.
   What do they do at the gym? _____

2. My new hobby is canoeing.
   What is my new hobby? _____

3. Building will start next week.
   What will start next week? _____

4. Anne's greatest talent was singing.
   What was Anne's greatest talent? _____

5. Jim's constant hiccuping annoyed me.
   Jim's constant **what** annoyed me? _____

6. We heard the neighing of the horses.
   What did we hear from the horses? _____

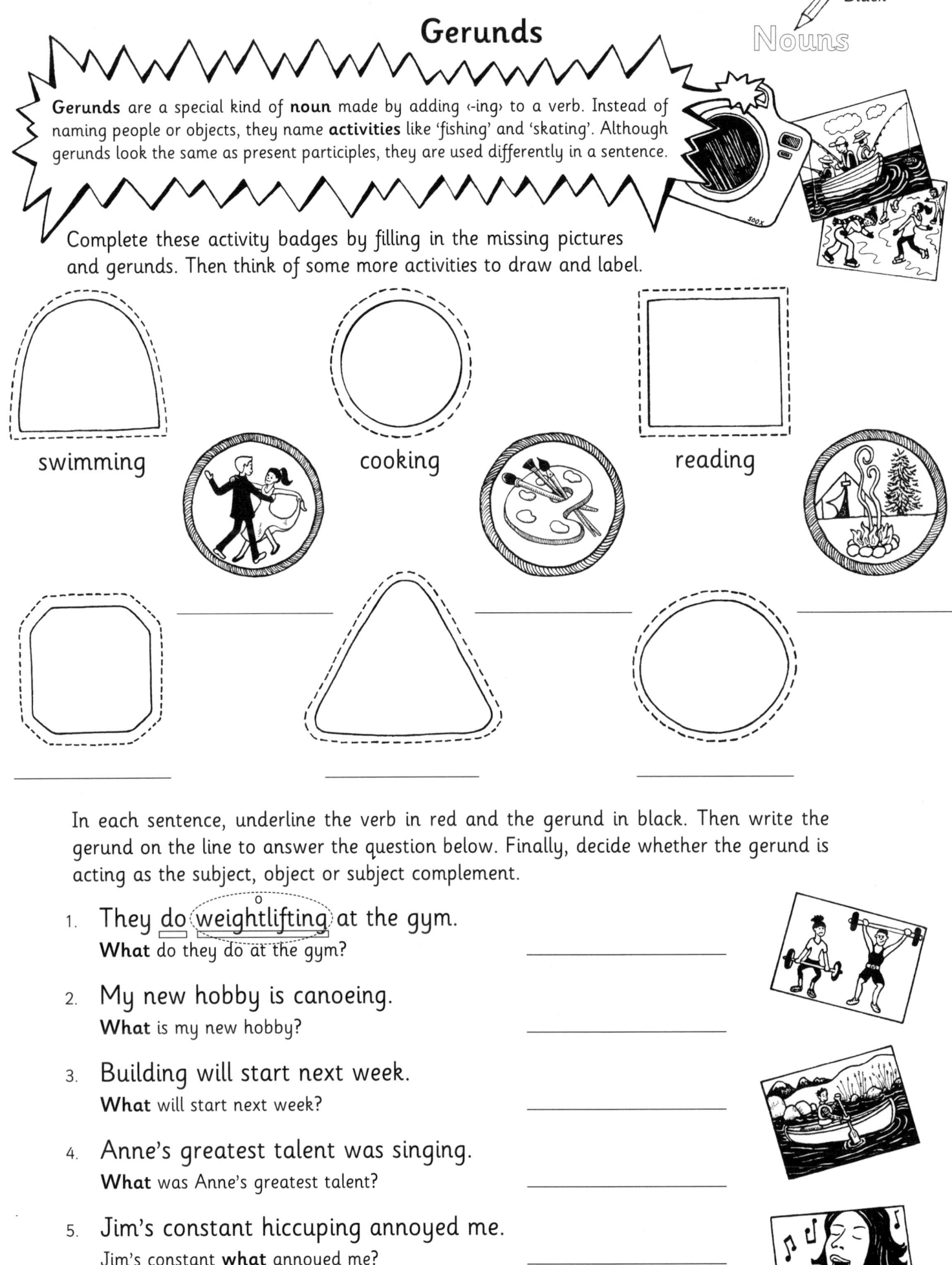

Spelling 24 – ‹gu›

Prepare...
Spelling Sheets 24a/b
Coloured pencils

Builds on...
JGH4: S16
JGH6: S23

Revision: Write these words on the board and ask the class to identify the ‹gh› or ‹gue› spelling in each one: din**gh**y, va**gue**, spa**gh**etti, lea**gue**, **gh**ost, ton**gue**, **gh**oul, merin**gue**. Discuss whether the spellings say /g/ or /ng/ in each one (if either spelling follows ‹n›, it usually says /ng/). Ask the children if they can think of other words with these spellings.

Main point: As well as ‹g› and ‹gh›, another spelling of the /g/ sound is the 'silent letter' digraph ‹gu›, which is found in words like '**gu**ide' and '**gu**ess'. Write these examples on the board and explain that words with this spelling originate from different languages, but usually come via Old or Middle English, when the ‹u› was added. Now write 'penguin' and 'language' on the board and ask what sound(s) ‹gu› is making now. In words like this, the ‹gu› says /gw/, which often reflects the pronunciation of the original word from which it is derived. In words seven to twelve in the spelling list, ‹gu› says /gw/.

Spelling list: Go through the list, discuss the meaning of any unfamiliar words, and ask the class to find and highlight the ‹gu› spelling each time. Point out other spelling features, such as the double ‹s› after the short, stressed vowel in 'guess', the way the ‹g› in 'language', 'penguin', 'anguish', 'extinguish' and 'distinguished' helps say /ng/ as well as making its own sound, the ‹age› saying /ij/ at the end of 'language', the ‹e› saying /i/ in '**e**xtinguish' and 'b**e**guile', the ‹ed› saying /t/ in 'distinguish**ed**', the ‹ee› in 'guarant**ee**', the compound word 'lifeguard', the ‹s› saying first /s/ and then /z/ in 'disguise' and the ‹i_e› saying /ee/ in 'guillotine'. It is a good idea to blend and sound out the spelling words quickly every day with the class, using the 'say it as it sounds' strategy where appropriate (stressing the pure sound of any schwas, for example, as in 'iguan**a**', 'guar**a**ntee', 'guardi**a**n' and 'guill**o**tine').

Spelling Sheet 24a: The children split each word into syllables to help remember the spelling *[1. guide, 2. guard, 3. guess, 4. guest, 5. guilt, 6. gui/tar, 7. lan/guage, 8. pen/guin, 9. i/gua/na, 10. an/guish, 11. ex/tin/guish, 12. dis/tin/guished, 13. guar/an/tee, 14. life/guard, 15. dis/guise, 16. be/guile, 17. guard/i/an, 18. guil/lo/tine].* They then work out the answers to the crossword clues and write them in *[1. guess (across) guilt (down), 2. language, 3. guarantee, 4. guest, 5. guitar, 6. anguish, 7. distinguished, 8. lifeguard, 9. disguise, 10. extinguish, 11. iguana, 12. guardian, 13. beguile, 14. guard, 15. guide, 16. penguin, 17. guillotine].*

Spelling Sheet 24b: The children add ‹-ing› to each verb, using the spelling rules. They then write in the missing word in each pair of sentences, underlining it in red when it is a present participle and in black when it is a gerund *[writing, playing, swimming, cooking, gardening, cycling, shopping, studying].* Then they parse the sentence and complete the wall *[Top: Ben - extinguished - flames / Bottom: (blank) - quickly - the/from the fire / Verb: active].* The adverb 'quickly' is made by adding ‹-ly› to the adjective 'quick'. 'From the fire' is a prepositional phrase describing 'flames', so it needs blue brackets.

Ben^N quickly^Adv extinguished^V the flames^N (from^Pre the fire^N)^Adj.

Noun^N (black), Verb^V (red), Pronoun^P (pink), Adjective^Adj (blue), Adverb^Adv (orange), Conjunction^C (purple), Preposition^Pre (green)

Dictation: (This can be done in the spelling lesson or at another time during the week.) Call out the sentences for the children to write down. Remind them to use speech marks with the correct punctuation in Sentence 1. 'Miss Beech' is a proper noun and needs capital letters.

1. "Welcome!" exclaimed Miss Beech to her guests.
2. The ghastly rogue was cleverly disguised as a guard.
3. The children saw the penguins and iguanas at the zoo.

Spelling List 24

1. guide

2. guard

3. guess

4. guest

5. guilt

6. guitar

7. language

8. penguin

9. iguana

10. anguish

11. extinguish

12. distinguished

13. guarantee

14. lifeguard

15. disguise

16. beguile

17. guardian

18. guillotine

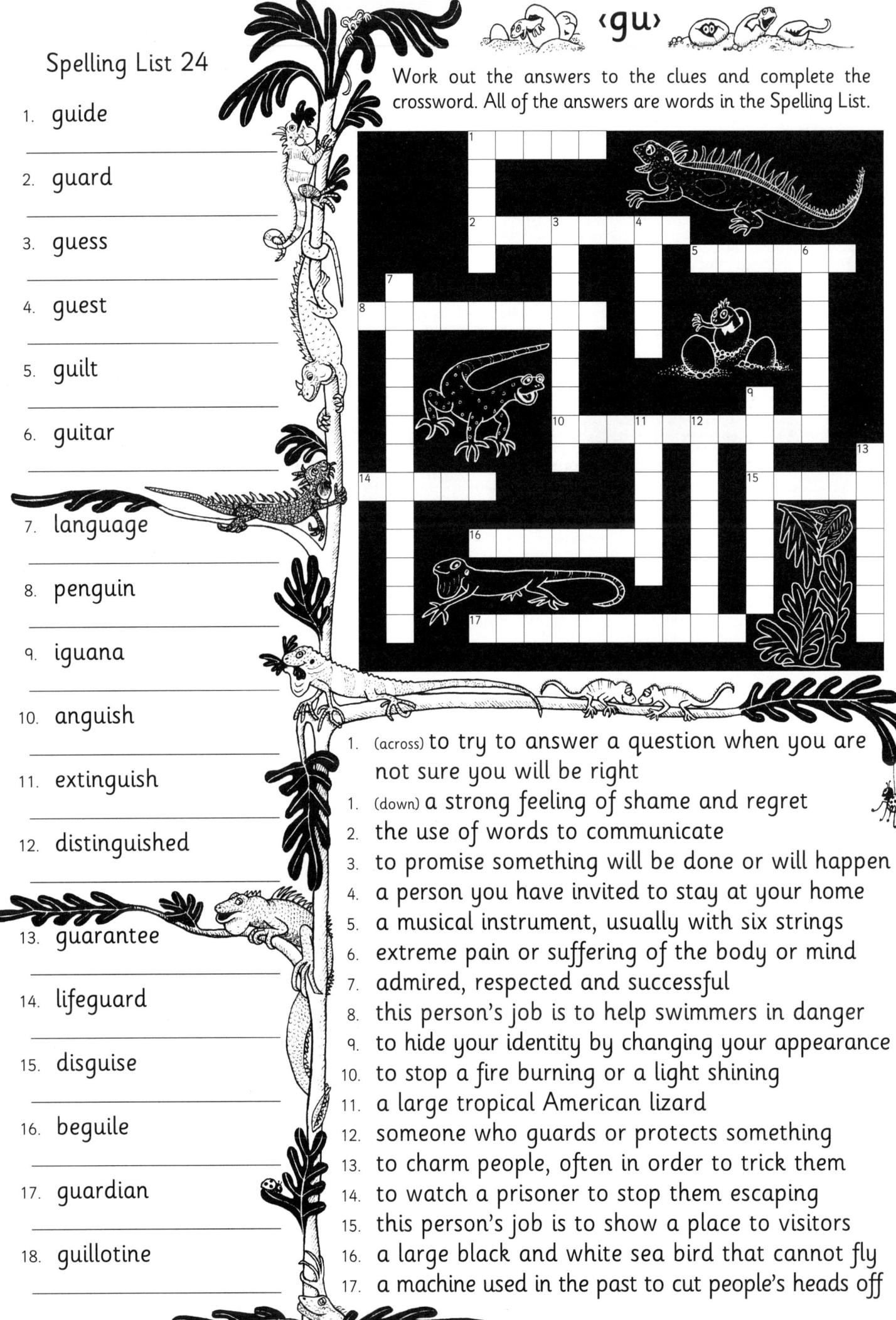

‹gu›

Work out the answers to the clues and complete the crossword. All of the answers are words in the Spelling List.

1. (across) to try to answer a question when you are not sure you will be right
1. (down) a strong feeling of shame and regret
2. the use of words to communicate
3. to promise something will be done or will happen
4. a person you have invited to stay at your home
5. a musical instrument, usually with six strings
6. extreme pain or suffering of the body or mind
7. admired, respected and successful
8. this person's job is to help swimmers in danger
9. to hide your identity by changing your appearance
10. to stop a fire burning or a light shining
11. a large tropical American lizard
12. someone who guards or protects something
13. to charm people, often in order to trick them
14. to watch a prisoner to stop them escaping
15. this person's job is to show a place to visitors
16. a large black and white sea bird that cannot fly
17. a machine used in the past to cut people's heads off

Dictation: ‹gu›

1. _____

_____

2. _____

_____

3. _____

_____

The present participle is used with the auxiliary verb 'to be' in the continuous tenses. A gerund is a special type of noun that names an activity. Add ‹-ing› to the verbs below, using the spelling rules, and fill in the gaps. Underline the present participles in red and the gerunds in black.

verb + ing = present participle or gerund

verb   present participle   gerund

write   I am _____ a long letter.   The children's _____ is neat.

play   Will you be _____ the guitar?   Little kittens enjoy _____.

swim   The penguins were _____.   _____ is a popular sport.

cook   Dad is _____ spaghetti.   Jane's _____ smells great.

garden   I was _____ this morning.   Jim does a lot of _____.

cycle   They were _____ very fast.   Fred is really good at _____.

shop   We were _____ for new shoes.   They will do the _____.

study   We are _____ French today.   Have you done any _____?

Parse the sentence and then write it on the wall.

Ben quickly extinguished the flames from the fire.

subject	verb	object
	active / passive	

Spelling Sheet 24b (JGH6)

Grammar 24 – Idioms

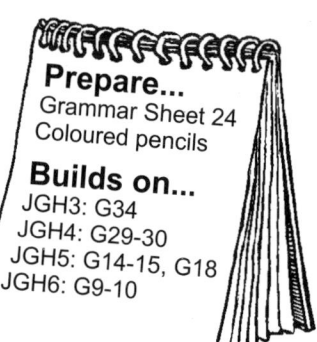

Prepare...
Grammar Sheet 24
Coloured pencils

Builds on...
JGH3: G34
JGH4: G29-30
JGH5: G14-15, G18
JGH6: G9-10

Aim: Introduce idioms, which are common expressions that have a special meaning that is not conveyed by the actual words used (so they have a 'figurative' meaning that is different to the 'literal' meaning). Idioms help us to describe events vividly and are especially used in stories and speech.

Introduction: Briefly revise sentences and phrases. A sentence must make sense, start with a capital letter, contain a subject and verb, and end in a full stop, question mark or exclamation mark. When a group of words makes sense but has no verb and subject, it is called a phrase. Ask the children what kinds of phrases they know *[noun phrases and prepositional phrases]*. Noun phrases consist of a main (or head) noun, together with all the words that describe it. They often represent the 'complete' subject or object of a sentence, as in '<u>The big blue ball</u> landed in the muddy puddle' or they can be part of a prepositional phrase, like 'in <u>the muddy puddle</u>'. Prepositional phrases often act as adverbs in a sentence (in the example here, the phrase tells us **where** the ball landed) but they can also be used as adjectives in bigger noun phrases, such as 'the dog <u>with the long tail</u>.' Ask the children to suggest some more phrases and then put them into sentences.

Main point: Now write the phrase 'at the drop of a hat' on the board and ask the children what they notice about it. They may recognise that this long prepositional phrase is made up of two smaller prepositional phrases *[at the drop/of a hat]*, but they may also notice that it is not like the other phrases discussed so far. Ask them to put it into a sentence, such as 'Dan is happy to go swimming at the drop of a hat', and discuss what the phrase actually means: Is Dan waiting for someone to drop a hat before he can go swimming? No, Dan loves swimming so much that he will go immediately, given the chance. Explain that there are many phrases or expressions like this in English that are used to describe something in a lively, vivid way. They are called 'idioms' and are usually old sayings with meanings that have become less obvious over time ('at the drop of a hat', for example, probably comes from the time when a hat was used to signal the start of a fight or race). Call out some more examples that the children will know, or ask them to suggest some examples of their own. Discuss them with the class, comparing what the words actually say with what the idioms really mean. Draw a picture on the board, showing the literal meaning of an idiom and see if the class can guess which expression it represents. Then ask some children to come and draw pictures of their own on the board for the rest of the class to guess. There are many examples of idioms, including 'a pain in the neck', 'a tall story', 'to beat about the bush', 'by the skin of your teeth', 'to cost an arm and a leg', 'down in the dumps', 'to get cold feet', 'to have a bee in your bonnet', 'in a nutshell', 'in the doghouse', 'to kick the bucket', 'to lend a hand', 'to play it by ear', 'to pull your leg', 'to rain cats and dogs' and 'to rock the boat'.

Grammar Sheet 24: The children read each idiom and draw a picture of what the words actually say. They then write the real meaning next to it *[answers should indicate the following meanings in the children's own words: 1. immediately/without delay, 2. to be mistaken, 3. unwell/ill/sick, 4. to keep quiet, 5. very rarely/not very often, 6. to reveal someone's secret]*.

Extension activity: The children think of some idioms and draw the literal meanings on the back of their grammar sheet. They then swap their sheet with a partner, who has to guess which idioms the pictures represent. The children should also be encouraged to start collecting idioms in their Spelling Word Books or to create a class book of illustrated idioms.

Rounding off: Go over the sheet with the children, discussing their answers. If they have done the extension activity, show the class some pictures and see if they can guess the idioms.

Idioms

 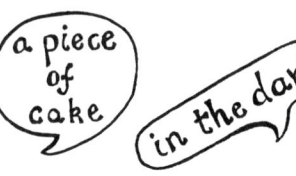

Idioms are common expressions that add variety and interest to our language. Every idiom has a special meaning that needs to be learnt. Look at each one below and draw a picture of what the words actually say. Then write the real meaning of the idiom next to it.

1. **at the drop of a hat**

_____

_____

_____

2. **to bark up the wrong tree**

_____

_____

_____

3. **under the weather**

_____

_____

_____

4. **to hold your tongue**

_____

_____

_____

5. **once in a blue moon**

_____

_____

_____

6. **to let the cat out of the bag**

_____

_____

_____

Spelling 25 – ‹ough›

Prepare...
Spelling Sheets 25a/b
Coloured pencils

Builds on...
JGH3: S34
JGH4: S16
JGH6: S23

Revision: Revise the spelling rule: 'If you want to say /ee/, it's ‹i› before ‹e›, except after ‹c›'. Write these words on the board and ask the class whether ‹ei› or ‹ie› is needed each time: shr(ie)k, n(ie)ce, rec(ei)ve, f(ie)nd, ach(ie)ve, conc(ei)ted, handkerch(ie)f, perc(ei)ve.

Main point: In Spelling Lesson 23, the children were reminded that ‹gh› is used in several spelling patterns, either to represent the consonant sound /f/ in words like 'rough' and 'laughter' or /g/ in 'yoghurt', or as part of a vowel spelling in words like 'light', 'height', 'weigh', 'daughter' and 'thought'. Write 'rough' and 'thought' on the board and point out how the ‹ough› says /uff/ in the first word and /or/ in the second. Explain that there are several other ways ‹ough› can be pronounced, including /ou/ (as in 'bough'), the schwa (as in 'thorough'), /oa/ (as in 'dough'), /off/ (as in 'cough') and /oo/ (as in 'through'). It can even say /up/ in 'hiccough', the alternative spelling of 'hiccup'. There are no rules to help us work out when these spellings are used, so they have to be learnt, but there are only a limited number of common words that use it for each of these sounds. This is why, when mastered, they can be remembered as '**o**h yo**u** **g**et **h**appy' words!

Spelling list: Go through the list, discuss the meaning of any unfamiliar words, and ask the class to find and highlight each ‹ough›, saying the sound that it is making. Point out other spelling features, such as the different spellings of /c/ in '**c**ough' and 'brea**k**through' the ‹e› saying /i/ in 'enough', the alternative spelling in '**al**though' and 'br**ea**kthrough' (and the way the ‹l› in 'although' also says its own sound), the compound words 'doughnut', 'throughout', 'overwrought', 'breakthrough' and 'afterthought' and the 'silent letter' digraph in 'over**w**rought'. It is a good idea to blend and sound out the spelling words quickly every day with the class, using the 'say it as it sounds' strategy where appropriate (stressing the pure sound of any schwas, for example, as in 'th**o**rough').

Spelling Sheet 25a: The children split each word into syllables to help remember the spelling *[1. cough, 2. dough, 3. bough, 4. rough, 5. tough, 6. bought, 7. though, 8. through, 9. e/nough, 10. drought, 11. al/though, 12. dough/nut, 13. sought, 14. thor/ough, 15. through/out, 16. o/ver/wrought, 17. break/through, 18. af/ter/thought]*. They then write them in the nests, grouped by sound *[/ou/: bough, drought;/uff/: rough, tough, enough; /or/: bought, sought, overwrought, afterthought; /oa/ or schwa: dough, though, although, doughnut/thorough; /off/: cough; /oo/: through, throughout, breakthrough]*. They then write the present tense *[buy, bring, fight, seek, think]* for each of the tricky past tenses shown on the tree.

Spelling Sheet 25b: The children write the meanings for each pair of homophones, using a dictionary to help them if needed. Then they parse the sentence and complete the wall *[Top: man - coughed - (blank) / Bottom: The thoughtless - loudly/throughout the play - (blank) / Verb: active]*. The adverb 'loudly' is made by adding ‹-ly› to the adjective 'loud'. 'Throughout the play' is a prepositional phrase acting as an adverb, so it needs orange brackets.

The thoughtless[Adj] man[N] coughed[V] loudly[Adv] (throughout[Pre] the play[N])[Adv].

Noun[N] (black), Verb[V] (red), Pronoun[P] (pink), Adjective[Adj] (blue), Adverb[Adv] (orange), Conjunction[C] (purple), Preposition[Pre] (green)

Dictation: (This can be done in the spelling lesson or at another time during the week.) Call out the sentences for the children to write down. Remind them to use speech marks with the correct punctuation in Sentence 2. 'Dad' is a proper noun and needs a capital letter.

1. The drought has damaged the bough of the tree.
2. "Have we bought enough doughnuts?" asked Dad.
3. The scientists will make a breakthrough very soon.

‹ough›

Spelling List 25

1. cough

2. dough

3. bough

4. rough

5. tough

6. bought

7. though

8. through

9. enough

10. drought

11. although

12. doughnut

13. sought

14. thorough

15. throughout

16. overwrought

17. breakthrough

18. afterthought

One of the trickiest spellings in English is ‹ough›, because it can say a number of different sounds. Match the Spelling List words to the sounds below.

/uff/

/ou/

/or/

schwa

/oa/

/off/

/oo/

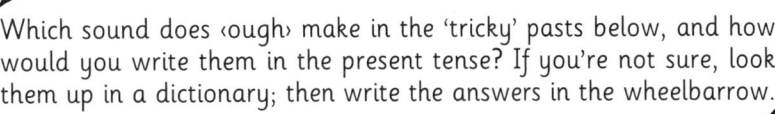

Which sound does ‹ough› make in the 'tricky' pasts below, and how would you write them in the present tense? If you're not sure, look them up in a dictionary; then write the answers in the wheelbarrow.

ough

bought
brought
fought
sought
thought

Spelling Sheet 25a (JGH6)

Dictation: ‹ough›

1. _____

_____

2. _____

_____

3. _____

_____

Write the meanings for these pairs of homophones. Use a dictionary if you need to check.

doe

dough

plain

plane

guessed

guest

bow

bough

Parse the sentence and then write it on the wall.

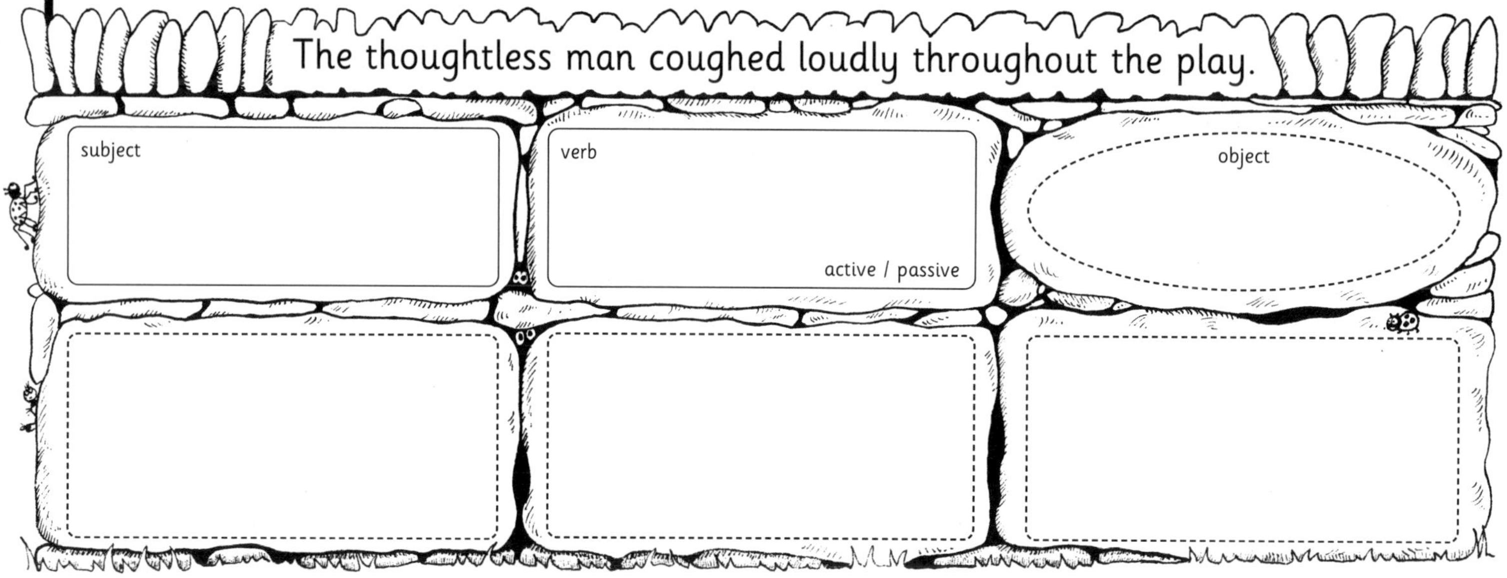

The thoughtless man coughed loudly throughout the play.

subject	verb	object
	active / passive	

Grammar 25 – Irregular Verb 'To Do'

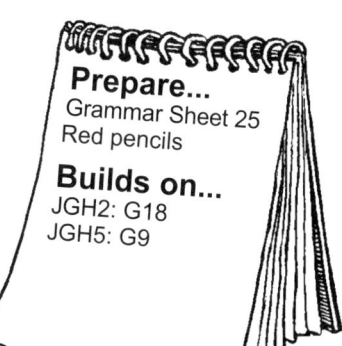

Prepare...
Grammar Sheet 25
Red pencils

Builds on...
JGH2: G18
JGH5: G9

Aim: Ensure the children can conjugate the irregular verb 'to do' in the past, present and future tenses (simple, continuous and perfect), and develop their understanding of how it can be used as a main verb.

Introduction: Remind the class that some verbs do not form the past tense and past participle by adding ‹-ed› to the root. Such verbs are irregular or 'tricky' and have to be learnt. The verb 'to do' is one of these verbs: it has the tricky past 'did'; its past participle is 'done'; and the third person singular in the simple present tense – 'does' – has the ‹-es› suffix rather than ‹-s›. Draw a simple grid of nine boxes on the board, fill in the tenses with the class (as shown on the worksheet), and discuss how each one is formed (see Verbs: pages 11 and 12), pointing out the regular and irregular parts. The children need to be able to conjugate 'to do' properly, as – like 'to be' and 'to have' – it is one of the most commonly used verbs in English, both as a main verb and as an auxiliary. Unlike 'to be' and 'to have', however, the auxiliary is not used to form tenses, but to add emphasis to a sentence, to make it negative, or to form a question, and the children learn more about this in the following two lessons.

Main point: The verb 'to do' has a number of meanings, mostly related to the idea of performing or taking part in an action *[What are you doing?]*, achieving or completing an activity or task *[I did... the crossword/my homework/some drawing/the ironing]*, studying *[We do French at school]*, or inquiring about someone's job *[What does Anna do?]*. Often it is used instead of another verb, particularly when the action described is obvious or routine, or when it includes several different tasks. For example, we can say that we 'do' our teeth and hair in the morning instead of using the verbs 'clean' and 'brush', or we will often say that we 'did' the gardening or cleaning, meaning that we undertook various activities like digging, weeding, mowing the lawn and watering the plants or dusting, polishing, vacuuming and tidying up. Point out that this list of activities is made up of gerunds (nouns formed by adding ‹-ing› to the root verb), which the children learnt about in Grammar Lesson 23; 'to do' is often used with gerunds, as the verb action is already obvious from the noun itself, as in 'to do the... cooking/sewing/shopping' and so on. Write some other 'to do' phrases on the board, discuss them with the children and see if they can think of other verbs to use instead. Possible examples include the following: to do... the dishes *[wash/ clean]*, ...our hair *[brush/tidy/style]*, ...their teeth *[brush/clean]*, ...the laundry *[wash/ dry/iron]*, ...the shopping *[buy]*, ...breakfast/lunch/dinner *[cook/make/prepare]*, ...sums *[work out/solve]*, ...a cartwheel/handstand *[perform]*, ...some damage *[cause/result in]*.

Grammar Sheet 25: The children write inside the outlined word Verbs, using a red pencil. They then find the different forms of the verb 'to do' in the sentences, underline them in red and identify the tense used each time *[1. will be doing/future continuous, 2. had done/ past perfect, 3. did/simple past, 4. is doing/present continuous, 5. has done/present perfect, 6. will have done/future perfect, 7. will do/simple future, 8. were doing/past continuous, 9. does/simple present]*. Then they complete each sentence by writing the correct form of the verb *[10. did, 11. did, 12. did, 13. does, 14. does, 15. do]* and think about what other verbs might be used instead *[for example: <u>completed</u> lots of work; <u>took part in</u> some exercise; <u>caused</u> a lot of damage; <u>brushes/cleans</u> his teeth; <u>undertakes</u> the gardening; <u>brush</u> my hair].*

Extension activity: The children rewrite some sentences from the worksheet in the other eight tenses. Alternatively, they can create their own sentences using 'to do', swap them with a partner, and then rewrite them in the other tenses.

Rounding off: Go over the sheet with the children, discussing their answers. If they have done the extension activity, ask some of the children to read out their sentences.

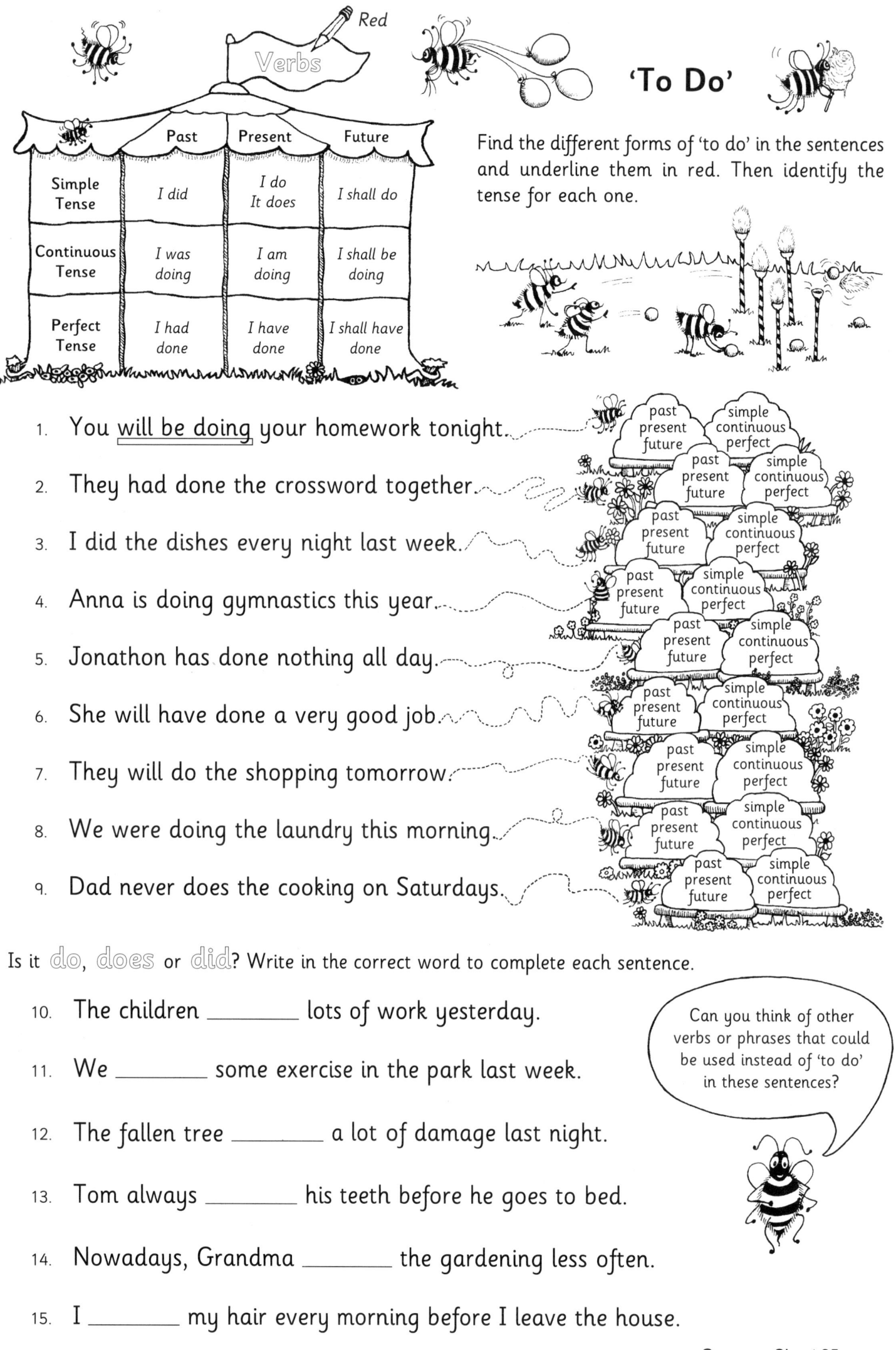

Red

Verbs

	Past	Present	Future
Simple Tense	I did	I do / It does	I shall do
Continuous Tense	I was doing	I am doing	I shall be doing
Perfect Tense	I had done	I have done	I shall have done

'To Do'

Find the different forms of 'to do' in the sentences and underline them in red. Then identify the tense for each one.

1. You <u>will be doing</u> your homework tonight.

2. They had done the crossword together.

3. I did the dishes every night last week.

4. Anna is doing gymnastics this year.

5. Jonathon has done nothing all day.

6. She will have done a very good job.

7. They will do the shopping tomorrow.

8. We were doing the laundry this morning.

9. Dad never does the cooking on Saturdays.

past present future — simple continuous perfect
past present future — simple continuous perfect
past present future — simple continuous perfect
past present future — simple continuous perfect
past present future — simple continuous perfect
past present future — simple continuous perfect
past present future — simple continuous perfect
past present future — simple continuous perfect

Is it do, does or did? Write in the correct word to complete each sentence.

10. The children _____ lots of work yesterday.

11. We _____ some exercise in the park last week.

12. The fallen tree _____ a lot of damage last night.

13. Tom always _____ his teeth before he goes to bed.

14. Nowadays, Grandma _____ the gardening less often.

15. I _____ my hair every morning before I leave the house.

Can you think of other verbs or phrases that could be used instead of 'to do' in these sentences?

Spelling 26 – Schwa ‹ure›

Prepare...
Spelling Sheets 26a/b
Coloured pencils

Builds on...
JGH2: S33
JGH3: S32
JGH5: S19-20

Revision: Write these words on the board and ask the class to identify the sound made by ‹ough› in each one: tough /uff/, cough /off/, drought /ou/, thorough (schwa), through /oo/, doughnut /oa/, afterthought /or/. Ask the children to use one of these words in a sentence.

Main point: Revise the ‹ure› spelling, which is often preceded by ‹t› or ‹s›, but can follow other letters as well. Remind the class that in monosyllabic words like 'pure' and 'cure', and in most words where the ‹ure› is stressed, it keeps its pure sound, /ue-r/, as in 'impure', 'secure' and 'manicure'; however, it can make other sounds too, such as a stressed /or/ in 'sure' and other words in that family (for example, 'unsure', 'ensure', 'insure' and 'reassure'), but more commonly it is unstressed and the vowel becomes a schwa. It is often added to words as a suffix to make abstract nouns indicating action or a group (as in 'failure' and 'legislature') but is also found in other types of word.

Spelling list: Go through the list, discuss the meaning of any unfamiliar words, and ask the class to find and highlight the ‹ure› spelling each time. Point out other spelling features, such as the ‹t› saying /ch/ in 'picture' and all the other ‹ture› words, the vowel saying its long sound in 'nature' and 'procedure', the alternative spelling in 'creature', the /y/ sound before the schwa in 'manufacture' and 'acupuncture', the ‹d› saying /j/ and 'soft ‹c›' in 'procedure', the ‹ea› saying /e/ and ‹s› saying /zh/ in 'treasurer', the ‹n› saying /ng/ in 'acupuncture' and the prefix and suffix in '**dis**figure**ment**'. It is a good idea to blend and sound out the spelling words quickly every day with the class, using the 'say it as it sounds' strategy where appropriate (stressing the pure sound of any schwas, for example, as in '**a**dventur**e**r' and 'pr**o**cedure').

Spelling Sheet 26a: The children split each word into syllables to help remember the spelling [1. pic/ture, 2. na/ture, 3. in/jure, 4. lec/ture, 5. tex/ture, 6. pas/ture, 7. sculp/ture, 8. crea/ture, 9. stat/ure, 10. tor/ture, 11. rup/ture, 12. cul/tured, 13. man/u/fac/ture, 14. ad/ven/tur/er, 15. pro/ce/dure, 16. trea/sur/er, 17. ac/u/punc/ture, 18. dis/fig/ure/ment]. They then put the spelling words into alphabetical order [1. acupuncture, 2. adventurer, 3. creature, 4. cultured, 5. disfigurement, 6. injure, 7. lecture, 8. manufacture, 9. nature, 10. pasture, 11. picture, 12. procedure, 13. rupture, 14. sculpture, 15. stature, 16. texture, 17. torture, 18. treasurer].

Spelling Sheet 26b: The children decide whether each word is a noun or verb, or whether it can act as both. They then write in the correct outlined word(s), using the appropriate colour(s): black for nouns and red for verbs [Nouns only: creature, nature, mixture, procedure; Verbs only: injure, conjure; Both: treasure, lecture, rupture, fracture, puncture]. Then they parse the sentence and complete the wall [Top: Sculptures - were bought - (blank) / Bottom: from ancient cultures - by the museum - (blank) / Verb: passive]. 'From ancient cultures' is a prepositional phrase describing 'sculptures', so it needs blue brackets. The passive verb uses the auxiliary 'were' with the irregular past participle 'bought'.

Sculptures[N] (from[Pre] ancient[Adj] cultures[N])[Adj] (were bought)[V] (by[Pre] the museum[N])[Adv].

Noun[N] (black), Verb[V] (red), Pronoun[P] (pink), Adjective[Adj] (blue), Adverb[Adv] (orange), Conjunction[C] (purple), Preposition[Pre] (green)

Dictation: (This can be done in the spelling lesson or at another time during the week.) Call out the sentences for the children to write down. Remind them to use speech marks with the correct punctuation in Sentence 3. 'Daisy' is a proper noun and needs a capital letter.

1. Daisy took a picture of the cows in the pasture.
2. The adventurer gave a lecture about her travels.
3. "The poor creature is badly injured!" exclaimed the vet.

Spelling List 26

1. picture
2. nature
3. injure
4. lecture
5. texture
6. pasture
7. sculpture
8. creature
9. stature
10. torture
11. rupture
12. cultured
13. manufacture
14. adventurer
15. procedure
16. treasurer
17. acupuncture
18. disfigurement

Put the words in the Spelling List into alphabetical order.

1. _____
2. _____
3. _____
4. _____
5. _____
6. _____
7. _____
8. _____
9. _____
10. _____
11. _____
12. _____
13. _____
14. _____
15. _____
16. _____
17. _____
18. _____

a b c d e f g h i j k l m n o p q r s t u v w x y z

Dictation: schwa ‹ure›

1. _____

_____

2. _____

_____

3. _____

_____

Are these words nouns or verbs or can they be both? Write inside the correct outlined word(s) in black (if it is a noun), red (if it is a verb) or black and red if they can act as both.

Black   Red

creature	noun	verb	noun and verb
treasure	noun	verb	noun and verb
nature	noun	verb	noun and verb
injure	noun	verb	noun and verb
lecture	noun	verb	noun and verb
mixture	noun	verb	noun and verb
conjure	noun	verb	noun and verb
rupture	noun	verb	noun and verb
fracture	noun	verb	noun and verb
puncture	noun	verb	noun and verb
procedure	noun	verb	noun and verb

Parse the sentence and then write it on the wall.

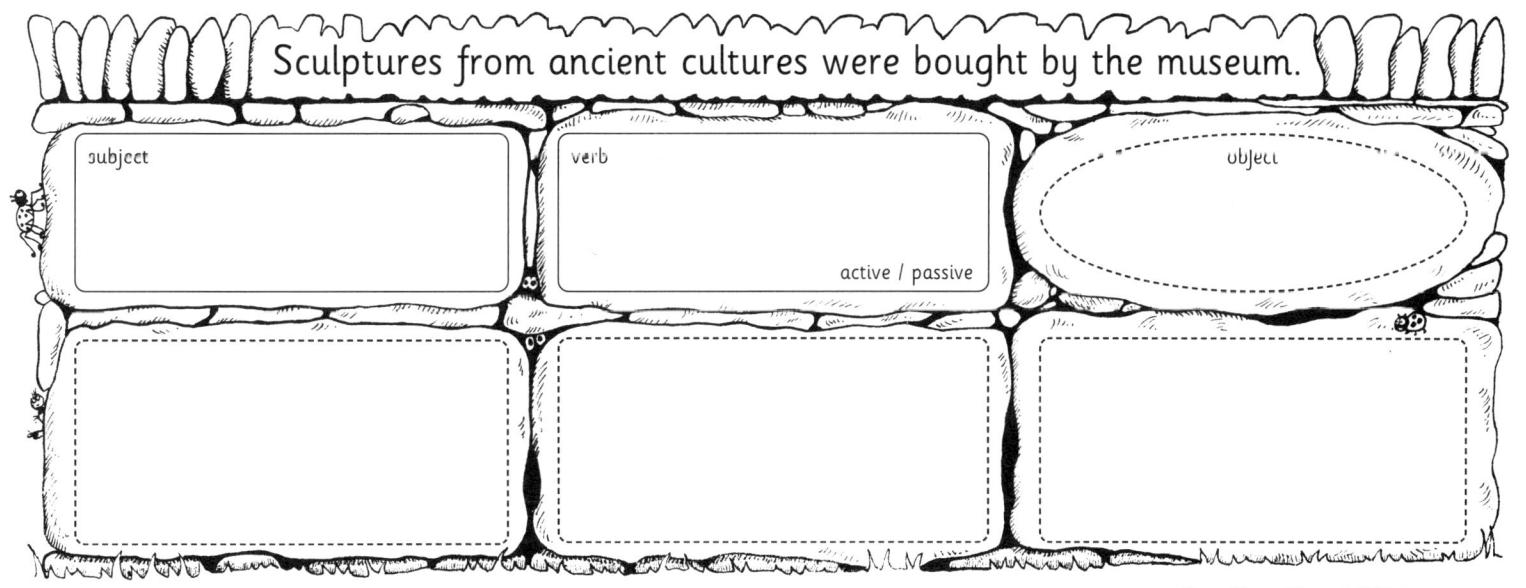

Sculptures from ancient cultures were bought by the museum.

subject

verb

active / passive

object

Grammar 26 – Using the Verb 'To Do' in Statements

Prepare...
Grammar Sheet 26
Red pencils

Builds on...
JGH5: G11

Aim: Develop the children's understanding of auxiliary verbs, which can help to emphasise a positive verb or to make it negative. If there is no auxiliary, we use the irregular verb 'to do' instead, along with the infinitive form of the main verb.

Introduction: Briefly revise sentences. Remind the class that all sentences must make sense, start with a capital letter, contain a verb and subject, and end with a full stop, question mark or exclamation mark. Sentences that state some information and end in a full stop are called statements, ones that ask for more information and end in ‹?› are called questions, and those that express something very strongly and end in ‹!› are called exclamations. Explain that sentences can be **positive**, expressing what **is**, or they can be **negative**, expressing what **is not**. Write the positive statement 'The cows were grazing in the pasture' and ask the children how they would turn this into a negative statement: the children should know how to put the adverb 'not' between the main verb and the auxiliary so that it becomes 'The cows were not grazing in the pasture'. Explain that if we wanted to add emphasis to this in our speech, we would stress 'not', but if we wanted to emphasise the positive statement we would stress the auxiliary, as in 'The cows **were** grazing in the pasture'. Call out some other positive statements in the continuous or perfect tenses (such as 'The painting is hanging on the wall' or 'They had buried the treasure') and ask the class to say them with emphasis or to make them negative.

Main point: Now write on the board 'The cows grazed in the pasture' and ask the children how this can be turned into a negative statement. Explain that the verb 'grazed' is in the simple past tense so 'not' cannot go in its usual place between the auxiliary and the main verb. Instead, we make the verb 'to do' the auxiliary, use the infinitive form of the main verb and put 'not' in between, so the sentence becomes 'The cows did not graze in the pasture'. Similarly, if we wanted to add emphasis to the positive statement, we would have to add 'to do' in the same way and stress the auxiliary, as in 'The cows **did** graze in the pasture'. Write some more positive statements on the board (in the simple past and present tenses) and rewrite them, firstly to show emphasis, and then as negative statements. Possible examples include: 'We like the sculpture' *[We do (not) like the sculpture]*, 'The adventurer returned safely' *[The adventurer did (not) return safely]*, 'The factory manufactures cars' *[The factory does (not) manufacture cars]*. Make sure the children use the correct form of 'to do' each time and revise the irregular parts of the verb if necessary.

Grammar Sheet 26: The children look at each sentence and underline the verb in red. They then add emphasis to the positive statement by adding 'do' or 'does' in the present tense, or by adding 'did' in the past tense, along with the infinitive form of the main verb. Then they add 'not' between the auxiliary and the main verb to turn it into a negative statement *[1. like/I do (not) like bananas, 2. made/We did (not) make pancakes, 3. went/ They did (not) go home, 4. builds/ He does (not) build boats, 5. ran/You did (not) run away, 6. stopped/The rain did (not) stop, 7. locked/I did (not) lock the door, 8. know/You do (not) know Sam, 9. met/We did (not) meet John, 10. plays/She does (not) play golf, 11. told/ They did (not) tell you, 12. saw/You did (not) see the thief]*. Lastly, the children write inside the outlined contractions and then write them out in full underneath, writing 'don't' as 'do not', 'doesn't' as 'does not' and 'didn't' as 'did not'.

Extension activity: The children rewrite some of their negative statements, using the correct contraction each time, such as 'They didn't go home', for example.

Rounding off: Go over the sheet with the children, discussing their answers. If they have done the extension activity, ask some of the children to read out their sentences.

Positive and Negative Statements

Auxiliary verbs can help to emphasise a positive verb or make it negative. We **stress** the auxiliary for emphasis (You **will** go the party!) and put 'not' between it and the main verb to make it negative (You will **not** go to the party!). The simple forms of the past and present tenses have no auxiliaries so we use the verb 'to do' together with the infinitive form of the main verb instead.

| do/does/did + infinitive = **positive** statement |
| do/does/did + **not** + infinitive = **negative** statement |

Underline each verb in red and decide whether it is in the past or present tense. Then rewrite each sentence using the correct form of 'to do' to a) show emphasis and b) make it negative.

1. I like bananas.   I do like bananas.   I do not like bananas.
2. We made pancakes.   We did make pancakes.   We did not make pancakes.
3. They went home.   _____   _____
4. He builds boats.   _____   _____
5. You ran away.   _____   _____
6. The rain stopped.   _____   _____
7. I locked the door.   _____   _____
8. You know Sam.   _____   _____
9. We met John.   _____   _____
10. She plays golf.   _____   _____
11. They told you.   _____   _____
12. You saw the thief.   _____   _____

'To do' is often contracted with 'not' in everyday speech. Trace over the contractions below and then write them out in full underneath, with no letters missing.

I do n o t   I don't

I don't   you don't   he doesn't   we don't   they don't

_____ _____ _____ _____ _____

I didn't   you didn't   she didn't   we didn't   they didn't

_____ _____ _____ _____ _____

Spelling 27 – Schwa ‹our›

Prepare...
Spelling Sheets 27a/b
Coloured pencils

Builds on...
JGH4: S7-12,
S22-24
JGH6: S26

Revision: Write these words on the board and ask the class to identify the schwa ‹ure› in each one: figure, structure, future, measure, feature, furniture, moisture, vulture. Ask the class to use one of these words in a sentence.

Main point: The ‹our› spelling can be pronounced in several ways in stressed syllables, such as /er/ in 'journey', /or/ in 'four', the little /oo/ followed by a schwa in 'tour', or the /ou/ and schwa in 'flour'. However, ‹our› is often found in a final, unstressed syllable, where it becomes a schwa sound, as in 'colour', 'flavour' and 'neighbour'. Ask the children to clap the syllables in each of these words and listen for the stress in the first syllable. Many words like this are derived from Latin nouns ending in ‹or›, but they have come via French, which uses the ‹our› spelling instead.

Spelling list: Go through the list, discuss the meaning of any unfamiliar words, and ask the class to find and highlight the ‹our› spelling each time. Point out other spelling features, such as the vowel saying its long sound in '**fa**vour', '**fla**vour', '**hu**mour', '**o**dour', '**la**bourer', '**sa**voury' and 'be**ha**viour', the ‹u› saying /oo/ in '**ru**mour', the ‹o› saying /u/ in 'c**o**lourful', the suffix in 'colour**ful**', 'labour**er**', 'savour**y**' and 'honour**able**', the ‹eigh› in 'n**eigh**bour', the ‹e› saying /i/ in 'b**e**haviour' and '**e**ndeavour', the ‹i› saying /y/ when it goes before ‹our› in 'behav**i**our', the ‹ea› saying /e/ in 'end**ea**vour', and the silent ‹h› in '**h**onourable'. It is a good idea to blend and sound out the spelling words quickly every day with the class, using the 'say it as it sounds' strategy where appropriate (stressing the pure sound of any schwas, as in 'labour**er**', or syllables that are almost swallowed, as in 'hon**our**able', for example).

Spelling Sheet 27a: The children split each word into syllables to help remember the spelling [1. arm/our, 2. fa/vour, 3. fla/vour, 4. hu/mour, 5. har/bour, 6. ru/mour, 7. o/dour, 8. clam/our, 9. col/our/ful, 10. neigh/bour, 11. la/bour/er, 12. vig/our, 13. val/our, 14. sa/vour/y, 15. splen/dour, 16. be/hav/iour, 17. en/deav/our, 18. hon/our/a/ble]. They then unscramble the letters and add them to ‹our› to make some of the spelling words [humour, flavour, harbour, armour, vigour, labourer, neighbour, colourful, clamour, valour, splendour, endeavour, behaviour, savoury].

Spelling Sheet 27b: The children turn the positive statements into negative ones by using the auxiliary verb 'to do', followed by 'not' and the infinitive form of the main verb [1. This cheese does not have an unpleasant odour, 2. I do not like this flavour of ice cream, 3. The ships did not sail into the harbour, 4. They do not often hear rumours about the old house, 5. Your neighbour does not do the gardening every day]. Then they parse the sentence and complete the wall [Top: armour - was worn - (blank) / Bottom: The splendid - by the king/in battle - (blank) / Verb: passive]. 'By the king' and 'in battle' are prepositional phrases acting as adverbs and need orange brackets. The passive verb uses the auxiliary 'was' with the irregular past participle 'worn'.

The splendid[Adj] armour[N] (was worn)[V] (by[Pre] the king[N])[Adv] (in[Pre] battle[N])[Adv].

Noun[N] (black), Verb[V] (red), Pronoun[P] (pink), Adjective[Adj] (blue), Adverb[Adv] (orange), Conjunction[C] (purple), Preposition[Pre] (green)

Dictation: (This can be done in the spelling lesson or at another time during the week.) Call out the sentences for the children to write down. Remind them to use speech marks with the correct punctuation in Sentence 1.

1. "Can you do me a favour?" I asked my neighbour.
2. Always reward your pet for good behaviour.
3. The sorbet had an interesting colour and flavour.

Schwa ‹our›

Spelling List 27

1. armour
2. favour
3. flavour
4. humour
5. harbour
6. rumour
7. odour
8. clamour
9. colourful
10. neighbour
11. labourer
12. vigour
13. valour
14. savoury
15. splendour
16. behaviour
17. endeavour
18. honourable

Unscramble the letters and add them to ‹our› to make words from the Spelling List.

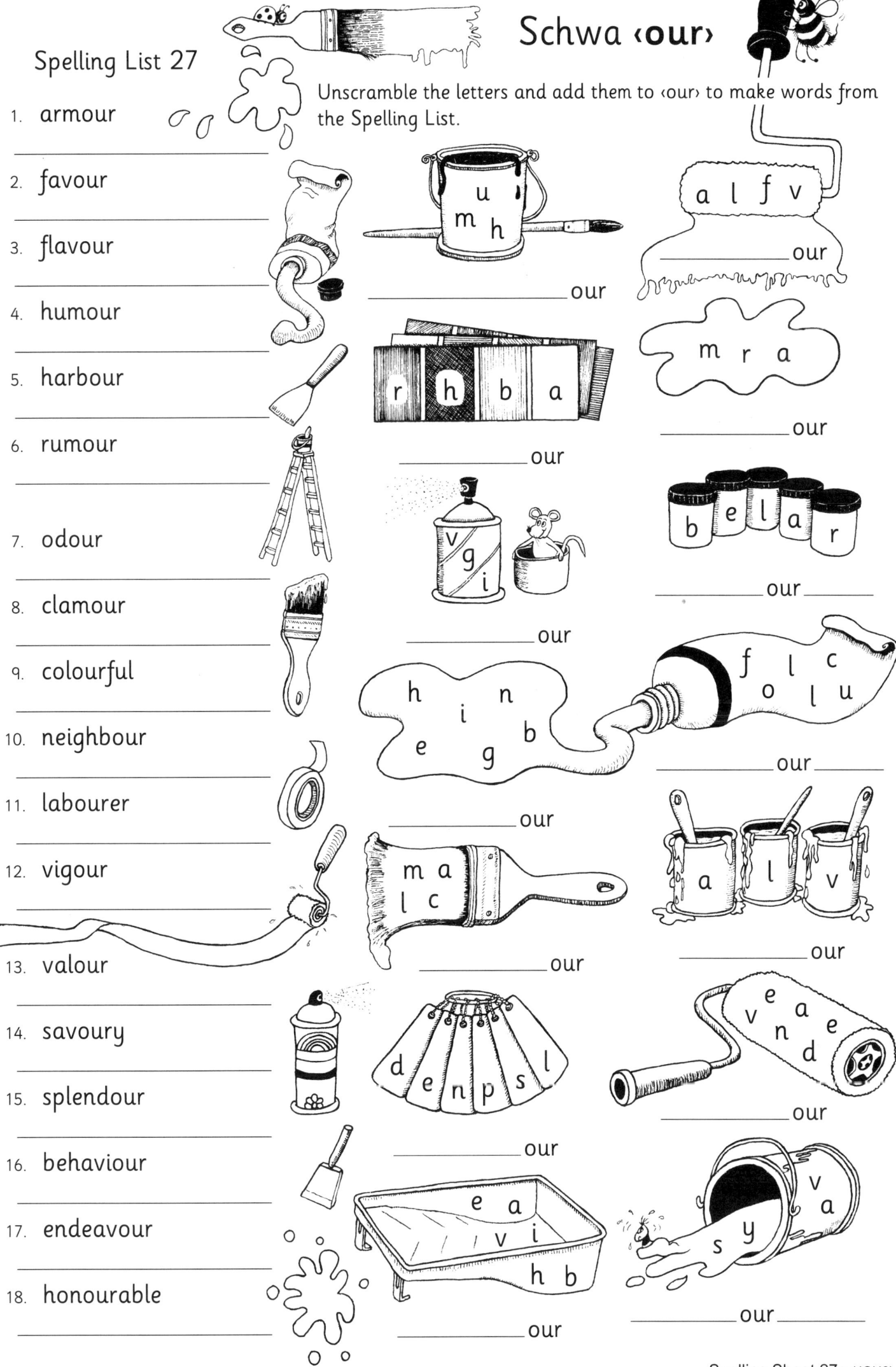

u m h _____ our

a l f v _____ our

r h b a _____ our

m r a _____ our

v g i _____ our

b e l a r our _____

h i n e g b _____ our

f l c o l u _____ our

m a l c _____ our

a l v _____ our

d e n p s l _____ our

v e a e n d _____ our

e a v i h b _____ our

s y v a _____ our _____

Spelling Sheet 27a (JGH6)

Dictation: schwa ‹our›

1. _____

_____

2. _____

_____

3. _____

_____

Turn these positive statements into negative statements, using the verb 'to do' as an auxiliary, followed by 'not' and the infinitive form of the main verb. If the original verb is in the present tense, use 'do' or 'does', and if it is in the past tense, use 'did'.

do/does/did + **not** + infinitive = **negative** statement

1. This cheese has an unpleasant odour.

_____

2. I like this flavour of ice cream.

_____

3. The ships sailed into the harbour.

_____

4. They often hear rumours about the old house.

_____

5. Your neighbour does the gardening every day.

_____

Parse the sentence and then write it on the wall.

The splendid armour was worn by the king in battle.

subject	verb	object
	active / passive	

Grammar 27 – Using the Verb 'To Do' in Questions

Prepare...
Grammar Sheet 27
Red pencils

Builds on...
JGH1: G2-3, G34-35
JGH2: G2, G4, G6
JGH4: G25-26
JGH5: G25
JGH6: G26

Aim: Develop the children's ability to turn statements into questions when the main verb is not 'to be' and it has no auxiliary. Explain that when this happens, we make 'to do' the auxiliary, put it at the beginning of the question and use the infinitive form of the main verb.

Introduction: Briefly revise the ways that the children know how to form a question or turn a statement into a question: for example, they could use one of the ‹wh› question words *[what, why, when, where, who, which, whose]*; alternatively, if 'to be' is the main verb, then it can be moved to the beginning to form a question *[The armour is heavy/Is the armour heavy?]*; similarly, if the verb has an auxiliary, this too can be moved to the beginning *[Her neighbours are moving soon/Are her neighbours moving soon?]*. Ask the children to think of some questions using the ‹wh› words and discuss them with the class. Then write some statements on the board in the continuous and perfect tenses and ask the children to turn them into questions by moving the auxiliary to the beginning and putting a question mark at the end, instead of a full stop.

Main point: Now write 'Her neighbours moved away' on the board, and ask the children how they think this statement could be rewritten as a question. Unlike the previous examples, this statement is written in the simple past *[moved]* and has no auxiliary to put at the beginning. Remind the class that when we want to add emphasis to a verb like this, we make 'to do' the auxiliary and use the infinitive form of the main verb, as in 'Her neighbours <u>did move</u> away'. Now explain that we can do the same thing to turn the statement into a question, only this time the auxiliary goes at the beginning and the full stop is replaced by a question mark, as in '<u>Did</u> her neighbours <u>move</u> away?' Write some more statements on the board in the simple past or present tense and ask the class to turn them into questions, such as 'We like the sculpture' *[Do we like the sculpture?]*, 'The adventurer returned safely' *[Did the adventurer return safely?]*, and 'The factory manufactures cars' *[Does the factory manufacture cars?]*. Each time, ask the children to answer their own question: they may say, for example, 'Yes, we do like the sculpture' or 'Yes, the adventurer did return safely', but they may also say 'Yes, we do' or 'Yes, he did'. Point out how, in these examples, 'to do' is used on its own as a substitute for the rest of the sentence. In addition, the verb is also used in what are called 'question tags' or 'tag questions' *[We like the sculpture, don't we?/The factory doesn't manufacture cars, does it?]*.

Grammar Sheet 27: The children write inside the outlined word Verb, using a red pencil. They then turn each statement into a question. First they add 'do' or 'does' *[present tense]* or 'did' *[past tense]* to the beginning of the sentence; then they use the infinitive form of the main verb; and finally they replace the full stop with a question mark *[1. <u>Do</u> I <u>like</u> bananas more than apples? 2. <u>Did</u> we <u>make</u> pancakes for breakfast? 3. <u>Did</u> they <u>go</u> home after the party? 4. <u>Does</u> he <u>build</u> boats for a living? 5. <u>Did</u> you <u>run</u> away from the fierce dog? 6. <u>Did</u> the rain <u>stop</u> during the concert?]*. Those children who need extra support can use their worksheet from Grammar Lesson 26 as a prompt. Then they rewrite the negative questions, using the contractions 'don't', 'doesn't' or 'didn't' *[7. Didn't I...? 8. Don't you...? 9. Didn't we...? 10. Doesn't she...? 11. Didn't they...? 12. Didn't you...?]*.

Extension activity: The children write some questions of their own starting with, for example, 'Do you...?' 'Did I...?' 'Does she...?' 'Didn't we...?' 'Don't they...?' 'Doesn't he...?' on the back of their worksheets.

Rounding off: Go over the sheet with the children, discussing their answers. If they have done the extension activity, ask some of the children to read out their questions.

Questions and the Verb 'To Do'

One way to write a question is to put the auxiliary verb at the beginning of the sentence (**Will** you go to the party?). There are no auxiliaries in the simple past and present tenses so we add 'do', 'does' or 'did' at the beginning instead and put the main verb in its infinitive form.

Rewrite these statements as questions using the verb 'to do'.

1. I like bananas more than apples.
   Do I like bananas more than apples?

2. We made pancakes for breakfast.
   _____

3. They went home after the party.
   _____

4. He builds boats for a living.
   _____

5. You ran away from the fierce dog.
   _____

6. The rain stopped during the concert.
   _____

Negative questions using 'to do' are usually contracted to 'don't', 'doesn't' and 'didn't' in everyday speech. Rewrite these questions, contracting the verb each time.

7. "Did I not lock the door?" said Dad, anxiously.
   "Didn't I lock the door?" said Dad, anxiously.

8. "Do you not know Sam?" they asked in surprise.
   _____

9. "Did we not meet John two years ago?" I queried.
   _____

10. "Does she not play tennis on Saturdays?" wondered Beth.
    _____

11. "Did they not tell you about their trip?" asked Grandpa.
    _____

12. "Did you not see the thief?" quizzed the police officer.
    _____

Spelling 28 – ‹-ity›, ‹-ety›

Prepare...
Spelling Sheets 28a/b
Coloured pencils

Builds on...
JGH4: S25-30
JGH5: S3-6

Revision: Write these words on the board and ask the class to identify the schwa ‹our› in each one: colour, labour, humour, savoury, honour, favour, clamour, vigour. Ask the class to use one of them in a sentence.

Main point: Write the words 'security' and 'safety' on the board and ask the children what they have in common. These words are synonyms (words with the same, or similar, meaning), and they also have similar suffixes: ‹-ity› and ‹-ety›. These suffixes are always unstressed and have a swallowed vowel that makes either the schwa or /i/ sound, so the spellings have to be learnt. They are found in abstract nouns with the quality or condition of the root word (so if there is a possibility of rain, for example, it is possible this will happen, or if there is a variety of choices, there are various options to consider). The less common suffix ‹-ety› is usually added to root words ending in ‹e› or is used to avoid having a double ‹i› in words like 'variety' and 'anxiety'. However, words with roots ending in ‹e› can also have the ‹-ity› suffix, as in 'activity' and 'security'.

Spelling list: Go through the list, discuss the meaning of any unfamiliar words, and ask the class to find and highlight the suffix ‹-ity› or ‹-ety› each time. Point out other spelling features, such as the way the final ‹e› of the root word has been removed before adding the suffix in 'activity', 'purity', 'security', 'safety', 'entirety', 'subtlety' and 'opportunity', the ‹e› saying /i/ in 's**e**curity', '**e**ntirety' and 're**s**ponsibility', the vowel saying its long sound in 'r**e**ality', '**i**dentity', '**a**nxiety', 'v**a**riety', 's**o**ciety' and 'opport**u**nity', the way the ‹e› in 'safety' and 'subtlety' is not pronounced, the ‹nx› saying /ng-z/ in 'anxiety', the 'soft ‹c›' in 'society', the 'silent letter' digraph in 'su**bt**lety', and the 'soft ‹g›' in 'generosity'. It is a good idea to blend and sound out the spelling words quickly every day with the class, using the 'say it as it sounds' strategy where appropriate (stressing the pure sound of any schwas, as in '**a**bility', for example).

Spelling Sheet 28a: The children split each word into syllables to help remember the spelling *[1. ac/tiv/i/ty, 2. a/bil/i/ty, 3. pu/ri/ty, 4. re/al/i/ty, 5. se/cu/ri/ty, 6. i/den/ti/ty, 7. safe/ty, 8. anx/i/e/ty, 9. va/ri/e/ty, 10. so/ci/e/ty, 11. en/tir/e/ty, 12. sub/tle/ty, 13. op/por/tu/ni/ty, 14. pos/si/bil/i/ty, 15. cu/ri/os/i/ty, 16. fa/mil/i/ar/i/ty, 17. gen/e/ros/i/ty, 18. re/spon/si/bil/i/ty].* They then write the spelling words that belong to the same word family as the adjectives *[ability, curiosity, variety, possibility, anxiety, society, opportunity, generosity, responsibility]* and add the correct suffix to the spelling words.

Spelling Sheet 28b: The children turn the statements into questions *[1. Does this cheese have an unpleasant odour? 2. Do I like this flavour of ice cream? 3. Did the ships sail into the harbour? 4. Do they often hear rumours about the old house? 5. Does your neighbour do the gardening every day?].* Then they parse the sentence and complete the wall *[Top: climbing - is\ activity (a popular) - (blank) / Bottom: Mountain - (blank) - (blank) / Verb: linking].* 'Mountain' is a noun acting as an adjective and should be underlined in blue. 'Climbing' is a gerund made by adding ‹-ing› to the verb 'climb'.

Mountain^Adj climbing^N is^V a popular^Adj activity^N.

Noun^N (black), Verb^V (red), Pronoun^P (pink), Adjective^Adj (blue), Adverb^Adv (orange), Conjunction^C (purple), Preposition^Pre (green)

Dictation: (This can be done in the spelling lesson or at another time during the week.) Call out the sentences for the children to write down. Remind them to use speech marks with the correct punctuation in Sentence 3.

1. They had a responsibility to ensure our safety.
2. We have the opportunity to create a better society.
3. "I will now reveal your true identity!" exclaimed the detective.

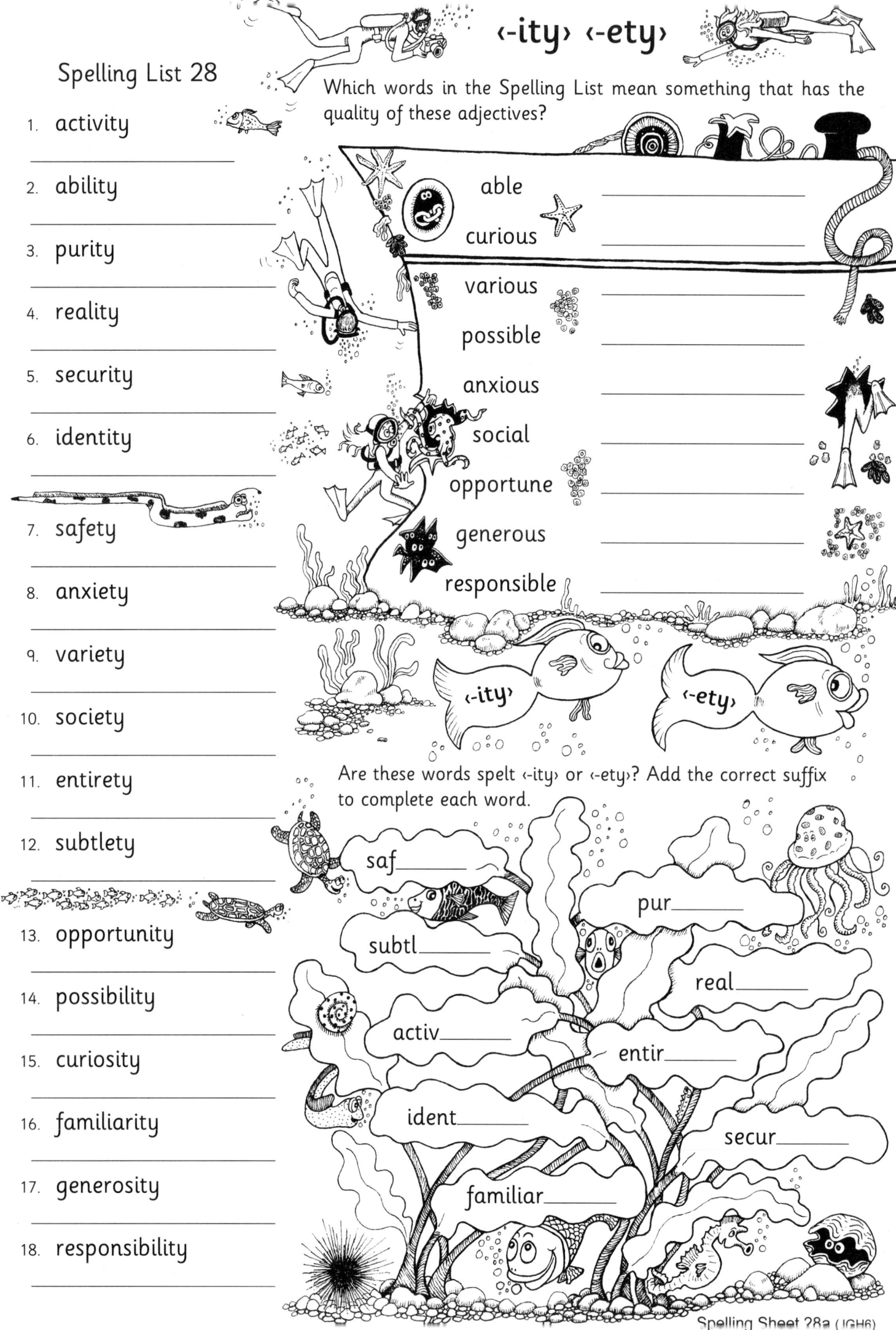

‹-ity› ‹-ety›

Spelling List 28

1. activity
   _____
2. ability
   _____
3. purity
   _____
4. reality
   _____
5. security
   _____
6. identity
   _____
7. safety
   _____
8. anxiety
   _____
9. variety
   _____
10. society
    _____
11. entirety
    _____
12. subtlety
    _____
13. opportunity
    _____
14. possibility
    _____
15. curiosity
    _____
16. familiarity
    _____
17. generosity
    _____
18. responsibility
    _____

Which words in the Spelling List mean something that has the quality of these adjectives?

able _____

curious _____

various _____

possible _____

anxious _____

social _____

opportune _____

generous _____

responsible _____

‹-ity›   ‹-ety›

Are these words spelt ‹-ity› or ‹-ety›? Add the correct suffix to complete each word.

saf_____

subtl_____

pur_____

real_____

activ_____

entir_____

ident_____

secur_____

familiar_____

Dictation: ‹-ity› ‹-ety›

1. _____

_____

2. _____

_____

3. _____

_____

Turn these statements (from Spelling Sheet 27b) into questions, adding 'do', 'does' or 'did' at the beginning and using the main verb in its infinitive form. If the original verb is in the present tense, use 'do' or 'does', and if it is in the past tense, use 'did'.

do/does/did + infinitive + ‹?› = question

1. This cheese has an unpleasant odour.

_____

2. I like this flavour of ice cream.

_____

3. The ships sailed into the harbour.

_____

4. They often hear rumours about the old house.

_____

5. Your neighbour does the gardening every day.

_____

Parse the sentence and then write it on the wall.

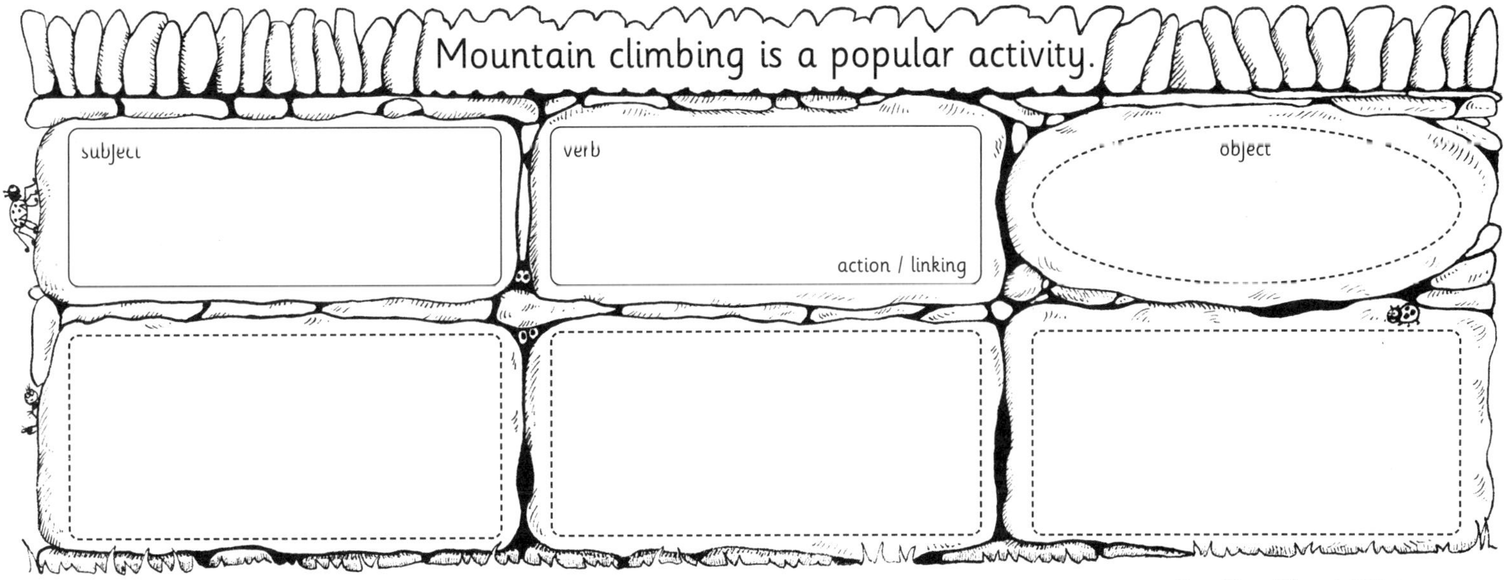

Mountain climbing is a popular activity.

subject	verb	object
	action / linking	

Grammar 28 – Modal Verbs

Prepare...
Grammar Sheet 28
Red pencils

Builds on...
JGH1: G18
JGH3: G8-9, G17
JGH4: G26
JGH5: G7
JGH6: G21-22, G26-27

Aim: Introduce modal verbs, which are a special kind of auxiliary verb. They are used with the infinitive of the main verb to help express things like certainty, obligation, permission or ability. The most common modal verbs are 'will', 'shall', 'can', 'could', 'may', 'might', 'should', 'would' and 'must'.

Introduction: Briefly revise auxiliary verbs and the different ways that they can 'help' the main verb in a sentence. They are often used to form different tenses: for example, 'shall' and 'will' help to indicate the future [*She* will *arrive soon/I* shall *go tomorrow*]; 'to be' forms part of the continuous tenses [*I* am/was/will be *doing the shopping*]; and 'to have' is used in the perfect tenses [*He* had/has/will have *lost his keys*]. Auxiliary verbs are also moved to the beginning of a sentence when we want to turn a statement into a question [*Are you going now?*] but, if there is no auxiliary, we use 'to do' instead, along with the infinitive form of the main verb [*They went home/*Did *they go home?*]. Similarly, 'to do' can be used to add emphasis to a positive statement [*We* **do** *like ice cream!*] or to make it negative [*We* **don't** *like ice cream!*]. Finally, 'to be' is paired with the past participle of the main verb when we want to write in the passive voice [*They* were *seen by the doctor*]. Write the examples on the board, identify the auxiliary verb each time, and make sure the children understand how each one is used.

Main point: We can also use auxiliary verbs to help us express how certain we are about something. For example, if we are very sure that we will go somewhere we can say 'I **will/ shall** go tomorrow'. However, if we are not entirely certain, we could say 'I **might/may** go tomorrow'. 'I **can** go tomorrow' suggests that it is possible and also likely, but 'I **could** go tomorrow' suggests that although it is possible it may not happen. If we feel it is important to go but there is some uncertainty, we can say 'I **should** go tomorrow', or if it depends on something else, we can say 'I **would** go tomorrow'. Also, if it is absolutely necessary to go, we can say 'I **must** go tomorrow', which rules out any uncertainty. Explain that 'will', 'shall', 'can', 'could', 'may', 'might', 'should', 'would' and 'must' belong to a special group of auxiliaries called 'modal verbs'. As well as expressing degrees of certainty and obligation, they can indicate ability [*She can ride a horse (present tense)/She could ride a horse (past tense)*]; or be used to ask or give permission [*Can/May/Could I go next? You can/may*]; or be used to give advice or make suggestions [*You should rest/We could go swimming*]. Modal verbs are always used with the infinitive form of the main verb and, unlike other auxiliary verbs, do not change depending on the grammatical person (so the verb stays the same whichever pronoun is used). Ask the children to suggest their own sentence for each of the modal verbs and discuss how it affects the meaning each time.

Grammar Sheet 28: The children write inside the outlined word Verbs, using a red pencil. They then read the definitions for each sentence and decide which one is correct [*1. A, 2. B, 3. A, 4. B, 5. A, 6. B, 7. A, 8. A, 9. B*].

Extension activity: Working in pairs, the children think of some more sentences using the modal verbs 'will', 'shall', 'can', 'could', 'may', 'might', 'should', 'would' and 'must'. They then discuss what they think the modal verb is doing in each sentence.

Rounding off: Go over the sheet with the children, discussing their answers. If they have done the extension activity, ask some of the children to read out their sentences and discuss what the modal verb is doing each time.

Modal Verbs

Modal verbs are a special kind of auxiliary verb. For example, they can help us express how certain something is, from uncertain (I **might** go to the party) to very certain (I **will** go to the party). Look at each sentence below and decide which definition is correct.

1. You **could** draw a colourful picture.
   - A. I suggest that you draw a colourful picture.
   - B. I demand that you draw a colourful picture.

2. She **can** speak three foreign languages.
   - A. She wants to speak three foreign languages.
   - B. She is able to speak three foreign languages.

3. He **must** polish his shoes thoroughly.
   - A. It is necessary that he polish his shoes thoroughly.
   - B. It is optional whether or not he polishes his shoes thoroughly.

4. If your tongue is numb, you **should** go to the doctor.
   - A. If your tongue is numb, I allow you to go to the doctor.
   - B. If your tongue is numb, I advise you to go to the doctor.

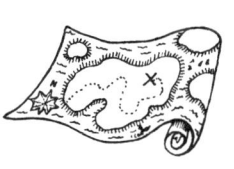

5. "We **shall** find the treasure!" cried the buccaneers.
   - A. "We are sure to find the treasure!" cried the buccaneers.
   - B. "We are likely to find the treasure!" cried the buccaneers.

6. I said that I **would** make the spaghetti dough today.
   - A. I said that I needed to make the spaghetti dough today.
   - B. I said that I intended to make the spaghetti dough today.

7. You **may** leave the table if you finish your fruit juice.
   - A. You are allowed to leave the table if you finish your fruit juice.
   - B. You are required to leave the table if you finish your fruit juice.

8. I **will** have another doughnut now.
   - A. I am going to have another doughnut now.
   - B. I am considering whether or not to have another doughnut now.

9. They **might** see the rhinos and penguins at the zoo.
   - A. It is certain that they will see the rhinos and penguins at the zoo.
   - B. It is possible that they will see the rhinos and penguins at the zoo.

Spelling 29 – ‹-ial›

Prepare...
Spelling Sheets 29a/b
Coloured pencils

Builds on...
JGH4: G19, S22
JGH5: S28-29

Revision: Write these words on the board and ask the class to identify the suffix in each one: saf**ety**, real**ity**, soci**ety**, abil**ity**, vari**ety**, curios**ity**, anxi**ety**, possibil**ity**. Ask the class to use one of them in a sentence.

Main point: Revise the suffix ‹-ial› – a variant of ‹-al› – often used when the root word ends in ‹y› or ‹ce›. When it appears in words ending in ‹tial›, ‹cial› and ‹sial›, the ‹i› helps make the /sh/ sound and the unstressed ‹a› becomes a schwa. However, when other letters precede it, the ‹i› usually makes a sound somewhere between /i/ and /ee/, as in 'burial' and 'trivial', and can also say /ie/, as in 'denial'. Remind the children that ‹-ial› often appears in adjectives that describe something as relating to or having the qualities of the (root) noun (so secretarial work is done by a secretary and a ceremonial uniform is worn at special ceremonies). Look again at the words 'denial' and 'burial' and point out that ‹-ial› is also found in nouns that name the action or practice of the root verb. Look at some more spelling words and identify the root word where possible.

Spelling list: Go through the list, discuss the meaning of any unfamiliar words, and ask the class to find and highlight the suffix ‹-ial› each time. Point out other spelling features, such as the ‹e› saying /i/ in 'denial' and 'secretarial', the ‹i› saying /ie/ in 'denial', the ‹u› saying /e/ in 'burial', the ‹o› saying its long sound in 'jovial' and 'ceremonial', the ‹er› saying /ear/ in 'material' and 'imperial', the double ‹r› in 'territorial', the ‹ar› saying /air/ in 'secretarial', the 'soft ‹c›' in 'ceremonial' and 'celestial', the spoken ‹i› in 'celestial' (rather than ‹tial› saying /shul/), and the ‹u› saying /oo/ in 'marsupial'. It is a good idea to blend and sound out the spelling words quickly every day with the class, using the 'say it as it sounds' strategy where appropriate (stressing the pure sound of any schwas, as in 'material' and 'memorial', for example).

Spelling Sheet 29a: The children split each word into syllables to help remember the spelling [1. de/ni/al, 2. triv/i/al, 3. bur/i/al, 4. jo/vi/al, 5. ma/te/ri/al, 6. im/pe/ri/al, 7. me/mo/ri/al, 8. ter/ri/to/ri/al, 9. ed/i/to/ri/al, 10. in/dus/tri/al, 11. sec/re/tar/i/al, 12. cer/e/mo/ni/al, 13. ce/les/ti/al, 14. sac/ri/fi/cial, 15. sub/stan/tial, 16. mar/su/pi/al, 17. prej/u/di/cial, 18. con/tro/ver/sial]. They then work out the answers to the crossword clues and write them in [1. denial, 2. ceremonial, 3. substantial, 4. industrial, 5. sacrificial, 6. trivial, 7. burial, 8. marsupial, 9. secretarial, 10. prejudicial, 11. celestial, 12. editorial, 13. jovial, 14. imperial, 15. memorial, 16. territorial, 17. material].

Spelling Sheet 29b: The children write the spelling word that belongs to the same word family as each noun or verb [Left-hand column: prejudicial, material, burial, trivial, sacrificial, ceremonial, controversial; Right-hand column: secretarial, memorial, denial, editorial, imperial, territorial, substantial]. Then they parse the sentence and complete the wall [Top: service - was held - (blank) / Bottom: A memorial - for their uncle - (blank) / Verb: passive]. The passive verb uses the auxiliary 'was' with the irregular past participle 'held'. 'For their uncle' is a prepositional phrase acting as an adverb, so it needs orange brackets.

A memorial[Adj] service[N] (was held)[V] (for[Pre] their[Adj] uncle[N])[Adv].

Noun[N] (black), Verb[V] (red), Pronoun[P] (pink), Adjective[Adj] (blue), Adverb[Adv] (orange), Conjunction[C] (purple), Preposition[Pre] (green)

Dictation: (This can be done in the spelling lesson or at another time during the week.) Call out the sentences for the children to write down. Remind them to use speech marks with the correct punctuation in Sentence 2. The proper adjective 'Australian' needs a capital letter.

1. The referee's decision was extremely controversial.
2. "The kangaroo is an Australian marsupial," she explained.
3. The imperial guards were wearing their ceremonial swords.

Spelling List 29

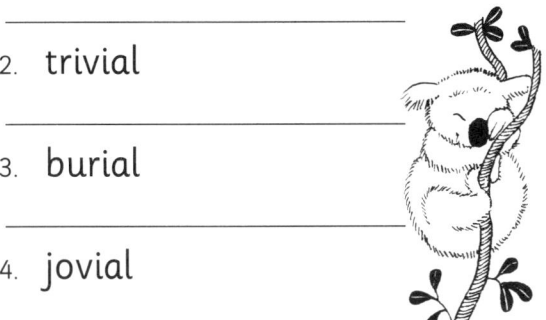

1. denial
_____
2. trivial
_____
3. burial
_____
4. jovial
_____
5. material
_____
6. imperial
_____
7. memorial
_____
8. territorial
_____
9. editorial
_____
10. industrial
_____
11. secretarial
_____
12. ceremonial
_____
13. celestial
_____
14. sacrificial
_____
15. substantial
_____
16. marsupial
_____
17. prejudicial
_____
18. controversial
_____

‹-ial›

Work out the answers to the clues and complete the crossword. All of the answers are words in the Spelling List.

1. a statement saying that something is not true
2. used at a formal event which has special traditions
3. large in size or amount
4. relating to the production of things we buy or to things we use, like oil, coal and steel
5. relating to a religious ceremony where an animal, food or special item is offered to a god as a gift
6. not important, serious or valuable
7. the act of putting something in the ground
8. an animal that carries its baby in a pocket of skin
9. relating to the work or skills of an office assistant
10. having a bad effect on something
11. relating to the sky, outer space or heaven
12. relating to the preparation of a book for printing
13. cheerful and friendly
14. relating to an empire or to the person who rules it
15. something built to remind us of a person or event
16. relating to land owned or controlled by a country
17. cloth used to make things like clothes or curtains

Dictation: ‹-ial›

1. _____

   _____

2. _____

   _____

3. _____

   _____

Which spelling word belongs to the same word family as each of these nouns and verbs?

prejudice _____   secretary _____

matter _____   memory _____

bury _____   deny _____

trivia _____   edit _____

sacrifice _____   empire _____

ceremony _____   territory _____

controversy _____   substance _____

Parse the sentence and then write it on the wall.

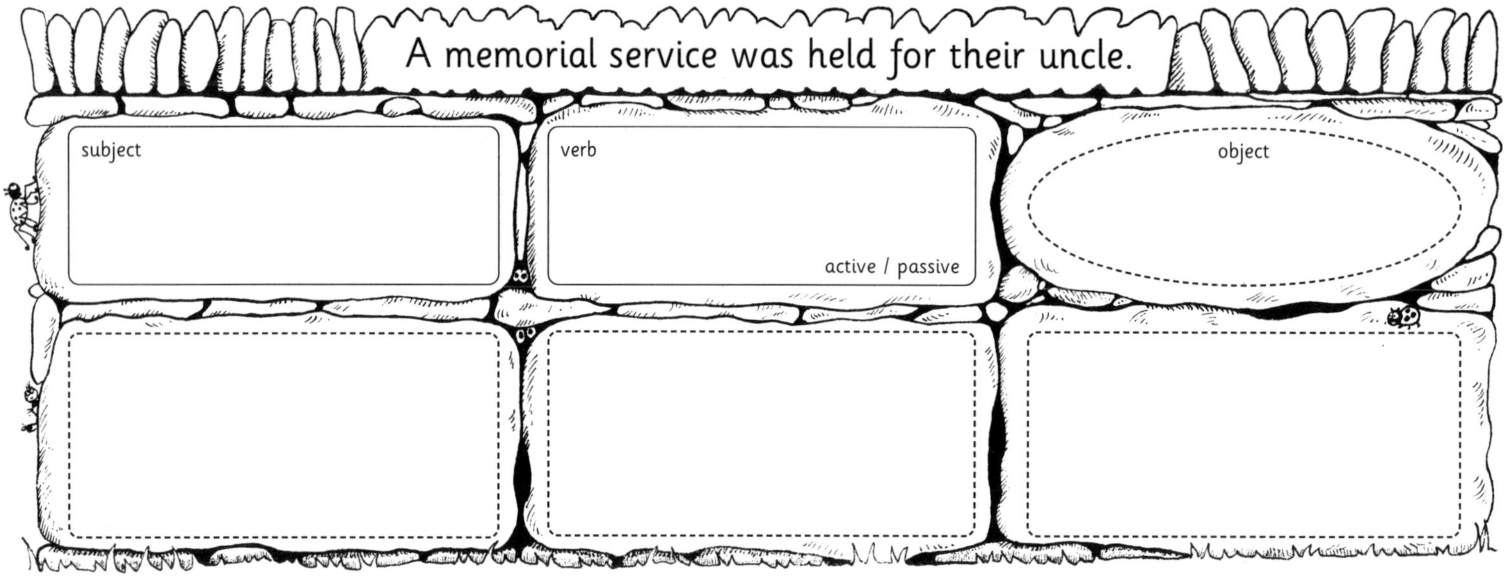

A memorial service was held for their uncle.

subject	verb	object
	active / passive	

Grammar 29 – Modal Adverbs

Prepare...
Grammar Sheet
29 Red & orange
pencils

Builds on...
JGH1: G27-28
JGH2: G15
JGH3: G21
JGH5: G11, G25-29
JGH6: G9, G11, G19,
G28

Aim: Introduce modal adverbs, which modify both main verbs and modal verbs to express different degrees of certainty. They range from **very certain** (as in 'surely', 'certainly', 'clearly', 'definitely', 'obviously' and 'absolutely') to **quite certain** (usually expressed by 'probably') to **less certain** (as in 'apparently', 'possibly', 'perhaps' and 'maybe').

Introduction: Revise adverbs with the class. Adverbs are words that usually describe or 'modify' a verb, telling us more about how, where, when, how much or how often something happens (as in 'quickly', 'away', 'yesterday', 'almost' and 'sometimes'). Although many adverbs, such as 'quickly', are made by adding ‹-ly› to an adjective, many others are not; in fact, some words that do end in ‹-ly› – such as 'lovely', 'silly' and 'friendly' – are not adverbs, but adjectives. Adverbs can also modify other adverbs and adjectives, as in 'really quickly' and 'really sad', and a few ('when', 'where' and 'why') are used in relative clauses to replace the more formal phrases 'in which', 'on which', 'at which' and 'for which'. Remind the class that any word, phrase or clause that acts as an adverb is called an adverbial and that when adverbials are at the beginning of a sentence they are usually followed by a comma. The most common adverbials are adverbs, noun phrases, prepositional phrases and subordinate clauses. Adverbial noun phrases always express time, telling us more about when *[next week]*, how often *[every day]*, or how long *[all year]* something occurs. Prepositional phrases and subordinate clauses sometimes tell us the reason why it occurred *[I got a bike <u>for my birthday</u>/I was running <u>because I was late</u>]*.

Main point: Remind the children that in the last lesson they learnt about the modal verbs 'will', 'shall', 'can', 'could', 'may', 'might', 'should', 'would' and 'must'. Modal verbs are a special kind of auxiliary which are used to express degrees of certainty and obligation, indicate ability, give or ask permission, offer advice or make suggestions. They are always used with the main verb's infinitive and stay the same whichever pronoun is used. Write 'Jane can sing' on the board and look at how the modal verb 'can' expresses certainty about Jane's ability to sing. Now write 'Jane can probably sing' and ask the class how this changes the meaning: it suggests that we do not know for sure whether Jane can sing but that we think it is quite likely. Change 'probably' to 'definitely' and look at the meaning again: this time there can be no doubt that Jane can sing. Finally, change the sentence to 'Perhaps Jane can sing' and ask the class whether it expresses a high or low degree of certainty: 'perhaps' suggests that while it is possible that Jane can sing, we are not really sure and so our degree of certainty is low. Ask the class what part of speech 'probably', 'definitely' and 'perhaps' are *[adverbs]* and explain that modal adverbs, like modal verbs, can be used to express degrees of certainty. They are used with modal verbs like 'can' (as in the example on the board) or with main verbs, as in 'I definitely like ice cream'. Replace 'definitely' in this sentence with some other modal adverbs and discuss how it affects the meaning each time. Point out that not all modal adverbs go so well with some modal verbs: for example, 'perhaps', which expresses a low degree of certainty, is not usually used with 'must', which expresses a high level of certainty.

Grammar Sheet 29: The children write inside the outlined word Adverbs, using an orange pencil. They then identify the modal verbs, underlining them in red *[1. could, 2. can, 3. must, 4. should, 5. might, 6. would, 7. May, 8. will]*. They then rewrite each sentence twice, using a different adverb. There is no wrong or right answer, as long as the sentence makes sense.

Extension activity: Working in pairs, the children look at their sentences and discuss what effect the different modal adverbs have on them.

Rounding off: Go over the sheet with the children, discussing their answers. If any modal adverbs do not work in a sentence, discuss the reasons why.

Modal Adverbs

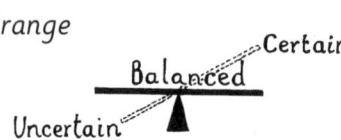

Orange
Certain
Balanced
Uncertain

Like modal verbs, we use adverbs of modality to express how certain we are, ranging from uncertain (**Perhaps** I will go to the party) to very certain (I will **definitely** go to the party).

apparently   surely   certainly   clearly

definitely   probably   perhaps

obviously   maybe   possibly   absolutely

Modal adverbs can be used with main verbs and modal ones. Identify the modal verbs below and then rewrite the sentences twice, using a different adverb each time. How does the meaning change? Do the adverbs work in some sentences but not in others?

1. The flavour of the soup could be improved.
   _____
   _____

2. Beth can play the guitar and accordion.
   _____
   _____

3. You must get some medicine for that cough.
   _____
   _____

4. The yacht should be in the harbour.
   _____
   _____

5. The sculpture might be genuine.
   _____
   _____

6. We would visit Thailand in the autumn.
   _____
   _____

7. May I have some new ballet shoes?
   _____
   _____

8. Tom will eat the steak but not the broccoli.
   _____
   _____

Spelling 30 – ‹-able›

Prepare...
Spelling Sheets 30a/b
Coloured pencils

Builds on...
JGH3: S18
JGH5: S21

Revision: Write these words on the board and ask the class to identify the suffix ‹-able› or ‹-ible› in each one: controllable, sensible, valuable, forcible, changeable, flexible, variable, enjoyable. Revise the rules for adding a suffix that starts with a vowel as you do so (see pages 39 and 40).

Main point: Revise the suffixes ‹-able› and ‹-ible›, which are found in adjectives that mean 'capable or worthy of being the root (word)'. (The adjectives' Latin roots determine which suffix is used.) The suffix ‹-able› is more common; it is often added to an identifiable root word, and always comes after words ending in a 'hard' ‹c› or ‹g›. The suffix ‹-ible› is less common and less likely to follow a whole root word; 'horrible', for example, comes from the Latin 'horrere' (to tremble or shudder) and is part of the same word family as 'horrid', 'horrify', 'horrifying' and 'horrific'. Sometimes we can use our existing knowledge to help us decide which suffix to use: knowing 'adoration', 'toleration' and 'application', for example, tells us that ‹-able› should be used in 'adorable', 'tolerable' and 'applicable'. (The same strategy can be used for other suffixes, as in 'applicant' and 'tolerance'.) There will always be exceptions, of course, and the children should use a dictionary if they are not sure.

Spelling list: Go through the list, discuss the meaning of any unfamiliar words, and ask the class to find and highlight the suffix ‹-able› each time. Point out other spelling features, such as the ‹e› saying /i/ in 'enjoyable' and 'reliable', the alternative spellings in 'enjoyable' and 'reasonable', the vowel saying its long sound in 'notable', 'reliable' and 'recognisable', the ‹o› saying /u/ in 'comfortable', the ‹ui› saying /oo/ in 'suitable', the ‹s› saying /z/ in 'recognisable', the ‹su› saying /sw/ in 'persuadable', the double ‹p› in 'applicable' and – in 'knowledgeable' – the silent ‹k›, the ‹ow› saying /o/ and ‹edge› saying /ij/. It is a good idea to blend and sound out the spelling words quickly every day with the class, using the 'say it as it sounds' strategy where appropriate (stressing the pure sound of any schwas, as in 'adorable', or syllables that are sometimes almost swallowed, as in 'comfortable', 'valuable' and 'fashionable', for example).

Spelling Sheet 30a: The children split each word into syllables to help remember the spelling *[1. en/joy/a/ble, 2. a/dor/a/ble, 3. a/void/a/ble, 4. a/vail/a/ble, 5. no/ta/ble, 6. rea/son/a/ble, 7. com/fort/a/ble, 8. val/u/a/ble, 9. re/li/a/ble, 10. suit/a/ble, 11. fash/ion/a/ble, 12. un/der/stand/a/ble, 13. con/sid/er/a/ble, 14. rec/og/nis/a/ble, 15. per/suad/a/ble, 16. tol/e/ra/ble, 17. ap/plic/a/ble, 18. knowl/edge/a/ble].* They then match the spelling words to the root verbs *[Left-hand column: avoidable, adorable, enjoyable, suitable, comfortable, valuable, applicable, considerable, persuadable; Right-hand column: reasonable, notable, available, reliable, understandable, fashionable, knowledgeable, recognisable, tolerable].*

Spelling Sheet 30b: The children add the correct suffix to complete each word *[Left: reliable, reasonable, convertible, incredible, applicable; Middle: forcible, knowledgeable, illegible, valuable, sensible; Right: suitable, possible].* Then they parse the sentence and complete the wall *[Top: bodybuilder - has achieved - success / Bottom: The - (blank) - considerable / Verb: active].*

The bodybuilder^N (has achieved)^V considerable^Adj success^N.

Noun^N (black), Verb^V (red), Pronoun^P (pink), Adjective^Adj (blue), Adverb^Adv (orange), Conjunction^C (purple), Preposition^Pre (green)

Dictation: (This can be done in the spelling lesson or at another time during the week.) Call out the sentences for the children to write down. Remind them to use speech marks with the correct punctuation in Sentence 1. 'Beth' is a proper noun and needs a capital letter.

1. "The puppy is adorable!" exclaimed Beth.
2. Playing the guitar is an enjoyable activity.
3. The variety of material available is notable.

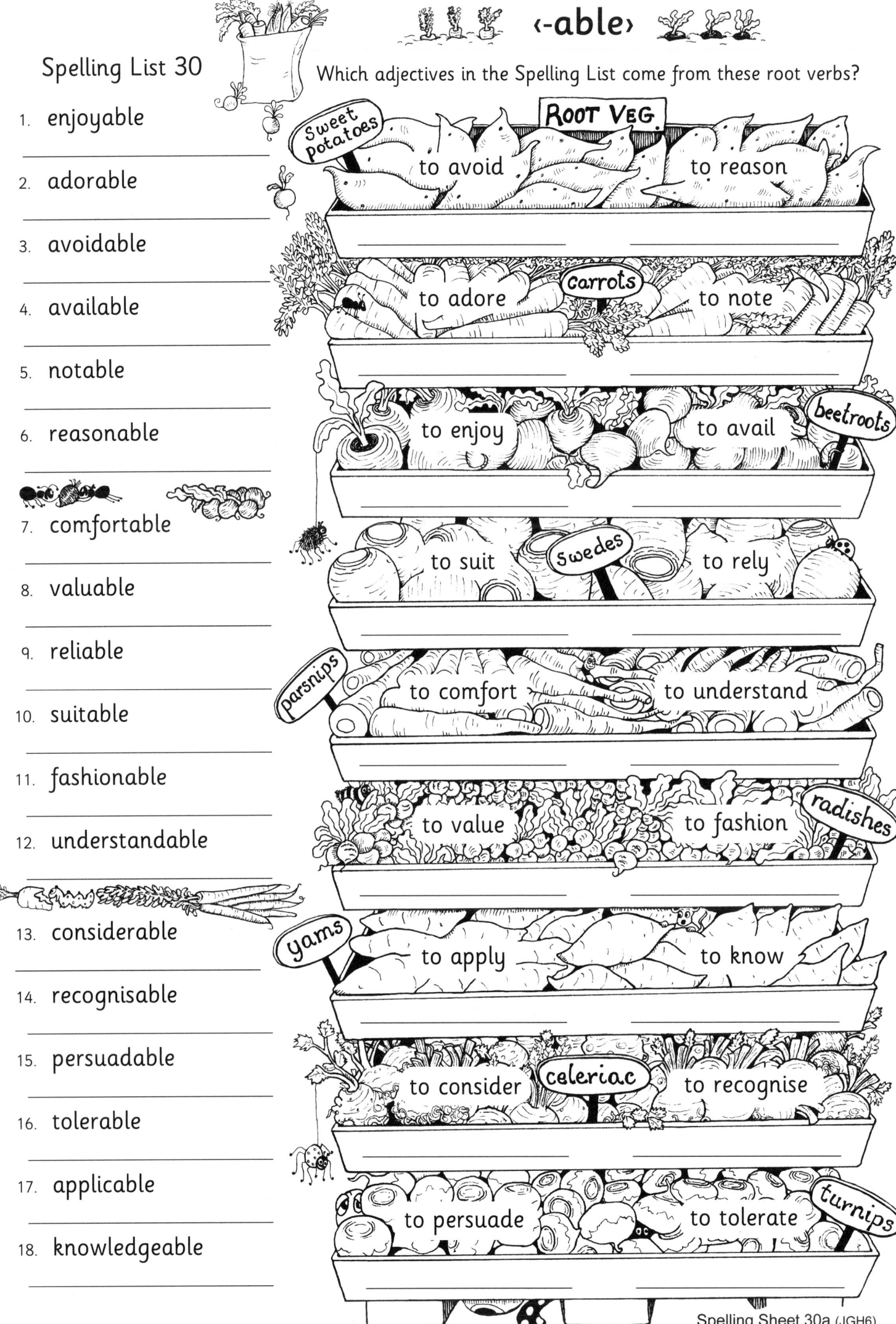

Spelling List 30

1. enjoyable

2. adorable

3. avoidable

4. available

5. notable

6. reasonable

7. comfortable

8. valuable

9. reliable

10. suitable

11. fashionable

12. understandable

13. considerable

14. recognisable

15. persuadable

16. tolerable

17. applicable

18. knowledgeable

‹-able›

Which adjectives in the Spelling List come from these root verbs?

Sweet Potatoes   ROOT VEG
to avoid   to reason

to adore   carrots   to note

to enjoy   to avail   beetroots

to suit   Swedes   to rely

Parsnips   to comfort   to understand

to value   to fashion   radishes

yams   to apply   to know

to consider   celeriac   to recognise

to persuade   to tolerate   turnips

Spelling Sheet 30a (JGH6)

Dictation: ‹-able›

1. _____

_____

2. _____

_____

3. _____

_____

Are these words spelt ‹-able› or ‹-ible›? Add the correct suffix to complete each word, and use a dictionary to check if necessary.

reli_____

reason_____

convert_____

incred_____

applic_____

forc_____

knowledge_____

illeg_____

valu_____

sens_____

suit_____

poss_____

Parse the sentence and then write it on the wall.

The bodybuilder has achieved considerable success.

subject	verb	object
	active / passive	

Grammar 30 – Imperatives

Prepare...
Grammar Sheet 30
Red pencils
Some dice and counters

Builds on...
JGH1: G34-35
JGH2: G4, G6
JGH4: G25-27
JGH6: G18, G26-27

Aim: Introduce the imperative, which is a special form of the verb that is used to give commands, warnings, instructions and advice or to make suggestions, invitations and requests. An imperative sentence usually ends in a full stop, unless it is a forceful command or warning, when it ends in an exclamation mark.

Introduction: Revise the different types of sentence that the children know. They have learnt, for example, that sentences can be simple (having a subject and verb), compound (consisting of two simple sentences joined by a coordinating conjunction or a hyphen) or complex (containing a main clause and a dependent clause). They also know that sentences can state facts, ask for information or make an exclamation and that these statements, questions and exclamations have their own punctuation, ending in a full stop, question mark or exclamation mark. Sentences can also be positive, expressing what is, or they can be negative, expressing what is not. Sentences are usually made negative by putting the adverb 'not' between the auxiliary verb and the main verb, as in 'The baby will not sleep'. If there is no auxiliary, we add the verb 'to do' and use the infinitive form of the main verb, as in 'I do not swim every week'.

Main point: Ask the class if they know the game 'Simon Says', the children's game where one player gives instructions (such as 'Stand up', 'Sit down', 'Jump in the air', 'Clap your hands' and 'Stamp your feet') and the other players obey, as long as the instruction begins with 'Simon says...'. Write some of these instructions on the board and ask the children what is unusual about them. The sentences make sense and have a verb, but the verb is in the infinitive form and the subject is not stated. Explain that these are 'imperative' sentences; the word 'imperative' comes from the Latin verb 'imperare' meaning 'to command', but actually, imperatives are used to give more than orders and commands: they can be used to give warnings *[Beware of the dog!]*, instructions *[Stir in the flour gradually]* and advice *[Use a sharp knife]*; or to make suggestions *[Try the apple pie]*, invitations *[Come and see us soon]* and requests *[Help me, please]*. Remind the class that when we talk directly to someone we use the second person, 'you', but this is not the case in imperative sentences. Instead, the 'you' is implied, although it can be used to add emphasis, as in 'You be quiet'. (We can tell that this is in the imperative form and not in the simple present tense, because the verb is 'be' rather than 'are'.) We make negative imperatives by using the auxiliary 'to do', as in 'Do not disturb', although they are often contracted in speech, as in 'Don't say anything!' or 'Don't go yet', for example. Also explain that imperative sentences usually end in a full stop, unless they are forceful commands or warnings, when an exclamation mark is used instead.

Grammar Sheet 30: The children write inside the outlined word Verbs, using a red pencil. They then write some positive and negative imperatives in the blank spaces, which could be similar to the existing instructions or could include some actions that can be done in the classroom, like 'Turn around three times'.

Extension activity: The children play the game in small groups. Each group will need a die and some counters, as well as a completed worksheet. The players take it in turns to throw the die and move their counter accordingly. When they land on a space with an imperative, they have to follow the instruction. The first person to finish is the winner.

Rounding off: Go over the sheet with the children. Ask them to read out some of their instructions.

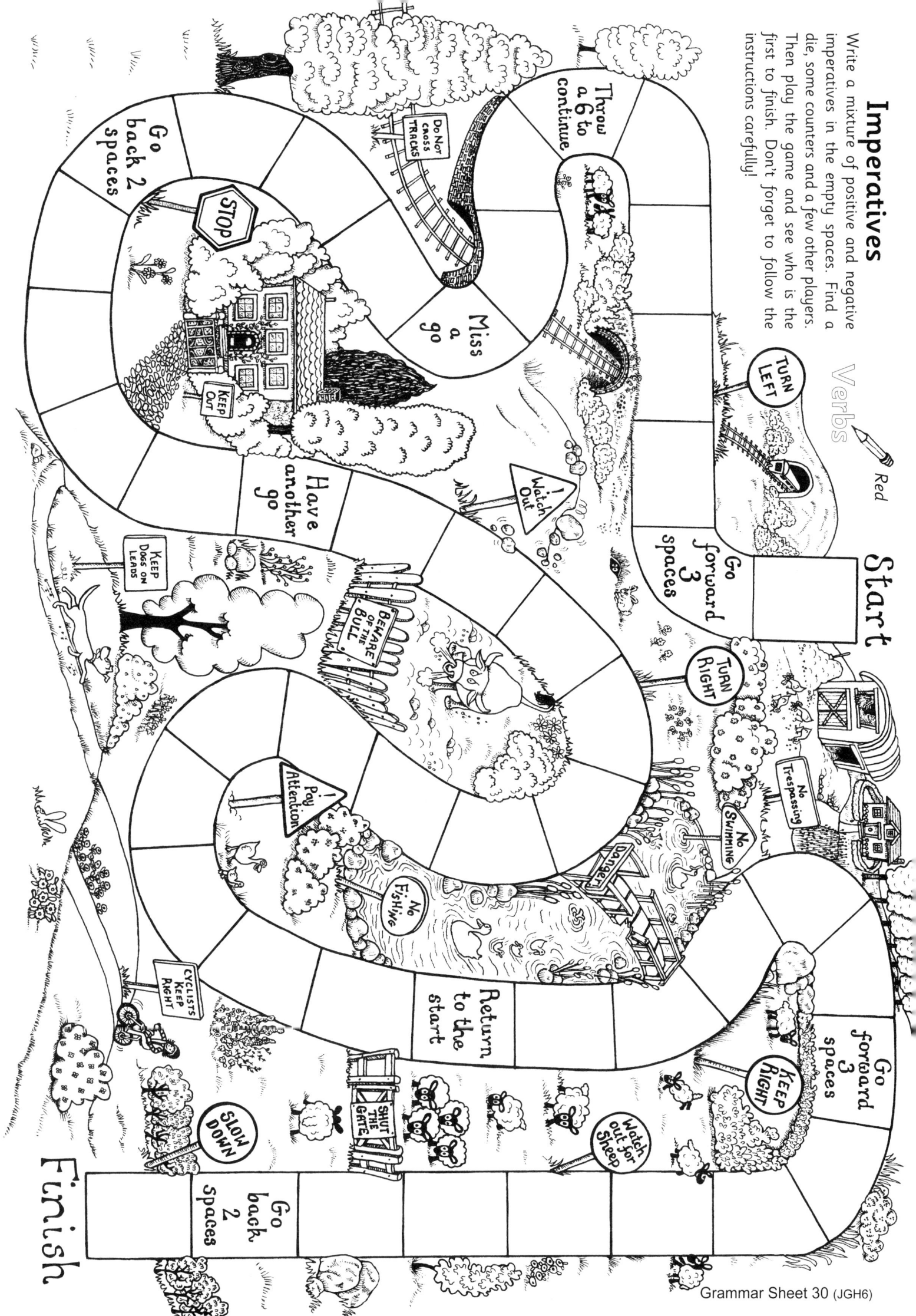

Imperatives

Write a mixture of positive and negative imperatives in the empty spaces. Find a die, some counters and a few other players. Then play the game and see who is the first to finish. Don't forget to follow the instructions carefully!

Verbs — Red

Start

TURN LEFT

Go forward 3 spaces

TURN RIGHT

Throw a 6 to continue

Miss a go

DO NOT CROSS TRACKS

! Watch Out

Go back 2 spaces

STOP

KEEP OUT

Have another go

KEEP DOGS ON LEADS

BEWARE OF THE BULL

No Trespassing

No Swimming

Danger

! Pay Attention

No FiSHing

Return to the start

CYCLISTS KEEP RIGHT

SHUT THE GATE

SLOW DOWN

Watch out for Sheep

KEEP RIGHT

Go forward 3 spaces

Go back 2 spaces

Finish

Go back 2 spaces

Grammar Sheet 30 (JGH6)

Spelling 31 – ‹que› for the /k/ Sound

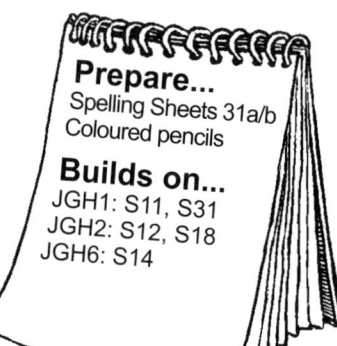

Prepare...
Spelling Sheets 31a/b
Coloured pencils

Builds on...
JGH1: S11, S31
JGH2: S12, S18
JGH6: S14

Revision: Write 'knowledgeable' on the board and discuss how the suffix ‹-able› has been added to the noun 'knowledge' to make an adjective. Point out the 'silent letter' digraph ‹kn› and ‹edge› saying /ij/ and revise the ‹dge› spelling, which always follows a short vowel. Explain that these words are in the same word family as 'know'; ask the class to think of some others (such as 'unknown', 'unknowingly', 'unacknowledged', 'acknowledge' and 'acknowledgement') and identify their parts of speech.

Main point: The main ways of writing the /k/ sound are ‹c›, ‹k› and ‹ck›. The letter ‹c› usually follows a short vowel, as in 'fact' and 'hectic'. This means that ‹c› is subject to the doubling rule and is written as ‹ck› at the end of short words like 'clock' or as ‹cc› in longer words without a suffix, like 'occasion'. The letter ‹k› usually follows vowels that are not short, as in 'book' and 'walk', and is used with ‹n› to make the /ng-k/ sound in words like 'bank' and 'sink' (although other spellings of /k/ are sometimes used, as in 'anchor' and 'conquer'); it is also used instead of ‹c› in words like 'kettle', 'kilt' and 'sky' to avoid the 'soft ‹c›' spellings. Two less commonly used ways to write /k/ are ‹ch› and ‹que›. These spellings both have foreign origins: words with ‹ch›, like 'chorus' and 'echo', are derived from Greek, but words with ‹que›, such as 'technique' and 'boutique', have often been 'borrowed' from French. The ‹que› spelling is usually found at the end of a word, although 'queue' is a notable exception.

Spelling list: Go through the list, discuss the meaning of any unfamiliar words, and ask the class to find and highlight the ‹que› spelling each time. Point out other spelling features, such as the vowel saying its long sound in 'unique', 'opaque' and 'grotesque', the ‹i› saying /ee/ in 'unique', 'antique', 'boutique', 'physique', 'mystique', 'pique' and 'technique', the ‹n› saying /ng/ in 'conquer', the way the first ‹e› in 'marquee' is part of both the ‹que› spelling and the /ee/ sound, the ‹ou› saying /oo/ in 'boutique', the alternative /f/ spelling and ‹s› saying /z/ in 'physique', the ‹y› saying /i/ in 'physique' and 'mystique', the ‹ture› saying /cher/ in 'picturesque', and the ‹ch› spelling of /k/ in 'technique'. It is a good idea to blend and sound out the spelling words quickly every day with the class, using the 'say it as it sounds' strategy where appropriate (stressing the pure sound of any schwas, for example, as in 'arabesque').

Spelling Sheet 31a: The children split each word into syllables to help remember the spelling *[1. u/nique, 2. an/tique, 3. queue, 4. mosque, 5. plaque, 6. con/quer, 7. mar/quee, 8. bou/tique, 9. phy/sique, 10. mys/tique, 11. o/paque, 12. pique, 13. gro/tesque, 14. pic/tur/esque, 15. mas/que/rade, 16. stat/u/esque, 17. tech/nique, 18. ar/a/besque].* They then write sentences for twelve of the spelling words.

Spelling Sheet 31b: The children look up 'masquerade' in the dictionary, check its meaning, and make as many words as they can with its letters. Then they parse the sentence and complete the wall *[Top: artists – have painted - valley / Bottom: Many - (blank) – this picturesque / Verb: active].*

Many^Adj artists^N (have painted)^V this^Adj picturesque^Adj valley^N.

Noun^N (black), Verb^V (red), Pronoun^P (pink), Adjective^Adj (blue), Adverb^Adv (orange), Conjunction^C (purple), Preposition^Pre (green)

Dictation: (This can be done in the spelling lesson or at another time during the week.) Call out the sentences for the children to write down. Remind them to use speech marks with the correct punctuation in Sentence 2.

1. The sculpture is a valuable antique.
2. "This technique is unique," said the scientist.
3. She bought her dress in a fashionable boutique.

 **‹que›** for /k/

Spelling List 31

Write a sentence for twelve of the words in the Spelling List.

1. unique

2. antique

3. queue

4. mosque

5. plaque

6. conquer

7. marquee

8. boutique

9. physique

10. mystique

11. opaque

12. pique

13. grotesque

14. picturesque

15. masquerade

16. statuesque

17. technique

18. arabesque

1. _____

2. _____

3. _____

4. _____

5. _____

6. _____

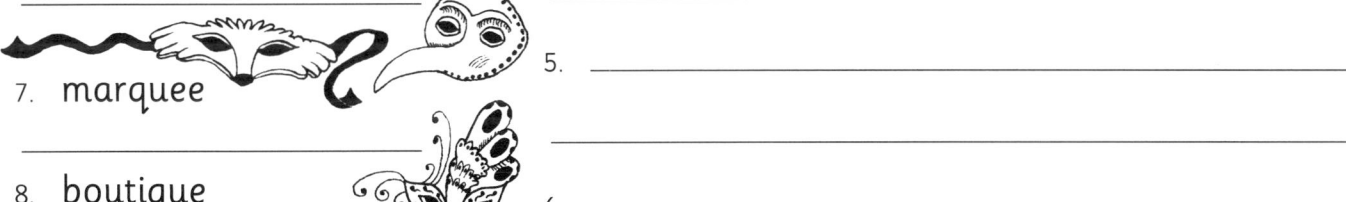

7. _____

8. _____

9. _____

10. _____

11. _____

12. _____

Dictation: ‹que› for /k/

1. _____
   _____

2. _____
   _____

3. _____
   _____

Check what this word means and see how many other words you can make with its letters.

m a s q u e r a d e

Parse the sentence and then write it on the wall.

Many artists have painted this picturesque valley.

subject	verb	object
	active / passive	

Grammar 31 – Using Paragraphs and Cohesion

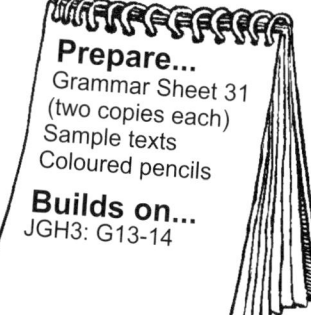

Prepare...
Grammar Sheet 31
(two copies each)
Sample texts
Coloured pencils

Builds on...
JGH3: G13-14

Aim: Introduce the children to the idea that a paragraph needs a beginning, a middle and an end. Also encourage them to use **cohesion** in their writing by using adverbs and conjunctions to link their ideas both within and between paragraphs.

Introduction: Revise paragraphs with the children. Remind them that paragraphs break down a longer piece of text into smaller sections so that it is easier to read and understand. Each one starts on a new line, which is usually indented, and is made up of sentences that describe one idea or topic. Show the children a page of writing: for example, part of a story, a magazine article, a letter, or a newspaper story. Identify the paragraphs with the class and read some of them out. Decide what each one is about and look at the order that they have been put in: could this be changed and, if so, what affect would it have? Look at some of the vocabulary used to move the story or argument along, and discuss how these words and phrases link ideas within a paragraph or link one paragraph to another.

Main point: Explain that, just like a story, a paragraph has a beginning, a middle and an end. The first sentence usually explains what the whole paragraph is about and is called the 'topic' sentence. The sentences that follow provide the evidence to support the main idea, and the final sentence usually acts as a conclusion, summing up what the paragraph is about (although not all paragraphs do this). Look again at some of the paragraphs from the piece of writing and find the topic, evidence and conclusion in each one. Explain that writing paragraphs in this way will help the children avoid repeating or contradicting themselves and allow their ideas to flow more naturally. Another way they can do this is to use 'cohesion', which means 'sticking together' in Latin and describes the use of words and phrases to link ideas and paragraphs together. Many adverbs and conjunctions (and phrases acting as these parts of speech) are used in this way and are often referred to as 'connectives'. Connectives can be categorised by function and include words that indicate time or sequence ('meanwhile', 'next', 'then', 'firstly', 'secondly', 'thirdly'); an opening ('at first', 'to begin with', 'initially'); a summing-up ('finally', 'after all', 'in conclusion'); place ('nearby', 'around the corner', 'down the road'); cause and effect ('because', 'since', 'therefore', 'as a result'); additional information ('also', 'as well as', 'moreover'); and contrast ('instead', 'although', 'however', 'unless').

Tell the children that they are going to think about something they would like to invent and then write about it. Remind them how to plan their work, starting by deciding what type of invention it will be, and then organising their ideas into three main paragraphs about what the invention will do, how it can be made, and how it will make life easier. Remind the class to put these ideas down in note form first, before expanding them into proper sentences, which can then be put together to make paragraphs, using cohesion where appropriate. Ask the children to suggest some ideas for inventions and write them on the board.

Grammar Sheet 31: Give each child two copies of the worksheet. On the first, they note down their ideas on what the invention will do (Box A), how it will be made (Box B) and its advantages (Box C). On the second, they expand these ideas into sentences, using some of the linking words and phrases shown. They should also give their invention a name and write an introductory paragraph and a closing paragraph. Ask the children to put their name at the top of the sheet and keep their essays for the next lesson.

Extension activity: The children draw a picture of their invention or create a diagram and label the different parts.

Rounding off: Ask some children to read out one of their paragraphs. Identify any connectives used and make sure each paragraph has a beginning, a middle and an end.

Using Paragraphs

Think of something you would like to invent and give it a name. Imagine a) what it could do, b) how you would make it and c) what the advantages would be. Note down your ideas, using the boxes to organise them into themes. Then write about your invention, using some of the linking words and phrases to connect your ideas and help your writing flow from one paragraph to another.

Title

Introduction

a)

b)

c)

Summary

to begin with	also	alternatively	next	for this reason	to sum up
first of all	similarly	otherwise	then	consequently	finally
at first	in addition	however	later on	accordingly	in short
firstly	as well as	nevertheless	eventually	as a result	after all
secondly	moreover	instead	for example	therefore	on the whole
thirdly	especially	although	in particular	since	in other words
initially	furthermore	even though	meanwhile	so	in conclusion

Spelling 32 – ‹ne› for the /n/ Sound

Prepare...
Spelling Sheets 32a/b
Coloured pencils

Builds on...
JGH2: S35
JGH3: S16
JGH4: S4-6, S17
JGH6: S19-20

Revision: Write 'mystique' on the board and revise words ending in ‹que›, which are often 'borrowed' from French. Point out the ‹y› saying /i/, the ‹i› saying /ee/ and the ‹que› saying /k/, and explain that 'mystique' belongs to the same word family as 'mystery'; ask the class to think of some other examples (such as 'mystic', 'mystical', 'mysterious', 'mysteriously', 'mystify', 'mystified', 'mystifying' and 'demystify') and identify their part(s) of speech.

Main point: It is not unusual for words in English to end in a silent ‹e›. For example, in Spelling Lessons 19 and 20 the children learnt the 'silent letter' digraphs (and trigraph) found at the end of words like 'tas<u>te</u>', 'pale<u>tte</u>' and 'awe<u>some</u>'. In previous years, they also learnt that silent ‹e› often appears in words ending in /s/, /z/, /v/ or /iv/, as in 'hor<u>se</u>', 'chee<u>se</u>', 'bron<u>ze</u>', 'twel<u>ve</u>' and 'mass<u>ive</u>'. Silent ‹e› also appears sometimes in words ending in /n/; write some of the words from the spelling list on the board and underline the 'silent letter' digraph ‹ne› in each one. Remind the class that these examples are different from 'magic ‹e›' words because the ‹e› at the end has no influence on any other vowel. For example, in the words 'gone' and 'examine', the preceding vowels ‹o› and ‹i› keep their short sounds, whereas in 'bone' and 'line' the influence of 'magic ‹e›' makes the vowels say their long sounds.

Spelling list: Go through the list, discuss the meaning of any unfamiliar words, and ask the class to find and highlight the 'silent letter' digraph ‹ne› each time. Point out other spelling features, such as the ‹o› saying /wu/ in 'one' and 'anyone' (but /u/ in 'none' and 'undone'), the 'soft ‹g›' in 'engine', 'imagine' and 'genuine', the prefix in '**un**done', the ‹a› saying /e/ and ‹y› saying /ee/ in 'anyone', the vowel saying its long sound in 'her**o**ine', 'gen**u**ine', 'mascul**i**ne' and 'migr**ai**ne', the ‹ex› saying /igz/ in 'examine', the ‹y› saying /ie/ in 'bygone', the 'soft ‹c›' in 'medicine', the 'silent letter' digraph in 'di<u>sc</u>ipline', and the ‹e› saying /i/ in 'd**e**termined'. It is a good idea to blend and sound out the spelling words quickly every day with the class, using the 'say it as it sounds' strategy where appropriate (stressing the pure sound of any schwas, as in 'feminine' and 'discipline', or swallowed syllables, as in 'medicine', for example).

Spelling Sheet 32a: The children split each word into syllables to help remember the spelling *[1. one, 2. none, 3. gone, 4. en/gine, 5. im/ag/ine, 6. un/done, 7. an/y/one, 8. fam/ine, 9. her/o/ine, 10. ex/am/ine, 11. by/gone, 12. gen/u/ine, 13. medi/cine, 14. fem/i/nine, 15. mas/cu/line, 16. dis/ci/pline, 17. mi/graine, 18. de/ter/mined]* and then find the eighteen spelling words in the word search. They then identify the correct antonym for each pair of synonyms *[1. c, 2. b, 3. c, 4. A]*.

Spelling Sheet 32b: The children rewrite each imperative twice: first they make it negative by starting the sentence with 'Do not' *[as in 'Do not forget what I told you']*; then they contract the negative imperative and put it in direct speech, *[as in "Don't forget what I told you," warned Dad]*. They then parse the sentence and complete the wall *[Top: expert - showed - antiques / Bottom: The - (blank) - some genuine / Indirect Object: us / Verb: action]*.

The expert^N showed^V us^P some^{Adj} genuine^{Adj} antiques^N.

Noun^N (black), Verb^V (red), Pronoun^P (pink), Adjective^{Adj} (blue), Adverb^{Adv} (orange), Conjunction^C (purple), Preposition^{Pre} (green)

Dictation: (This can be done in the spelling lesson or at another time during the week.) Call out the sentences for the children to write down. Remind them to use speech marks with the correct punctuation in Sentence 1.

1. "Imagine that!" exclaimed the heroine.
2. We were determined to examine the engine.
3. He took some medicine to cure his migraine.

‹ne› for /n/

Spelling List 32

1. one
2. none
3. gone
4. engine
5. imagine
6. undone
7. anyone
8. famine
9. heroine
10. examine
11. bygone
12. genuine
13. medicine
14. feminine
15. masculine
16. discipline
17. migraine
18. determined

Find the words from the Spelling List.

n	b	y	g	o	n	n	o	m	e	n	g	i	n	p
i	m	a	b	y	g	i	n	e	f	a	m	m	a	s
m	e	d	i	c	i	n	e	x	e	n	u	g	o	n
a	h	e	r	o	w	e	x	a	m	i	n	e	n	r
g	r	t	u	m	i	g	r	a	i	n	e	n	g	i
i	n	e	z	d	e	t	e	r	n	d	o	u	i	n
n	e	r	o	i	n	e	v	e	i	h	r	i	u	e
e	o	m	a	s	c	u	l	i	n	e	p	n	f	n
b	e	i	s	c	i	p	l	n	e	r	t	e	a	g
y	x	n	l	i	n	e	b	y	g	o	n	e	m	i
g	a	e	x	p	m	i	g	r	a	i	s	h	i	n
o	m	d	g	l	c	k	n	t	u	n	d	o	n	e
g	e	n	u	i	m	a	o	n	f	e	m	i	e	t
v	i	m	a	n	y	o	n	e	q	u	i	n	r	h
n	g	o	n	e	s	s	e	m	a	s	c	u	l	i

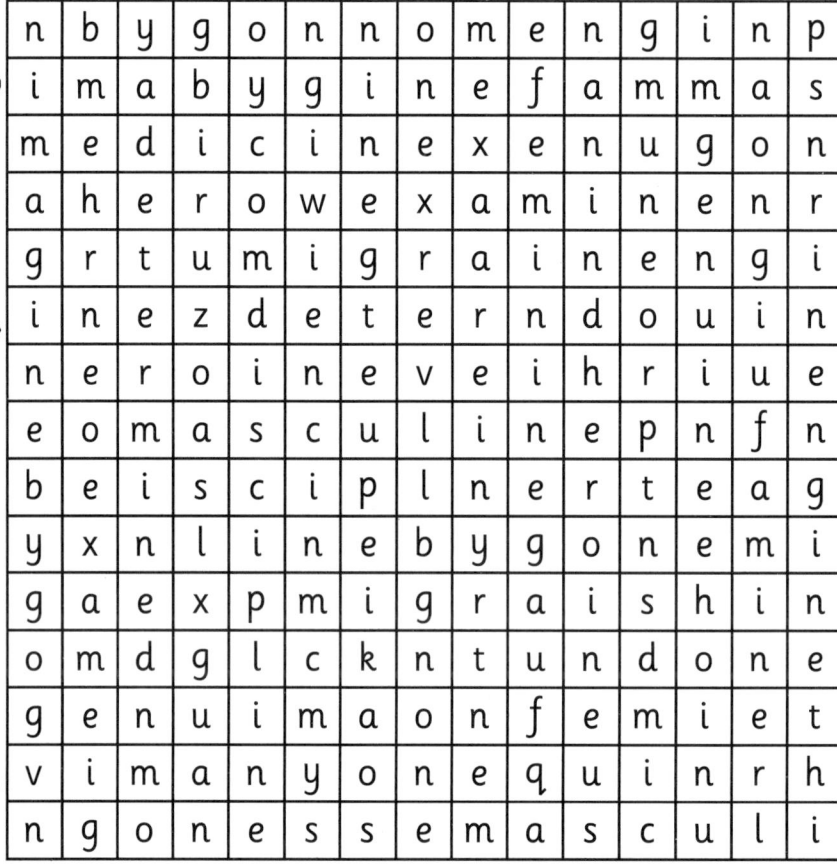

Which is the correct antonym for each pair of synonyms?
Use a thesaurus to help you, if necessary.

1. **false, fake**
   A. undone
   B. determined
   C. genuine

2. **villain, rogue**
   A. famine
   B. heroine
   C. migraine

3. **all, everything**
   A. one
   B. anyone
   C. none

4. **recent, modern**
   A. bygone
   B. feminine
   C. masculine

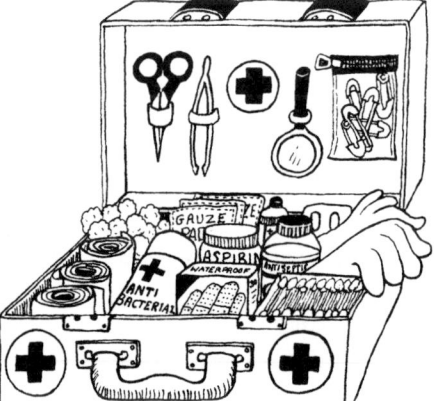 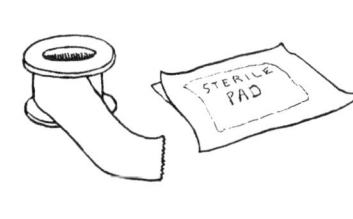  

Spelling Sheet 32a (JGH6)

Dictation: ‹**ne**› for /n/

Throat
Cough
ULTRA SOFT
TISSUES

Antiseptic Ointment
NASAL SPRAY

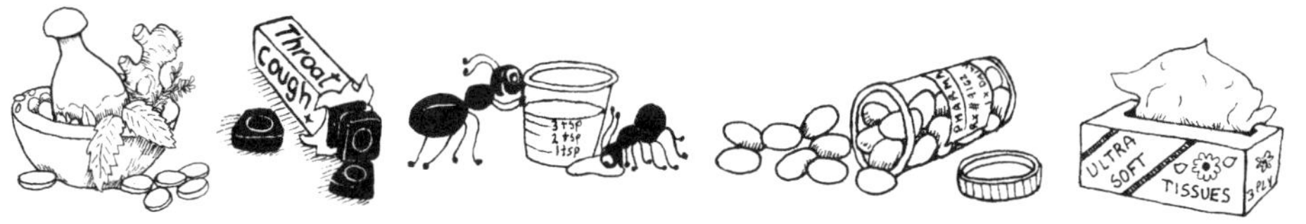

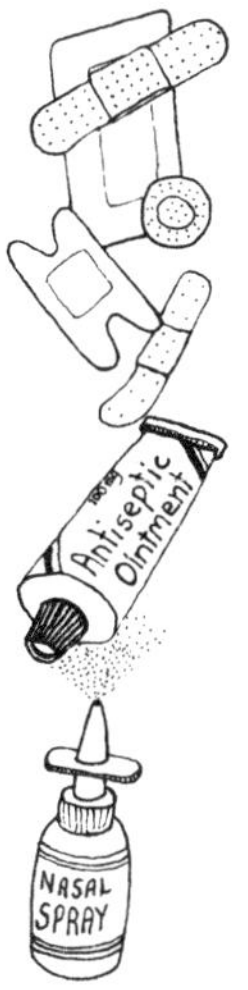

1. ______________________________

____

2. ______________________________

____

3. ______________________________

____

Rewrite each imperative twice. First, make it negative by starting with ‘Do not’. Then contract the verb to ‘don’t’ and write a sentence with direct speech. Try not to use the verb ‘to say’ each time, but vary it with other verbs, such as ‘to warn’, ‘to advise’, ‘to instruct’ or ‘to order’.

1. Forget what I told you.

Do not ______________________________

“Don’t ______________________________

2. Plant the seeds in large pots.

____

____

3. Come to the house today.

____

____

4. Use the scissors in the drawer.

____

____

5. Take your medicine now.

____

____

Parse the sentence and then write it on the wall.

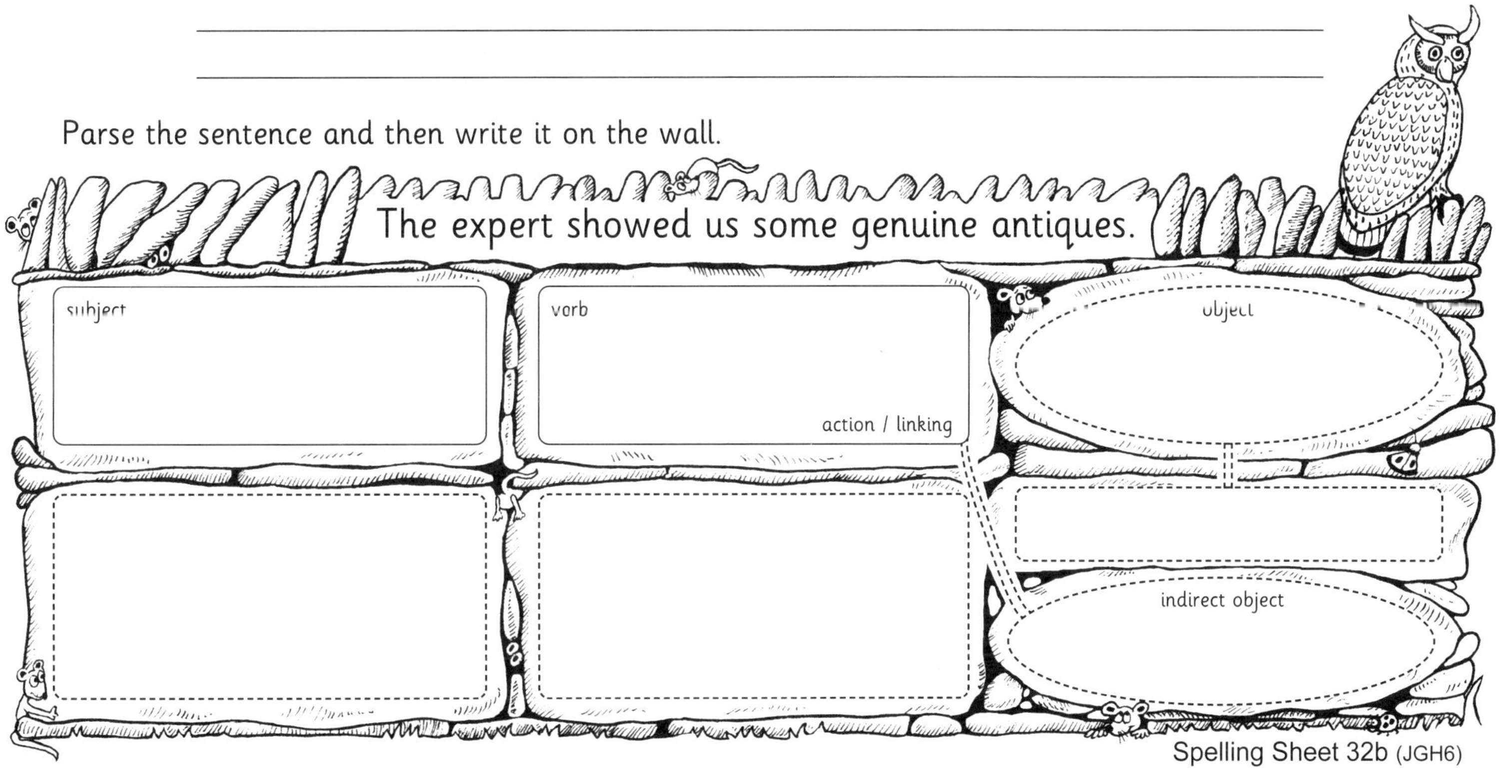

The expert showed us some genuine antiques.
subject
verb
action / linking
object
indirect object

Grammar 32 – Formal and Informal Writing

Prepare...
Grammar Sheet 32
Last week's essay
Ext. Sheet, p234
Sample texts
(formal & informal)
Thesauruses
Scissors

Builds on...
JGH6: G31

Aim: Introduce the children to the idea that writing can be formal or informal. Develop their ability to write in both styles and refine their understanding of when to use each one.

Introduction: Remind the children that a sentence can be written in the first, second or third person, with the person being singular or plural. The first person refers to the author and uses 'I' and 'we'; the second person addresses someone directly with 'you'; and the third person refers to someone else and uses 'he', 'she', 'it' and 'they'. These are personal pronouns, so called because they relate mostly to people; we use the first and second person when we communicate directly with someone either in speech or in writing, and the third person is used to describe something from another person's point of view or to keep things impersonal. Call out a few sentences and ask the children to identify the grammatical person each time.

Main point: Write 'c u l8ter' on the board and ask what kind of writing this is and when it might be used. Would the children write this in class, for example? Explain that it is 'text speak', which we only really use when sending a text or chatting online with someone we know very well. Show the children some examples of writing that include things like slang, idioms, contractions and words like 'well', 'like' and 'anyway' that are often added unnecessarily, and discuss when this kind of writing is appropriate. For example, we may write in this relaxed, informal style in notes to ourselves or in a letter to a friend, but we would use a more formal style when addressing someone we do not know or when it concerns something more serious, like a letter of complaint. Show the class a more formal piece of writing, such as a report or an instruction manual, and compare the styles: the tone is more polite in the formal writing; standard punctuation is used; the vocabulary is more sophisticated; there are no contractions; and there is a greater use of the third person and the passive voice.

Now ask the children what differences there might be between a formal and an informal letter. Write two short messages on the board, one in each style. The informal one could read something like: 'Hi Zack! Is it OK if I stop by on Saturday to chat about that stuff you've decided to chuck out? Cheers! Sam'. The other should be a more formal request: 'Dear Zack, I am writing to ask if I can visit you on Saturday, 12th May, to talk about the items that you wish to throw away. Many thanks, Sam.' Discuss them with the class, asking what makes the second one more formal, and compare the punctuation, the tone, and the synonyms chosen, like 'hi/dear', 'stop by/visit', 'chat/talk', 'stuff/items', 'chuck out/throw away' and 'cheers/many thanks'. Look at synonyms that are even more formal, like 'discuss' for 'talk', 'discard' for 'throw away' and 'kind regards' instead of 'many thanks', and remind the children that a thesaurus can help them to vary the words they write. Look at some more examples, such as those on the Extension Activity sheet, and discuss them with the class.

Grammar Sheet 32: The children write a formal letter to a business, asking whether it would like to make and sell their invention from Grammar Lesson 31; then they write an informal one to a friend, telling them about the invention and their plans to sell it. Before they start, remind the children where to write the date and their address, and make sure they know when to use 'Dear Sir or Madam', 'Yours sincerely' and 'Yours faithfully'. Remind them to use paragraphs and cohesion, and make sure they have their essays from last week.

Extension activity: The children cut out the triangles on the Extension Activity Sheet (page 234) and then put them back together, matching the formal and informal synonyms.

Rounding off: Ask some children to read out a paragraph from one of their letters, and discuss whether it is written in a formal or informal style.

Formal and Informal Writing

Write two letters about your invention from Grammar Lesson 31. Write a formal letter to a local business who might be interested in making and selling your invention. Then write an informal one, telling a friend all about your plans.

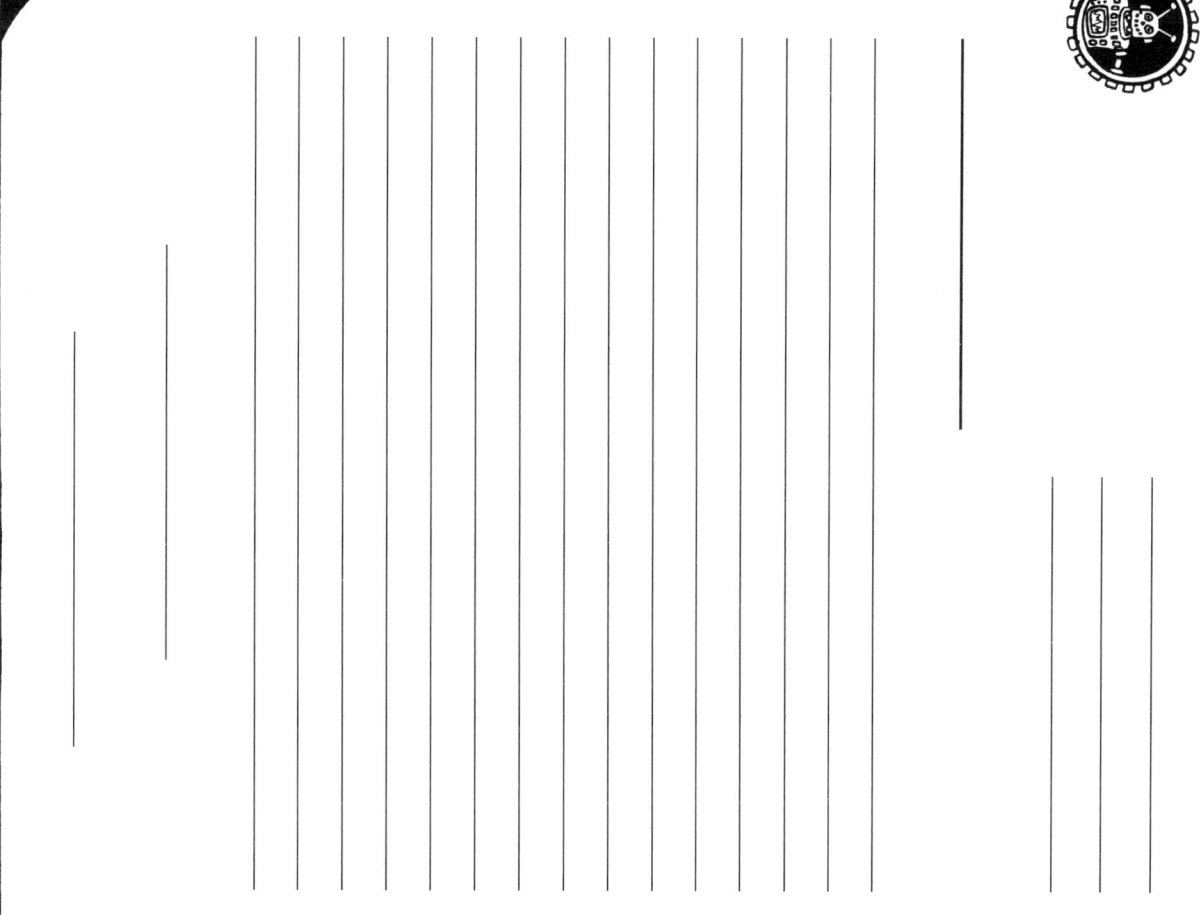

Spelling 33 – Commonly Confused Words

Prepare...
Spelling Sheets 33a/b
Coloured pencils

Builds on...
JGH2: G12, G31
JGH3: G29-30, S30
JGH4: S2, G4, G14,
G17-18, G28, G35
JGH5: G33
JGH6: G1

Revision: Write 'imagine' on the board and point out the 'soft ‹g›' spelling and 'silent letter' digraph ‹ne›. Explain that this word belongs to the same word family as 'image', and ask the class to think of some other examples (such as 'imagery', 'imaginary', 'imagination', '(un)imaginative(ly)' and 'unimaginable'). Identify the part(s) of speech for each word.

Main point: Revise the word 'homophone', which means 'same *[homos]* sound *[phone]*' in Greek. Homophones sound similar to one another but have different spellings and meanings and include words like 'our', 'hour' and 'are' and 'where', 'wear' and 'were'. Explain that 'are' and 'our' and 'were' and 'where', which are not strictly homophones but sound similar enough to cause confusion, are called 'near homophones'. Look at the near homophones 'lose/loose', 'lightning/lightening', 'breath/breathe', 'desert/dessert', 'angle/angel' and 'island/Ireland' and discuss how they differ in pronunciation and meaning. Point out that the verb 'desert' (to abandon) and the noun 'dessert' (a sweet course at the end of a meal) are homophones, as they both stress the second syllable, but that the noun 'desert' (a dry, arid region) is a near homophone, because its stress is on the first syllable.

Spelling list: Go through the list, and look at the differences in meaning and spelling between each pair of words. Point out other spelling features, such as the suffix saying /t/ in 'pass**ed**', the ‹o› saying /oo/ in 'lose', the ‹s› and ‹ss› saying /z/ in 'lose', 'desert' and 'dessert', the 'silent letter' digraph (or trigraph) in 'lo<u>s</u>e', 'loo<u>s</u>e', 'brea<u>the</u>', 'mu<u>sc</u>le' and 'i<u>s</u>land', the ‹igh› in 'lightning' and 'lightening', the ‹ea› saying /e/ in 'breath' but /ee/ in 'breathe', the ‹e› saying /i/ in 'd**e**sert' (to abandon) and 'd**e**ssert', but /e/ in 'd**e**sert' (a dry arid region), the different spellings of /ool/ in 'mus**cle**', 'muss**el**', 'ang**le**' and 'ang**el**', the way the ‹g› in ‹ng› also says /g/ in 'angle', the vowel saying its long sound in 'a**ngel**', 'i**sland**', 'st**ationary**' and 'st**ationery**', the 'soft ‹g›' in 'angel', and the suffixes in 'station**ary**' and 'station**ery**' and the ‹tion› saying /shun/. It is a good idea to blend and sound out the spelling words quickly every day with the class, using the 'say it as it sounds' strategy where appropriate (saying /is-land/ for 'island' or stressing the pure sound of any schwas, as in 'light**e**ning' and 'Irel**a**nd', for example).

Spelling Sheet 33a: The children split each word into syllables to help remember the spelling *[1. passed, 2. past, 3. lose, 4. loose, 5. light/ning, 6. light/en/ing, 7. breath, 8. breathe, 9. des/ert (noun), de/sert (verb), 10. des/sert, 11. mus/cle, 12. mus/sel, 13. an/gle, 14. an/gel, 15. is/land, 16. Ire/land, 17. sta/tion/a/ry, 18. sta/tion/e/ry]*. They then write the meanings for each pair of spelling words, using a dictionary to help them if needed. Then the children read the four words below and draw pictures to illustrate them.

Spelling Sheet 33b: The children match the synonyms *[thanks/thank you, TV/television, kids/ children, loads of/a great deal of, you're/you are, ASAP/as soon as possible, hi/dear, love/yours truly, I've/I have, it's about/it concerns, can you?/would you mind?]* and then parse the sentence and complete the wall *[Top: tree - was struck - (blank) / Bottom: The old oak - by lightning - (blank) / Verb: passive]*. The passive verb has the irregular past participle 'struck'.

The old^{Adj} oak^{Adj} tree^N (was struck)^V (by^{Pre} lightning^N)^{Adv}.

Noun^N (black), Verb^V (red), Pronoun^P (pink), Adjective^{Adj} (blue), Adverb^{Adv} (orange), Conjunction^C (purple), Preposition^{Pre} (green)

Dictation: (This can be done in the spelling lesson or at another time during the week.) Call out the sentences for the children to write down. Sentence 2 needs a question mark. Remind them to use speech marks with the correct punctuation in Sentences 3.

1. The ship sailed past the desert island.
2. How many angles are there in a triangle?
3. "Don't lose that key," warned my mother.

Word Mix-Ups

Spelling List 33

Write the meanings for each pair of spelling words.

1. passed

2. past

3. lose

4. loose

5. lightning

6. lightening

7. breath

8. breathe

9. desert

10. dessert

11. muscle

12. mussel

13. angle

14. angel

15. island

16. Ireland

17. stationary

18. stationery

loose _____

lose _____

breath _____

breathe _____

past _____

passed _____

island _____

Ireland _____

mussel _____

muscle _____

Draw a picture to illustrate each word.

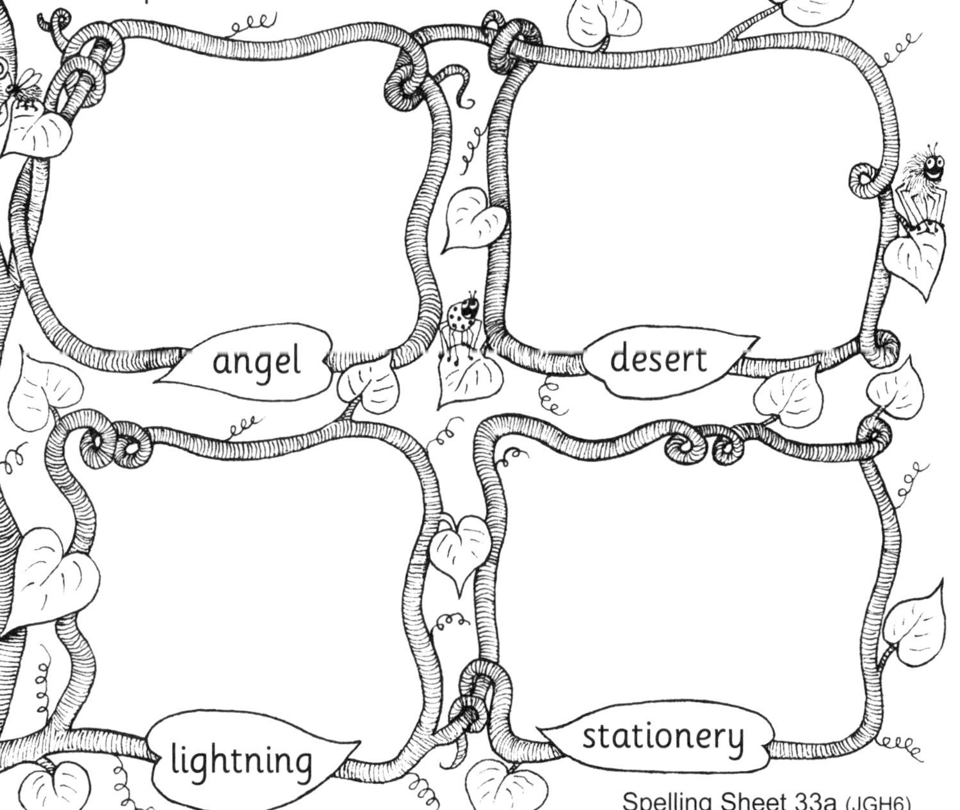

angel

desert

lightning

stationery

Spelling Sheet 33a (JGH6)

Dictation: word mix-ups

1. _____

   _____

2. _____

   _____

3. _____

   _____

Can you match the formal and informal synonyms below?

dear

a great deal of

it's about

would you mind?

TV

thank you

you are

thanks

television

love

as soon as possible

I have

loads of

I've

children

it concerns

you're

hi

yours truly

ASAP

can you?

kids

Parse the sentence and then write it on the wall.

The old oak tree was struck by lightning.

subject

verb

active / passive

object

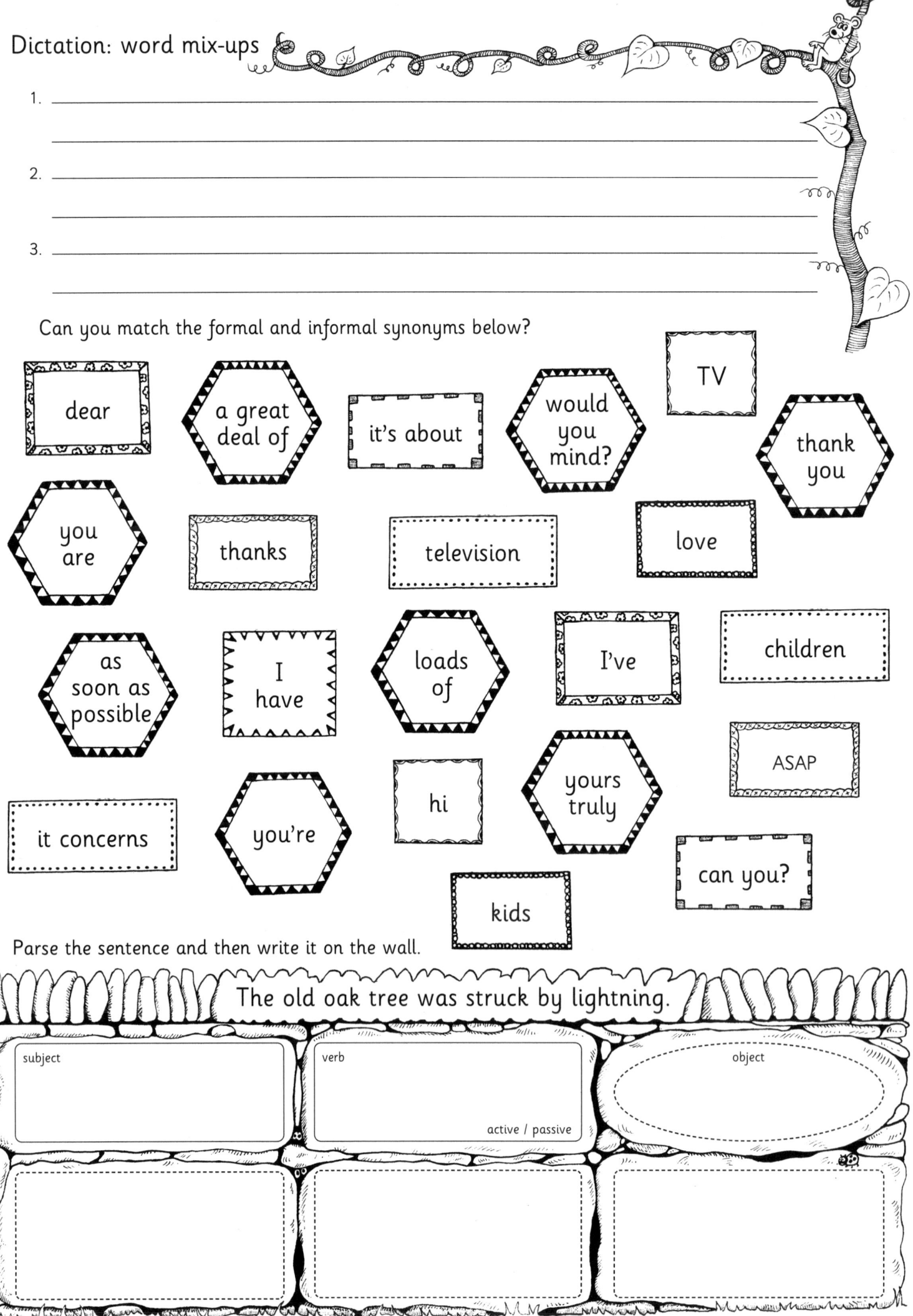

Grammar 33 – Alliteration

Prepare...
Grammar Sheet 33
Coloured pencils

Builds on...
JGH4: S17 (Ext. Act.),
G32

Aim: Introduce the children to the idea of 'alliteration': the use of repeated sounds in a series of words, which can be used to grab our attention and make the words more memorable.

Introduction: Say the alphabet with the class and write it on the board in capital letters. Remind the children that when we say the alphabet we use the letter **names**, but when we want to read and write words, we use the letter **sounds**. Point to various letters in the alphabet and ask the class to say the sounds. Then take one of those sounds and go around the class, asking each child to think of a word that begins with that sound. Write the words on the board and repeat the activity with other sounds from the alphabet. Now write 'The knowledgeable naughty knight knew a lot about knives' and read it with the children. Ask them what they notice about it *[most of the words begin with the /n/ sound]* and discuss the effect this has on them. Some children may find it a bit of a tongue twister, others might think it is funny, while others in the class might like the way it makes the silent ‹k› words memorable.

Main point: Explain that when we repeat a sound like this, it is called 'alliteration', and the effect is used in writing to grab our attention, make something memorable or to create a particular mood. Look again at the words that the class called out earlier and ask the children to make some alliterative sentences of their own. Remind them that it is the initial sound that matters, and not the way the sound is spelt, so not all the words have to start with the same letter. Also, not all the words have to start with the same sound: smaller words like articles, pronouns and prepositions can be used regardless of their initial sound. Look at some of the children's suggestions and discuss the effect the alliteration has: some sentences may seem quite poetic; others might sound like a line from a song or nursery rhyme; others could be quite catchy, like a newspaper headline, advertising slogan or an idiom (as in 'curiosity killed the cat'); and some might resemble well-known tongue twisters like 'Peter Piper picked a peck of pickled peppers' or 'She sells seashells on the seashore' (in this last example there are two repeated sounds – /s/ and /sh/ – which do not always come at the beginning of the word). Alliteration is not just used in sentences and long phrases: it is used in brand names and television shows, and many characters in children's literature, television, film, cartoons and video games have alliterative names. Ask the children if they can think of any examples and discuss them with the class.

Grammar Sheet 33: The children write the first letter of their name in the frame and decorate it. They then think of as many words beginning with that letter as they can and write them in the box below. (If a child's name starts with a particularly difficult letter, like ‹X›, they can choose another one). Then they use as many of these words as possible to make an alliterative sentence, before writing alliterative sentences or phrases for the five words underneath.

Extension activity: Ask the children to think back to Grammar Lesson 31 and the names they gave to their inventions. Working in pairs or small groups, they decide whether these names are alliterative or not and, if not, think of alliterative names that they could use instead to make them catchy and memorable. The children could also be encouraged to write down alliterative idioms and short phrases in their Spelling Word Books or to collect real-life examples for a class project.

Rounding off: Go over the sheet with the children, discussing their sentences and phrases. If they have done the extension activity, ask some of the children to read out the names of their inventions.

All About Alliteration

She sells seashells on the seashore

Peppers

Peter

Piper picked a peck of pickled

ALLITERATION is when we use several words together that begin with the same sound. It gives our writing a certain rhythm, which can be used to create different moods, get the reader's attention, or make something memorable. Alliteration is used to make tongue-twisters and is often found in poetry.

Write the first letter of your name in the frame and decorate it. Then think of as many words beginning with that letter as you can and write them below. Finally, write a sentence, using as many of the words as possible.

_____

_____

Write an alliterative phrase or sentence using these words.

F

1. fashionable _____

   _____

T

2. treasure _____

   _____

D

3. doughnut _____

   _____

P

4. penguin _____

   _____

G

5. ghastly _____

Spelling 34 – ‹-ly›

Prepare...
Spelling Sheets 34a/b
Coloured pencils

Builds on...
JGH3: G21
JGH4: S21

Revision: Write 'breath' and 'breathe' on the board and discuss the different pronunciations of ‹ea› in each one. Ask the class to suggest other words in this word family (such as 'breathable', 'breathless', 'breathing', 'breathtaking' and 'breathy') and identify their part(s) of speech.

Main point: Remind the class that the suffix ‹-ly› is added to an adjective to make an adverb. Because ‹-ly› begins with a consonant, it is usually just added to the root word, so 'actual', 'frequent', 'sincere', 'physical' and 'accidental' become 'actually', 'frequently', 'sincerely', 'physically' and 'accidentally'. However, there are some exceptions that the children should be familiar with: if the word ends in a consonant plus ‹y›, 'shy ‹i›' replaces 'toughy ‹y›' before the ‹-ly› is added, so 'hearty' and 'necessary' become 'heartily' and 'necessarily'; if a word ends in ‹le›, the ‹le› is removed before adding ‹-ly›, so 'probable' becomes 'probably'; and if a word ends in ‹ic›, the suffix ‹-ally› is added instead of ‹-ly›, so 'symbolic' and 'systematic' become 'symbolically' and 'systematically'. Go through the other words in the spelling list and identify the adjective root each time.

Spelling list: Go through the list, discuss the meaning of any unfamiliar words, and ask the class to find and highlight the ‹-ly› suffix each time. Point out other spelling features, such as the 'soft ‹c›' in 'centrally', 'excellently', 'sincerely', 'necessarily' and 'accidentally', the ‹ear› saying /ar/ in 'heartily', the vowel saying its long sound in 'frequently', 'immediately' and 'environmentally', the alternative /f/ spelling and ‹s› saying /z/ in '**ph**y**s**ically', the ‹y› saying /i/ in 'ph**y**sically', 's**y**mbolically' and 's**y**stematically', the way /ear/ is spelt in 'sinc**ere**ly', the ‹ie› saying /i/ in 'mischievously', and the ‹e› saying /i/ in '**e**nvironmentally'. It is a good idea to blend and sound out the spelling words quickly every day with the class, using the 'say it as it sounds' strategy where appropriate (stressing the pure sound of any schwas, as in 'frequ**e**ntly', 'indiv**i**du**a**lly' and 'exc**e**ll**e**ntly', or any syllables that are almost swallowed, as in 'actu**a**lly', 'physi**ca**lly', 'des**per**ately' and 'mar**vel**lously', for example).

Spelling Sheet 34a: The children split each word into syllables to help remember the spelling [1. ac/tu/al/ly, 2. prob/a/bly, 3. cen/tral/ly, 4. heart/i/ly, 5. fre/quent/ly, 6. in/di/vid/u/al/ly, 7. ex/cel/lent/ly, 8. phys/i/cal/ly, 9. sin/cere/ly, 10. nec/es/sar/i/ly, 11. des/per/ate/ly, 12. ac/ci/den/tal/ly, 13. im/me/di/ate/ly, 14. mar/vel/lous/ly, 15. sym/bol/ic/al/ly, 16. mis/chie/vous/ly, 17. sys/tem/at/ic/al/ly, 18. en/vi/ron/men/tal/ly]. They then complete the 'word family' trees, writing the correct adjective and spelling list adverb each time [act: actual(ly); excel: excellent(ly); heart: hearty/heartily; despair: desperate(ly); marvel: marvellous(ly); accident: accidental(ly); centre: central(ly); environment: environmental(ly); mischief: mischievous(ly); symbol: symbolic(ally); system: systematic(ally)].

Spelling Sheet 34b: The children write an alliterative sentence for each word. Then they parse the sentence and complete the wall [Top: Seth - ate - dessert / Bottom: (blank) - immediately (almost) - his / Verb: active]. The adverb 'almost' modifies the adverb 'immediately'.

Seth^N ate^V his^{Adj} dessert^N almost^{Adv} immediately^{Adv}.

Noun^N (black), Verb^V (red), Pronoun^P (pink), Adjective^{Adj} (blue), Adverb^{Adv} (orange), Conjunction^C (purple), Preposition^{Pre} (green)

Dictation: (This can be done in the spelling lesson or at another time during the week.) Call out the sentences for the children to write down. Remind them to use speech marks with the correct punctuation in Sentence 3. 'Ireland' is a proper noun and needs a capital letter.

1. Her parents visit Ireland quite frequently.
2. Their products are environmentally friendly.
3. "I have probably passed my test," I replied.

‹-ly›

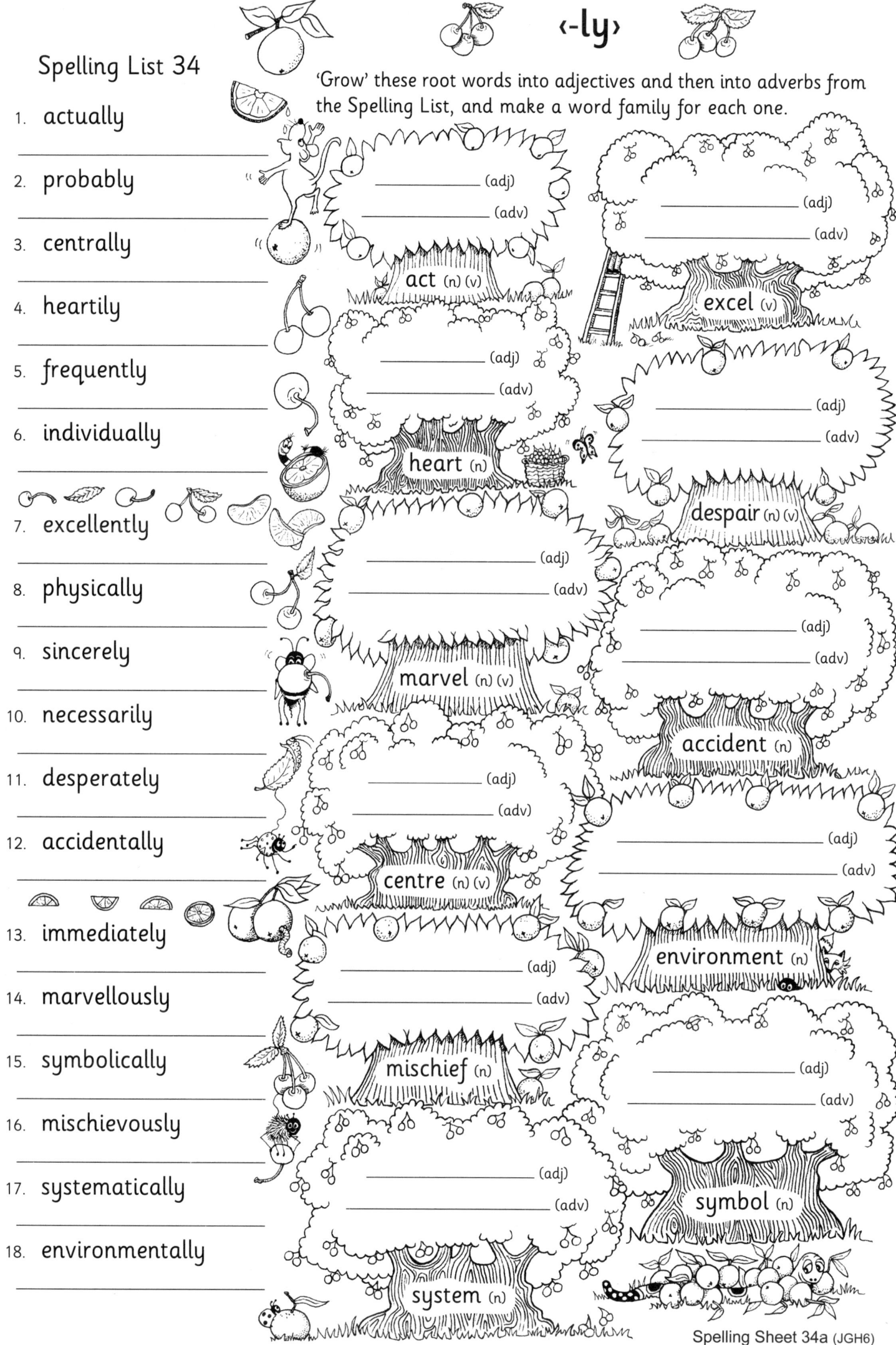

Spelling List 34

1. actually
_____
2. probably
_____
3. centrally
_____
4. heartily
_____
5. frequently
_____
6. individually
_____
7. excellently
_____
8. physically
_____
9. sincerely
_____
10. necessarily
_____
11. desperately
_____
12. accidentally
_____
13. immediately
_____
14. marvellously
_____
15. symbolically
_____
16. mischievously
_____
17. systematically
_____
18. environmentally
_____

'Grow' these root words into adjectives and then into adverbs from the Spelling List, and make a word family for each one.

_____ (adj)
_____ (adv)
act (n) (v)

_____ (adj)
_____ (adv)
heart (n)

_____ (adj)
_____ (adv)
marvel (n) (v)

_____ (adj)
_____ (adv)
centre (n) (v)

_____ (adj)
_____ (adv)
mischief (n)

_____ (adj)
_____ (adv)
system (n)

_____ (adj)
_____ (adv)
excel (v)

_____ (adj)
_____ (adv)
despair (n) (v)

_____ (adj)
_____ (adv)
accident (n)

_____ (adj)
_____ (adv)
environment (n)

_____ (adj)
_____ (adv)
symbol (n)

Dictation: ‹-ly›

1. _____

2. _____

3. _____

Alliteration is when we use several words together that begin with the same sound. Write an alliterative sentence for each of these words.

H M G D C

1. heartily _____

2. medicine _____

3. grotesque _____

4. dessert _____

5. comfortable _____

Parse the sentence and then write it on the wall.

Seth ate his dessert almost immediately.

subject	verb	object
	active / passive	

Grammar 34 – Homophone Mix-Ups

Prepare...
Grammar Sheet 34
Dictionaries

Builds on...
JGH2: G12, G31
JGH3: G29-30, S30
JGH4: S2, G4, G14, G17-18, G28, G35
JGH5: G33
JGH6: G1, S33

Aim: Reinforce the children's understanding of homophones and develop their ability to choose between similar-sounding words in their writing.

Introduction: Ask the children to call out some homophones that they know. The most commonly confused ones usually include parts of the verb 'to be', possessive adjectives or contractions, as in 'our', 'hour' and 'are'; 'their', 'there' and 'they're'; 'your' and 'you're'; 'its' and 'it's'; and 'where', 'wear' and 'were'. 'Our' is more properly pronounced /ou-r/ to sound like 'hour', but in practice it is often pronounced /ar/ and can be confused with 'are'. 'Were' is not strictly a homophone of 'where' either, but it looks and sounds similar enough to cause confusion. Remind the children that words like this are called 'near homophones'. Some numbers are also homophones: one ('won'), two ('to', 'too'), four ('for') and eight ('ate'). Quickly go through these words, as well as any others that the children called out, and make sure that they know which meanings go with which spellings.

Main point: Remind the children that it is important to use the correct spelling when writing homophones, otherwise their writing will not make sense. They need to pause before writing a homophone, decide which meaning is needed, and think how the word with that meaning is spelt. Write the homophones from Grammar Sheet 34 on the board, look at the spellings, and check that the class know what they mean: herd/heard, who's/whose, serial/cereal, ascent/assent, father/farther, dissent/descent, draft/draught, principle/principal. If the children are unsure of any meanings, ask them to look up the words in the dictionary and see who can find them first. Remind the children that they can sometimes use their existing knowledge to help them choose the correct homophone: for example, 'heard' is the simple past tense and past participle of the verb 'to hear', so if the homophone needed is the verb, they should use this spelling; 'whose' is either a question word or a relative pronoun, whereas 'who's' is a contraction of either 'who is' or 'who has'; 'serial' is an adjective meaning 'forming part of a series'; and 'farther' is a comparative meaning 'more far'. Ask the children to think of a sentence for some of the homophones and discuss which spellings they would use.

Grammar Sheet 34: The children write the meaning for each homophone. Encourage them to use a dictionary, if needed, to look up the meaning or to check the spelling. They then use each homophone in a sentence, writing it on the back of their worksheet. Alternatively, this could be done as part of the extension activity.

Extension activity: The children can work in pairs, dictating one of their sentences to their partner, and then checking whether the correct spelling has been used.

Rounding off: Go over the sheet with the children, discussing their answers. If they have done the extension activity, ask some of the children to read out their sentences and check that they have used the correct spelling.

Homophone Mix-Ups

Write the meanings for these pairs of homophones.
If you are unsure, look them up in the dictionary.

herd

heard

who's

whose

serial

cereal

ascent

assent

father

farther

dissent

descent

draft

draught

principle

principal

Now write a sentence for each word on the back of the sheet.

Spelling 35 – ‹ere› and /oa/

Prepare...
Spelling Sheets 35a/b
Coloured pencils

Builds on...
JGH1: S16, S23
JGH2: S11, S16, S24, S27-28
JGH3: S5, S22-23, S31, S35
JGH6: S9

Revision: Write 'individually' on the board and discuss how the suffix ‹-ly› has been added to the adjective 'individual' to make an adverb. Explain that these words are in the same word family as 'divide'; ask the class to think of some others (such as '(un)divided', '(in)divisible', 'division', 'divisive(ly)' and 'individuality') and identify their part(s) of speech.

Main point: The most common spellings for /oa/ are ‹oa›, ‹ow› and ‹o_e›, but ‹o› can also say its long vowel sound, as in 'soldier'. There are other less common spellings too, as found in 'toe', 'brooch', 'sewn' and 'mauve'. Remind the class that ‹oe› usually says /oa/ in plurals like 'potatoes' and 'tomatoes'. Now revise ‹ere›, which is an alternative spelling of both the /ear/ and /air/ sounds, as in 'here' and 'there'. See if the children can think of any other words with this spelling and write them on the board (such as those from the spelling list, as well as 'sphere', 'cereal', 'mere', 'coherence', 'atmosphere', 'somewhere', 'wherewithal' and 'elsewhere'). Point out that the word 'werewolf' can be pronounced in both ways.

Spelling list: Go through the list, discuss the meaning of any unfamiliar words, and ask the class to find and highlight the ‹ere› or /oa/ spelling each time. Point out other spelling features, such as the ‹e› saying /i/ in 'severe', 'revere' and 'persevere', the ‹di› saying /j/ in 'soldier', the silent ‹e› in 'mauve' and 'therefore', the ‹o› saying /oo/ in 'werewolf', the ‹a› saying /e/ and ‹y› saying /ee/ in 'anywhere', the ‹wh› spelling in the compound words 'anywhere', 'wherever', 'whereupon' and 'whereabouts', the way the middle ‹e› in 'wherever' belongs to both 'where' and 'ever', the 'soft ‹c›' in 'sincere', and the prefix in '**inter**fere'. It is a good idea to blend and sound out the spelling words quickly every day with the class, using the 'say it as it sounds' strategy where appropriate (stressing the pure sound of any schwas, as in 'shoulder', 'soldier', 'interfere', 'whereupon' and 'whereabouts', for example).

Spelling Sheet 35a: The children split each word into syllables to help remember the spelling *[1. toe, 2. brooch, 3. sewn, 4. se/vere, 5. re/vere, 6. cash/mere, 7. shoul/der, 8. sol/dier, 9. mauve, 10. were/wolf, 11. an/y/where, 12. wher/ev/er, 13. sin/cere, 14. there/fore, 15. in/ter/fere, 16. per/se/vere, 17. where/up/on, 18. where/a/bouts]* and add the missing letters in the shawl *[br**oo**ch, s**o**ldier, sinc**ere**; wher**e**upon, cashm**ere**; s**e**vere, sh**o**ulder, rev**ere**; th**ere**fore, any**where**; t**o**e, mau**v**e, s**ew**n; pers**ev**ere, wher**e**abouts; wher**e**ver, inter**fere**, were**wolf**]*. They then sort the spelling list words by sound and write them in the correct scarf *[/air/: werewolf, anywhere, wherever, therefore, whereupon, whereabouts; /oa/: toe, brooch, sewn, shoulder, soldier, mauve; /ear/: severe, revere, cashmere, (werewolf), sincere, interfere, persevere]*.

Spelling Sheet 35b: The children write the meanings for each pair of commonly confused words, using a dictionary to help them if needed. Then they parse the sentence and complete the wall *[Top: soldier - had - toe / Bottom: The - (blank) - a severely broken / Verb: active]*. The adverb 'severely' modifies the adjective 'broken' (which is the past participle of 'to break').

The soldier^N had^V a severely^Adv broken^Adj toe^N.

Noun^N (black), Verb^V (red), Pronoun^P (pink), Adjective^Adj (blue), Adverb^Adv (orange), Conjunction^C (purple), Preposition^Pre (green)

Dictation: (This can be done in the spelling lesson or at another time during the week.) Call out the sentences for the children to write down. Remind them to use speech marks with the correct punctuation in Sentence 2.

1. The mauve buttons had been sewn on securely.
2. "I cannot find my brooch anywhere," I admitted.
3. She draped the cashmere scarf over her shoulders.

‹ere› and /oa/

Spelling List 35

1. toe
2. brooch
3. sewn
4. severe
5. revere
6. cashmere
7. shoulder
8. soldier
9. mauve
10. werewolf
11. anywhere
12. wherever
13. sincere
14. therefore
15. interfere
16. persevere
17. whereupon
18. whereabouts

Add the missing letters to complete the Spelling List words in the cashmere shawl.

br____ch   s____ldier   sinc____

wh____upon   cashm____

sev____   sh____lder   rev____

th____fore   anywh____

t____   m____ve   s____n

persev____   wh____abouts

wh____ver   interf____   w____wolf

Match the Spelling List words to the sounds below.

/air/   /oa/   /ear/

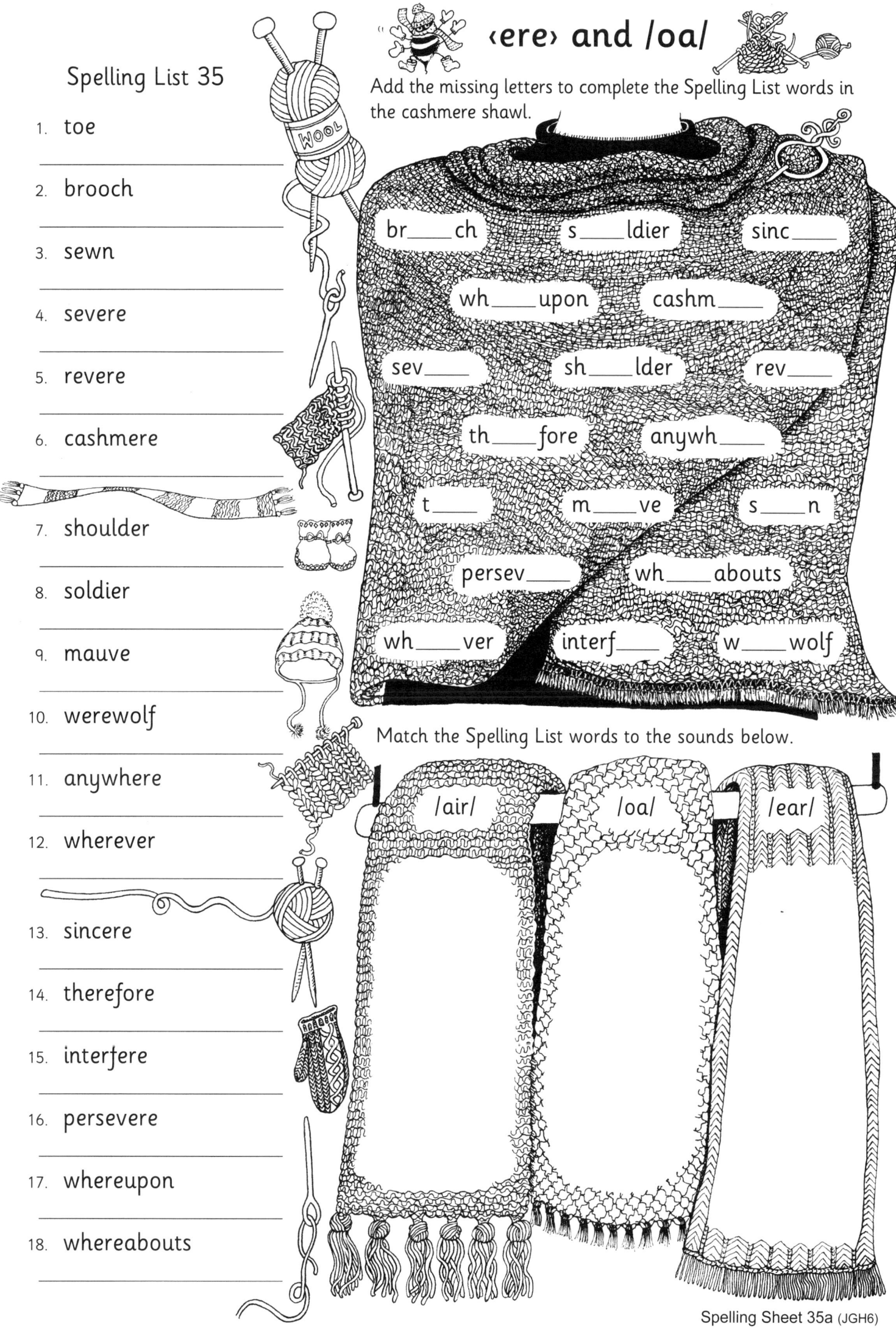

Spelling Sheet 35a (JGH6)

Dictation: ‹ere› and /oa/

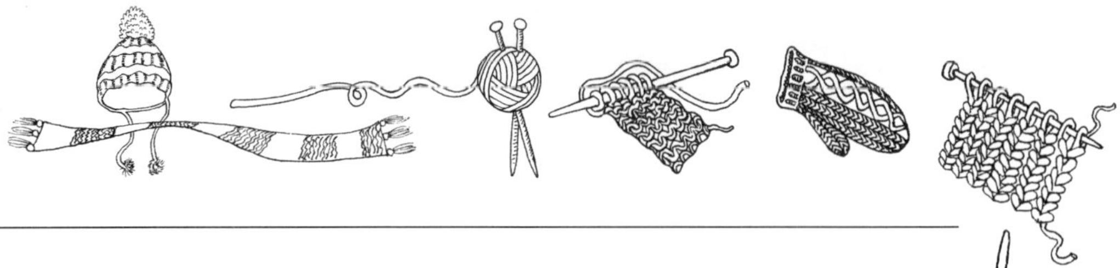

1. _____
_____
2. _____
_____
3. _____
_____

Write the meanings for these commonly confused words. Use a dictionary to check, if needed.

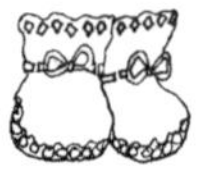

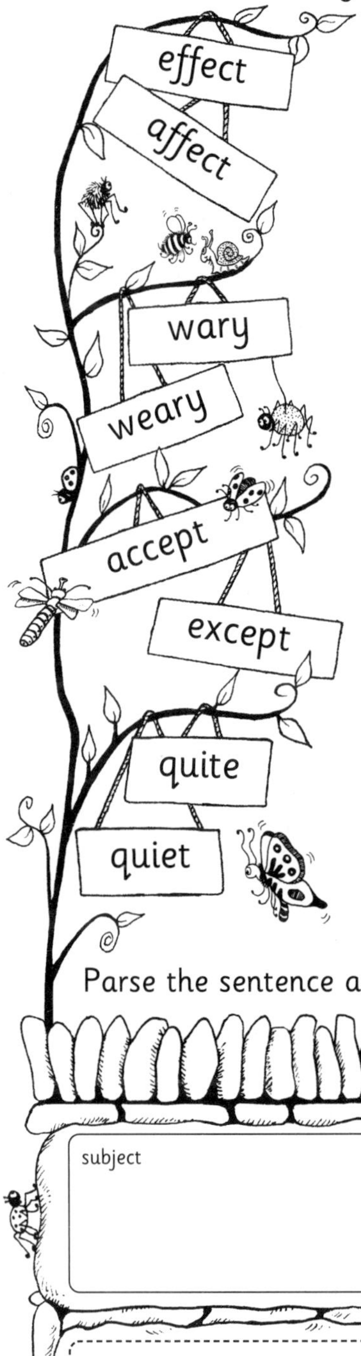

effect

affect

wary

weary

accept

except

quite

quiet

Parse the sentence and then write it on the wall.

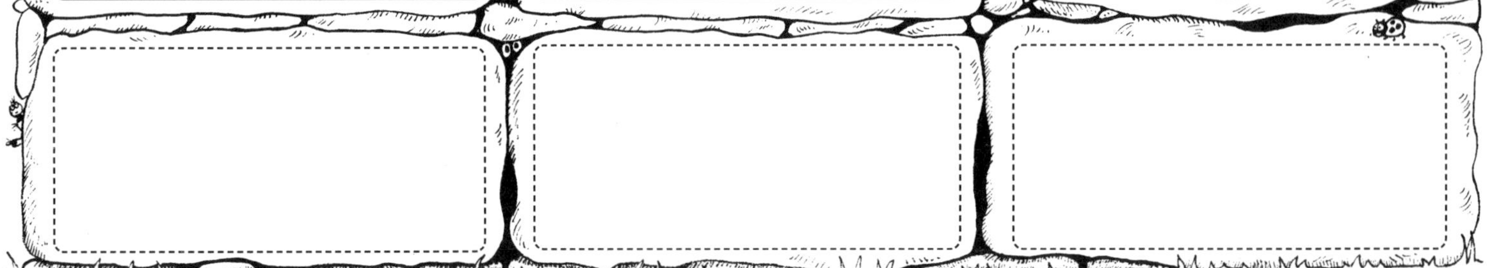

The soldier had a severely broken toe.

subject	verb	object
	active / passive	

Grammar 35 – Antonyms and Synonyms

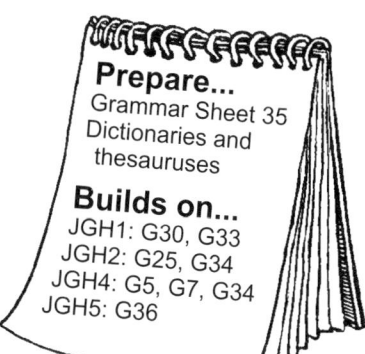

Prepare...
Grammar Sheet 35
Dictionaries and thesauruses

Builds on...
JGH1: G30, G33
JGH2: G25, G34
JGH4: G5, G7, G34
JGH5: G36

Aim: Reinforce the children's understanding of antonyms and synonyms and develop their ability to use a wider variety of words in their writing.

Introduction: Briefly revise dictionaries and thesauruses. Remind the children that we use a dictionary to check a word's meaning or its spelling and that a thesaurus helps us to find synonyms and antonyms for a particular word. Make sure that the children know the difference between synonyms and antonyms, both of which are words with a Greek origin: the word 'synonym' means 'with name' and is used for words with the same or similar meanings, while 'antonym' means 'opposite name' and is used for words with opposite meanings. Make sure that everyone in the class has access to either a dictionary or a thesaurus and call out some words. The children race to look up each one and whoever finds it first can read out its meaning in the dictionary or call out some of its synonyms and antonyms from the thesaurus. This is a good opportunity to look again at this week's (or other recent) spelling list words.

Main point: Remind the children that using a more varied vocabulary will help them avoid overusing certain words and can make their writing more interesting. Write some overused words on the board (possible words include 'big', 'small', 'nice', 'nasty', 'good', 'bad', 'hot', 'cold', 'happy', 'sad', 'angry', 'dirty', 'run', 'go', 'pretty', 'fun' and 'say') and ask the children to think of other words (synonyms) that they could use instead. Then see if the children can think of any words that mean the opposite of these words (antonyms) . Remind them that many prefixes and some suffixes can be used to make antonyms, as in '**un**happy', '**dis**like', '**mis**understand', '**il**legal', '**im**possible', '**in**capable', '**ir**relevant', '**non**sense', '**de**activate' and '**anti**social'. Also, some prefixes have opposite meanings so that when they are added to the same root word, they create pairs of antonyms, as in '**pre**-war' and '**post**-war', '**super**script' and '**sub**script', '**in**clude' and '**ex**clude', '**in**flate' and '**de**flate'. This is also true of the suffixes ‹-less› and ‹-ful›, as in 'thought**ful**' and 'thought**less**', 'fear**ful**' and 'fear**less**', 'hope**ful**' and 'hope**less**'.

Grammar Sheet 35: The children read each group of words and cross out the one that is not a synonym of the word in the web *[Top: reliable, constant, ignore; Middle: decorated, retreat, hobby; Bottom: eventually, carefully, politely]*. They then match the pairs of antonyms and synonyms with the correct word in the drawers *[weird: bizarre, strange/ordinary, normal; enjoyable: fun, amusing/unpleasant, boring; jovial: jolly, cheerful/miserable, gloomy; antique: old, ancient/new, modern; grotesque: ugly, hideous/beautiful, gorgeous; bygone: past, former/ present, recent; genuine: real, true/fake, insincere; frequently: regularly, often/occasionally, rarely; valuable: precious, expensive/cheap, worthless]*. The children may want to use a thesaurus or dictionary to check whether they are correct.

Extension activity: The children choose some words from the drawers on the worksheet and write a sentence for each one. Then they rewrite each sentence twice, first using one of the synonyms and then using one of the antonyms.

Rounding off: Go over the sheet with the children, discussing their answers. If they have done the extension activity, ask some children to read out their sentences.

Antonyms and Synonyms

Cross out the word in each group that is **not** a synonym of the word in the spider's web.

...and **antonyms** are words that have the opposite meaning.

REMEMBER! **Synonyms** are words which have the same, or a similar, meaning...

large
considerable — reliable — gone
plentiful

missing
absent — examine
constant

test
inspect
ignore

decorated
picturesque — pretty — conquer
attractive

beat
defeat — technique
retreat

skill
hobby
method

eventually
immediately — instantly — heartily
straightaway

eagerly
carefully — sincerely
warmly

politely
truly
honestly

synonyms

regularly · often

old · ancient

fun · amusing

past · former

real · true

ugly · hideous

bizarre · strange

jolly · cheerful

precious · expensive

For each word in the drawers, there are two words that have the same meaning and two that have the opposite meaning. Can you match them correctly?

weird · enjoyable · jovial

antique · grotesque · bygone

genuine · frequently · valuable

antonyms

occasionally · rarely

miserable · gloomy

cheap · worthless

fake · insincere

new · modern

present · recent

ordinary · normal

unpleasant · boring

beautiful · gorgeous

Grammar Sheet 35 (JGH6)

Spelling 36 – The Schwa

Prepare...
Spelling Sheets 36a/b
Coloured pencils
Builds on...
JGH1: S7, S13
JGH2: S19, S29-30, S33, S36
JGH3: G12, S13, S32
JGH4: S7-12, S22-29
JGH5: S3-6, S13-17, S19-21, S25-29
JGH6: S11-12, S25-30

Revision: Write 'sincere' on the board and point out the 'soft ‹c›' and the ‹ere› spelling of /ear/. Ask the class to think of some other words in this word family (such as 'insincere', '(in)sincerer', '(in)sincerest', '(in)sincerely' and '(in)sincerity') and identify their part(s) of speech.

Main point: Revise syllables, which are units of sound that contain a vowel sound. In spoken English, if a word has two or more syllables, we stress one of them by saying it a little louder and lengthening the vowel slightly, which keeps the vowel sound pure; however, the vowel in an unstressed syllable is often swallowed and becomes – most commonly – a neutral 'schwa', sounding something like /uh/, but it can sometimes change to an /i/ sound instead. Go through the spelling list words with the class and listen for these swallowed vowels. *[Letters in bold indicate a schwa; underlined letters say /i/; underlined letters in bold can say either: bargain, certain, perhaps, develop, continue, remember, decide, relevant, amateur, category, strengthen, dictionary, vegetable, stomach, criticise, cemetery, restaurant; there is also a schwa sound in the ‹le› in 'vegetable' and 'vehicle'.]*

Spelling list: Go through the list, discuss the meaning of any unfamiliar words, and ask the class to find and highlight the swallowed vowel(s) each time. Point out other spelling features, such as the 'soft ‹c›' in 'certain', 'decide', 'criticise' and 'cemetery', the ‹t› saying either its own sound or /ch/ in 'amateur', the /ng/ in 'strength', the ‹tion› saying /shun/ in 'dictionary', the 'soft ‹g›' in 'vegetable', the ‹o› saying /u/ and ‹ch› spelling of /k/ in 'stomach', the ‹s› saying /z/ in 'criticise', the silent ‹h› and ‹e› saying its long vowel in 'vehicle', and the ‹a› saying /o/ in 'restaurant'. It is a good idea to blend and sound out the spelling words quickly every day with the class, using the 'say it as it sounds' strategy where appropriate (stressing the pure sound of any swallowed syllables, as in 'vegetable' and 'cemetery', or syllables that are almost swallowed, as in 'category' and 'dictionary', for example).

Spelling Sheet 36a: The children split each word into syllables to help remember the spelling *[1. bar/gain, 2. cer/tain, 3. per/haps, 4. de/vel/op, 5. con/tin/ue, 6. re/mem/ber, 7. de/cide, 8. rel/e/vant, 9. am/a/teur, 10. cat/e/go/ry, 11. strength/en, 12. dic/tion/a/ry, 13. vege/ta/ble, 14. stom/ach, 15. crit/i/cise, 16. ve/hi/cle, 17. cem/e/tery, 18. res/tau/rant]*. They then unscramble the letters in the dinner plates to make some of the spelling words *[Left-hand column: continue, perhaps, amateur, relevant, strengthen, stomach, vegetable / Right-hand column: certain, remember, dictionary, category, vehicle, criticise, restaurant]*.

Spelling Sheet 36b: The children try to write down a fruit or vegetable that starts with each alphabet letter *[for example: apple, beans, carrot, date, endive, fig, grape, horseradish, iceberg lettuce, Jerusalem artichoke, kiwi fruit, leek, melon, nectarine, onion, potato, quince, radish, spinach, turnip, ugli fruit, vine leaves, watercress, xigua, yam, zucchini]*. They then parse the sentence and complete the wall *[Top: shawl - was\bargain (a) - (blank) / Bottom: The cashmere - (blank) - (blank) / Verb: linking]*. The verb 'was' links 'bargain' to 'shawl', which it defines.

The cashmere[Adj] shawl[N] was[V] a bargain[N].

Noun[N] (black), Verb[V] (red), Pronoun[P] (pink), Adjective[Adj] (blue), Adverb[Adv] (orange), Conjunction[C] (purple), Preposition[Pre] (green)

Dictation: (This can be done in the spelling lesson or at another time during the week.) Call out the sentences for the children to write down. Remind them to use speech marks with the correct punctuation in Sentence 1. 'Dad' is a proper noun and needs a capital letter.

1. "Do you remember that restaurant?" asked Dad.
2. They sorted the books into certain categories.
3. We must continue to develop our dictionary skills.

Schwas

Spelling List 36

1. bargain
2. certain
3. perhaps
4. develop
5. continue
6. remember
7. decide
8. relevant
9. amateur
10. category
11. strengthen
12. dictionary
13. vegetable
14. stomach
15. criticise
16. vehicle
17. cemetery
18. restaurant

Unscramble the letters to make words from the Spelling List.

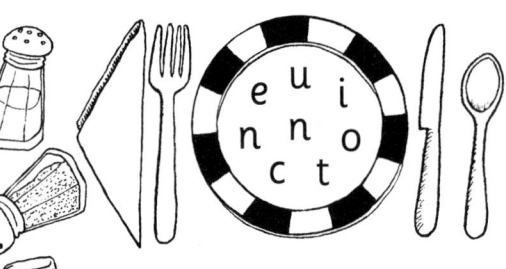  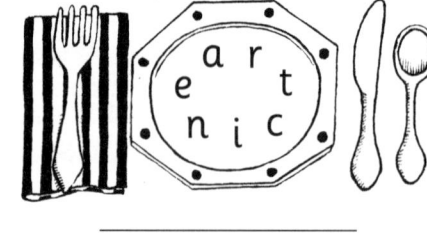

 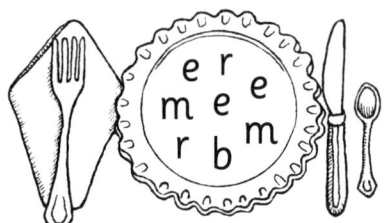

 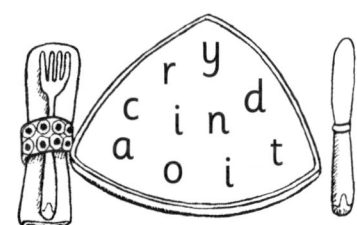

 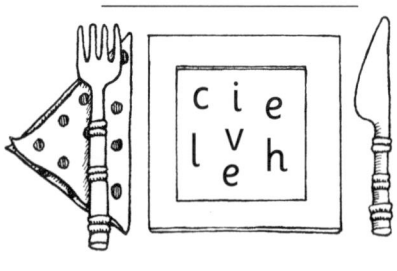

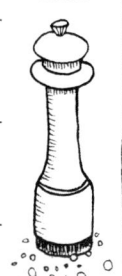 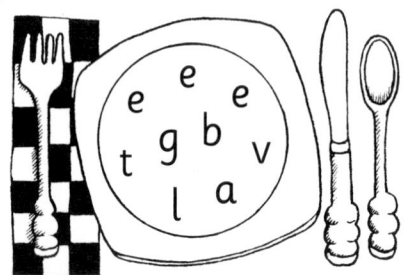 

Dictation: schwas

1. _____
   _____
2. _____
   _____
3. _____
   _____

Can you think of a fruit or vegetable that starts with each letter of the alphabet? Look in a dictionary or other reference book if you get stuck!

a b c d e f g h i j k l m

n o p q r s t u v w x y z

Parse the sentence and then write it on the wall.

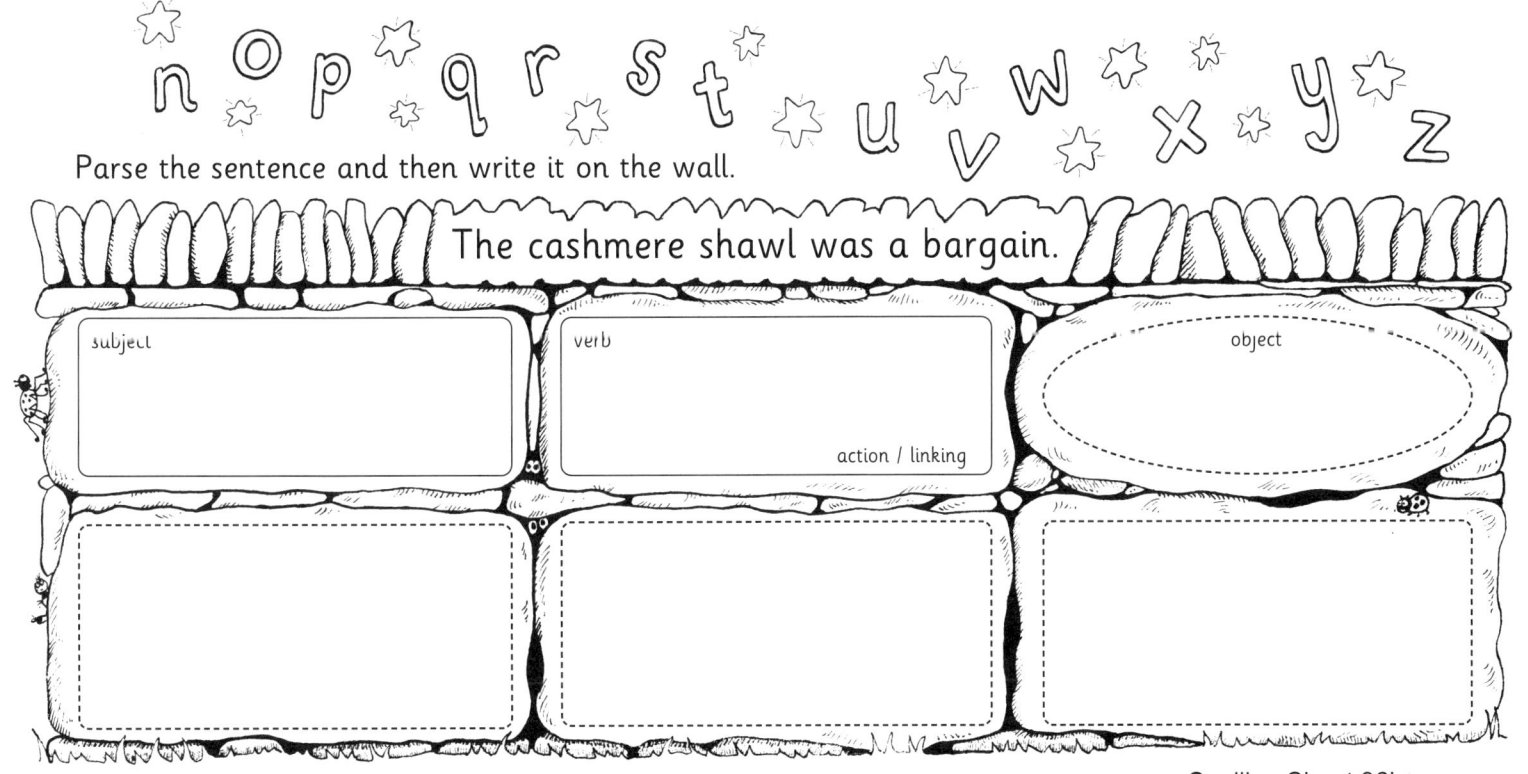

The cashmere shawl was a bargain.

subject	verb	object
	action / linking	

Grammar 36 – 'Grammar Consequences' Game

Prepare...
Grammar Sheet 36
Coloured pencils
Action cards,
pp 232–233

Builds on...
JGH1: G36
JGH2: G36
JGH3: G2
JGH5: G1
JGH6: G5

Aim: Have fun revising the different parts of speech. Play Grammar Action Sentences and a new game called Grammar Consequences.

Introduction: Briefly revise the different parts of speech and the nine verb tenses, using the action cards from Grammar Lesson 5. Hold up each card and ask the class which part of speech it represents. Do the actions with the children and revise the colour associated with each one: nouns (black), pronouns (pink), adjectives (blue), verbs (red), adverbs (orange), prepositions (green) and conjunctions (purple). Remind the children of the actions for the definite and indefinite articles, which are a special kind of adjective, and discuss the different ways to write the past, present and future tenses (simple, continuous and perfect). More information about this can be found in the Introduction on pages 4 to 20. Remind the class that many words can act as more than one part of speech, depending on how they are used in a sentence.

Main point: Play Grammar Action Sentences, either by doing the actions or using the action cards from Grammar Lesson 5. The actions should be ordered in a sequence, following the pattern of a simple sentence; the children think of a suitable word for each part of speech and create a sentence. Try to use a different sequence each time, perhaps from the following examples, and specify which article and tense should be used:

- article / adjective / common noun / verb / adverb
- article / adjective / adjective / common noun / verb
- pronoun / verb / preposition / article / common noun
- proper noun / conjunction / proper noun / verb / adverb
- article / common noun / verb / adverb / conjunction / adverb
- proper noun / verb / preposition / article / adjective / common noun

As you create each sentence, it may be necessary to rethink some of the words used in order for it to make sense; the verb chosen, for example, may not work if it precedes a preposition. However, it can also be fun to see how more random choices affect the meaning. Play the game again but this time ask a different child to think of the word each time, without revealing what it is. At the end of the sequence, the children call out their words and see if the sentence makes any sense. This can also be done by playing a version of the game Consequences, using Grammar Sheet 36.

Grammar Sheet 36: The children write inside each of the outlined parts of speech in the appropriate colour (see above); the articles could be done in pencil or in blue, as preferred. The children then play Grammar Consequences as a class. Hold up the first card in the sequence (or do the action), and ask the children to think of a suitable word, without telling anyone else what it is. They write it in the first empty space on their sheet, using the appropriate colour, and fold the top of the sheet over so that it covers the word. They then pass the sheet to their right-hand neighbour and continue the game. At the end of the sequence, the children unfold their sheets and read their 'silly' sentence.

Extension activity: The children can draw a picture to illustrate their Grammar Consequences sentence or they can play the game again, only this time the children decide which sequence to use for the sentence.

Rounding off: Ask some of the children to read out their sentences to the rest of the class.

How to play: Each player thinks of a word for the chosen part of speech. They write it in the first space and fold the paper over to hide it. Then they pass their sheet to their right-hand neighbour and continue the game. At the end of the game, the players unfold their sheets and read the sentence.

Fold --

Fold --

Fold --

Fold --

Fold --

Fold --

Fold --

Fold --

Fold --

Fold --

A / An   The
Articles

Adjectives

Proper   Common
Nouns

Pronouns

Adverbs

Verbs

Past   Present   Future

Prepositions

Conjunctions

Grammar Sheet 36 (JGH6)

Photocopy Section 2

Spelling List Sheets

Each week the children have a list of spelling words to take home and learn. The word list is divided into three groups of six. The words in the first group are usually short, regular and fairly common; those in the second group are a bit longer and may have more alternative spellings in them; and the third group has longer words with more varied spellings.

Those children who struggle with spelling can be given the first group of spelling words, others can be given the first two groups, and those who find it easy to learn their spellings can be given all three.

The six sheets on pages 226 to 231 provide all the spelling lists, which are ready to be photocopied, cut up, and stuck into the children's spelling homework books. Alternatively, the children can write the words in themselves.

To encourage parents to help their child, a parents' advice sheet has been provided. This can be copied, cut and stuck at the front of the children's spelling homework books. When the spelling tests have been marked, the results can be written into each book to show the parents how well their child has done. Including the parents in this way, and giving them regular feedback, will encourage them to help their child with his or her spellings.

Parents' Advice Sheet

Dear Parent,

Every week your child will be given some spellings. Please help him/her to learn them.

Each week the focus is on a particular sound or spelling pattern.

If a word is regular, it can be spelt by listening for the sounds and writing the letter(s) for them.

If a word is not completely regular, the tricky part can be identified and learnt. The spelling for the remainder of the word can be worked out just like regular words.

It is a good idea to look at the spelling words with your child several times in the week, concentrating on those words that he/she finds most difficult.

Dear Parent,

Every week your child will be given some spellings. Please help him/her to learn them.

Each week the focus is on a particular sound or spelling pattern.

If a word is regular, it can be spelt by listening for the sounds and writing the letter(s) for them.

If a word is not completely regular, the tricky part can be identified and learnt. The spelling for the remainder of the word can be worked out just like regular words.

It is a good idea to look at the spelling words with your child several times in the week, concentrating on those words that he/she finds most difficult.

Dear Parent,

Every week your child will be given some spellings. Please help him/her to learn them.

Each week the focus is on a particular sound or spelling pattern.

If a word is regular, it can be spelt by listening for the sounds and writing the letter(s) for them.

If a word is not completely regular, the tricky part can be identified and learnt. The spelling for the remainder of the word can be worked out just like regular words.

It is a good idea to look at the spelling words with your child several times in the week, concentrating on those words that he/she finds most difficult.

Dear Parent,

Every week your child will be given some spellings. Please help him/her to learn them.

Each week the focus is on a particular sound or spelling pattern.

If a word is regular, it can be spelt by listening for the sounds and writing the letter(s) for them.

If a word is not completely regular, the tricky part can be identified and learnt. The spelling for the remainder of the word can be worked out just like regular words.

It is a good idea to look at the spelling words with your child several times in the week, concentrating on those words that he/she finds most difficult.

Dear Parent,

Every week your child will be given some spellings. Please help him/her to learn them.

Each week the focus is on a particular sound or spelling pattern.

If a word is regular, it can be spelt by listening for the sounds and writing the letter(s) for them.

If a word is not completely regular, the tricky part can be identified and learnt. The spelling for the remainder of the word can be worked out just like regular words.

It is a good idea to look at the spelling words with your child several times in the week, concentrating on those words that he/she finds most difficult.

Dear Parent,

Every week your child will be given some spellings. Please help him/her to learn them.

Each week the focus is on a particular sound or spelling pattern.

If a word is regular, it can be spelt by listening for the sounds and writing the letter(s) for them.

If a word is not completely regular, the tricky part can be identified and learnt. The spelling for the remainder of the word can be worked out just like regular words.

It is a good idea to look at the spelling words with your child several times in the week, concentrating on those words that he/she finds most difficult.

Spelling Lists 1 to 6

1. ‹uni-›, ‹mono-›

1. unit
2. unicorn
3. uniform
4. monogram
5. monorail
6. monotone
7. unify
8. unicycle
9. union
10. universe
11. monocle
12. monologue
13. monosyllable
14. universal
15. monochrome
16. monolith
17. unification
18. monopoly

2. ‹bi-›, ‹di-›, ‹du-›

1. duo
2. duet
3. biceps
4. biplane
5. bicycle
6. duel
7. dilemma
8. biathlon
9. binary
10. diverge
11. duplicate
12. digraph
13. billion
14. biennial
15. binoculars
16. bicentenary
17. bilingual
18. bicentennial

3. ‹tri-›

1. trio
2. triple
3. trident
4. triplane
5. tricycle
6. tripod
7. trilogy
8. triathlon
9. triangle
10. triplet
11. triceps
12. tricolour
13. triceratops
14. triangular
15. triplicate
16. triennial
17. tricorn
18. trillion

4. Prefixes: 4, 5, 6

1. quad
2. quintet
3. quadrant
4. quartet
5. sextet
6. hexagon
7. pentagon
8. quarter
9. quadruple
10. hexagonal
11. pentathlon
12. sextant
13. quadrangle
14. pentagram
15. quadruped
16. pentameter
17. sextuplet
18. quadrilateral

5. Prefixes: 7, 8, 9

1. septet
2. octet
3. heptagon
4. octagon
5. nonagon
6. octopus
7. octave
8. octagonal
9. September
10. October
11. November
12. heptathlon
13. septuplet
14. octuplet
15. octahedron
16. septuagenarian
17. octogenarian
18. nonagenarian

6. ‹dec-› and more

1. decagon
2. decade
3. twice
4. forty
5. hundred
6. December
7. twelfth
8. twentieth
9. percent
10. centurion
11. decibel
12. decimal
13. percentage
14. millennium
15. decathlon
16. millionaire
17. billionaire
18. decathlete

Spelling Lists 7 to 12

7. ‹ei›, ‹eigh› for /ai/

1. vein
2. veil
3. rein
4. reign
5. feint
6. weigh
7. weight
8. beige
9. feign
10. eighth
11. neigh
12. unveil
13. freight
14. inveigle
15. deign
16. weightlifter
17. surveillance
18. neighbourhood

8. ‹ei›, ‹ie› for /ee/

1. shriek
2. wield
3. siege
4. yield
5. ceiling
6. fiendish
7. niece
8. deceit
9. receive
10. deceive
11. achieve
12. conceited
13. hygiene
14. retrieve
15. perceive
16. reprieve
17. handkerchief
18. inconceivable

9. ‹ei›, ‹eigh›, ‹eir›

1. weir
2. their
3. heir
4. weird
5. forfeit
6. either
7. height
8. surfeit
9. foreign
10. heifer
11. feisty
12. sovereign
13. seismic
14. heirloom
15. eiderdown
16. counterfeit
17. kaleidoscope
18. Fahrenheit

10. ‹ci› for /sh/

1. ancient
2. unsocial
3. species
4. sociable
5. specially
6. multiracial
7. efficient
8. sufficient
9. suspicion
10. conscience
11. proficient
12. especially
13. appreciation
14. insufficient
15. coercion
16. inefficient
17. beneficiary
18. excruciating

11. ‹cious›

1. graciously
2. conscious
3. viciously
4. unconscious
5. semi-precious
6. suspiciously
7. malicious
8. atrocious
9. luscious
10. vivacious
11. tenacious
12. ferociously
13. audacious
14. auspicious
15. officious
16. voracious
17. precocious
18. subconscious

12. ‹-eous›

1. hideous
2. gorgeous
3. piteous
4. gaseous
5. righteous
6. outrageous
7. courageous
8. courteous
9. bounteous
10. erroneous
11. nauseous
12. advantageous
13. extraneous
14. simultaneous
15. spontaneous
16. miscellaneous
17. instantaneous
18. discourteous

Spelling Lists 13 to 18

13. Double Letters

1. address
2. arrive
3. suppose
4. attached
5. committee
6. equipped
7. programmed
8. aggressive
9. apparent
10. harass
11. possession
12. community
13. interruption
14. communicate
15. embarrass
16. exaggerate
17. recommend
18. correspond

14. ‹cc› for /k/

1. hiccup
2. occur
3. acclaim
4. account
5. raccoon
6. soccer
7. broccoli
8. moccasin
9. occupy
10. according
11. accurate
12. accomplish
13. piccolo
14. buccaneer
15. occasionally
16. accommodate
17. accompany
18. accordion

15. ‹fer›

1. refer
2. referral
3. infer
4. inferred
5. transfer
6. transferring
7. prefer
8. preferred
9. defer
10. deferred
11. confer
12. conferring
13. offer
14. offered
15. conference
16. deference
17. inference
18. reference

16. Long /oo/

1. fruit
2. suit
3. soup
4. youth
5. movie
6. prove
7. shoe
8. route
9. canoe
10. group
11. juice
12. bruise
13. wound
14. recruit
15. removal
16. approval
17. disapprove
18. improvement

17. /ai/

1. they
2. prey
3. break
4. great
5. steak
6. ballet
7. heyday
8. fete
9. buffet
10. convey
11. obey
12. sorbet
13. sachet
14. straight
15. bouquet
16. gourmet
17. survey
18. cabaret

18. Silent ‹h›

1. Sikh
2. ankh
3. khaki
4. rhyme
5. rhythm
6. Buddhism
7. rhino
8. jodhpurs
9. rhubarb
10. rhombus
11. rhapsody
12. sheikh
13. dhoti
14. sadhu
15. gymkhana
16. rhinoceros
17. rheumatism
18. rhythmically

Spelling Lists 19 to 24

19. /t/

1. debt
2. doubt
3. paste
4. baste
5. thyme
6. Thailand
7. yacht
8. subtle
9. rosette
10. palette
11. definite
12. favourite
13. suite
14. baguette
15. statuette
16. brunette
17. silhouette
18. redoubtable

20. /m/

1. numb
2. bomb
3. come
4. some
5. hymn
6. autumn
7. welcome
8. column
9. dumb
10. solemn
11. condemn
12. gruesome
13. income
14. outcome
15. handsome
16. thumbnail
17. tombstone
18. honeycomb

21. Silent ‹p›

1. psalm
2. psyche
3. pseudo
4. tempt
5. prompt
6. attempt
7. receipt
8. pneumonia
9. pneumatic
10. psychiatry
11. psychology
12. pterodactyl
13. psychiatrist
14. pseudonym
15. ptarmigan
16. psoriasis
17. psi
18. psychological

22. ‹ui›, ‹u› for /i/

1. build
2. built
3. busy
4. busily
5. biscuit
6. rebuilt
7. lettuce
8. minute
9. builder
10. building
11. cuisine
12. business
13. built-in
14. circuit
15. busybody
16. businesslike
17. outbuilding
18. bodybuilder

23. ‹gh›, ‹gue›

1. dinghy
2. rogue
3. plague
4. vague
5. league
6. ghastly
7. meringue
8. intrigue
9. tongue
10. fatigue
11. spaghetti
12. ghostwriter
13. colleague
14. dialogue
15. prologue
16. epilogue
17. harangue
18. ghoulishly

24. ‹gu›

1. guide
2. guard
3. guess
4. guest
5. guilt
6. guitar
7. language
8. penguin
9. iguana
10. anguish
11. extinguish
12. distinguished
13. guarantee
14. lifeguard
15. disguise
16. beguile
17. guardian
18. guillotine

Spelling Lists 25 to 30

25. ‹ough›
1. cough
2. dough
3. bough
4. rough
5. tough
6. bought
7. though
8. through
9. enough
10. drought
11. although
12. doughnut
13. sought
14. thorough
15. throughout
16. overwrought
17. breakthrough
18. afterthought

26. Schwa ‹ure›
1. picture
2. nature
3. injure
4. lecture
5. texture
6. pasture
7. sculpture
8. creature
9. stature
10. torture
11. rupture
12. cultured
13. manufacture
14. adventurer
15. procedure
16. treasure
17. acupuncture
18. disfigurement

27. Schwa ‹our›
1. armour
2. favour
3. flavour
4. humour
5. harbour
6. rumour
7. odour
8. clamour
9. colourful
10. neighbour
11. labourer
12. vigour
13. valour
14. savoury
15. splendour
16. behaviour
17. endeavour
18. honourable

28. ‹-ity›, ‹-ety›
1. activity
2. ability
3. purity
4. reality
5. security
6. identity
7. safety
8. anxiety
9. variety
10. society
11. entirety
12. subtlety
13. opportunity
14. possibility
15. curiosity
16. familiarity
17. generosity
18. responsibility

29. ‹-ial›
1. denial
2. trivial
3. burial
4. jovial
5. material
6. imperial
7. memorial
8. territorial
9. editorial
10. industrial
11. secretarial
12. ceremonial
13. celestial
14. sacrificial
15. substantial
16. marsupial
17. prejudicial
18. controversial

30. ‹-able›
1. enjoyable
2. adorable
3. avoidable
4. available
5. notable
6. reasonable
7. comfortable
8. valuable
9. reliable
10. suitable
11. fashionable
12. understandable
13. considerable
14. recognisable
15. persuadable
16. tolerable
17. applicable
18. knowledgeable

Spelling Lists 31 to 36

31. ‹que› for /k/

1. unique
2. antique
3. queue
4. mosque
5. plaque
6. conquer

7. marquee
8. boutique
9. physique
10. mystique
11. opaque
12. pique

13. grotesque
14. picturesque
15. masquerade
16. statuesque
17. technique
18. arabesque

32. ‹ne› for /n/

1. one
2. none
3. gone
4. engine
5. imagine
6. undone

7. anyone
8. famine
9. heroine
10. examine
11. bygone
12. genuine

13. medicine
14. feminine
15. masculine
16. discipline
17. migraine
18. determined

33. Word Mix-Ups

1. passed
2. past
3. lose
4. loose
5. lightning
6. lightening

7. breath
8. breathe
9. desert
10. dessert
11. muscle
12. mussel

13. angle
14. angel
15. island
16. Ireland
17. stationary
18. stationery

34. ‹-ly›

1. actually
2. probably
3. centrally
4. heartily
5. frequently
6. individually

7. excellently
8. physically
9. sincerely
10. necessarily
11. desperately
12. accidentally

13. immediately
14. marvellously
15. symbolically
16. mischievously
17. systematically
18. environmentally

35. ‹ere›, /oa/

1. toe
2. brooch
3. sewn
4. severe
5. revere
6. cashmere

7. shoulder
8. soldier
9. mauve
10. werewolf
11. anywhere
12. wherever

13. sincere
14. therefore
15. interfere
16. persevere
17. whereupon
18. whereabouts

36. Schwas

1. bargain
2. certain
3. perhaps
4. develop
5. continue
6. remember

7. decide
8. relevant
9. amateur
10. category
11. strengthen
12. dictionary

13. vegetable
14. stomach
15. criticise
16. vehicle
17. cemetery
18. restaurant

Extension Activity Sheets

The following extension sheets are provided for further grammar practice. They are ready to be photocopied and cut up for use in the lessons mentioned below.

The grammar action cards can be cut out and given to the children to make up their own 'grammar action' sentences, either with a partner or working in groups. If the cards are laminated, they can also be used as a 'morning' or 'filler' activity. Alternatively, the cards can be enlarged and mounted onto card for whole-class work.

A copy of the formal and informal writing sheet can be given to each child. The children cut the large triangle up into smaller triangles, mix them up, and then rebuild the triangle, matching the formal and informal words and phrases.

Further instructions on how to use these sheets can be found in the corresponding lesson notes (Grammar 5, page 67; Grammar 32, page 202).

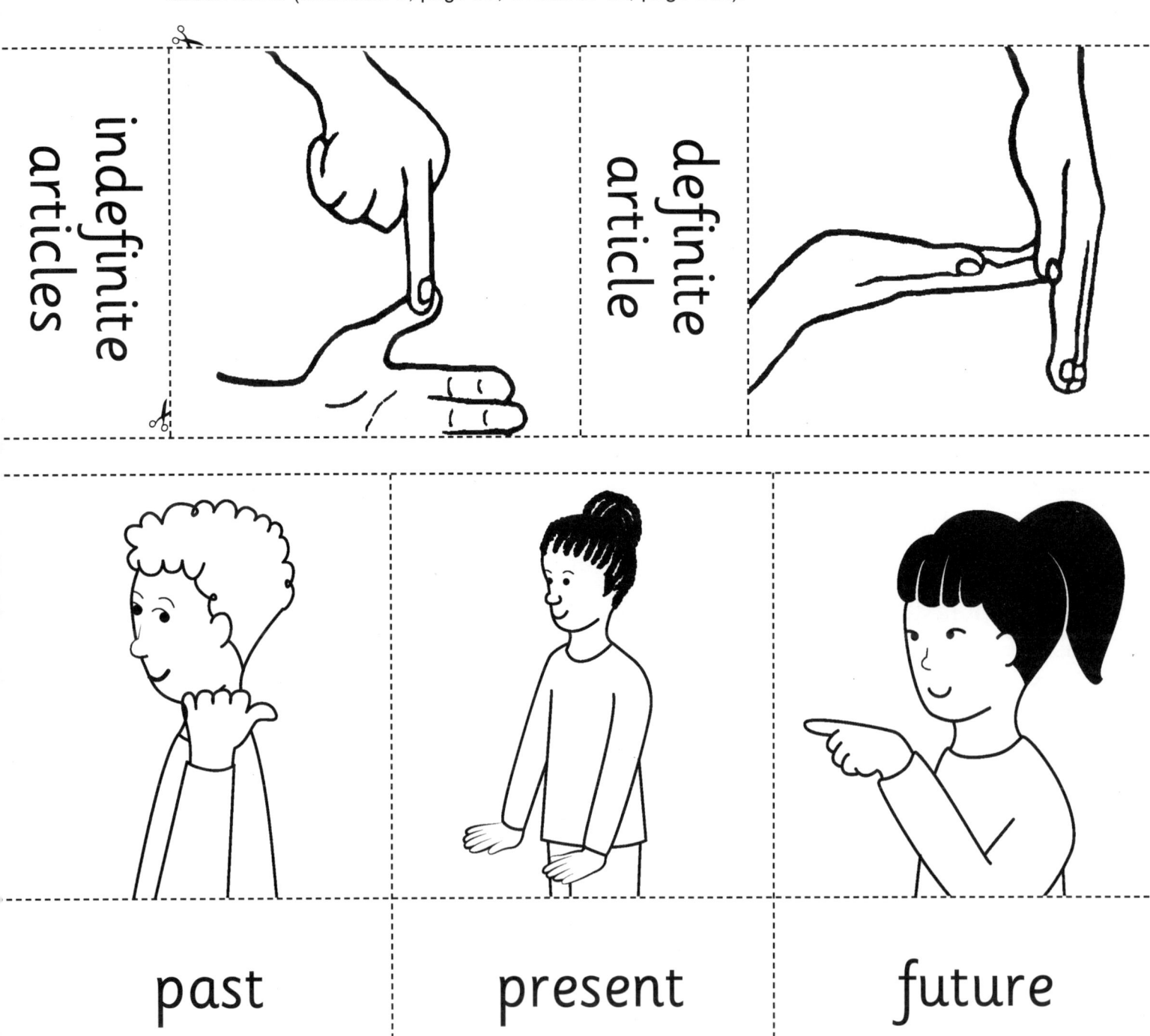

Grammar Action Cards (Grammar Lesson 5, page 67)

proper nouns

common nouns

pronouns

adjectives

verbs

adverbs

prepositions

conjunctions

Formal and Informal Writing

There are many ways to say the same thing and, when we speak or write, we choose different words for different reasons. We think about who we are talking to and what our purpose is, and use words that we think are suitable.

When we talk about something serious to someone we do not know or who is important, we are more formal and use advanced words, but when we talk to a friend or someone we know well, we are relaxed and use a more informal style.

Cut up the large triangle below and mix up all of the smaller triangles. Then put them back together, matching the formal and informal words and phrases.

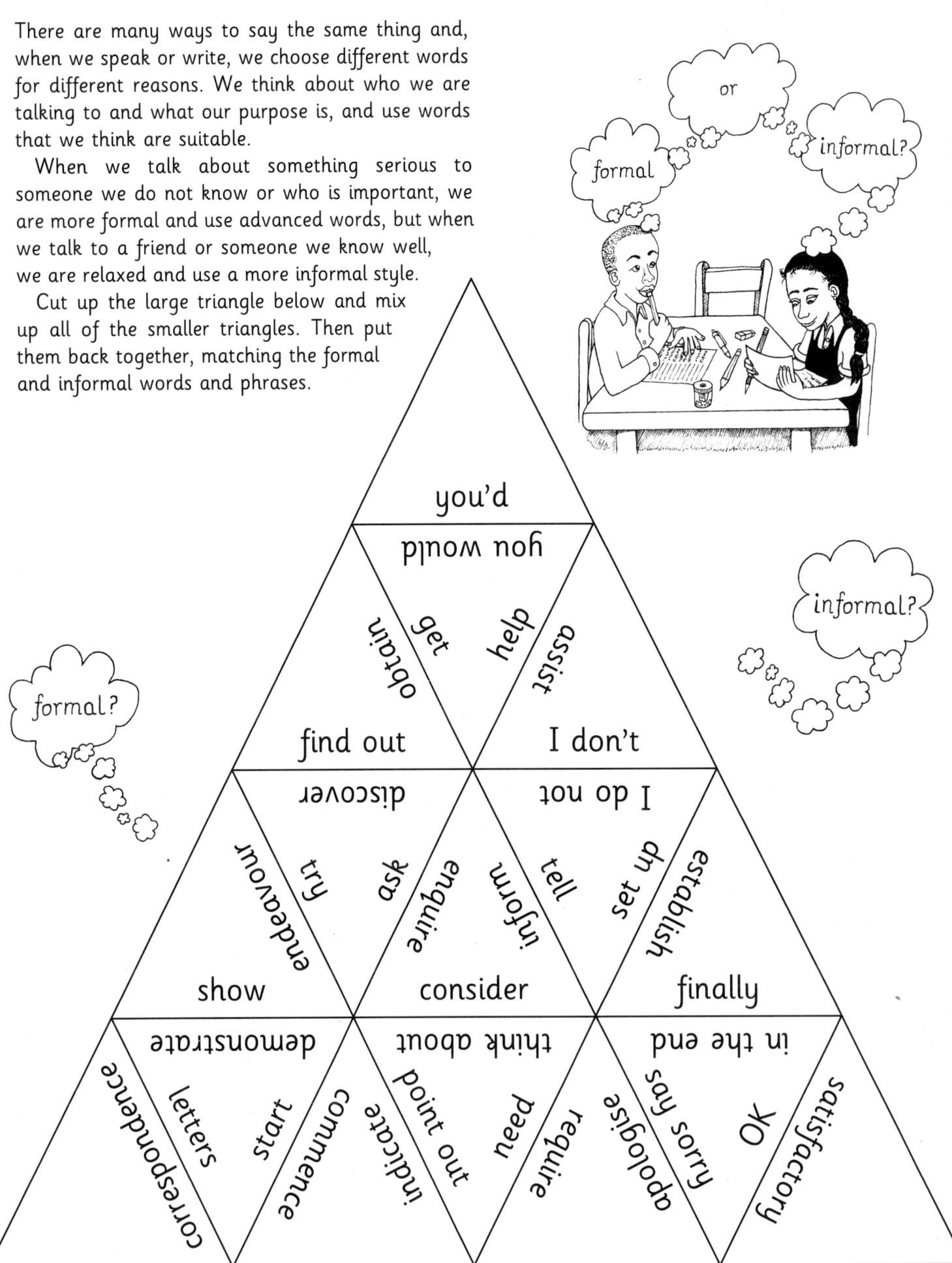